Six Galleons for the King of Spain

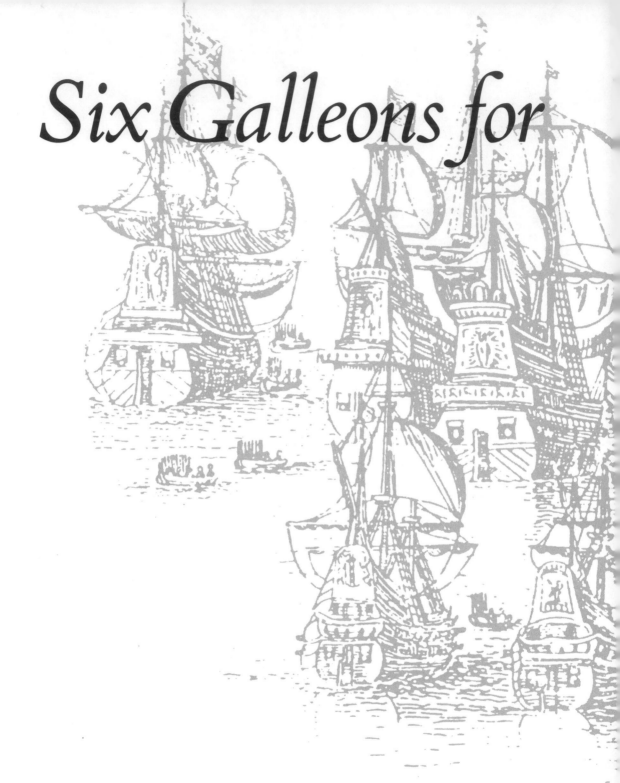

Six Galleons for

The Johns Hopkins University Press
Baltimore and London

the King of Spain

Imperial Defense
in the Early
Seventeenth Century

Carla Rahn Phillips

This book was brought to publication with the generous assistance of the Program for Cultural Cooperation between the Spanish Ministry of Culture and North American Universities.

The Johns Hopkins University Press
701 West 40th Street
Baltimore, Maryland 21211
The Johns Hopkins Press Ltd., London

∞ The paper used in this publication meets the minimum requirements of American National Standard for Information Sciences—Permanence of Paper for Printed Library Materials, ANSI Z39.48-1984.

Library of Congress Cataloging-in-Publication Data

Phillips, Carla Rahn, 1943–
  Six galleons for the king of Spain.

  Bibliography: p.
  Includes index.
  1. Galleons—Spain—History—17th century. 2. Spain. Armada—History—17th century. 3. Spain—Colonies—Defenses. I. Title.
VA583.P48   1986   359.3′ 21′ 0946   86-45444
ISBN 0-8018-3092-3 (alk. paper)

TO Wim

Contents

Tables

Most of us who become interested in Spanish galleons on the Indies run are, I suspect, neither sailors, nor shipbuilders, nor treasure hunters. The romance of the sea, especially the legendary life and times of the Spanish silver fleets, attracts everyone who was raised on stories of pirates and shipwrecks and buried treasure. Even when their romantic appeal fades as we learn the grim realities of life at sea, the topics are still endlessly fascinating. Yet they should be enlightening as well. Too often in the past, studies of European shipbuilding and shipping have degenerated into nationalistic essays unsupported by reliable evidence, or have dealt only superficially with the subjects at hand. That is neither desirable nor necessary, given the wealth of documentation available, and the work of scholars in the last several decades has moved the field in the right direction. This study will provide evidence for the Spanish experience, which, unfortunately, has been neglected even by some of the best recent surveys.

Using as a focus six galleons built for the crown in 1625–28, I will discuss three sets of topics in the lives of armada ships. The first will involve their construction, including the costs and availability of labor and raw materials on the north coast of Spain where they were built. To place the six galleons in context, I will examine the background of ship construction in Spain and the effects of inflation and royal policies on the shipbuilding industry in the sixteenth and seventeenth centuries. The next set of topics will focus on the preparation of galleons for the Indies run, an impressive feat of logistics. Discussion of where the food and equipment came from, what they cost, and how difficult they were to procure will contribute to a better understanding of bureaucratic responses to the challenge of defending the empire. Finally, I will examine the lives of the men and the ships that composed Spain's imperial fleets, concluding with a sketch of the life histories of the six galleons, from their first voyage to the Indies in 1629, to 1640 after the Battle of the Downs.

This study began far from Spain, at the University of Minnesota, where the James Ford Bell Library owns a packet of inventories describing the six ships delivered to the crown. The documents name the ships, their builder, and the royal officials who prepared the documents. They also give a fairly detailed inventory of the equipment and characteristics of each ship, but they do not mention the measurements or even the tonnage of any of them, nor reveal why they were built. In an attempt to find out more about the ships, I searched for mention of them in various Spanish archives. At first I suspected that the ships were built primarily for European duty, perhaps as part of a squadron to patrol the Baltic, a major concern of the government in 1625. Instead, as I soon discovered, their first voyages were to the Indies, leaving behind an extraordinary amount of documentation at the Archivo General de Simancas, the Archivo General de la Marina (Museo Naval) in Madrid, and the Archivo General de Indias in Seville. The search reminded me once again that imperial Spain created one of the world's great bureaucracies. Once the logic of its filing system becomes clear, the paper trail is there to follow, even in a matter so specific as the life histories of six galleons.

In the course of following that paper trail, I benefited greatly from the cataloging efforts and professional skills of the archivists at the collections mentioned above. They serve as invaluable guides through the millions of documents generated by the early Spanish empire. I am personally grateful for their help and kindness over the years, and professionally grateful for the obvious dedication and sense of mission they bring to their work.

Institutional support has been of the utmost importance in the years devoted to this project. The University of Minnesota, where the project began, funded a summer's research in 1982 through its graduate school, the McMillan Travel Fund, and the Office of International Programs. John Parker and Carol Urness of the Bell Library served as a steady source of encouragement as the project progressed, and John Jenson of the Rare Books Collection prepared the index. The generous support of the Edward Laroque Tinker Foundation of New York City provided a full year's uninterrupted research and writing in 1983, which enabled me to draft most of the book. And a Faculty Summer Research Fellowship from the university in 1984 allowed me to complete the manuscript undistracted by teaching duties. Without this generous support, the book would have taken much longer to appear, and I am grateful to everyone who helped me along the way.

Finally, I thank my husband, William D. Phillips, Jr., for his unstinting love, advice, and encouragement as the manuscript took shape, and for his calming presence during the terrors and traumas of computerized word processing. This book is dedicated to him.

Six Galleons for the King of Spain

Figure 1. Spain, showing the principal ports and mountain ranges. (Map prepared by the Cartography Laboratory, Department of Geography, University of Minnesota.)

ONE

Challenge and Response

On Thursday morning, the eighteenth of May 1634, a solemn procession wound its way through the streets of Seville. Starting at the door of the Royal Court of Justice, the participants walked down the winding street called Sierpes and then passed through narrow lanes named after the crafts practiced there: locksmithing, carpentry, belt making, mercery. Official processions were common enough in Seville, one of the most impressive cathedral cities in Europe, but they generally followed a less obscure route. This procession was different. Its destination was the Plaza de San Francisco, the traditional site of public executions, and its purpose was solemn and terrible—to put to death don Juan de Benavides, native of the town of Úbeda, gentleman of the noble military Order of Santiago, and ill-fated captain-general of the fleet returning from New Spain (Mexico) in 1628.[1]

A series of miscalculations by Benavides had allowed that fleet to fall into the hands of the Dutch admiral Piet Heyn, at Matanzas Bay in Cuba, the first and only time that an entire Spanish fleet fell to an enemy.

The Dutch had launched a major attack on Portuguese possessions in Brazil in 1624, three years after the expiration of their truce with Spain. As king of the united crowns of Spain and Portugal, Philip IV had responded immediately, ousting them from the Brazilian seaport of Bahia in 1625. The Dutch were by no means finished in the New World, however. Piet Heyn, who began his career as a pirate and ended it as an admiral, unsuccessfully tried to capture a merchant fleet of forty ships in 1626 and continued to harass Portuguese colonies and shipping in Brazil the following year. The richest prize of his life came in 1628 at Matanzas, when the New Spain fleet fell into his hands.[2]

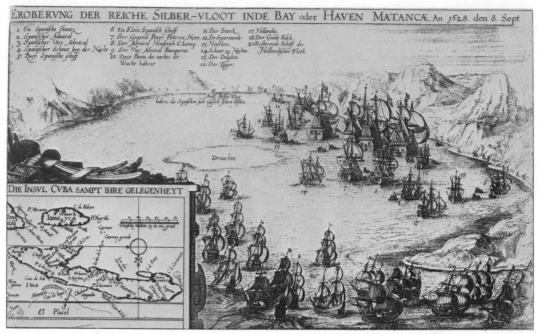

Figure 2. Matanzas Bay, Cuba. Capture of the New Spain fleet on September 8, 1628. (*Nederlandsche reizen, tot bevordering van den koophandel, na de Westindien.* Amsterdam: P. Conradi, 1787. Courtesy of the James Ford Bell Library, University of Minnesota.)

There was no possibility that Benavides could avoid the blame for Matanzas, although the disaster was due at least as much to bad luck as to any incompetence on his part. There has been enough misrepresentation of the events at Matanzas to warrant a brief summary here.

The Dutch had thirty-two ships and more than thirty-five hundred men when they surprised the exceptionally small fleet en route from New Spain to Havana on the homeward voyage under Benavides's command. (See figure 2.) In all there were just fifteen ships—two galleons and eleven merchantmen from New Spain and two more galleons that had joined them from Honduras. In other years the New Spain fleet would have been several times that size. In 1628 the four galleons carried silver bars and coins, gold coins, dyestuffs, and silk, plus a variety of more mundane items such as hides, wood, and chocolate. The eleven merchant vessels, as was customary, carried most of the trade goods. Had the fleet been larger, they would probably have carried nearly all the trade goods. The galleons would have been reserved to transport the silver, gold, pearls, and precious stones that we think of as the treasures of the Indies, belonging both to the crown and to private persons.

When the Dutch blocked the way into Havana, Benavides and the officers on his ship decided to head for the nearby port of Matanzas, planning to unload the treasure and secure it before heading out again to meet the enemy fleet. Benavides did not consult his second in command, Admiral Juan de Leoz, nor the officers on other ships, and that would weigh heavily in the charges against him later. This error was compounded by the failure of his plan.

Benavides's pilots thought they knew the area, but the ships ran aground in uncharted shallows as they headed for the port. Though all but the rear guns on his galleons were rendered useless by the grounding, Benavides at first ordered his men—outnumbered at least two to one by the Dutch—to prepare for battle. He then changed his mind, ordering his ships abandoned and destroyed to keep them out of enemy hands. Confusion set in as the Dutch closed in to board and the Spanish tried to send their men ashore under enemy fire. Benavides later claimed that his officers had asked him to establish order in the landing operations. In any case, he left his flagship mined with explosives and went ashore. His admiral surrendered to the Dutch rather than sacrifice his ship and his men. All fifteen ships were lost.[3] The Dutch burned half of them and took the rest back to Holland, along with booty reportedly worth 12 million florins.[4]

Shortly after Matanzas, King Philip IV appointed don Juan de Solórzano from his Council of the Indies to draft charges against Benavides and his admiral; Solórzano's brief, which ran to ninety printed folio pages, argued that both men should be punished severely, as an example to others, even if they were absolved of negligence.[5] Admiral Leoz, first imprisoned by the Dutch, returned to Spain and served four years in solitary confinement. Captain-General Benavides spent five years imprisoned in the castle fortress of Carmona between Córdoba and Seville, awaiting resolution of the charges against him.[6] The initial sentence of death was handed down in Madrid on January 18, 1633, but a judicial review and aristocratic protests dragged on for nearly another year and a half.

Once royal officials had issued the definitive sentence, they moved swiftly and secretly to carry it out. This secrecy was ordered by the king, to avoid arousing the ire of the nobles at court, who had previously importuned him on Benavides's behalf and who might cause even more embarrassment if they knew about the execution in advance. The death sentence was registered at the Royal Court of Justice in Seville on May 15, and that night officials traveled to Carmona to fetch Benavides. Interned in the public jail in Seville, he heard the death sentence and received a long mourning gown to wear over his prison serge. He was forbidden to wear the habit of the noble Order of Santiago or any other badge of his rank and social position, except for a cross of Santiago around his neck. Thus attired, between ten and eleven on the morning of May 18, he was mounted on a mule—a distinction reserved for gentlemen—for his final journey. At the portal of the Royal Court of Justice he listened as the solemn proclamation was read, announcing his crimes and his sentence. "This is the justice that the king our Lord and his royal councils order done to this man for his lack of care in the loss of the New Spain fleet, taken by the enemy this past year of 1628. He who did so, thus shall he pay."[7] After a distinguished career in royal service, Benavides was to die, not for criminal misdeeds, but because he had been careless. It is no wonder that the king worried about the reaction from his high-ranking subjects, who claimed Benavides as one of their own.

The place of execution in the Plaza de San Francisco was very near the Royal Court of Justice. The king had ordered that the scaffold be erected no sooner than the afternoon before the execution and that the official procession follow as inconspicuous a route as possible. Even though Seville was far from the court in Madrid and the nobles who lived there, it had a large contingent of aristocrats, who could be expected to be as difficult as their counterparts in the capital if given the chance. The official orders even specified that the entrances to the Plaza de San Francisco be blocked off to prevent coaches from approaching the place of execution. If any of the nobility attended they would have to come on foot.

The execution had to be a public spectacle to achieve its desired effect, and despite the crown's careful plans, news of it inevitably spread throughout Seville. A large crowd waited at the Plaza de San Francisco for the procession to arrive, surrounding a simple scaffold draped in baize cloth with a chair fixed in the middle. Benavides dismounted his mule and climbed the scaffold, with the long skirt of his mourning gown slung over his right shoulder. A guardian appointed from the order of St. Francis ascended with him, accompanied by several other Franciscans. Behind them came the constable of the Royal Court of Justice, with a notary. Benavides knelt next to the chair and conferred for a time with the guardian, who heard his last confession and granted him absolution. Then the condemned man rose from his knees and sat in the chair, clutching in his right hand the emblem of the Order of Santiago that he wore around his neck, and told the executioner to proceed. Benavides's feet, arms, and body were bound to the chair and his eyes blindfolded. Then, with a sharp knife, the executioner slashed Benavides's throat three times in rapid succession from the front, as the condemned's noble rank warranted, rather than from behind, as was the custom with commoners. Death came quickly. The official crier repeated the proclamation he had delivered at the door of the Royal Court of Justice, then Benavides's body was unbound, placed to one side of the scaffold, and covered with a mourning drape. After warning that the death penalty awaited anyone who removed the body without permission, the ministers of the crown departed, leaving the Franciscan friars to attend the body.

For having failed in his duty to the crown, Benavides had died ignominiously, attended by a few mendicant friars, a crowd of onlookers, and the royal officials who carried out the sentence. But in death, he was once again claimed by his brother noblemen and buried with the dignity due his birth and rank. There can be little question that the pomp arranged for his burial served as a gesture of defiance by the local nobility against the policies of the crown. Don Álvaro de Colón, as Duke of Veraguas and Admiral of the Indies, bore all the expense of the funeral with exemplary liberality. At his order, as soon as the royal officials had left, large torches were placed on the scaffold near Benavides's body, and the nearby Franciscan church and convent began to toll a solemn death knell that would last until the burial. About midday, when the crowd had thinned, the Franciscan friars attending the body uncovered it and dressed it in the habit of their order. Onlookers noted with respect that in death Benavides, with his gray hair and beard, took on the aspect of St. Paul.

A gentleman sent from the Duke of Veraguas then arrived at the scaffold with a shroud and wrapped it round the body. At four in the afternoon the funeral ceremonies began, attended by the duke and all the other noblemen of Seville, who had gathered at the Franciscan convent for the event. As the clergy of the metropolitan church of St. Francis filed out of the sacristy, the religious community of more than 250 Franciscan friars began a procession to the scaffold. There they said a solemn response in the presence of the deceased. As they finished, the clergy and nobility arrived from the church, escorted by more than a hundred noble pages carrying large candles. With the rest of the nobility looking on, members of the Order of Santiago climbed the scaffold and brought down the shrouded body of Benavides, covering it with a cloth of black velvet and the habit of Santiago. The layers of cloth binding his body thus marked Benavides's progression that day, from prisoner and condemned criminal, to penitent, corpse, and reaffirmed member of the Order of Santiago. Benavides was carried to the convent of St. Francis for a funeral mass sung by the religious community. He was given a resting place in an alcove donated by the Marquis of Ayamonte and his wife in the principal chapel of the church.

We can only guess at the conflicting emotions with which the nobles attended this tragic occasion. One of their own had brought shame not only upon himself but upon them as well, and for his mistakes in royal service the king had demanded the ultimate penalty. Like Benavides, they too were obligated to serve the crown, and his death must have reminded them all of the potential weight of that obligation. To the nobility the severity of the penalty undoubtedly seemed disproportionate to Benavides's offense; even worse was the ignominy of his imprisonment and execution. From their perspective, the king and his ministers had acted too harshly; yet their perspective necessarily differed from that of the king. Philip IV, a man known for his icy reserve, would later write that merely mentioning the Matanzas disaster made the blood boil in his veins.[8]

Even in ordinary times, the crown could not excuse mistakes of the magnitude of Matanzas, and 1628 was no ordinary time. With the start of the Thirty Years' War in 1618 and the renewal of hostilities with its former subjects in Holland in 1621, Spain faced nothing less than a threat to its power in Europe and to the very existence of its empire abroad.

The main theaters of the Thirty Years' War in the Germanies claimed enormous amounts of Spain's financial and human resources. At the same time, the maritime strength of the Dutch, the French, and the English—separately and together—tried to take control of Spain and Portugal's rich overseas possessions. The best—and perhaps the only—hope of surmounting that threat lay in the continued and regular arrivals of treasure from Spain's American empire. Only with regular infusions of the crown's share of that treasure could Spain meet its global obligations. The loss of the New Spain fleet at Matanzas was therefore not only serious in itself, but also in its portent. It presaged a major effort by the Dutch to destroy Spanish power, both in the New World and in Europe.

The Dutch had established their national identity in the course of their rebellion against Spanish Habsburg rule, and they brought zeal as well as military and financial strength to the ongoing struggle. In the early seventeenth century, Spain was their hereditary enemy. French rivalry with Spain, equally heated, was even older, dating from dynastic rivalry for territory and prominence in the late fifteenth century. England was by far the least of the maritime powers in Europe, but it could also present a threat to Spain when acting in concert with the French or the Dutch. For most of the Thirty Years' War in Europe, England remained neutral, and this worked to Spain's benefit. On the other hand, the English were at least as active as the French and Dutch in challenging Spanish claims to monopoly in the New World.

The 1620s and 1630s thus saw a major challenge to Spanish power all over the globe, a challenge that the crown faced by mobilizing every available resource, both material and human. Its response acknowledged that shipping played a major role in maintaining the lines of communication to pieces of the far-flung empire, and in protecting the shipments of men, money, and trade goods that kept Spanish power and its empire alive.

Spain was the major political power in sixteenth-century Europe, with a collection of European territories as well as a worldwide empire. What is not always realized, however, is the logical corollary that Spain was also the major shipping power in Europe in the sixteenth century. This was true even before the Spanish assumption of the Portuguese throne in 1580 under Philip II. Together, the two Iberian powers had about 300,000 tons of shipping, considerably more than the Dutch at 232,000, and out of sight of lesser shipping powers such as France and England.[9] Fernand Braudel estimated that Europe as a whole had some 600,000–700,000 tons of merchant shipping in 1600, a figure that is at least a useful minimum.[10] Spain alone was said to have more than a thousand oceangoing vessels in about 1583, which probably totaled 250,000 tons.[11] Even though the rise of the Dutch as an economic power is one of the salient features of the sixteenth century, it is important to remember that Spain retained its dominant role as a naval power. Only in the seventeenth century can we see the decline of Spain in shipping, dragged down by a prolonged crisis of production and population at home and by the enormously increased expense of maintaining its position in Europe and the empire against its rivals.

Spain's seventeenth-century decline, as it is usually called, was actually a century-long economic depression lasting from about 1580 to 1680. This affected the internal economy in all its facets, including a sharp drop in population and corresponding declines in agricultural production and manufacturing. The depression also affected trade with the rest of Europe and with the colonies in the New World. When the unfavorable economic conjuncture turned upward again in the late seventeenth century, Spain was no longer among the contenders for primacy in Europe either politically or economically. With one notable exception, Spain's depression left it a second-rank power, even after a considerable resurgence in the eighteenth century. The one exception was the empire, still immensely rich and still in Spanish hands until the colonies themselves broke away in the nineteenth century. Whatever else happened to Spain's position among European powers, thanks to the fleets the empire remained virtually intact, a coveted source of income and prestige. That fact was of great importance to Spanish governments throughout the more than four hundred years that the empire lasted, though European concerns often claimed their attention and the bulk of their resources.

Shipping was the lifeline of the empire, not only in the sixteenth century when Spanish power was at its peak, but right through the depression of the early seventeenth century and the moderate recovery of the late seventeenth and eighteenth centuries as well. At one point, from the late 1630s until the late 1640s, when the Thirty Years' War occupied Spain on every front, the expense would have been impossible to bear without treasure receipts from the colonies, despite crushing taxes at home. And, we should remember, even attempting such expenses would have been impossible for any country except Spain. As Europe's first modern imperial power, only Spain had the resources to attempt so much and to fail on so grand a scale. This broader context is necessary to understand fully the importance of shipping and trade on the Indies run.

The monumental and pioneering work of Pierre and Huguette Chaunu in the archives of Seville has made the scholarly world aware of the enormous scope of the Indies trade (*carrera de las Indias*) and of the bureaucratic machinery that regulated it.[12] In addition to the taxes and tribute that the crown collected from the inhabitants of the Americas, it also taxed the treasure and trade in private hands. The city of Seville, which was the legally designated port for shipments to the Spanish Indies, attracted trade goods and military supplies from all over Europe: cloth, dyestuffs, glassware, paper, munitions, metals, wood, cable, and all sorts of food. In return, the New World sent to Seville hides, dyestuffs, sugar, and medicinal plants, in addition to treasure. Thanks to the efforts of the Chaunus, we can trace the volume of trade from 1500 to 1650. Yet we know much less, ironically, about the royal ships that protected the annual trading fleets and carried New World treasure back to Spain. Although these ships of the Armada de la Guardia were usually mentioned in the registers noted by the Chaunus, it is rare to find much about them or their cargoes, except for the treasure shipments. Often one cannot even be sure of their size or their commanders' names. As disappointing as this is, it is not surprising. The House of Trade (Casa de Contratación) in Seville was established in 1503 to regulate private trade and the vessels that carried it, not the royal escorts that accompanied them. Even that early the organization of Spain's American trade was the product of a compromise of interests between the crown and its subjects. During Columbus's initial voyages of discovery in the late fifteenth century, Ferdinand and Isabella made royal interests central to the venture. And they founded the House of Trade to supervise private commerce and the payment to the crown of taxes and tribute from the New World, defined and defended as a Castilian monopoly.

In those early years of the American empire, Spanish ships crossed the Atlantic alone, for the most part, without any protection. The newness of the route, full of dangers for the uninitiated, and its unproven value kept interlopers and pirates at bay. But by the second decade of the sixteenth century, French pirates had already become a problem to Spanish vessels as they neared home in the eastern Atlantic. In 1522 the merchants of Seville asked King Charles I of Spain, who also served as Charles V of the Holy Roman Empire, to provide a fleet to guard their sea lanes.[13] The first contingent involved four warships, funded by a tax called the *avería* on merchandise going to and from America.[14] The patrol route eventually stretched from Cape St. Vincent in Portugal to the Canaries and the Azores, but organized defense for the merchant fleets was a hit-and-miss affair. This was particularly true after the third decade of the sixteenth century, when war with the Ottoman Turks in the Mediterranean and the dynastic wars between Spanish Habsburgs and French Valois placed heavy demands on ships suitable for warfare.

In many respects, the best way for merchant vessels to assure their safety was to arm themselves and travel in groups, however inconvenient that was. Merchants ordinarily preferred to set their own timetables, the better to take

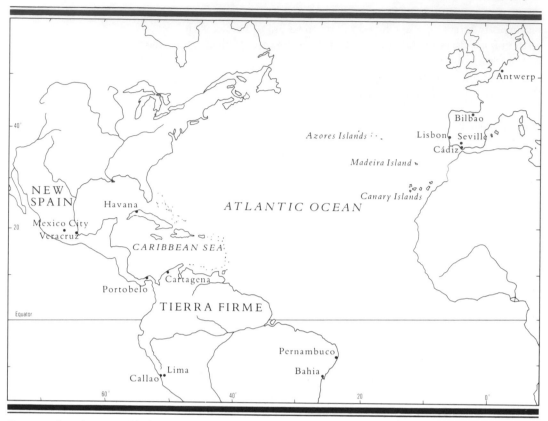

Figure 3. The Atlantic World, showing the principal ports of the Spanish and Portuguese empires in the Western Hemisphere. (Map prepared by the Cartography Laboratory, Department of Geography, University of Minnesota.)

advantage of changing market conditions. Nonetheless, in 1526 the king ordered merchant vessels to travel in convoys, and in 1536 and 1543 the crown issued detailed ordinances about the ships, officers, and sailing orders for the merchant fleets. Generally speaking, between 1543 and 1554 one fleet each year sailed for the Indies, dividing into two parts in the Caribbean. (See figure 3.) One convoy sailed on to New Spain (Mexico) and the other to Tierra Firme (northern South America) and then to Panamá. A single warship with each convoy provided some degree of added protection.[15]

The intensified struggle with France toward midcentury called for even more controls, and stiff penalties awaited ships that failed to travel in convoys. Not only were all the merchant ships to be armed, but the crown planned to provide each convoy with an escort of four heavily armed warships (*naos de armada*), funded by the *avería*. At the same time, plans began for a permanent fleet in Santo Domingo on the island of Española to guard the Caribbean sea lanes, and another fleet in Spain to patrol the eastern Atlantic. For lack of money, neither of the permanent fleets was established then, but under the pressure of war, the transatlantic run began to settle into a pattern that would last to the mid-seventeenth century and well beyond.

Conditions of wind and weather at both ends of the run helped to shape the timetable of the convoys. The dangers of winter sailing in the Atlantic

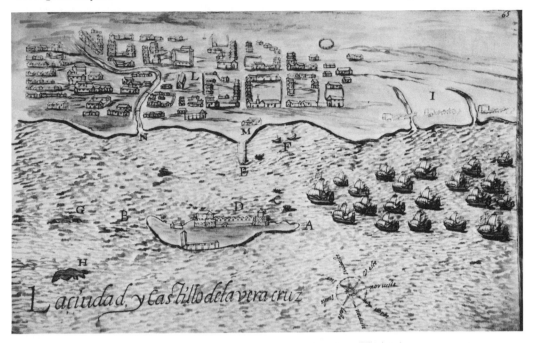

Figure 4. Veracruz, the major port on the Mexican coast, ca. 1615. The fleets entered the channel (C) from the north, under the protection of the island castle at D. At the city's docks (E) they unloaded their merchandise and registered it at the custom's house (M). The mule-drawn carts shown at I supposedly carry wine destined for inland markets. (Man uscript of Nicolás de Cardona, *Descripciones geographicas, e hydrographicas de muchas tierras y mares del norte, y sur, en las Indias* [Madrid, 1632]. Courtesy of the Biblioteca Nacional, Madrid.)

were well known to Spanish seafarers by the mid-sixteenth century, as was the equally dangerous and violent Caribbean hurricane season in late summer and fall. As the naval hero don Fadrique de Toledo would remark in 1630, to delay departure for Spain beyond August was to tempt God.[16] Moreover, the climate in many Caribbean ports created a singularly unhealthful atmosphere for both human beings and ships in hot weather. To avoid these hazards, the Indies fleets tried to follow a tightly organized timetable, which has been variously defined, depending on the sources consulted.

From 1555 on, the ideal evolved of having two annual convoys, one to New Spain and the other to Tierra Firme, accounting for nearly all the authorized trade with the New World. An official schedule, developed by the crown in 1561–64 in consultation with the Council of the Indies and the House of Trade, called for the New Spain fleet to leave Spain in April and the Tierra Firme fleet to leave in August. The actuality was somewhat different, although it retained an internal logic and rhythm that responded to the prevailing wind and weather conditions.[17] According to the research of the Chaunus, the New Spain fleet tended to leave Cádiz about July 1, following the prevailing currents southwest to the Canaries, then west across the Atlantic to the Caribbean. On the average, the fleet arrived at the outer Caribbean islands sometime in August, and on the Mexican coast sometime in September. This exposed the ships and men to summer storms, but

Figure 5. Cartagena de Indias, the main port for Tierra Firme, ca. 1615. The entrance to the port was from the northwest at A, a deep channel for large ships. Fortifications are indicated at B and I, with the beginnings of a walled enclosure for the city at H. Large ships could anchor near D, a place called Boqueroncillo Fuerte. Fragatas and medium sized ships could anchor at G or several other locations. (Manuscript of Nicolás de Cardona, *Descripciones geographicas, e hydrographicas de muchas tierras y mares del norte, y sur, en las Indias* [Madrid, 1632]. Courtesy of the Biblioteca Nacional, Madrid.)

avoided the worst of the pestilential summers on the Mexican coast. The bulk of the fleet could winter over fairly safely in Veracruz, doing business in the cool winter and spring. (See figure 4.) For a safe return home, it left Veracruz sometime in May or early June for Havana. After staying there for several weeks, the fleet departed for Spain.[18]

The Tierra Firme fleet typically left Spain sometime from March to May, reaching Cartagena de Indias (see figure 5) by about June and moving on to the Isthmus of Panamá when its business in Cartagena was finished, which usually took two months. From Cartagena, the captain-general of the fleet sent a dispatch boat to Panamá with official correspondence for the viceroy of Perú, on the Pacific side of South America. Once the viceroy received his instructions, he sent the assembled treasure and merchandise from the port of Callao near Lima to the Isthmus of Panamá, then overland to Portobelo, which had replaced Nombre de Dios as the principal port in the late sixteenth century. Ideally, the Tierra Firme fleet and the shipment from Perú arrived in Portobelo at the same time. The great Portobelo fairs that celebrated this exchange of money and goods achieved enormous importance, but the site itself was quite unhealthful. If possible, the fleet stayed only briefly at the isthmus, returning to Cartagena to meet the ships that had split off to visit other ports in the Caribbean.[19] The Tierra Firme fleet usually wintered over

Figure 6. Havana and its harbor, ca. 1615. The castle of El Morro (B) guards the entrance to the port, shown at the lower (northern) part of the map. Havana was the last major stopover for the homeward-bound fleets. (Manuscript of Nicolás de Cardona, *Descripciones geographicas, e hydrographicas de muchas tierras y mares del norte, y sur, en las Indias* [Madrid, 1632]. Courtesy of the Biblioteca Nacional, Madrid.)

in Cartagena and left for Spain the following summer, either alone or joined by the fleet from New Spain in Havana (see figure 6).

Several galleons accompanied the Tierra Firme fleet but did not necessarily follow the same timetable once they arrived in Cartagena. The crown preferred that the galleons return to Spain as soon as possible with the year's silver, and that meant leaving Cartagena for Havana and then home in the same sailing season. These galleons, called the Armada de la Guardia, followed that pattern for most of the first quarter of the seventeenth century. In some years, the galleons were forced to winter in Cartagena, which became a major refitting station in the seventeenth century, large enough to handle the men and their ships. When the galleons wintered over, they escorted the same Tierra Firme fleet for the whole voyage. Otherwise, they escorted one fleet out and the previous year's fleet back.

On the way home, both fleets aimed to get through the Bahama Channel before August. Usually the New Spain fleet, which left Veracruz in late spring, arrived in Seville by about October 1, followed by the Tierra Firme fleet about a month later. The two fleets returned together only fourteen times during the reign of Philip II in the late sixteenth century, although combined fleets would become the norm in the seventeenth. As one pair of fleets prepared to leave the New World, another pair prepared to leave Spain. With luck, they would both sail the Atlantic and the Caribbean during the most favorable seasons.[20]

These ideal timetables could be delayed on both sides of the Atlantic for a variety of causes: a money shortage might slow the fleet's outfitting; merchants in Seville might have trouble filling their ships because of trade disruptions in Europe; merchants in the New World might have trouble selling their wares and so be reluctant to return to Spain on schedule. If all went according to plan, however, the regular rhythm of the Atlantic trade followed the pattern described from the mid-sixteenth century on.[21] Although the convoy system was not as all-inclusive as its planners intended, the bulk of the Atlantic trade undoubtedly sailed in the great fleets organized by the Spanish crown after 1550.[22] It was those fleets that the Armada de la Guardia was designed to protect. Some authors claim that the Armada de la Guardia originated in 1522, with the first organized protection financed by the avería.[23] Its formal existence, however, did not begin until the late sixteenth century, under pressure from French and English corsairs and pirates.[24] Thereafter a fleet of six to eight galleons habitually accompanied the Tierra Firme fleet, because most of the treasure was coming from the immensely rich silver mine at Potosí in the viceroyalty of Perú, now part of modern Bolivia. The New Spain fleet had as its protection two galleons funded by the avería, and sometimes another heavily armed ship or two. In 1595, an extraordinary year, twenty galleons accompanied the fleets, with a separate mission to find the English pirates Francis Drake and John Hawkins—both of whom were to die that year.[25] Although American colonists and Spanish merchants continually asked for more permanent protection in the sixteenth century, the crown could never afford to send it.[26] Instead, the crown concentrated its few available resources on protecting the fleets. By the late sixteenth century, the galleons accompanying the fleets had come to replace other ships as carriers of treasure from the New World, both for private individuals and for the crown. The ships named to carry treasure on a given fleet were often called the *galeones de la plata* (silver). Although the crown could legitimately claim that the treasure was better protected on galleons than on private ships, the change also made it easier to enforce registration and thwart smuggling.

For much of the sixteenth century, both fleets were called *flotas,* the traditional designation of merchant fleets. When a merchant fleet was reinforced with one or more warships, it was usually called an *armada y flota,* or a *flota y galeones.* The galleon came to be the most typical armed ship in Indies convoys, though other types of ship often participated as well.[27] Once the galleons of the Armada de la Guardia began to accompany the Tierra Firme fleet regularly, many distinctions began to blur. During the seventeenth century, the Tierra Firme fleet came to be called simply the *galeones,* with the term *flota* applying only to the New Spain fleet, which retained its largely mercantile character. This change of names symbolized a deeper change in the character of the Indies fleets and the warships that accompanied them. The stunning rise in treasure returns from the New World after about 1545 funded Spain's ambitious foreign policy in the late sixteenth and early seventeenth centuries. This was not so much because of the absolute value of New World treasure—it rarely exceeded 20 percent of total royal income—but because it was readily negotiable to pay for expenses outside Spain.[28] Although the crown could never commit sufficient resources to the protection of its American trade and colonies, there was at least a sort of balance in the royal approach during much of the sixteenth century. From the late sixteenth century on, however, treasure returns became the main focus of royal efforts on behalf of New World trade. It was a logical choice, but it left the Indies settlements to defend themselves most of the time.

Protection for the Indies fleets often came from ships reassigned from the Armada del Mar Océano, the Atlantic naval force charged with protecting Spanish interests closer to home. It came into existence in about 1580 and acquired its name formally in 1594. The force grew rapidly in the last two decades of the sixteenth century and could muster forty to sixty ships when it had to, some 20,000 to 30,000 *toneladas* (see appendix B for definitions of the tonelada). In extreme situations, the Armada del Mar Océano could call upon over ninety ships with some 50,000 toneladas, according to one estimate.[29] The nucleus of this more or less permanent navy was the squadron called the galleons of Portugal, but other squadrons were part of it at one time or another, named for the place they were most recently outfitted.[30] Under Philip III in the early seventeenth century, the Armada del Mar Océano had three principal squadrons, their main mission being to guard the Iberian coasts and secure navigation routes in three areas: (1) the north coast, patroling from the northwest tip of Spain to the mouth of the English Channel, with galleons based in the Basque provinces of northern Spain; (2) the Atlantic gateway to the Indies, patroling from Portugal's Cape St. Vincent and the Azores, with galleons based in Lisbon; and (3) the Strait of Gibraltar, with galleons based in the southern ports of Andalusia.[31]

All three squadrons were formed of warships owned or leased by the crown; they could be enlarged when the need arose by embargoing and leasing more private vessels. The Lisbon squadron was the standard-bearer for the Armada del Mar Océano as a whole, but, by the reign of Philip IV, the armada had taken on a life of its own, distinct from the various squadrons that composed it.

Of necessity, various squadrons of the Armada del Mar Océano often traveled farther afield than their main patrol areas—to the Indies, deep into the Mediterranean, to Flanders, and beyond. In periods of active warfare in one area, additional forces would be sent to the main trouble spot, leaving the others with reduced defenses. Given the global interests of Spain and Portugal, the united Iberian monarchy had an extraordinary problem in supplying ships, commanders, and men for everything at once. The problem became acute in the 1620s and 1630s, with Dutch attacks in the New World and continentwide warfare in Europe.

One way to increase available naval forces was to license private vessels to prey on enemy shipping in wartime, an expedient practiced by most European powers. A formal decree to license such corsairs or privateers, issued by Philip IV in 1621, coincided with the renewed outbreak of war against the Dutch provinces that had broken away from Spanish rule.[32] Some of the most effective corsairs sailing for Spain were based in Flanders, inflicting considerable damage on Dutch fishing and merchant fleets in the English Channel and beyond. One widely used estimate is that corsairs sailing for Spain took five times as many Dutch prizes as their enemies took Spanish ones.[33] The legal distinction between pirates and corsairs is often hard to draw. The same activity that would qualify as licensed corsairing or privateering in wartime would become piracy in peacetime. If governments issued clandestine licenses during peacetime, however, even that distinction blurred. The Spanish empire had to contend with all sorts of piracy, sanctioned or not, during the sixteenth and seventeenth centuries. In defense, the Spanish crown licensed its own corsairs on both sides of the Atlantic, though they could hardly do the job that a permanent defense fleet could have done. Funds for the corsairs came from a variety of sources, scraped together as the occasion demanded.

The averías and the Armada de la Guardia that they financed were supposed to provide more stable protection for the Indies trade, because the averías taxed both public and private merchandise and treasure in the trade itself. In reality, it was a rare year when the crown paid its share willingly, and the merchants' share on the outgoing fleets was collected at the last minute, after money for the Armada de la Guardia had already been spent. In short, the Administración de la Avería, a committee of the House of Trade, found itself in chronic difficulties. Bankers often had to be found to advance money to prepare the Armada de la Guardia, and in years when no merchant fleets sailed, the avería administration ran further into debt. Despite those difficulties, however, the roughly 5,000 toneladas of warships funded by the avería in the early seventeenth century provided the most important means of defense for the Indies fleets, in large part because they sailed regularly and had become an integral part of military planning.[34] Massive war fleets sailed too infrequently to help commerce, even if that had been their primary mission, which it was not.

Interestingly enough, by the seventeenth century the Spanish merchant community did not wholeheartedly welcome more protection for the fleets, since they were the ones asked to pay for it.[35] Every plan for armadas invariably rested on an increase of the avería or on special levies on local trade in the New World. In 1625 merchants in Seville even offered the king a one-time subsidy of 400,000 *ducados* for an armada in the eastern Pacific, rather than submit to a permanent increase of 1 percent on the avería.[36] The merchants shipping to the Indies did benefit from the monopoly that the crown tried to enforce, however, taking their privileged position so much for granted that they priced their goods as if the monopoly had no competition from contraband. In many ways, contraband trade represented the invasion of the real market into the official monopoly. To the extent that smuggled goods could supply local demand in the Indies, colonists had less interest in officially approved trade goods, which contributed to declines in officially sanctioned trade. When a renewed enemy presence in the Caribbean in the 1620s seriously threatened the very existence of their trade, however, the merchants supported royal policies more enthusiastically, seeing in monopoly, however unenforceable, their only hope of holding at least part of the Indies market. As Chaunu so memorably put it, "They could only choose the sauce; they could not choose not to be eaten."[37]

Plans for permanent protection of local trade and colonies in the New World appeared from time to time in the sixteenth and early seventeenth centuries, but they invariably foundered on a lack of money. When English and French corsairs plundered the Caribbean in the late sixteenth century, the idea of a permanent armada for the area gained currency. Very specific proposals passed through the bureaucracy in Madrid, which found money to build at least six galleons and two smaller warships in Vizcaya. Other priorities overtook the project, however, and the ships themselves passed into the Armada del Mar Océano. A similar story occurred in the years around 1600, with planning activity reaching a peak in 1605 for a large Caribbean Armada de Barlovento. Once again, however, funds, ships, and men had to be diverted to more pressing needs. The idea was in limbo from about 1610 to 1636, when such a fleet actually came into existence, if only for a few years. Although few doubted the need for permanent defense of the Caribbean, the resources simply could not be spared to provide it.[38]

One of the reasons that interest in defense of the Caribbean faded in the early seventeenth century was that Spain was generally at peace with its neighbors during the reign of Philip III—after 1598 with France, after 1604 with England, and after 1609 with the northern Netherlands. Peace did not mean inactivity, however. Philip III and his ministers used the respite from international wars to launch a campaign against pirates, foreign traders trying to interlope on the Spanish monopoly, and Spanish colonists who cooperated with them. The campaign was carried out largely by local authorities and resources. One governor of Cartagena de Indias, don García de Loaysa, took a particularly active role in local defense. When a squadron of English and French pirates appeared and menaced the town in 1620, the governor put together a small fleet and pursued them all the way to the southern coast of Cuba. He defeated the pirates and returned in triumph to Cartagena with the enemy ships and all their cargo.[39]

To provide incentives for the colonists to deter illegal trade, the crown let them keep the goods they captured from interlopers, and even to summarily execute the interlopers. Furthermore, a royal decree ordered colonists in several areas that were hotbeds of smuggling to move inland, away from the temptation to engage in illegal trade. Local authorities on the coast of Venezuela filled in the salt pans of Araya that had attracted Dutch interlopers to the area, hoping to discourage them from returning.[40]

Although peace took some of the urgency from comprehensive plans for imperial defense, the government of Philip III made it quite clear that Spain intended to enforce its monopoly of Indies trade and colonization. Royal policies had considerable success. There is no question that smuggling activities declined in the first two decades of the seventeenth century, although the start of a general decline in trade played some role in that. Such policies were costly, however. The forced relocation of colonists on the islands of Española and Cuba caused much resentment and left some important coastal areas open to later foreign incursions.[41] Once war resumed in 1621, foreign interlopers and enemy fleets would test the improved Spanish defense of the Caribbean.

Concern for the silver fleets was never far from the center of royal planning as Spain defended its trade monopoly in the New World. The less uncontrolled activity there was in the Caribbean, the less threat to the regular and unimpeded flow of treasure to Spain. That became paramount in the reign of Philip IV (1621–65), when Spain made its last great bid to remain the most powerful country in Europe. The government of Philip IV had what has been called an "absorbent need for ready cash," as increasing demands for funds pressed upon an Indies trade that had entered a serious slump.[42] That made it all the more necessary to maintain protection for the treasure fleets, even if it meant shifting scarce resources to the Armada de la

Guardia from other needs. During the 1620s and 1630s, the Spanish crown would fight to keep control of its American empire, which included Portuguese Brazil, since Portugal remained united to Spain until it rebelled in 1640. In this struggle, the galleons of the Armada de la Guardia would play a crucial role. Various authors have charged that Spanish Indies fleets were lightly defended in the seventeenth century,[43] yet it is worth noting that in the entire life of the empire only one fleet fell into enemy hands—the New Spain fleet of 1628, commanded by the luckless don Juan de Benavides. Stung by this blow to its prestige and control, as well as by the damage to the royal fisc, the government of Philip IV launched a major effort to defend the fleets and rid the New World of enemies.

To understand better the crisis created by foreign threats to the Spanish empire, we need to know more about the ships that formed its seaborne lifeline. How to assemble and maintain the fleets, how to supply them with provisions and men when Spain was short of both, all these were vital concerns as long as the empire lasted. Yet in considering a subject so vast, historians must make choices. It would be useful to be able to focus on years and ships that would be representative of the imperial experience as a whole, but the flow of history rarely produces average years or typical experiences. Another approach would be to trace royal armadas over a long span, noting changes in strategies of imperial defense, but that presents problems of superficiality. Instead, this study will focus on the critical period of the first four decades of the seventeenth century, a time in which limited resources, both public and private, were subjected to increasing strains.

To illustrate the functioning of the royal bureaucracy during that difficult time, I will follow the life histories of six ships in royal service, commissioned by the crown in 1625, the *annus mirabilis* when the young king and his ministers were flushed with a series of recent victories in Europe and the New World.[44] Among other successes, Iberian forces had ousted the Dutch from Bahia, Brazil, and repelled an Anglo-Dutch attack on Cádiz. In many ways this time marked the peak of Spanish power. But when the ships were ready to set sail for the crown in 1628, not another month passed before the New Spain fleet was captured at Matanzas Bay by Piet Heyn. In a few short years the tide had turned, and Spain found itself threatened on every front. The empire was in the throes of a crisis that affected the government from top to bottom, including the naval bureaucracy that oversaw the imperial fleets.

*Spanish Shipbuilding and
the Contract of
Martín de Arana*

The needs of defending the empire from its enemies prompted Spain to focus on ways to enhance its naval power, among other things by encouraging private shipbuilders to work for the crown. This was not a new policy, but it underwent several interesting changes in the first decades of the seventeenth century.

Early in 1625 Martín de Arana, a gentleman of the military Order of Alcántara and a native of Bilbao, offered to build six ships for King Philip IV of Spain. A subcommittee of the Council of War called the Junta de Armadas reviewed the terms he wished to present to the king.[1] Without giving precise specifications, Arana promised to build the ships in Bilbao according to legally prescribed measures and to the satisfaction of the king's representatives, "with all the fortification and perfection necessary for war."[2] He would provide the finished ships and their skiffs, cables, anchors, and other necessary equipment for a price of 32 ducados per tonelada, half in silver and half in copper *vellón,* payable in thirds during the course of the construction.[3] Arana also offered to supervise the first levy of seamen and artillerymen for the ships if the king would provide additional funds for that purpose.

The king's response to Arana's proposal gave specific requirements for the construction. First of all, the six ships had to be galleons (meaning suitable for warfare), two of 500 toneladas, two of 400, and two of 300. The anchors had to be made from Bilbao iron, the masts and yards from Prussian pine, and the first crew had to come from Vizcaya, the province in which Bilbao was located. Finally, the king was willing to pay only 30 ducados per tonelada, but otherwise he accepted the financial details. Arana agreed to the king's terms, and the official contract (*asiento*) was drawn up; it was signed in Madrid, March 14, 1625.

There is nothing in the straightforward language of the documents to warn us that this agreement signaled an important change in the way the Spanish crown procured the ships it needed. During the sixteenth century there had been no permanent navy, and the crown generally used private vessels rented voluntarily or forcibly from their owners, paying a standard fee for their time in royal service. A variety of incentives such as government subsidies encouraged private shipbuilders to produce vessels that could be used for both warfare and trade. This saved money in both the long and the short term and provided ambitious and patriotic subjects with a chance to serve the crown. But the policy came under attack in the last half of the sixteenth century, as Spanish shipbuilding declined in volume and warship design became more specialized. The crown tried several remedies, including building ships directly with royal funds and employees, but this proved insufficient for the empire's growing shipping needs. In the early seventeenth century, the crown took a renewed interest in shipbuilding, subsidizing private construction, or in effect hiring private builders to work for the crown. Arana's contract was one of the first examples of this latter arrangement.[4] There will be more to say about the contract and its terms later, but it is important here to establish its context in the history of Spanish shipbuilding.

Ever since the twelfth century, there had been important commercial and fishing fleets based in the provinces of Spain's northern coast.[5] A combination of assets (such as abundant forests and iron deposits) and liabilities (such as isolation from the Castilian interior and a lack of cereal production) turned the Basques and Cantabrians naturally toward seafaring.[6] Successive medieval kings of Castile, reigning over the Basque provinces as well, granted concessions to coastal cities to aid commerce and stimulate maritime construction.[7] Although they were by no means alone in developing maritime trade and shipbuilding, the Basques became particularly prominent in these enterprises. As the only major seafarers between Scandinavia and the Mediterranean, the Basques came to dominate shipping and shipbuilding in a wide area of northwestern Europe, including England, western France, and the Netherlands. Basque and Cantabrian ships aided in the reconquest of Seville from the Moslems in 1248, and Basque expansion into the Mediterranean was one of the key developments in fourteenth-century trade.[8] Some Basques were active in the export of Vizcayan iron, and Bilbao, capital of the Basque province of Vizcaya, eventually became the chief commercial port of the entire northern coast.[9] The Basques excelled as shipbuilders and shippers for hire. As merchants, however, they were overshadowed by natives of the inland city of Burgos, who dominated Spanish trade to northern Europe and controlled the lucrative export of wool to Flanders.[10]

During the fifteenth century, the crown intervened regularly in shipping matters, providing subsidies for ship construction as trade increased.[11] The merchants of Burgos, the best customers for Vizcayan shipping, in 1502 helped finance port work to change the course of Bilbao's river and to maintain passage over the sandbar downriver from the town. Intermittent hostilities with France increased the attractions of an upriver port such as Bilbao, and, in the early sixteenth century, five hundred ships were estimated to be registered there.[12] Spanish shipping and shipbuilding on the north coast reached a peak in the sixteenth century, aided in many ways by royal policy.[13] In 1500 the Catholic monarchs Isabella and Ferdinand prohibited the loading of merchandise in foreign ships, as long as Spanish ones were available.[14] But royal policy, even that early, was not always attuned to northern coastal interests. In 1501 the same Catholic monarchs prohibited the sale of Spanish ships abroad, in effect making illegal a major source of income for north coast shipbuilders.[15] Neither ban was absolute, however, and the crown could and did grant exemptions in particular circumstances.[16]

The Bilbao area where Martín de Arana was to build his ships was highly reputed among shipbuilders. What was not available on the banks of the Cadagua and Nervión rivers could easily be brought there.[17] This reputation rested on a combination of resources—extensive nearby oak forests and a complementary iron industry that made ship fittings and equipment—and the renown of particular families of shipbuilders such as the Aranas. Pedro de Medina noted in 1548 that one shipbuilder in Bilbao was wealthy enough to produce three or four ships a year financed out of his own pocket.[18] From the late fifteenth to the late sixteenth century Bilbao shipbuilders produced a steady stream of ships for public and private use, each bearing the famous Vizcayan flag: two crossed red harpoons on a white field. Although its larger ships were better known, Bilbao also produced a range of smaller oceangoing vessels that accompanied the great fleets and served in other capacities as well.[19]

Yet by the mid-sixteenth century there were signs of strained resources. In 1551 the crown granted a petition that foreigners be banned from building ships on the north coast, since Italian and Ragusan immigrants were blamed for the depletion of local forests and hence rising prices of building materials.[20] Although Vizcaya could lend three hundred shipbuilders to Barcelona in 1562 to aid that city's decayed industry, the north coast had troubles of its own.[21] Despite continuing production, Philip II was warned that the industry needed more help from the crown if it was to meet the increasing demands of European trade and imperial defense. Reports in 1574 from Vizcaya and Guipúzcoa on the northeast coast, and from the Santander area farther west, all said the same thing—that the once-flourishing shipbuilding industry had declined alarmingly.[22]

Perhaps because of this decline, Philip II has often been faulted by historians for neglecting naval matters.[23] Yet he responded promptly to reports of the crisis in shipbuilding, and it could be argued that Spanish shipping and shipbuilding reached their zenith in his reign. In 1563, when Spanish trade was still flourishing, the king instructed Cristóbal de Barros, an expert in nautical matters, to survey shipbuilding on the north coast and to seek remedies for local distress. For the remainder of Philip's reign, Barros would be the king's man on the north coast, overseeing the enforcement of royal decrees to protect timber supplies, setting up instruction programs for mariners, and organizing the disbursement of government loans to underwrite ship construction. A fund of 10 million *maravedís* was set up to provide interest-free loans to those who built ships of 300 toneladas and above, with the loan due when the builder sold the ship.[24] The subsidy was 2 ducados for each *tonel*, a Basque measure about 1.2 times the size of a tonelada. Administrative costs used up much of the loan fund, and, despite Barros's efforts and the continued preference for native over foreign ships, the production of new ships could not keep up with demand, and even declined.[25]

Juan Escalante de Mendoza, author of a pioneering treatise on shipping, wrote in 1575 of a slump in the industry as a whole.[26] The preference for native shipping had to be suspended in the 1580s for several years because of the shortage of Spanish ships, even though trade with the Netherlands had declined as those provinces began their rebellion against Spain.[27] This points out one of the contradictions in royal commercial policies. Protective legislation giving preference to native shipping could help only if native industry was strong enough to take advantage of it. Otherwise, the protectionism may have done no more than impede the flow of trade.[28] Although shipbuilding revived strongly in the 1580s both before and after the Great Armada was sent against England, it seems clear that shipbuilding and shipping were in a state of crisis from the 1560s on. The question is why.

The standard answer has been that foreign competition, especially from the technically advanced Dutch, caused the decline of Spanish shipbuilding. There is some logical appeal to this argument, although it cannot be separated from many other potential causes. There is no doubt that Dutch shipbuilding grew rapidly during the great expansion of trade that marked the late sixteenth and early seventeenth centuries, just at the time that Spanish shipbuilding declined. It is also clear that the Dutch made technical advances in building the types of ships that suited their needs, especially the wide, shallow-draft *fluyts* that were ideal for trade to the Baltic.[29] What is not clear is how those developments affected Spanish shipbuilding.

Did the Dutch ships take potential buyers from the Spanish shipbuilders? In the mid-sixteenth century, the Spanish problem was not in finding buyers for their ships but in finding enough ships for their own uses. Did the Dutch take part of the carrying trade away because of their greater efficiency? That is a reason commonly given in Spanish documents, and it has been adopted by many later historians. In 1608 Tomé Cano passionately denounced foreign shippers for their part in the decline of Spanish shipbuilding and shipping. Not hampered by government regulations, corsairs, or foreign enemies, they underbid Spanish shipping and increased their fleets as Spanish fleets declined.[30] But we need to look carefully at the date of Cano's remarks, which many historians have failed to do. Although Cano defines the situation that existed in the early seventeenth century, when he wrote, his remarks cannot be used as evidence for the 1560s, when the problem was not foreign competition but a shortage of tonnage for Spanish needs. When the rules giving preference to Spanish ships were relaxed, it was to supplement insufficient shipping, assuring supplies of foodstuffs and other vital items to areas such as the north coast that could not feed themselves without imports.[31] Once a pattern developed of letting foreign shipping into the home trade, it may have depressed Spanish shipbuilding further, but foreign competition did not initiate the crisis in shipbuilding. Instead, it moved in to fill a gap created once the crisis developed.

At least initially, the great pressure of demand precipitated the crisis. As Spain's New World trade grew, its European trade grew as well. In about 1550, just the shipments of Spanish wool to northern Europe would have required some 14,000 to 35,000 toneladas of shipping capacity each year. The estimate comes from comparing numerous lists of cargo and ship tonnages, most of them in the General Archive of Simancas. Tomé Cano estimated that there were more than a thousand large oceangoing vessels in

Spain in about 1583, all owned by natives. Taking a moderate estimate of 250 toneladas as an average for those vessels would mean an estimated 250,000 toneladas for large ships alone.[32]

The average length of time a ship could remain serviceable varied widely according to the nature of its service. Although a few ships on strenuous runs might last fifteen years or more with frequent refittings, a recent study of Dutch shipping reveals surprisingly low life-spans for most of the ships involved—five to ten years.[33] Similarly, ships in the carrera de las Indias rarely seem to have served for more than four round trips across the Atlantic. Thereafter, they were generally assigned elsewhere, if they were royal ships, or sold off for easier service in local trade, if they were privately owned. Given the short life spans of the average oceangoing vessel, the creation and maintenance of Spain's combined fleets presented enormous problems of supply and organization.

Complicating matters was the admitted scarcity of some of the key materials for ship construction. Although the area around Bilbao was rich in wood for hull planking and superstructures, near the coast the long timbers needed for masts and spars had been used up by the early sixteenth century. Those were imported from the Baltic, along with pitch and other naval stores, while much of the sail canvas came from Holland and France.[34] Political upheavals could threaten foreign supplies, as when the Dutch embargoed shipbuilding materials to Spain after 1622.[35] That was long after the Spanish industry had entered a decline, however; in general, foreign supplies remained available, even though at a higher price during wartime.

In war and in peace, prices are the most likely key to the decline of Spanish shipbuilding, since they relate to so many of the contributing causes of that decline. From the late fifteenth century on, Spain experienced a dramatic rise in prices of all sorts, including the cost of skilled labor. Fueled by population increases, then by the expanded trade to Europe and the New World, Spain's experience was part of the great inflation of the sixteenth century, one of the shaping forces of economic and social change in many areas of Europe.[36] According to Tomé Cano, a ship that had cost about 4,000 ducados in the first half of the sixteenth century would have cost about 15,000 ducados shortly after 1600. The price of every part of the construction and equipment of the ship, and the labor that assembled it, had risen enormously.[37] In the sixteenth century, such inflation was unprecedented. It was highly disturbing to those who lived through it, and damaging to individuals and industries that could not profit from it.

Raw materials for shipbuilding, particularly wood in the necessary sizes and varieties, became scarcer in the sixteenth century. As scarcity increased, so did prices. The obvious technical solution was to develop methods of ship construction that used less wood but were still acceptable for the tasks at hand. Northern European shipbuilders, especially the Dutch, moved in that direction with the specialized cargo carrier called the fluyt, which was light for its size and had very little interior wood bracing. It was not suitable for warfare, nor could it carry many guns, but the unfortified cargo ship was cheap to build, very inexpensive to use, and suitable wherever conditions were peaceful.[38] The Dutch had always had to worry about wood supplies, importing virtually all they used, and they devised cheaper construction methods to solve the problem posed by the scarcity and rising price of wood.

In Spain, on the other hand, lighter ships could not answer the dual needs of commerce and defense. If the Dutch "Mother Trade" was in the peaceful Baltic, the main avenues of Spanish trade went to the Mediterranean, the Atlantic, and the Caribbean, waters that rarely enjoyed a respite from warfare. Even in peacetime ships had to be heavily braced and go in armed convoys to protect themselves from pirates and privateers—many of them Dutch (as well as French and English) by the late sixteenth century. In addition, Spanish trade was in warm waters, which increased the damage from several kinds of shipworms.[39] Only costly hull sheathing and frequent careenings could protect ships from these destructive pests. Thus Spanish shipbuilders, looking for ways to overcome rising prices in the sixteenth century, could not take advantage of the two most obvious savings: building lighter ships and careening them less often.[40]

As the cost increased, it is probable that the margin of profit from shipbuilding and the carrying trade shrank, even with royal loans and subsidies. Tomé Cano says as much in his famous treatise, the product of fifty-four years' experience on the Indies run.[41] Elsewhere in Europe as well, there is evidence that the carrying trade was much less lucrative than historians have assumed, with annual profits running below 5 percent even among the highly successful Dutch in the late sixteenth century. The costs of insurance alone could exceed that figure, which may explain why so few commercial voyages seem to have been insured.[42] Given the short life span of a ship, inflationary pressures helped to drive Spaniards out of shipbuilding and the carrying trade in the late sixteenth century.

Adding to and reinforcing the ill effects of inflation was the naval policy of the Spanish crown. Royal policy followed its own agenda, based on the needs of European politics and imperial defense, and the great interest the crown took in shipbuilding was not solely, or even mostly, designed to help the industry. Instead, private shipbuilding was fostered as the source of royal fleets, as mentioned earlier in this chapter. When ships were needed for royal service in war or in peace, most often they were rented or embargoed out from under their owners in exchange for a monthly fee (*sueldo*). If the fee were high enough, and the ship had no other opportunities that would have paid better, a royal embargo was not entirely unwelcome. A little trade on the side, perhaps some privateering during wartime, and the ship owner might come out considerably ahead. But embargoes were rarely popular, and kings often had to follow one embargo with a promise not to impose another in the near future in the same town.[43]

The effects of embargo worsened as the crown's obligations expanded during the sixteenth century. Losses to the royal treasury due to piracy and warfare, and the expenses of the empire in Europe and abroad, all took their toll on the royal budget, and ship owners found increasing difficulty in getting paid for their service to the crown. The archives abound with embargo documents, and the complaints about them seem to have increased in the 1550s, a period in which the crown and the merchant community of Spain were in direct competition for the limited supplies of transport. Warfare with France and campaigns in the Mediterranean against the Ottomans drained shipping away from profitable trading voyages to Europe and the New World. Ship masters and merchants also started to complain about the inadequate rental fees for the use of their ships and about the high-handed treatment they received from royal officials in charge of the embargoes.[44] The embargo fee doubled during the sixteenth century—from about 3.2 to 6.5 *reales* per month for each tonelada "ready to sail," with 20 percent added to a ship's official size when it was put in royal service. With the rate of inflation, however, ship owners complained that royal compensation for their services was both too little and too late.[45]

The local government of Guipúzcoa indicted the embargo policy in a long memorandum in 1584, complaining that embargoes used to be for short terms and that local ship owners had been promptly paid by the crown. Lately, ships were embargoed before they were actually needed, then dismissed without either serving or being paid for the time they were unproductive. Foreigners took advantage of the situation and moved cargoes that Spanish ships could not, and at much cheaper rates, because their ships were poorly outfitted and required fewer sailors to man them. Merchants chose the cheapest carriers, covering the risk with insurance, and this hurt Spanish shipping. In addition, England had passed laws restricting the use of foreign ships, so that Spanish ships trading there could not get return cargoes. Thus, Spanish royal policy combined with market pressures to discourage the building and buying of ships.[46] The Guipúzcoan memorandum ignored war and rebellion, which were surely affecting trade northward in 1584, but the points it mentioned clearly contributed to the decline of shipbuilding.

The government of Guipúzcoa spoke for local shipbuilders, but obviously not for merchants. It is worth noting that the interests of merchants, shipbuilders, and cargo carriers were often opposed to one another, and each group had its own ideas about the causes and cures for the decline in shipping. Royal policy, in meeting its own needs and responding to those of divergent interest groups, rarely pleased everyone. In the late sixteenth century, the crown waged a tug of war with merchants and private shipbuilders over the proper size of ships for trade and service in royal armadas. In general, merchants who traded with northern Europe favored smaller ships than those required for European warfare, whereas those who traded with the New World were happier with even larger ships than the crown required.[47]

In a memorandum to the king in 1610, local government officials of Vizcaya gave their analysis of shipbuilding declines, concentrating their complaints on the royal preference for large ships. At the peak of the Flanders trade, they said, some forty ships of 200–500 toneladas had sailed each year, completely crewed by local men. Since that trade had decayed, "no one has wanted to build large ships because of the great wealth that is necessary for it and because the times are very changed and the materials and wages much raised in price and the finances [of local inhabitants] impaired; and if some large ships have been made in these years in the Señorío of Vizcaya it has been to sell them in Seville to carry merchandise for the carrera de las Indias." Local residents were not even disposed to make small ships, because royal regulations favored larger ones.[48]

Whatever their preference, merchants saw royal policy as detrimental to trade. They blamed royal subsidies of large ships for raising costs, and they blamed the favor shown to native ships for lessening their access to cheaper foreign carriers.[49] Given the scarcity of good ships and their high cost, some merchants deliberately bought old, cheap hulks for their cargoes to the

Indies, planning to sell them off or break them up after one voyage.[50] This inclined them to avoid royal regulations about maximum loads and safety standards, and put them at odds not only with the crown but with shipbuilders and owners as well.

The great advocate for shipbuilders and owners was Tomé Cano, who strongly denounced royal policy. Given the requirements for ships serving in royal armadas, a character in his dialogue said,

> I think there would be no private person who would dare to make a warship, or even a merchant ship, for the little sueldo that His Majesty pays per tonelada when the ships serve in the armada; even with 20 percent added to the tonnage allowed, it costs more to build a ship for the king than for oneself, and I cannot think of anyone who would act so against his own finances as to do this, even more so when one considers the many ship owners who have been bankrupted in these years, living with the penance of seeing their children and their family ruined, and finding no one to offer them any more than condolences to raise themselves up again.[51]

There is strong reason to accept Cano's argument as at least a partial explanation of the problem. Faced by ever-increasing costs in the sixteenth and early seventeenth centuries, shipbuilders had to trust in the profit-making potential of building and owning ships, or else to have another reason as compelling as profit, to continue in business. In the late sixteenth century, Spanish trade to northern Europe was seriously disrupted by war, rebellion, and piracy; and the American trade, while potentially lucrative, was quite risky. Even at the best of times, transatlantic trade often saw long delays between expenditures and receipts. Royal embargo policy and inadequate sueldos added both to the costs and to the risks of shipbuilding and shipping. Some of the difficulties faced by Spanish shipbuilders, such as rising costs for raw materials, were to some extent shared by shipbuilders in other countries. But no other group faced as damaging a combination of circumstances. The magnitude of shipping requirements for warfare and commerce undoubtedly had stimulated shipbuilding in Spain for a time, even as it drove up prices. But cost-cutting was thwarted by the very nature of a worldwide trade in often hostile and worm-infested seas. Having taken the risks involved to build and outfit a ship, the Spanish builder had a good chance of seeing his vessel embargoed by the crown at a cut rate for the best years of its life. In short, it would seem that the chances for profiting from shipbuilding and shipping had been reduced enough in late sixteenth-century Spain to drive many shipbuilders either to ruin or to other forms of enterprise.

Although the crown helped to create the problem, it had done so not deliberately but as a result of its own limited choices and the vast responsibilities that it faced. It is noteworthy that the government of the Venetian republic, committed to the promotion of seaborne trade and far less burdened than Spain by global responsibilities, was equally powerless to reverse a decline in shipbuilding there.[52] The Spanish crown knew that the decline in shipping, whatever its causes, was a threat to the entire empire. To combat that threat, in the seventeenth century royal policy-makers expanded their options in procuring ships for imperial defense. As in the past, ships might be rented from their owners, either in the Indies or in Spain. They might be purchased from foreign shipyards; they might be fabricated directly by the crown; or they might be built on contract, as had been suggested more than once. In 1601 the Duke of Medina-Sidonia urged royal construction of armada ships and an end to embargoes.[53] Each of these options had its day during the early seventeenth century, but none was without problems. The overriding concern was that the ships met the needs of imperial defense and commerce.

In general, contemporaries agreed that the policy of embargoing private vessels was the least desirable method of providing for the country's requirements and that the crown needed to secure a permanent navy. Direct construction by the crown in the late sixteenth century had been too expensive, although the ships built by this direct *administración,* as it was called, had the reputation of being better built than private vessels. Building ships on contract (asiento) with private individuals undoubtedly cost less and shifted much of the risk and bother to the contractor and away from the crown. Although administración remained the ideal in the seventeenth century, the practicality of asiento won out.

We still have no clear verdict on the relative merits of these two methods of ship construction. One recent author sees the tendency toward private contracting as an abrogation of both governmental responsibility and sovereignty. He takes as given that the government could have produced a better product, falling too easily in line with contemporary critics of contracts and contractors. In addition, he makes no distinctions among the various types of contracts for ship construction.[54] There is no question that contemporaries resented the privileges granted to government contractors, as well as the occasional fraud and regular profits made while serving the crown. And there is no question that tensions could arise among contractors, bureaucrats, and military men in the matter of naval procurement. Yet even contemporaries saw the undoubted value of contracting out, in both efficiency and cost-effectiveness. Since ancient times rulers had regularly farmed out many governmental functions, and few states in the twentieth century could survive without the services of private contractors. By itself, private contracting hardly constitutes an abrogation of sovereignty, in Habsburg Spain or anywhere else. The important thing is the control that governments exercise over contracted services. As we shall see in following the contracts of Martín de Arana and others involved in military procurement, the government of Habsburg Spain exercised a very tight supervision over those who served it.

The early years of the seventeenth century have often been characterized as a time of stagnation for the Spanish fleets, especially after the country made peace with its European neighbors.[55] That may be true for the total tonnage afloat belonging to the crown, but it does not reveal the whole of naval policy in that period. With the start of the reign of Philip III in 1598, the Spanish monarchy began to exercise closer control over the shipbuilding industry, to bring private construction in line with public needs. Not only were the sizes and configurations of ships regulated, but the crown specified where ships were to be built and where materials and labor could be recruited. Potentially at least, royal regulation was a powerful tool to revive the ailing shipbuilding industry and to encourage subsidiary industries as well. There has been much debate about the effects of this regulation.[56] It is worth examining in some detail, as the ships built by Martín de Arana would be defined almost completely by the specifications that evolved between 1600 and 1625.

During the heyday of Spanish shipbuilding, the crown did little to intervene in the industry, except to subsidize the construction of large ships and regulate their use for trade.[57] Charles I in the early sixteenth century, and his son Philip II later in the century, were both vitally concerned with Spanish shipping capacity and quality, and each of them traveled by sea a good deal. Both Charles I and Philip II preferred Vizcayan ships for their own travels, and northern ships in general predominated in the far-flung trade and warfare of their reigns.[58] Nonetheless, they left the crucial business of ship design and construction in private hands.

In all of Europe, craftsmen's traditions continued to govern ship construction in the sixteenth century, but eventually the need for a more standardized approach was felt. Spurred by the demands of the Indies trade, Spaniards published the first European treatises on ship construction. Juan Escalante de Mendoza briefly discussed the ideal proportions for oceangoing ships in his work on navigation in 1575.[59] It was Diego García de Palacio, however, who published the first full-blown treatment of ship construction and design. His *Instrucción náutica,* published in Mexico City in 1587, gave detailed mathematical proportions for the hull and the rigging, as well as discussing ship construction, sailmaking, and other topics.[60] In addition to these important works, the reign of Philip II saw both the famous naval victory at Lepanto (1571) and the equally famous defeat of the Great Armada sent against England (1588).

Ironically, the reign of Philip III (1598–1621), a king who almost never traveled by sea, saw the most thorough attempt to revive, improve, and regulate ship construction in Spain. With experienced mariners serving as catalysts, three major sets of shipbuilding ordinances appeared during the reign—in 1607, 1613, and 1618—accompanied by lively government-sponsored public debate on the topic. That is an extraordinary record for a king who is usually considered a cipher by historians of imperial Spain, a king whose only claims to fame are that he made peace with his European neighbors and expelled his converted Muslim subjects. In the matter of naval policy, however, his reign marks a turning point, though he is usually credited with only "spasmodic efforts" to aid naval construction.[61] At first the king and his advisors continued trying to make the policy of private shipbuilding and public embargo work. When that proved inadequate, they began a new strategy of building armada ships with private contractors. Throughout, royal policy-makers showed a willingness to experiment, not only with methods for the procurement of ships, but also with their size and configuration, searching for the ideal ship for the Indies trade.

Very early in the reign, on December 28, 1602, the crown wrote a contract with General Martín de Bertendona that was to be a model for royal involvement in ship construction. With a sizable government loan, Bertendona contracted to build ten ships in Vizcaya. They would be in royal service at a monthly fee of 7 reales per tonelada for four years, during which time Bertendona was to repay the loan. After further negotiations, Bertendona actually built seven galleons and two "galeoncetes," fashioned according to the design used in Dunkirk, "which ships sail well and are the best design for warfare currently sailing the seas.''[62] Others who argued for changes in ship design favored Italian, Flemish, or English models but showed an equal willingness to experiment.[63] Although Bertendona's contract mentioned only a maximum size of 500 toneladas for the ships, their official measurement showed a range from 127.4 to 889.6 toneladas. The crown provided their artillery. More will be said later about their configurations, but for now it suffices to say that they were somewhat deeper in the hold than the warships that would follow them, but shallower than some traditional merchant ships.

All nine ships began to serve the crown on March 1, 1604, but only four of them effectively served the full four-year term. Two were lost in an encounter with Dutch interlopers off the coast of a Caribbean island before two years had passed, and three more were lost in a storm off the French coast just short of three years into their contract. The one benefit to Bertendona was that he did not have to repay the loan for the ships lost at sea. One of the surviving vessels was purchased from Bertendona by the crown and served for several more years. The average length of service for the original four-year contract was 37.8 months, counting the full time for three ships dismissed early in the final winter when the fleet was idle. It is possible that the Dunkirk design was not suited to conditions faced by Spanish fleets. But, whatever the reason, if such a short life span was typical of embargoed ships, it put the ship owner at a great disadvantage: there was little chance that the ships would be productive much beyond the term of royal service. In the years that followed, the crown would move to regulate ship design and to make contracts more attractive to private owners.

A royal ordinance of December 21, 1607, specified for the first time the dimensions for ships to be used in the carrera de las Indias. Compared to traditional designs, the regulations proposed longer, narrower hulls and a greater depth in the hold. (See appendix C, table 2.) The new rules proposed an average keel-to-beam ratio of 2.59 to 1 (the figure for traditional sailing ships was generally below 2.5). In fact, the rule of thumb still widely accepted was that for every unit of beam there should be two units of keel and three of length, though actual ships rarely followed those proportions exactly.[64] For comparison, a Mediterranean galley propelled largely by oars could have a ratio as high as 7 to 1.[65]

The speed and maneuverability of the galley as a war machine inspired several Spanish attempts to develop larger sailing ships that could also be oar-propelled. Pedro Menéndez de Avilés, the *adelantado* of Florida, built eight such "galizabras" in Vizcaya in 1568.[66] Unfortunately, the ships handled badly, and Menéndez's experiment must be qualified as an interesting failure rather than a success. Nonetheless, he is often credited with beginning the general lengthening of sailing vessels for the Atlantic. Later warships in Spain and elsewhere would succeed in combining greater length with stability, and design changes in the seventeenth century saw a slow but steady lengthening of the hull.

Before 1550 don Álvaro de Bazán had also experimented with oars and sails together, but his more lasting innovations included strengthened hull bracing, improved topmast yards, and more efficient artillery placement.[67] If the galleass (oars and sails) was an unproductive direction in ship design, there were many better ways to improve the warship. Design improvement proceeded slowly and incrementally, relying more on changes to proven designs than on introducing radically different new ones.

According to the 1607 rules, the maximum size for ships in the carrera was to be 567 toneladas, much smaller than some of the ships in the late sixteenth century, which had trouble crossing the sandbar at Sanlúcar de Barrameda downriver from Seville. Embargoed ships should be paid 8.5 reales per month per tonelada, up from the 7 reales paid to Bertendona. Other provisions raised the wages of workers in royal shipyards but ended the custom of providing them with tools.[68] Although the rules were not to take effect until March 1609, the outcry against them was loud and immediate. The province of Guipúzcoa protested that the rules undercut their traditional privileges.[69] Workers did not like the rules pertaining to them, and merchant shipbuilders generally disliked the new proportions, saying they were more suitable for warfare than trade, with less cargo space than traditional designs. Several shipbuilders even criticized their value as warships, citing several potential difficulties. They claimed the new ships would be so long, with so little depth in the hold, that they might roll too much on the open sea, especially during storms. They would also be hard to maneuver in and out of ports, particularly those upriver. Moreover, with so little depth, even a small surge could bring the water level even with the lower gunports. Experience had shown the value of ships that sat high in the water, the critics continued; their fighting men were at an advantage in both boarding and firing guns at an enemy.[70]

Even before the rules went into effect, the crown responded to the critics by calling together a conference of "persons practiced in navigation and the fabrication of oceangoing ships, to try to emend some defects that experience has found in the General Ordinances of 1607 on the making of ships of war and of commerce."[71]

The debate continued for several years. Among those consulted was don Diego Brochero, a distinguished naval commander and a member of the king's Council of War. Another of the many participants, Juan de Veas, an experienced mariner and shipbuilder, suggested an alternative both to traditional measures and to the 1607 rules: ships that were longer, shallower-draft, and more flat-bottomed than normal.[72] Veas's proposed design followed the Dutch example, blending speed with ample cargo space, a seemingly ideal combination. Tomé Cano pointed out, however, that such ships were hard to handle and had a tendency to pitch and toss even in light seas.[73] Speed was less important than safety in the commercial voyages to the Indies. While the debate continued, the crown extended its policy of subsidizing large ships suitable for warfare, thus providing incentives for merchants to fall in line with shipbuilding regulations.[74]

A new set of rules in 1613 showed the results of the years of sponsored debate. (See appendix C, table 2.) The proposed ratio of keel to beam—averaging between 2.55 and 2.71 to 1—was still higher than it had been in traditional ships, and higher than it had been in the 1607 rules. The depth in the hold, which was traditionally designed in proportion to the widest point (beam) of the ship, was set at half the beam, because the lengthened keel would presumably allow for more cargo with less depth. In addition, the raised superstructure at the rear of the ship (the aft-castle) was supposed to be lowered for greater stability.[75] In short, whether ships were to be used for warfare or for cargo on the Indies run, they were to be shaped more like warships, or at least so the merchants claimed.[76]

The crown sponsored the building of many ships according to the 1613 ordinances, persuading provinces to share in underwriting them. One such arrangement with Vizcaya in 1617 was quite similar to the 1602 contract with Martín de Bertendona but more favorable to the shipbuilder. The crown would advance enough money to buy wood to build eight galleons of 325 toneladas each, guaranteed by a bond posted by the *señorío* of Vizcaya. Once the ships were finished, the crown would return the bond to Vizcaya, in effect taking over the loan to the builder/owner. The finished ships were obligated to serve for four to five years in royal armadas, for a fee of 9 reales per tonelada per month, a rate that would remain in effect at least until 1636.[77] The crown would provide all the armament and ammunition required, and advance six months' rent for the ships plus enough money to cover any remaining debts for their construction. Any damage to the ships while in royal service would be borne by the crown; if a ship sank, the owner would bear the loss but would not have to repay any balance still outstanding from his loan. In four or five years, ships still fit for service in the carrera would be purchased by the crown for a fair price plus other benefits.[78]

If all went according to the theoretical accounting in the contract, such an arrangement would not have been disadvantageous for the owner, and in fact a similar contract was made with Guipúzcoa in 1618. However, the practice was soon dropped. That suggests that private shipbuilders still lacked adequate compensation for providing vessels for the crown. Moreover, the rules of ship construction continued being revised, and private builders were understandably reluctant to serve as part of the experiment.

The Seafarers' Guild (Universidad de Mareantes) in Seville, whose members included shipwrights, owners, and merchants, played for time regarding the 1613 regulations, asking that ships currently in service be exempted from compliance. They claimed that the new proportions were so bad that ships' carpenters feared to follow them because no one would buy the product of their labors. Yet it is clear that self-interest was their strongest motivation. They also complained about new requirements for increased hull bracing and bans on outboard platforms (*embonos* and *contracostados*). These platforms, as well as enlarged castles fore and aft, increased the cargo space of smaller ships but decreased their maneuverability and stability. In banning these accretions, the 1613 regulations tried to make merchant ships safer, albeit at the cost of cargo space. Faced by such strong merchant opposition, however, the crown exempted existing ships from the new rules and surveyed all the ships in Seville and Cádiz to see how well they conformed to the new proportions. Surprisingly, given the vehemence of merchant opposition, the royal inspectors found thirty-three of the seventy-six ships acceptable as they were, and another twenty that could be remodeled easily. Only twenty-three were judged usable just once more before retirement, because of either questionable seaworthiness or unsatisfactory proportions.[79]

On June 16, 1618, the crown published another new set of ordinances for ships destined for the carrera de las Indias. Although these rules by no means met universal applause, they were accepted by merchants as the best compromise they were likely to get from the crown. (See appendix C, table 2.) The new ordinances provided for ships with a keel-to-beam ratio of about 2.59 to 1, and a depth in the hold of half the beam. The maximum size for Indies ships was set at 624 toneladas, presumably large enough for cargo and still small enough to pass the bars at Sanlúcar de Barrameda and at San Juan de Ulúa on the Mexican coast, both exceedingly dangerous for large ships. Increased cargo space in the new design supposedly reduced the need to haul cargo in the forecastle and aft-castle (usually called the *alcázar* or fort in Spanish).[80] The new rules moved in the direction of longer, shallower vessels with less superstructure, all to make the ships faster, easier to handle, and livelier in battle. Nevertheless, they were still supposed to be good cargo carriers. The size restrictions were designed not only to aid in the movement of goods in and out of ports, but also to make it easier to regulate trade. Ships without an excuse to avoid Seville because of the bar at Sanlúcar would find it harder to engage in smuggling.

At first it may seem surprising that ships on the Indies run would be smaller in the early seventeenth century, after having reached a peak in the late sixteenth, but medium-sized ships had proven their worth over the years, not only in Spain but elsewhere in Europe as well. Indies pilots in Escalante's time (around 1575) seem to have preferred ships of no more than 500 toneladas, presumably because they handled better than the larger vessels common in the late sixteenth century.[81] The nature of Spanish-American trade, with many small ports over a broad expanse of pirate-infested waters, also made medium-sized ships more desirable than large ones, even if the system of regulated convoys prevented their taking full advantage of the shorter turnaround time of smaller vessels. The Duke of Medina-Sidonia in 1610 proposed a maximum size for Indies ships of 300–500 toneladas.[82] The Spanish crown nearly met that in 1628 by reducing the maximum size for the Indies run to 550 toneladas, although by then the general trend in Spanish and other European shipbuilding was edging upward again.

Though Spain participated in the general upward trend, there were those who argued against it, and in the period under study, Spanish ships could easily be dwarfed by foreign vessels.[83] A registry of twenty-one ships in port at Seville in 1625 ranged from 338.5 to 736 toneladas, with an average size of just 507.[84] In July 1636, facing a French fleet in the Mediterranean, don Antonio de Oquendo wrote the king, ''We have news that the enemy's armada is of seventy ships, forty of them large, and some of such excessive size that they are over 2,000 toneladas, a thing never before seen on the sea . . . and of the ships that I have here, only the two that came from Vizcaya are as much as 700 toneladas, plus the capitana of Mambradi at 600, and the *San Carlos* and the *Begoña* at 500. None of the rest exceed 400 toneladas, and some are of 300, the size of the dispatch ships that the enemy has.''[85]

The six galleons that Martín de Arana was to build for the crown in 1625–28 were sized to obey the 1618 ordinances and to follow the trend toward medium-sized ships. Some larger ships would continue to serve in the armadas in this period, however, usually sailing as capitanas of their squadrons, the flagship of the captain-general, a distinction traditionally reserved for the largest and strongest ships.

With the publication of the 1618 ordinances, the major naval legislation of Philip III's reign was completed. Although the ordinances dealt with many aspects of the carrera de las Indias, the most important innovations were in reducing ship sizes and proportions to predictable formulas and thus moving away from the traditional method in which every ship was a unique creation, shaped from the experience of the master builder and the specifications of the owner. Shipbuilding was still far from being a science, yet there was a recognizable scientific method at work in producing and revising the ordinances. The first rules in 1607 were an attempt to substitute theory for blind tradition, basing changes on the principle that longer, narrower ships would be faster. Past and present experience combined to test that theory and to interject other practical concerns into the question of the ideal shape and size for Indies ships. The result was a compromise of theory, tradition, and the needs of the Indies trade that produced the ordinances of 1613 and 1618, much in the way that scientific method generates, tests, and revises theory.

Of course, the men summoned by Philip III to consider nautical matters were not scientists. They were seamen and shipbuilders with practical experience and with definite ideas about what the ideal ship would be like. Unfortunately, those ideas were based on a very limited knowledge of the physical world in the early seventeenth century, when serious work on mechanics, the resistance of solid bodies in fluids, and other crucial ingredients of scientific ship design were still in the future. Not until the late eighteenth century was there enough experimentally based science to support the first European treatise on nautical construction and navigation that fully blended scientific knowledge and experience. That treatise was Jorge Juan y Santacilia's *Examen marítimo* (1771), a product of the author's career in the Spanish navy, his broad study of mathematics, and his own controlled experiments.[86]

A seventeenth-century Spanish physician noted that experience is the mother of science.[87] But theory is the father, even though in the period under study experience and tradition counted for more than theory in the final determination of ship configurations. In the absence of scientifically based designs, that was not necessarily bad. Each traditional ship type in Europe had developed through the specific requirements of the tasks it had to perform. Some modern writers on the evolution of ship design keep this clearly in mind. Others write as if every sailing vessel from ancient times onward was merely a stage in the evolution of the clipper ship, rather than being designed for a specific time and place and task. Understanding this is the key to understanding the role of the galleon in the Spanish empire, and the minutely detailed ordinances the crown developed for its construction.

There has been a great deal of confusion about the definition of the galleon, in part because, although the ship saw considerable changes over the years, its name remained the same. Some of the confusion can be cleared away by a brief description of the evolution of its ancestor, the full-rigged sailing ship of the fifteenth century.

Several characteristics are generally used to classify ship types: origin, function, type of propulsion, size and tonnage, the form of the hull, the type and amount of rigging, and so on. The most inclusive classification is the method of propulsion, which in our period meant the distinction between ships moved primarily by oars and those moved primarily by sail. Of the principal seagoing ships in Europe, only the galley was designed with the demands of oared propulsion as a paramount consideration. Oars moved the ship during combat, beaching, and entering and leaving port in periods of calm. Sails were carried for periods of extended cruising. Long, narrow, and oar-propelled, the galley was most useful on inland seas and rivers, where it could transport trade goods on a fairly reliable schedule. Not surprisingly, the galley was the archetypal ship of the medieval Mediterranean, excelling as both a warship and a cargo carrier. It was not very efficient at the latter job, however, because the enormous rowing crews and their provisions took up much of the available space.[88]

The other principal ships were moved primarily by sail, and these were the ancestors not only of the galleon but of diverse other ships as well. Much of the evidence we have for the evolution of the sailing ship comes from paintings, illuminated manuscripts and books, town seals, and votary statues. As unrealistic as these designs may seem to the casual observer, they can illustrate the slowly changing shape of the hull and rigging of European ships. As a general rule of thumb, the date of a work of art is a better gauge of the date of any ships represented therein than the date of the event it supposedly commemorates.[89] Unfortunately, the illustrations and models upon which historians must rely are often difficult to identify or date with precision. The few documents available also lack the kinds of specific information needed to study ship evolution. All this means that there are varying opinions about nearly every aspect of the topic, some well documented, others more the product of national pride and wishful thinking than of scholarship. It is important to bear this in mind as one surveys the evidence.

One major generalization is certain. During the fourteenth and fifteenth centuries, the blending of characteristics from northern and southern European ships eventually produced the ancestors of the galleon. Some stages in this evolution are fairly well known; others are not. One tradition places the introduction of northern ships to the Mediterranean in 1303, when Basque pirates from the Bay of Biscay sailed a northern ship into the Mediterranean.[90] Another tradition holds that northern ships appeared in the Mediterranean at the time of the Crusades.[91] But regardless of when they could first be compared side by side, northern and southern ships were quite different in the late Middle Ages. Northern ones usually carried a large square sail on one upright mast, most efficient for sailing with the wind and easily divisible into several parts to take advantage of variable wind conditions. Southern ships usually had two or three forward-leaning masts carrying triangular (lateen) sails; they were able to sail closer to the direction of the wind, but more difficult to alter in response to wind changes.[92] Both types of vessels were steered by oars fixed at the stern, the northern ships generally with one and the Mediterranean ships with two. A single hinged rudder began to replace steering oars as early as the late twelfth century and came into general use on large ships by the mid-fourteenth century,[93] perhaps even earlier.[94] Finally, the hulls of northern ships were built of overlapping planks with little internal bracing (known as clinker built), whereas southern ones were built over a skeleton, with planks edge to edge and caulking in the seams (carvel built).[95]

Regular voyages between northern Europe and the Mediterranean were facilitated, if not initiated, by the reconquest of southern Spain and Gibraltar from the Muslims in the mid-thirteenth century. Once northern and southern ships came into regular contact with one another, a hybrid style of ship gradually developed, the product of mutual borrowing as the pace of European trade quickened. As we trace the process, we should remember that old and new styles could and did exist at the same time, even on the same ship. Moreover, even when a new style was introduced, decades could pass before it was generally adopted; the sternpost axial rudder mentioned above took 150 years to become standard equipment.

Mediterraneans adopted the one-masted square rig of the north, as well as a northern-style platform on the mast. By the mid-fourteenth century, large ships both north and south often had a second, smaller mast, generally with a square sail,[96] though it could be lateen in Mediterranean ships.[97] Higher permanent castles fore and aft aided sailors working the lines of the large square sails in both northern and southern versions of this square-rigged ship; the castles also served as fighting platforms in warfare. Generally called a cog, this hybrid ship was double-ended, with a straight sternpost and a forward-raking stempost, straight on northern and curved on southern ships. Many examples of these ships exist in paintings of the era. By the early fifteenth century a third mast with a lateen sail, placed at the rear of the ship, had been added for balance, and the southern type of hull construction had come to be used in both north and south for larger ships, though it took a while for northern builders to master the technique.[98]

The result of this combination of styles was the so-called full-rigged ship, the great technical innovation of the fourteenth and fifteenth centuries. In general it had three masts, the front two (called the foremast and the mainmast) with square sails, and the mizzenmast behind them with a lateen sail. It was steered with a sternpost rudder. Just as the one- or two-masted square-rigged ship of the time was commonly called a cog, the new full-rigged ship was commonly called a carrack. In contemporary artwork, it was usually depicted as a large rounded ship with a high, protruding forecastle, a smaller aft-castle, and a deeply cut waist in between (see figures 7 and 8). Neither the styles of sailing ships nor their configurations followed rigid definitions in that period, however. The only surviving model of a mid-fifteenth-century ship is an *ex voto* of a carrack or *nao* (as the Spanish often call it) from the sanctuary of San Simón de Mataró in Catalonia.[99] The full-rigged ship in Sandro Botticelli's "Judgment of Paris" lacks a forecastle, and it is not clear what it might have been called by contemporaries.[100]

The origin of the full-rigged ship has not been settled. Some claim it was an Italian invention.[101] Most, however, credit it to the Basques, because of their experience of both Atlantic and Mediterranean navigation and their familiarity with various types of oceangoing ships. It is possible that other seafarers from Spain's northern coast also contributed to the evolution. Whatever their role as inventors, Basque shipbuilders became famous for the quality and design of their vessels, and they were probably most responsible for the spread of the full-rigged ship to northern Europe in the early fifteenth century. There is documentary evidence that such ships were imported to the Netherlands directly from northern Spanish shipyards in the fifteenth century.[102]

With its three-masted combination of square and lateen sails and its sternpost rudder, the full-rigged ship was balanced and maneuverable, able to withstand conditions on the open seas and to enter and leave ports with some degree of grace and efficiency. Once developed, the rigging and sail

Figure 7. Carrack, with its characteristic protruding high forecastle, full-rigged sails, and high continuous aft-castle. (Woodcut published by Georg Stuchs, Nuremberg, 1505–06, supposedly showing Americo Vespucci landing in America at the mouth of the River Plate, in service to the Portuguese crown. Courtesy of the James Ford Bell Library, University of Minnesota.)

plan on the full-rigged ship evolved further: the number of sails gradually was increased and their size was decreased. This allowed a wide range of sail area aloft, to respond to changing wind conditions. Topsails were added above the sails on the foremast and the mainmast. A spritsail was added to a forward-pointing mast on the prow (the bowsprit). The same principle was applied to the lateen sails by adding another mast (the bonaventure) behind the mizzen with its own lateen sail, although this was not universally adopted.[103]

From its basic hull design, the full-rigged ship would develop in several directions, each one suitable for a particular set of needs and circumstances. The type of full-rigged ship known as the hulk was designed for cargo capacity rather than for speed or warfare. The most characteristic hulks were wide, shallow vessels such as the barge; the Dutch fluyt would also be in this general category. Hulks characterized northern more than southern Europe, although the model for the fully developed hulks of the sixteenth and seventeenth centuries was the modified carrack transmitted from the south. The generally peaceful conditions of northern trade meant less interest in hull reinforcement in the north and more interest in developing the cargo hulk rather than the other variations of the full-rigged ship.[104]

Quite different from the hulk was the caravel, generally a long, narrow,

Figure 8. Carrack. *Llibre appellat Consolat de mar.* Barcelona: J. Rosembach, 1518. (Photograph courtesy of the James Ford Bell Library, University of Minnesota.)

and agile ship, useful for coastal exploration and liaison duty (see figure 9). Strictly speaking, the caravel was not always a full-rigged ship, as it probably began with a two-masted lateen rig. Such lateen caravels were developed and widely used from the 1430s on by the Portuguese, following their own seafaring experience as well as the general evolution of Mediterranean sailing ships. Lateen caravels proved to be ideal for the historic Portuguese explorations down the African coast and for many subsequent discovery voyages, and they were praised by sixteenth-century sailors. The first mention of a caravel in Spain was in 1434, in a royal chronicle describing a flood in Seville. It is likely that shipwrights in southern Spain added square sails to the rigging, making the caravel more suitable for long voyages.[105] This full-rigged caravel, or *carabela redonda* as the Spanish called it, represents one branch of the development of the full-rigged ship.[106] (See figure 10.) The fine handling qualities of both types of caravel were well known, but the redonda performed better on the open sea. Columbus's *Pinta* was a full-rigged carabela redonda from the beginning of his famous voyage, and the *Niña* was rerigged in the Canary Islands from a two-masted lateen rig to a full rig for better handling. Columbus often mentioned the superior handling qualities of both the *Niña* and the *Pinta* over his own flagship the *Santa María,* which was a nao.[107]

Caravels in Columbus's time were quite small, no larger than 50 toneles or so. During the sixteenth century, full-rigged caravels used in Spain's transatlantic fleets could be as large as 150 or 200 toneladas. By the end of the century, some large caravels had moved away from the full rig, carrying four masts with lateen sails on all but the foremast.[108] Smaller caravels persisted in the sixteenth century as well, having proved useful as coastal patrol vessels,

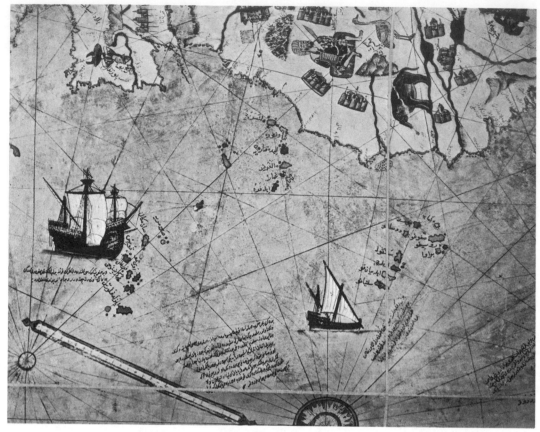

Figure 9. Carrack and lateen caravel. Facsimile of a map showing America drawn by the Turkish admiral Piri Reis in 1513, compiled from maps captured from Spanish and Portuguese mariners. (Photograph courtesy of the James Ford Bell Library, University of Minnesota.)

dispatch boats, and light gunboats. In 1577, Galicia in northwest Spain had more small caravels than any other region, presumably because they handled well along that difficult stretch of coastline.[109] In short, ships called caravels showed great variety, not only in size but also in rigging and equipment. The safest generalization is that caravels were long, narrow, and fairly light, relying on speed and agility rather than on size and strength for their defense. Because of its adaptability, the caravel became one of the two most important types of ships on the transatlantic run to the Spanish Indies in the early sixteenth century.

The other important type was the nao, in many ways the logical successor to the fifteenth-century carrack. Although *carrack* was a general term used for the full-rigged merchant ship of the fifteenth century, in the sixteenth century it generally meant an enormous oceangoing ship, sometimes as large as 1,000 toneladas, apt for long trading voyages. Although it was used by many Europeans, the carrack was particularly favored by the Portuguese for their East Indies trade. Because of its size and its height above the water line, the large carrack was a virtual floating fortress, easily able to defend itself against poorly armed local enemies in the Indian Ocean.[110] But it was not

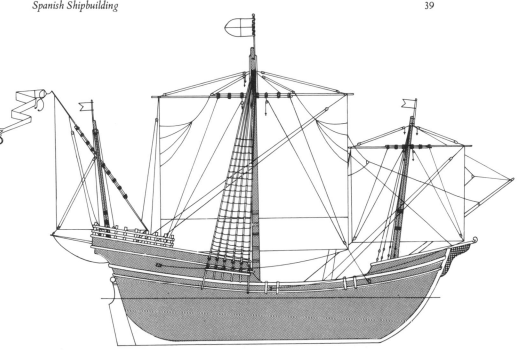

Figure 10. "Carabela redonda," with square sails on the fore and mainmasts, and a lateen sail on the mizzen.

suitable against European interlopers in or voyages to the West Indies. The Spanish therefore developed the smaller nao for their Indies trade. At times Spanish authors call a ship a large nao that other authors would call a carrack, and there were certain similarities in the shape of their hulls and their rigging. That helps to explain the confusion surrounding the names of large oceangoing ships in the sixteenth century. As a Portuguese author observed in about 1565, "The names of the species, or manners, of ships and boats, of one type or another, are almost incomprehensible; as much because there are so many of them, as because there have been many changes over time, and from place to place. The same species of ship or boat will have one name in Spain, another in France, and another in Italy. In Spain they call naos what in Italy are called carracks, and in Germany hulks."[111]

Some authors have considered the word *nao* to be a general term, yet before the late seventeenth century contemporaries seem to have meant a particular sort of ship. Judging from their comments, a nao was fairly large and wide, short in the keel and deep in the hold, as one can easily see in the best reconstructions of the *Santa María*. When the word first appeared in a royal chronicle in 1343, it seems to have denoted a kind of warship, but later it would most often denote a cargo carrier.[112]

After the initial voyages of discovery, the nao grew in importance on the Indies run, for reasons that are not hard to discern. To make the Atlantic crossing at all required a ship of about 50–60 toneladas; Columbus's ships were just large enough. Smaller ships did not have enough extra space even to carry provisions for the crew on that long a voyage, once the weight and bulk of the rigging, hull, and crew itself were accommodated. To make the Atlantic crossing profitable required much larger ships. Those engaged in regular long-distance trade needed enough space to carry not only crew, soldiers, and provisions, but also trade goods, passengers, and their belongings. A nao was large enough to carry cargo, strong and fast enough for naval warfare, and seaworthy enough for long voyages, although it was not as efficient as more specialized ships in any of these tasks. Its combination of characteristics made it the ideal cargo ship for the early Indies run.

Hulks, caravels, and naos represent three distinctive types of full-rigged ships that developed from the fifteenth century onward. In the sixteenth century, all seafaring peoples in Europe had adopted characteristic types of sailing ships based on these three types, designed to serve their particular needs. As Juan Escalante de Mendoza observed in 1575, the Venetians still used very large carracks, both to fight the Turks and other enemies in the Mediterranean and to carry large loads of merchandise to and from their accustomed ports. The Portuguese also used very strong, large naos—which others called carracks—so that a few ships could handle their trade to the remote East Indies, as well as carry passengers and withstand attacks from the small pirate craft in those waters. The Castilians and the Vizcayans, whom Escalante considered separately, also made large, strong ships for the dual purposes of trade and defense, in addition to smaller craft of all sorts. The French, English, and Flemish had requirements different from those of the great long-distance trading powers. The French tended to have small and medium-sized ships, ideal for their shallow ports and the conditions of Atlantic fishing. The English also had small ships that suited their home ports and their limited-range European trade. And the Flemish specialized in very large, flat-bottomed ships that could in their various manifestations manage both the Baltic trade and the shallow ports and canals of their homeland.[113]

Among the ships used by Spain, the galleon became the characteristic vessel of the Indies route by the late sixteenth century. The distinguished Spanish naval historian Julio Guillén y Tato once remarked that the galleon came into general use in the Mediterranean about 1517, to combat Barbary pirates, but its origins are not that clear.[114] Venice used oared *galleoni* in the fifteenth century and later for river patrols, and full-rigged ships called galleons were in use in both Italy and Spain before 1530. Matteo Bressan is usually credited with designing and building Venice's first galleon, about 1526–30, but his achievement proved hard to duplicate.[115] For Spain, the earliest archival reference I have found is 1526, when several *galeones* appeared on a list of ships sailing for the crown, with no indication that they were new or unusual vessels.[116] Moreover, the famous 1529 "Carta Universal" of Diego Ribero, cosmographer to the king of Spain, depicts several unmistakable galleons.[117] Whatever the stages in its evolution, the Mediterranean origins of the galleon are also supported by early sixteenth-century documents from the archives of Bordeaux in southern France, which mentioned galleons as feared warships from Spain.[118] The late fifteenth and sixteenth centuries were times of great innovation in ship design, and it is not surprising that the early years of the galleon are not clearly known. Yet, if its name and reputation as a warship owed something to the medieval galley, its shape seems to have owed a great deal more to the caravel and the nao.

Edward García has been studying the pictorial evidence for some years and is convinced that the caravel was the direct ancestor of the galleon.[119] Although it was considerably larger than the caravel, the Spanish galleon of the sixteenth century had a very similar profile. The forecastle was much lower than the aft-castle, unlike most naos and carracks, giving the galleon, like the caravel, a distinctive low-slung crescent shape. It was full-rigged like the carabela redonda, but it featured a beakhead below the bowsprit, which the caravel usually lacked. The major differences, apart from size, were that the galleon was more heavily armed than the caravel and more effectively braced for battle and heavy seas. Moreover, although many historians estimate the galleon's ratio of length to beam at 4 or 5 to 1,[120] the galleons analyzed in this study had ratios between 3.11 and 3.26 to 1 (see appendix C, table 1), no narrower than the best estimate for Columbus's caravels.[121]

The overall characteristics of the galleon have led most authors to think it evolved from the nao rather than the caravel type of full-rigged ship. Even though traditional Castilian naos had very prominent forecastles, some mid-fourteenth century versions lacked them altogether. Naos had a closed aft-castle called a *tolda* on the Cantabrian coast and an *alcázar* (fortress) in the south. The nao adopted a full rig and a sternpost rudder as they became generalized, and measured in a range of 100–600 toneladas. Primarily a merchant vessel that carried some artillery, it could sail as a warship with the addition of more guns.[122]

The traditional nao was not really strong enough to serve as an all-purpose vessel for the transatlantic run, however. Even before 1520, it had begun to change in response to the needs of the Indies trade. Following the design of braced Flemish hulls, Castilian naos became stronger and acquired a northern-style rounded stern, which would become very popular in Mediterranean ships. In addition, the forecastle was pulled back from the prow for easier handling of the sails, foreshadowing the characteristic silhouette of the galleon.[123] New regulations in 1522 improved the quality and quantity of artillery that merchant naos carried, and other changes regulated mast height and sail volume, required bilge pumps, and established strict rules for the use of fire on board. Ships were also required to carry spare parts and the means to make repairs, as well as sufficient provisions for increased crews on longer voyages.[124] Thus, conditions of the transatlantic trade early on forced the evolution of the nao as a more seaworthy and self-sufficient vessel, able to serve as both a cargo carrier and as a warship, with minor changes in equipment.

As the galleon developed in the early sixteenth century, it took features from both the caravel and the nao, the two favored ships of the early Indies trade; in its various manifestations, it might resemble either one. What it did not resemble was the large carrack, typical of Portuguese trade, whose high castles fore and aft clearly set it apart from the crescent shape of the Spanish galleon. Much of the confusion about the nature and origins of the galleon seems to come from confounding carracks with galleons, an error that pervades the historical literature.[125]

Another point of confusion has to do with the uses of the galleon. In the Spanish context galleons were most often ships that sailed for the crown, or had at some time; by the mid-sixteenth century, the crown often referred to warships as galleons. Because of this, historians have often tended to regard the galleon as a specialized warship, just as the Dutch fluyt was a specialized

cargo ship.[126] A recent historian has argued that by the late sixteenth century, the use of the same type of ship interchangeably for war or for cargo,
"still common in the fifteenth century, no longer prevailed,"[127] but that
statement needs to be modified. The Portuguese evidently did make a clear
distinction between naos or carracks used for commerce, and galleons used
for war. The vessels were different in size, shape, appearance, and function.[128] In Spanish usage, on the other hand, the distinction was much less
clear. Continuing into the seventeenth century, the same ship might serve as
a galleon on one voyage and then as a merchant vessel on the next.[129] The
confusion between merchant and war vessels was particularly acute in the
transatlantic fleets of Spain, which surely had more galleons and naos afloat
in the late sixteenth century than any other nation.

Very few of the ships going to the Indies were identified by type in the first
half of the sixteenth century, but of those identified, 35.4 percent were
galleons. In an average Indies fleet of 1551–1600, some 44 percent of the ships
of known type were identified as either galleons or naos. Chaunu mentions
that Spanish ships to the Indies were enormous, and they were, compared to
the average trading or fishing vessels in European use. Nonetheless, the
largest ships in the Indies fleets were rarely over 600–700 toneladas, so that a
few leviathans of 1,000 or even 1,200 toneladas were always worthy of
note.[130] Naos in late sixteenth-century fleets were usually more numerous,
generally smaller, and more lightly manned than the galleons, but that was
not always the case. Both naos and galleons changed in size during the course
of the sixteenth century. A list of naos from the north coast in royal service in
1505, before the galleon developed, included ten ships with an average size of
271.7 toneladas and a manning ratio of 22 sailors per 100 toneladas (1 man for
each 4.5 toneladas).[131] It is sometimes unclear if ship sizes are in toneladas or
the larger toneles, but the rather high manning ratio on these naos is borne
out by a variety of contemporary documents.[132] In 1537 an inventory of
shipping on the northwest coast of Spain showed eight naos with an average
of 204 toneladas, and two galleons with an average of 120 toneladas.[133] In the
same year the ports of Asturias, also in the northwest, registered seven naos
with an average size of 147.1 toneladas (perhaps toneles) and four galleons
with an average size of 97.5.[134] Early galleons in Spain could thus be considerably smaller than merchant ships, as they evidently continued to be in
France. In addition, they often carried oars as well as sails, for better
handling near ports and along difficult coasts.[135]

The situation had changed somewhat by 1554. A list of thirty-one new
naos from Guipúzcoa and Vizcaya in that year had an average capacity of 283
toneladas.[136] Another list of sixteen naos in royal service had an average
capacity of 390.4 toneladas when used as merchant ships, and a manning
ratio of 10.3 sailors for 100 toneladas, or 1 to each 9.7 toneladas. Thirteen
galleons listed with them averaged 333.6 toneladas, with a manning ratio of
8.1 sailors to 100 toneladas (1 to each 12.3 toneladas).[137] Unless the lists are
incomplete, the naos were not only larger than the galleons, but they had a
higher manning ratio, surely not what one would expect. In 1554 Spain was
at war, but even so it is noteworthy that both the naos and the galleons had
much lower manning ratios than naos in the early sixteenth century. This
suggests that changes in hull and rigging had made the ships more efficient
to sail.

In an important armada assembled in 1558 to fetch Philip II from Flanders, a list of eight naos included a galleass at 648 toneladas, a galleon at 156, and the other six averaging 367 toneladas. Accompanying them and carrying shipments of wool were eleven naos that averaged 448.4 toneladas. Here the word *nao* was used in a general sense as a large ship, and it sometimes happened that the same ship could be referred to as both a nao and as a *galeón* in the same document.[138] These merchant ships were heavily armed for the voyage to and from Flanders, with one piece of artillery for every 10 toneladas.[139] Clearly, in this fleet neither ship size nor armament defined how cargo ships differed from warships.

In 1540, when Álvaro de Bazán contracted to build several "galleons of new invention" for coastal defense, he called them armada ships rather than merchant vessels. The distinction, evidently, was that his ships would be very strong, heavily reinforced and braced inside, with improved placement of the artillery, a shallow draft, and oars as well as sails. The oars proved useless and were abandoned on later galleons, but the stronger hull certainly defined Bazán's galleons as more specialized warships than their precursors.[140]

Because of the innovations of Bazán and others, by the mid-sixteenth century the Spanish galleon was approaching its classic form. Yet in size and function it was still hard to distinguish from the nao. An armada to Flanders in 1567 seems to show a degree of specialization. It contained twenty-eight naos with an average capacity of 541 toneladas and a manning ratio of 10 sailors per 100 toneladas (1 for each 10 toneladas), and five galleons averaging 201 toneladas and a manning ratio of 15 sailors per 100 toneladas (1 for each 6.7 toneladas).[141] Official ordinances called for 20 mariners per 100 toneladas in the 1570s after rebellion had erupted in the Netherlands, and particularly dangerous voyages were urged to take as many as 50 per 100 toneladas, three-quarters of them able-bodied seamen and only one-quarter apprentices and pages.[142] These manning ratios are quite high, at least double those for a fluyt to the Baltic.[143] However, they illustrate the need for defense on Spanish vessels more than they illustrate requirements for sailing the ship. Even as late as 1700, fourteen Spanish war galleons in European service carried an average of 30.9 sailors and 26.4 soldiers per 100 toneladas.[144]

Carlo Cipolla, along with other historians, supports the idea that the Spanish developed the classic galleon, based on its name and Spain's familiarity with the Mediterranean galley. Cipolla's reasoning is somewhat hard to follow, however, as is his assertion that the English and the Dutch "adopted and perfected the new type of vessel most quickly and got the best out of it . . . eventually."[145]

A quite different approach in *The Oxford Companion to Ships and the Sea* credits the English privateer John Hawkins with developing an improved carrack after 1570 that eliminated the high forecastle. Hawkins's improved design supposedly reached Spain about seventeen years later, just in time for the Spanish to produce proper galleons to send against England in 1588. The statement cannot withstand close scrutiny, however. It is at least possible that Hawkins's inspiration came less from his own invention than from his experience with already existing Spanish galleons in the West Indies. He would have had ample opportunity to observe them close hand during his disastrous encounter with a Spanish armada at San Juan de Ulúa in 1568.

Even more puzzling is the remainder of the *Oxford Companion*'s entry on the galleon, which credits Spain with its development as a warship, then with its subsequent alteration over the next thirty or forty years to replace the carrack as a trading ship. The conclusion that "although the design was essentially English, the actual name was never adopted in England or among the northern European nations" is flatly absurd.[146] The name "gallyon" appeared as early as 1545 in a list of King Henry VIII's ships, though what type of ship it denoted can only be conjectured.[147] Moreover, Flemish galleons were used to great effect by the Spanish crown, which also investigated the possibility of having galleons built on contract in the Baltic during the early seventeenth century. The ship type, and probably the word as well, must have been well known in northern Europe to make the plan feasible. With this sort of confusion in the available literature, it is no wonder that the galleon's evolution remains obscure, quite apart from the legitimate confusion caused by changing design coupled with unchanging nomenclature.

Long before 1570 the Spanish unquestionably had ample experience with building what they called galleons, although the ships are difficult for us to distinguish from naos in documents of the time. Galleons as large as 700 toneladas were to be found in the province of Guipúzcoa in the 1570s, although the average would probably have been about 350 toneladas.[148] Merchant naos might still have been somewhat larger. A list of thirty-three on the north coast in 1572 averaged 462 toneladas.[149] In general, Guipúzcoa preferred larger ships than Vizcaya, partly because its port of Pasajes near San Sebastián could handle them, whereas Vizcaya's main port of Bilbao could not.[150]

All this illustrates the confusion that comes when we try to sort out galleons and merchant naos even in the late sixteenth century. Galleons could be smaller and carry less crew and artillery than merchant ships, and both types of ship tended to grow larger in the later sixteenth century, encouraged and subsidized by Philip II. By the 1570s, as we have seen, shipbuilding on the north coast was in a slump, and local residents were decrying the shortage of large ships in their ports.[151] The situation did not last, however, and there were ships averaging more than 500 toneladas in many ports on the north coast in the 1580s, many of which would be gathered into the ill-fated Great Armada against England.[152] By then the galleon had acquired its classic shape: a high aft-castle; low, set-back forecastle; beak protruding below the bowsprit; high, flat stern; and full rigging, complete with topsails on the fore and main masts (see figure 11). It was faster, more maneuverable, and better able to sail into the wind than earlier galleons.[153] But the nao, and even the carrack, had adopted some of these features as well, which should warn us against rigid distinctions based solely on shape, size, or presumed function.

By the first third of the seventeenth century, when Martín de Arana contracted to build six ships for the crown, the galleon had become more specialized for warfare than it had been before, but it was still not a dedicated warship. To be sure, it had heavy internal hull bracing and carried a full complement of artillery and a much larger crew than would be needed simply to man the ship. But most galleons also carried cargo on the Indies run, on both the outward and homeward voyages, despite regulations to the contrary. To allow that the galleon *could* carry cargo fairly efficiently, as

Figure 11. Spanish galleon of the late sixteenth century. Despite the crude sketch, the characteristic features are plainly visible: high aft-castle, low forecastle, beak, flat stern, and full-rigged sail plan. In Artiñano, *Arquitectura naval,* page 92, from a map of the fortifications of San Juan, Puerto Rico, in the AGI. (Photo courtesy of the James Ford Bell Library, University of Minnesota.)

Unger's recent study presents it, misses the point.[154] On the Indies run, it nearly always *did* carry cargo, as well as the specialized accoutrements of its military function. The legal cargo included mercury, royal documents, papal bulls, and extra supplies on the outward voyage, and treasure and official documents on the homeward voyage.[155] That placed restrictions on the extent to which it could develop as a dedicated fighting ship. There were all sorts of specialized craft on the Indies run in the sixteenth and seventeenth centuries, such as caravels, hulks, dispatch boats, and others. But the galleon could not be too specialized, because it had to be seaworthy both as a cargo carrier and as a warship.

The merchant naos in the Indies fleets in the seventeenth century were somewhat smaller on the average than the ships called galleons, but they differed little in hull type and rigging.[156] One expert, in fact, discounts structural differences entirely, favoring an entirely functional definition of the galleon. To him, a galleon was a ship that (1) served for both war and commerce, and (2) was destined for use on transatlantic voyages. Both conditions were necessary for a ship to function as a galleon.[157] That definition covers many galleons, but not all of them, and it does not resolve the main points of confusion between naos and galleons. A merchant nao would have had less internal bracing, much less artillery, and a smaller crew than a galleon of similar size. However, if the need arose, it might be refitted with the addition of more bracing timbers, guns and gunports, and additional crew and soldiers. Moreover, even galleons that were part of the Armada de la Guardia might engage in commercial trade when they were not needed for military use.[158] As one recent historian has put it, "Compared to the galley—*essentially* a warship—the nao, the galleon, and in general, all 'round' ships, alternated, for a long period, their utilization as military and merchant ships. Reinforced, gunned and outfitted for war, the merchant nao became an armada ship. Maritime power, more than ever, was the support of naval power."[159]

When a ship sailed for the crown, it typically underwent a refitting and full careening, if time permitted, and the additional load carried by the ship in royal service was calculated at 20 percent. In other words, the same ship defined as a merchant vessel with a 500-tonelada capacity, would be defined in royal service as having a 600-tonelada capacity. It is not clear if the refitted nao would then have been called a galleon, but there continued to be a certain looseness between the two terms, as well as between galleon and *navío*. The latter term, which came to designate a warship in the eighteenth century, was in the sixteenth and seventeenth centuries most often used as a general term for a large ship, regardless of how that ship might be used.[160]

A partial list of ships that sailed for the crown from 1600 to 1665 included detailed information for thirteen galleons and nine naos. The galleons had an average capacity of 753.5 toneladas, with 1 piece of artillery for each 20.6 toneladas and 16 mariners and 44 soldiers for each 100 toneladas. The naos had an average size of 651.3 toneladas, with 1 piece of artillery for each 30.7 toneladas and 12 mariners and 29 soldiers for each 100 toneladas.[161] Although the galleons had become more specialized for warfare than the ships defined as naos, the distinction between them was still not clear-cut. Besides, given the circumstances, both galleons and naos could serve on either European or American voyages. The diverse requirements of Spanish shipping thus led to a continued need for multi-purpose vessels, just as the characteristics of Atlantic navigation and American ports of call helped to define their ideal size and hull dimensions.

The ships Martín de Arana built for the crown in 1625–28 were a product of all of these forces: the historical evolution of the galleon, the requirements of the Indies trade, the tug of war between crown and merchants in drafting official rules for ship construction, and the raw materials and traditions of shipbuilding in the Basque country of northern Spain.

THREE

The Construction of Arana's Six Galleons

When Martín de Arana offered to build six galleons for Philip IV, he was following long family traditions of both shipbuilding and service to the crown. Mention of ancient Basque shipping families almost invariably includes the Aranas, and one encounters the name frequently in official records of shipbuilders and shippers.[1] In the first decade of the fifteenth century, a Juan López de Arana was in the Flemish town of Bruges where he commandeered a ship called the *San Juan de Lequeitio* loaded with cloth.[2] It is not clear just what his involvement was in this incident, although it is possible that he claimed to own the ship. In 1465 a Juan de Arana of Bilbao received a sea loan of 1,440 ducats from a Milanese and a Catalan, in a contract dated in Genoa on May 24, 1465. Such loans were very important to finance voyages, since Basque shippers tended to be sole owners of their ships. Without partners, they had few internal sources of capital. That Basques could find financing so far from home testifies to the extent of their shipping network.[3]

The sixteenth century saw continued involvement of Aranas in shipping. In 1554 an earlier Martín de Arana of Bilbao owned a galleon called *Santa María de Begoña,* with a capacity of 350 toneladas and a crew of thirty-five. It was embargoed in January 1554 to be part of the armada that carried Prince Philip to England to join his bride, Mary Tudor.[4] Captain Martín Díez de Arana, identified in 1563 as a local official (*alcalde ordinario*) of Bilbao, was also a shipbuilder of some distinction. When King Philip II sent three hundred Vizcayan shipwrights to Barcelona in 1562, Martín Díez de Arana accompanied them at the request of the king.[5] Without a thorough search of local archives, it is impossible to know the relationships among these various

Aranas, but there is a good chance they were related to the man who offered his services to the crown as a shipbuilder in 1625.

The Martín de Arana with whom we are concerned must have been somewhat over forty years old by then, according to testimony offered in support of his entry into the noble military Order of Alcántara in 1622. All of the twenty-four witnesses questioned spoke of the widely known Christian ancestry and nobility of the family, whose members were principal land-holders in many towns in Vizcaya. His paternal grandfather had been a gentleman of the Order of Santiago, so the family had transcended merely local prestige and position two generations before.[6] Although simple noble status was common in the Basque provinces because of services to the crown in the Middle Ages, Arana's family was several cuts above that, and Martín must have enjoyed considerable wealth and prestige. Otherwise he could not have undertaken the task he set himself, at a time when shipbuilding was in decay and many of his colleagues had been ruined. As a gentleman of Alcántara, he was in the middle ranks of the Spanish nobility, which meant not only that he was able to offer his services to the crown but that he was also duty-bound to do so.

Shipbuilding was an activity perfectly compatible with nobility in Spain, since it was of such great benefit to crown and country. It was an Arana family tradition as well, which at least one of Martín's sons would continue. As chapter 2 demonstrated, one needed compelling reasons to engage in shipbuilding by the early seventeenth century, even with the crown directly involved in the project. For Arana, the reasons were evidently tied up with his personal and family ambitions, as we shall see. He was willing to under-take the construction of royal ships, even at a potential loss, to gain prefer-ment for himself and his children. The government of Philip IV (1621–1665) continued the active naval policy of the first two decades of the century, encouraging ship construction by private builders and commissioning fur-ther construction at crown expense.[7] By a judicious use of patronage, the king could capitalize on the ambitions of men such as Martín de Arana.

The formal contract drawn up after Philip IV accepted Arana's services specified that the ships were to be built in the royal shipyards at Zorroza in the *ría* (estuary) of Bilbao. The phrase "royal shipyards" may suggest that the Zorroza yards were permanent installations, perhaps similar to the fifteenth-century *atarazanas* in Barcelona, the enormous stone building that now houses the Maritime Museum. It is more likely that the Zorroza yards were much less permanent and served as royal shipyards only when a con-tract with the crown was in effect. In fact, they may have lacked any buildings more impressive than sheds to store materials. The Spanish word for shipyard, *astillero*, comes from the same root that gives us the word for the framing of a ship, suggesting that astilleros were simply places where the framing was built. This would have been typical of most shipyards of the times, which were often merely designated sites along riverbanks or in protected harbors by the sea (see figure 12). A good example of this was the shipyard at Bordeaux in southern France, which nonetheless produced siz-able numbers of ships. There, props and struts were used to form rudimen-tary dry docks on the banks of the Garonne River, in the open air.[8] The ships produced in Bordeaux tended to be quite small, but there is ample evidence that even facilities that produced much larger ships had the same informal

Figure 12. Shipbuilding at Seville. Seventeenth-century oil on canvas, artist unknown. (Courtesy of the Hispanic Society of America.)

arrangements.[9] (See figure 13.) This makes the job of the historian difficult, since few physical traces remain to teach us about shipbuilding and shipwrights during the sixteenth and seventeenth centuries.

The crucial element in choosing a site was the availability of wood suitable for framing and shaping the hull and the means for transporting other materials to the site efficiently. There were ample supplies of oak and other sorts of wood for hull planking and bracing in the mountains near Bilbao. Even in the late seventeenth century, Nicolaes Witsen considered Bilbao oak superior to that of Bohemia and Westphalia.[10] In addition, the Bilbao area was the center of the Basque iron industry, supplying shipbuilders with anchors, chains, nails, and even some of the artillery that warships required. Given the location of Bilbao and its difficult access to the Spanish interior, it was often easier and cheaper to import cable, as well as canvas and other items, by sea. The long timbers required for masts and spars, as well as pitch, tar, resin, and oils—the famous "naval stores" mentioned in introductory textbooks—were generally supplied from northern Europe. The site at Zorroza was therefore well located for shipbuilding in a number of ways.

Oddly enough, the Zorroza shipyards were not mentioned by name in Pedro Texeira's famous survey of the ports and harbors of Spain, commissioned by the king in 1622, presumably because he included them in the ría of Bilbao.[11] Pedro de Medina, writing in 1548, had also mentioned shipbuilding in Bilbao "and its area," without naming the shipyards.[12] Perhaps that is

why Zorroza is not as well known as it should be. Today it is an interchange
on the superhighway from Bilbao northwest to Santander, and there is little
to suggest that large oceangoing vessels were ever built there. In the sixteenth and seventeenth centuries, however, the Zorroza yards were vital
centers of activity.

When King Philip III underwrote the construction of the squadron of
Vizcaya in 1617, the contract specified that the ships be built at the royal
shipyards at Zorroza. We know quite a bit about how the yards functioned
then, because of the king's concern for the spiritual welfare of the shipwrights working there. A royal document from 1617 mentions that three
hundred men were ordinarily employed in the two royal astilleros at Zorroza, quite a large number for any enterprise at that time. Because of the
urgency of their work, the yards functioned seven days a week, with normal
work shifts on religious feast days as well as on Sundays. When the men
were not working, they were free to go to mass, but that presented a
problem. The shipyards were 1.5 leagues (nearly 4 miles) from the populated
parts of Bilbao, which meant a long walk for those who wished to attend
mass. Moreover, the men had to ford the river first, which in certain seasons
could be extremely difficult. More serious, however, even if they braved the
river and the walk to attend mass, they could not get back in time to work
their shifts. So the men were forced to go without spiritual comfort, and this
troubled the king greatly. He asked his ambassador in Rome to seek a papal
license allowing mass to be said at the Zorroza shipyards, in a rustic chapel
(*barraca*) built of planks and fixed up "as decently as possible." This had been
done in the past, the king wrote (although he did not specify when), and he
urged his ambassador to send the license with all possible speed, so that the
situation might be remedied.[13]

Besides relating the impressive number of workers employed at Zorroza,
the document confirms the lack of permanent facilities there. The description of the modest chapel indicates that there were probably no other suitable
structures available, as the Church was very particular about where it
allowed mass to be celebrated in those days. Another salient point is the

seven-day work schedule. We tend to think that work was less regimented in the seventeenth century, yet the more we learn, the more we have to allow for large operations such as glassmaking, soap boiling, and shipbuilding, which could have the atmosphere of an industrial factory of later centuries. Even so, there were provisions for the workers' welfare at Zorroza that did not necessarily continue into the industrial age. Those whose homes were far from the yards were paid a small sum on religious holidays, as they paid for local board and lodging whether or not they worked. The same assistance—one-third the working wage—was paid to all the workers when, for lack of materials or in bad weather, they could not work.[14] Martín de Arana would also employ several hundred workers at Zorroza to build his six galleons, which enabled him to work on all the ships more or less simultaneously.

Chapter 2 mentioned that the method of shipbuilding in the early seventeenth century depended upon the traditions that had shaped the shipbuilder and his workers more than it depended on theory or precise plans. Nonetheless, royal ordinances from 1607 on prescribed the ideal configurations for Indies ships. Traditional methods of shipbuilding then had to be changed to conform to the ordinances, or the ordinances had to be changed to conform to tradition. In Arana's case, the result was a bit of both. He was technically bound by the measurements in the 1618 ordinances, as well as by contract provisions that his six galleons should include two ships of 500 toneladas, two of 400, and two of 300. As the ships rose in their frameworks, tradition and legislation would blend.

Hull construction methods in the Mediterranean were centuries in the making and changed very little throughout the entire era of wooden seagoing ships. The first step was to select the wood, a matter of great importance. If the master builder or carpenter could arrange to go the forests himself, so much the better. Otherwise, he would select appropriate logs from the lumber brought to the shipyards. The accepted wisdom was that trees should be cut during the winter when they had no leaves and little sap. Most varieties were better cut during a waning moon, though cedar, cypress, and olive trees were supposed to be cut during a full moon. For bracing inside the hull, shipbuilders looked for curved pieces of particular sizes and shapes. The roots made ideal treenails. Hull planking would be sawn from the selected logs, with varying plank widths for particular parts of the hull and superstructure. All the wood needed proper drying and aging before use.[15] In general, it was assumed that one-quarter would be lost in trimming the wood to size.

The first step in the actual construction of the ship (see figure 14) was to lay the keel—the spine of the ship's body—made of several pieces of joined heavy timber.[16] In traditional shipbuilding, the keel was then braced by pieces of wood set into the ground, with additional bracing added as the ship took form. Attached to the front end of the keel was a forward-curved stempost called the *roda* in Spanish. Attached to the back end of the keel was a straight sternpost (the *codaste* in Spanish), set at an angle leaning backward from the keel. According to the 1618 ordinances, the forward curve of the stem should extend farther from the front of the keel than the sternpost extended from its aft end. The precise amount was calculated by dropping a plumb line from a particular point on both stempost and sternpost to the ground below. The distance from the plumb bob to the keel was called the

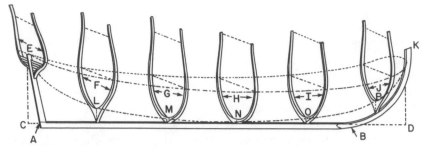

Figure 14. Schematic diagram of a partially framed ship, showing some of the ribs in place (Adapted from Jorge Juan y Santacilia, *Examen marítimo,* plate 2; drawing by Tom Lund and Rich McLaughlin, Space Science Graphics Center, University of Minnesota.)

AB	keel	BK	stempost
CD	length	AE	sternpost
H	location of master rib	BD	lanzamiento a proa
E,F,G,I,J	location of other ribs including E, called the aletas	AC	lanzamiento a popa

Line EFGHIJ, called the "linea de fuerte" in Spanish, divides the upper dead work of the hull from the lower live work.

Line ELMNOP divides the convex main body of the hull from the concave section extending up from the keel. Called the "raising line" in English, there is no one- or two-word Spanish equivalent.

lanzamiento. According to the 1618 ordinances, the *lanzamiento a proa* at the prow end should be just over twice the length of the *lanzamiento a popa* at the stern end.

The length of the keel itself was determined by the proportions established for the finished ship.[17] In other words, as Escalante stressed as early as 1575, by the time the keel was laid in the astillero, the future owner, the master builder, and the master carpenter should already know the mathematical proportions of the ship they would be making. Only in that way could each piece of wood have its proper place and the geometry of the ship be structurally appropriate and pleasing to the eye.[18] (See figure 15.) In Escalante's day, not all master builders were mathematically inclined, but by Tomé Cano's day (1608), and certainly by Arana's, this was an accepted principle. For Arana, it was absolutely necessary if he was to follow the terms of his agreement with the crown. If he deviated more than a certain amount from the overall measures of the ships, he would be subject to a stiff fine.

The key variable in the ship's configurations in Arana's time was the breadth of the hull at its widest point, called the beam (*manga*). From this measure, all the others followed in proportion, from the length of the keel (*quilla*), to the length of the ship at the level of the lower deck (*eslora*), to the depth of the hold (*puntal*) and the breadth of the floor (*plan*). On the basis of these five measures, the total tonnage of the ship could be calculated, according to strict rules. Once the hull had been shaped, it was virtually impossible to change it, so Arana and his workers had to get it right the first time for each of the six galleons. A knowledge of the mathematical propor-

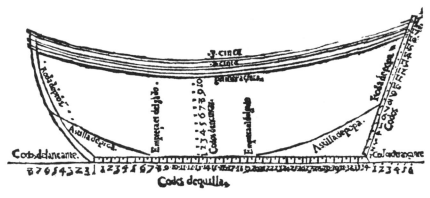

Figure 15. Shipbuilding diagram for a nao of 400 toneladas.

Beam	16 codos
Length	51.75
Keel	34
Depth	10.5

(Diego García de Palacio, *Instrucción náutica para navegar* [1587], fols. 93v–94.)

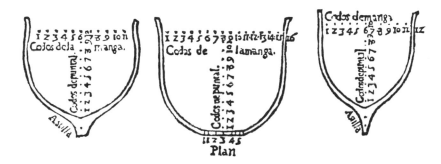

tions for each part of the construction made this possible. In a very real sense, then, the royal ordinances from 1607 to 1618 reinforced the evolution of shipbuilding toward codified and standardized engineering practice and away from art. Yet art was still important, and even within the prescribed measures, many variations were possible that determined how well a ship would sail. That is where the experience of both workers and supervisors played an important role.

With minor variations from country to country, the ship rose from the keel in the time-honored fashion of skeleton construction in southern Europe. The largest and fullest pair of ribs was placed first, perpendicular to the keel. In Arana's galleons, these master ribs (*cuaderna maestra*) were located just a little more than one-third the length (*eslora*) measured from front to back. Their curve was set by a combination of geometry and tradition; for a galleon, their shape was approximately a U. Each part of the ribs had a precise name in Spanish usage, from the first curved piece of wood at the bottom (the *varenga*) to each of the futtock timbers bracing the top (*genol*). The breadth of the master ribs defined the beam of the ship.

The next step was to form and attach a smaller pair of ribs called the *aletas* to the sternpost. Shaped more like a Y than a U, they were set anywhere from one-half to two-thirds the distance from the keel to the top of the sternpost, at the same angle as the sternpost. A piece of wood running from one rib of the aletas to the other through the sternpost was called the *yugo* or yoke. The 1618 ordinances made the yugo half the beam plus one-quarter codo. The codo, the standard measure of Spanish shipbuilding, was equivalent to 22 inches or 565 millimeters. This would produce a fairly wide poop and provide more support for the ship in careening.[19] At a point 2 or 2½ codos below the yugo, the aletas were to widen by an additional quarter codo.

With the first two pair of ribs in place, a traditional shipbuilder could have formed the rest of the ship, shaping the curve of the hull by relying on his experienced eye. He would attach four thick but narrow strips of wood (the *cintas* or wales) to the aletas at the poop, the master ribs, and the stempost, curving them between each two points as experience dictated, perhaps providing measuring devices to aid his carpenters. The highest strip of wood traditionally was fullest at two points, about one-fourth the distance from each end of the ship. Because the master ribs were forward of the middle of the ship, they were closer to the point in front, called the *mura,* than to the one in back, called the *cuadra.* A pair of ribs was placed at each of the two points, with the bottom of each pair higher above the keel than that of the master ribs, lengthening the U shape into a modified Y. This would reverse the curve of the ribs from convex to concave near the keel in the sections of the hull forward and aft of the master ribs.

Arana used more advanced methods than experience alone to place the first four pair of ribs, given the years when he built and the precise measures he had to follow. The 1618 rules told how to place the ribs and provided that every pair except the ones at each end of the ship have the same curve, so that the hold would be as ample as possible. The ribs at the mura had to be 1 codo narrower than the beam, and those at the cuadra 2 codos narrower. The ribs between the cuadra and the aletas needed to be one twenty-fifth wider than half the breadth of the floor, providing a proportional narrowing of the hull toward the rear of the ship.[20] To follow all these regulations, one needed to calculate the breadth and height of each pair of ribs precisely, including the shape of the reverse curve at the bottom of each pair of ribs near the keel. A model for the curve was calculated, probably using diagrams of curves, circles, and tangents. Then a piece of wood, notched to show the deviation in height of each pair of ribs above the keel, could serve as a pattern for the carpenters as they worked.

Once the first four pair of ribs were in place and braced, the shape of the hull was set.[21] The rest of the ribs would be set at even intervals to fill in the skeleton framework and attached to the keel by a strong jointed beam called the *sobrequilla* (keelson). For the galleons built by Martín de Arana, the 1618 regulations dictated the number of ribs for each size of ship. A galleon of 17 codos in beam, which was the average of the six galleons he would build, required thirty seven pair of ribs in all, eighteen on either side of the master ribs.[22] This resulted in a stronger hull than had characterized earlier ships. Juan de Veas in 1608 had advocated three-fourths as many ribs as the keel had codos, plus the master rib. For a ship of 17 codos beam and 42 codos keel, this would have meant only thirty three pair of ribs bracing the hull.[23]

Arana waited to begin construction until he received precise measurements, which delayed the start of work considerably. In Madrid the crown was consulting shipbuilding experts who urged changes in the 1618 rules, just as they had urged changes in the 1607 and 1613 versions. On April 24, 1626, more than a year after the date of Arana's official contract with the crown, the royal secretary Juan de Pedroso sent Arana some of the changes agreed upon. In essence, the changes increased the depth in the hold and narrowed the floor, bringing the 1618 ordinances closer to traditional practice. The matter was still not resolved, however, and Pedroso wrote further that if Arana could find master builders and persons conversant with shipbuilding to agree that other measurements were better, he should go ahead and follow their advice. In effect, this gave Arana considerable discretion in determining the measures the galleons should have. It is clear from Pedroso's letter that the king was anxious for the construction to begin without further delays.[24] On June 11 Pedroso wrote again to Arana with a further modification. The widest point of the ship (the beam) should be one-half codo (about a foot) below the first deck, which was traditionally the lower gun deck on warships.[25] Although Pedroso gave no reason for this, it would have provided more stability by having the gun deck narrower than the beam, thus putting the weight of the artillery closer to the center of the ship.

The work began in May 1626 on the largest four of the six galleons, and it was already well advanced by late July, when General don Martín de Vallecilla, a gentleman of the military Order of Santiago, was sent to report on Arana's progress. The care and good materials going into the construction impressed him, as well as the strong bracing and the shape of the curve ("*garbo*" or *gálibo*) being used to form the hull.

Vallecilla seems to have been sent to Zorroza in part to settle the first of many disputes involved in Arana's contract. As the contract provided, the crown had sent 24,000 ducados to Bilbao at the start of construction, which represented the first third of the total sum of 72,000. It was kept in a traditional Spanish *arca de tres llaves,* a chest with an intricate lock and three keys. One key was held by the *proveedor* (purveyor), a royal official charged with provisioning and overseeing the construction of ships on the north coast. Another key was in the hands of the *pagador* (paymaster), who was in charge of logging the funds in and out. The third was held by Arana himself. The box could be opened only by the simultaneous action of all three keys.

Tomé Cano had complained a few decades earlier that many shipbuilders experienced a lack of cooperation from royal officials, but he had the royal accountants chiefly in mind. Martín de Arana had his own particular adversary in the person of the *veedor* (inspector) of shipbuilding on the north coast, Domingo Ochoa de Yrazagorria, also a native of Bilbao. In July 1626 Arana complained that no more than 12,000 ducados had been released to him because of the foot-dragging of the *veedor,* who "for private reasons was no friend of his, which was notorious in the town of Bilbao." Despite the delays in payment, by July 1626 the two largest galleons had been partially planked, with the heavy timbers or bows to support the hull and the lower deck in place. Arana had spent much more money on this work than the 12,000 ducados released to him, and the favorable report of Martín de Vallecilla on his progress was appended to his request to the Junta de Armadas to order the rest of the funds released. There were materials to buy and more than a hundred workers to pay. The king responded with a royal decree on August 3, 1626, ordering the release of the other 12,000 ducados to Arana.[26] Still, it would be some time before Arana ceased to blame the personal animosity of Ochoa for the difficulties he had with the royal bureaucracy.

Spanish shipwrights enjoyed a high reputation in Renaissance Europe, and their methods were widely copied by nations just developing major shipbuilding industries.[27] Part of the 1607 ordinances for ship construction required workers in royal shipyards to provide their own tools, and this provision was repeated in great detail in the 1618 version.[28] Each carpenter had to bring a hatchet, a saw, three sizes of auger, a claw hammer, a sledge hammer, and two chisels. Each caulker had to bring a mallet, five sizes of caulking irons (*hierros*), a centering chisel (*gubia*), a rave hook (*magujo*), a sledge hammer, a claw hammer, an oakum remover (*saca estopa*), and three sizes of auger. The *cabillador,* who affixed the treenails or spikes that attached the planking, had to bring augers, caulking augers, gimlets (*taladros*), and sledge hammers.[29] Each worker needed to register his tools with the veedor and to display them, marked as his, in order to receive his pay. The crown provided the oakum, treenails, grease, and all other materials required; should a worker be found guilty of pilferage, he was liable to a steep fine or five years as a galley slave.[30]

The duplication of certain tools for different sorts of workers illustrates the overlapping duties of shipwrights. Carpenters were responsible for preparing the wood to size and shape and for erecting the framework. Once the frame was ready to be planked, the carpenters moved on to the internal bracing and decks, and the caulkers and cabilladores worked on attaching the hull planking.[31] Special care was needed to match the sizes of the planks and the nails, treenails and spikes used to attach them. Many different sizes of planks were used for different parts of the ship, and, just as in modern woodworking, if a fastener was too thick it would splinter the wood. The dowels or treenails (*cabillas*) used in Spanish shipbuilding could be made either of wood or of iron. The wooden sort were always round, but the iron ones could be either round or square. Shipwrights in Vizcaya often used iron treenails; Arana certainly used them.[32] Anyone who knows a bit about modern woodworking would be comfortable with the methods used. First a hole was drilled, the proper size for the plank and the treenail so that it would fit tightly in the hole without splitting the wood. The foreman (*capataz*) of each work crew supervised this phase of the work carefully, since the safety of the ship depended upon it.

The work of caulking the seams between the planks followed, according to methods that had been proven over the centuries.[33] Traditionally, oakum (*estopa*) or hemp fiber (*cáñamo*) was forced into the open seams. That was not the ideal method, according to a famous treatise on caulking written in about 1640.[34] Its anonymous author wrote that if the seams were of uneven widths or too narrow to allow sufficient caulking, they should be chiseled out. The thicker the plank, the deeper the V-shaped gouge that the caulkers should make, sometimes cutting all the way to the ribs. The result would be a deep, even channel for the caulking and a more watertight ship. The prescription for channels that deep is perhaps excessive, but there is no doubt of the importance of proper caulking. Nail and treenail holes, seams and other joinings, knotholes and other flaws in the wood all had to be made as watertight as possible. In Vizcaya, knotholes and other flaws were placed facing toward the inside of the ship, an acceptable method if they were properly caulked, but one that could cause trouble if the flaw were missed.

Throughout the process of caulking, a foreman watched the work carefully, but especially before the caulking material was coated with tar. Once tar had been added to the seams, it was nearly impossible to see flaws in the caulking. To protect against shipworms, tarred cloth and a thin layer of lead sheathing were often nailed to the hull below the water line. As a final step, the entire hull was coated with a mixture of tar and some sort of grease, lard, or tallow to make the tar stick to the hull. If fish grease were used, the best sort came from dogfish, small sharks, or other light fish, since less sulfur had to be used to get it to mix with the tar. Sardine oil, the greasiest of all, was also recommended. The worst fish oil came from tuna, which, if used in cold temperatures, prevented the tar from adhering to the hull. Besides animal fats, one could use heated pitch or pine tar, or alquitrán, a mixture of pitch, grease, resin, and oil. There was some evidence that alquitrán was superior to animal fat; it was the admixture used in every careening account examined for this study. Even when everything was done properly, leakage was a major problem on most large ships; that is why pumps were a standard part of their equipment.[35] Because of the nature of their work, caulkers worked more days on a given ship than carpenters, and major ports often faced a shortage of caulkers to handle a sudden influx of business, despite government efforts to increase their numbers.[36]

By January 1627, Arana's galleons were rapidly approaching completion. Following royal orders, the proveedor and the pagador went to Zorroza on an inspection tour of the construction site and the materials on hand. They visited the ships with four master carpenters who were employed there and asked each one about the progress being made. The carpenters said under oath that already more than 40,000 ducats had been spent on the six galleons, and that the work was being done with care. Accompanying the official report of the visit was a record of over 23,000 ducados in gold that had been spent between September and December 1626 on wood, labor, and caulking materials. Evidently, the veedor had presented accounts only for the first 12,000 ducados delivered to Arana, and the other two royal officials asked in their report that he be ordered to account for the balance. It is hard to avoid the suspicion that Arana was right in claiming the veedor was dragging his feet.[37]

By then the construction had advanced far enough that the ships could be officially measured. This was easiest to do before a ship was completed, because the bracing and superstructures got in the way of the measurements. Consequently, on February 13, 1627, the king ordered don Fernando de la Rivaherrera, the general purveyor of armadas and superintendent of ship construction on the north coast, to proceed to Bilbao. There he was to measure each ship thoroughly, inspect them all for conformity to the 1618 rules, and report back with an estimate of when they would be ready to sail.[38]

Winter on the Cantabrian coast can be wet and miserable, and Rivaherrera was not in the best of health. Arana wrote to the Junta de Armadas when Rivaherrera delayed his arrival, complaining that his workers had little to do until the official measurement (*arqueamiento*) had been carried out. The Junta received the letter on March 28 and decided to give the job instead to General Martín de Vallecilla, who was about to leave for Vizcaya anyway. By then, however, Rivaherrera had already carried out his commission, though with rather poor grace. In the surprisingly bold terms common to many royal officials, Rivaherrera wrote the king that he had carried out the royal order, "leaving my house in bad weather, when I was in poor health."[39] Despite his pique at being dragged from his home in the winter, he did not take it out on Arana, whom he reported to be a careful man desiring more to serve the king than to make money. It was clear even then that the ships would exceed the price the crown was paying for them.

Delays in sending funds from Madrid had begun to slow the construction, and in a separate letter sent with Rivaherrera's packet, Arana made a special plea to be paid. Though he had not received any money for seven months, he noted, he had underwritten the work with his own money, "with such punctuality, toil, and care that in this particular no human man could have surpassed me." Although by the terms of the contract, the delays in payment entitled him to an extra year to finish the ships, he still planned to have them done by August, with the help of divine favor. So that nothing should impede his progress, he asked the king to send the last half of the second payment, and the third payment, augmented to include the increased tonnage ordered by the crown. "If God gives me life," Arana concluded, he would finish the ships soon, made as handsome, strong, and well constructed as any that had ever come from Vizcaya. In a separate letter to Rivaherrera, Arana asked for his support in getting the rest of the money owed, since he had received no more than 35,300 ducados of the total 72,000 promised.[40]

In Rivaherrera's opinion, the work could be finished as Arana promised, if he were able to continue with his present work force of 130 carpenters plus the master carpenters, and 50 caulkers. In general, he found the work to be proceeding well, with handsome wood and conformity to the royal ordinances. Arana had managed to assemble all the wood he needed to finish, and even more. The masts were on hand, including some in reserve. Pitch, tar, nails and treenails, tackle, ropes, cables, and hemp—everything had arrived. Only the sail canvas was missing, and it was promised any day from France. The effort required to assemble all these supplies in less than a year was noteworthy.

Rivaherrera found only a few faults with the construction, which was in general "very good and very strong." The empty bows beneath the lower deck on each ship lacked four additional curved braces (*corbatones*), two on each side at the extreme ends of the hull. As it was, they had no more braces than the bows supporting the deck above them. When questioned, Arana had responded that the master craftsmen thought they had included quite sufficient bracing, the same amount recommended by General Vallecilla. Reminded that his contract required additional bracing, Arana bowed to the king's will. Rivaherrera also found the poop of each ship to lack a specific type of strengthening; the meaning of the word used (*calimes*) is not clear, though he mentioned that each ship carried three or at most four calimes. The defect was evidently impossible to correct at that stage, and Rivaherrera judged that the ships would probably be strong enough as they were.

Fully half of Rivaherrera's letter to the king concerned his own health and his service to the crown. The task of inspecting Arana's ships had been very great, and he was not suited to such long trips from his home. Fourteen years before, the late King Philip III, realizing how sickly he was from liver ailments and stone (kidney stone, presumably), had granted him a special dispensation in his work. Since the north coast climate exacerbated these ailments, the king had permitted him to live where it best suited him, delegating his duties to his brother Francisco.[41] Since the brother subsequently gained a royal post of his own in about 1623, the duties of superintendent on the north coast had been carried out by Juan de Sala, who was experienced, zealous, and faithful in the work. In other words, Rivaherrera had been an absentee official for the past twelve years, a situation that the new king and his ministers had evidently decided to correct. Nonetheless, Rivaherrera asked for a confirmation of the royal decree, so that he might live out the few remaining days of his life in some alleviation of his pain. He further asked to be allowed to come to the court (as Madrid was known) to seek a cure. If this mercy were to be granted, he assured the king, royal interests would not be compromised, since he had trained a good team for the work, and he himself would not leave the coast the coming summer until the troops and sailors had been gathered for Arana's ships.[42] Rivaherrera was sincere enough about his poor health; he died a few years later.[43]

These official reports provide a glimpse into the personal relationships that allowed the government to function. The developed world in the twentieth century functions with a system of bureaucracy in which the principle of reciprocity—favors for services—is hidden by official rules and impersonality. In Habsburg Spain, the personal relationships between clients and patrons instead were on the surface, openly acknowledged by all concerned parties. This is clear in Rivaherrera's report, which is a frank request for special treatment in return for services rendered. The fact that those services were part of his job had little to do with it. Royal government would have been paralyzed without the voluntary compliance of royal officials who were perfectly capable of "obeying but not complying," as the old phrase went. Bureaucracy and royal service were still personal contracts between the sovereign and the subject. Rivaherrera had been granted a special favor by the late King Philip III. The new king owed him nothing, until he had performed some service to the crown. Carrying out the inspection and measurement of Arana's ships and supervising the levy to crew them constituted that service. The reciprocal nature of royal service is less clear in Arana's case. He already had wealth and position, and he seemed to be acting out of duty and zeal to serve the king, to the detriment of his own finances. A cynical modern mind might wonder what was in it for him. The simple answer is that building the six galleons was his claim to royal favor in the future. He knew that perfectly well, and so did the king. That was the way the system worked, and there is no need to interpret it cynically or to question Arana's loyalty or his zeal. He did work hard, and he did spend some of his own money in constructing the six ships. It was his duty, and also his privilege, to do so, because it put the king in his debt.

At the end of March 1627 when Rivaherrera made his inspection, Arana's six galleons were so far along that they had acquired names as well as individual characteristics. Spanish ships, especially those in royal service, usually had religious names, often connected in some way to the place where they were built or to a saint with special significance for their owners. A ship might later be given a nickname by its crew, or it might have its name changed when it changed ownership or status. Among important ships in royal service, there seems to have been only one of a given name at a given time.[44] When a ship was lost at sea or left royal service, its name was often given to a new ship serving the crown, just as parents in those days sometimes gave a new child the name of one they had lost.

Nuestra Señora de Begoña, the largest of Arana's six galleons, measured 541.5 toneladas by Rivaherrera's calculations (with the fractions in the documents expressed here as decimals). *Begoña* was a very popular name for a ship built in Bilbao, as Our Lady of Begoña was the patroness of Vizcaya. Her sixteenth-century basilica is in the northeast part of Bilbao, and local residents have always felt a special devotion to her. When Rivaherrera first saw the galleon called *Begoña* it was completely planked and caulked halfway up, ready to be hauled into the water after Easter. The *San Felipe* at 537.375 toneladas was named for the patron saint of the king. It was also planked and completed to the top of the hull, and workers had just begun to caulk. *San Juan Baptista* at 455.75 toneladas was less far along. Planking had been applied from the wale (*cinta*) that marked the widest point of the ship (called the *linea de fuerte*) on up—the part called the dead work (*obra muerta*). (See figure 14.) It was half planked from the linea de fuerte on down—the part called the live work (*obra viva*), which carried heavier planking. The wales were strips of wood applied to the outside of the ribs from stem to stern, setting the shape of the hull and the curve (*arrufo* or sheer) for the planking to follow. Spanish ships had four wales, with the so-called principal wale (*cinta principal*) on the linea de fuerte.[45] The galleon *Los Tres Reyes,* whose name was actually *Nuestra Señora de los Tres Reyes,* measured 455 toneladas. The first deck and the bridge (*puente*) or second deck were finished by March 1627, along with their braces and supporting beams. One side had been planked from the cinta to the keel, and the other side was half finished. The *San Sebastián,* named for another popular saint on the north coast, measured 330.25 toneladas. The first deck (*cubierta*) was in place, everything was half planked, and the inside bracing was finished from the deck on down. The *Santiago,* named for the patron saint of all Spain, measured 338.5 toneladas. It was completely planked from top to bottom and ready to be caulked.

To calculate the tonnages of the six galleons, Rivaherrera followed a precise set of instructions. In Cristóbal de Barros's time in the late sixteenth century, only the beam, length, and depth in the hold had been used to measure the ships, and the rules assumed that the decks had not yet been planked.[46] There had been a great deal of criticism of this, most notably from Tomé Cano, who pointed out that increases in the keel and decreases in the depth in the hold meant that the old method greatly underestimated the size of the ships.[47] Responding to this and other criticisms, the crown issued a new set of rules for measurement in 1613, but they were not destined to please the critics. The beam (*manga*) was to be measured from side to side on the lower deck at its widest point, whether or not that was the greatest breadth of the ship. If any obstructions such as reinforcing timbers were in the way, the way around them would be part of the beam as well. The length (*eslora*) was to be measured along the same deck from stem to stern, with the way around any obstruction likewise included. The depth in the hold (*puntal*) was to be measured from the planks of the floor to the upper surface of the same deck, including the thickness of the planking of that deck. In foreign ships with a compartment at the bottom of the hold for grain and other bulky goods, the area would have to be opened up to get to the rib, with the depth then measured as if floor planking were in place on top of the rib. The breadth of the floor (*plan*) itself was to be measured at the bottom curve of the master ribs, as if the floor were flat. Finally, the keel was to be measured along its flat part alone, ideally with the ship out of the water or fully careened to expose the keel. If the ship were in the water, complicated rules provided for figuring the keel based on its length measured from inside the ship.

The 1613 rules gave three methods to figure the tonnage of a ship, using all five of these principal measures, and differing according to whether the floor was equal to, less than, or more than half the beam. All three methods assumed that the surfaces of the floor and the breadth on deck diminished at a predictable rate from their midpoints toward the prow and the poop. The simplest method was the third one, which worked regardless of the width of the floor.[48] The 1613 rules gave a figure that was considerably smaller than Barros's method, about 14 percent smaller on the average for the ships' measures I have calculated using both methods. As these new rules were clearly to the crown's advantage, both in renting ships and in paying for their construction by tonnage, there should have been strong protests against them, but I have found no evidence of it. The crown did rescind the new rules in 1618, however, returning to the method used by Barros.[49] The configurations given in the 1618 ordinances seem to have used Barros's method in full, which subtracted 5 percent from the cubic measure to allow for the space taken by internal bracing, and added 20 percent to the calculated tonnage for ships sailing in royal armadas (method 2 in Table 1). The calculations for Arana's ships made by Rivaherrera must have used a simplification of Barros's method, without subtracting for bracing or adding for armada use (method 1 in Table 1). That would explain why the given tonnages for Arana's ships fall far below the tonnages for ships of similar configurations in the 1618 ordinances. By using the simplified method, the crown greatly reduced the amount it had to pay for the construction. Recalculating the tonnages of Arana's ships using the complete Barros method (method 2) gives a result quite close to the tonnages in the 1618 ordinances, certainly close enough for Arana's ships to have been approved by royal officials. All together, the six galleons measured 2,658.375 toneladas, exceeding the contract specifications of 2,400 toneladas, because of changes ordered by the crown.[50]

Evidently Arana took the royal secretary Juan de Pedroso at his word and virtually ignored the changes to the 1618 ordinances that had been made in 1626. In general, we may assume the ships conformed fairly closely to the 1618 ordinances, which specified not only the five principal measures but many others as well. If we look at a theoretical ship with a beam of 17 codos (the average size of the ships Arana built), we can follow the specifications in detail. (See figure 16.) Besides the five measures listed in Table 1, the ship would have had its lower deck at 8.5 codos from the floor, or .5 codo above the upper limit of the hold. The lanzamiento at the prow (see below) was 8 codos, and that at the poop 4 codos. The ship would have 37 ribs and a yugo measure across the aletas of 8.75 codos, narrowing from the 17 at the master ribs. The concave rise above the keel and below each pair of ribs, called the *astilla muerta,* was given as a single measure, with two-thirds of it to be at the master ribs and the other third divided into as many equal parts as there were

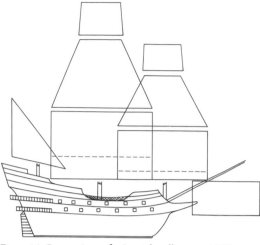

Figure 16. Proportions of a Spanish galleon ca. 1625[a]

Hull

Beam	17	codos
Breadth at mura	16	
Breadth at cuadra	15	
Keel	44	
Length on lower deck	56	
Depth in the hold	8	
Height of first deck above keel	8.5	
Lanzamiento a proa	8	
Lanzamiento a popa	4	
Width of floor	8.5	
Width of yugo	8.75	

Tonnage according to 1618 rules	530 toneladas
Tonnage calculated by Method 1 (See Table 1)	476
Tonnage calculated by Method 2 (See Table 1)	543

Masts

Mainmast	46	codos long
Its yard	38.25	
Main-topmast	28.4	long
Its yard	17	
Main-topgallant mast	14	long
Its yard	15.5	
Foremast	42	long
Its yard	34	
Fore-topmast	23	long
Its yard	15.5	
Fore-topgallant mast	11.5	long
Its yard	14.5	
Bowsprit	40	long
Its yard	27	
Mizzenmast	31.4	long
Its yard	34	

Sails

Mainsail	17.5	codos long
	38.25	wide
Bonnet	8.5	long
	38.25	wide
Topsail	26	long
	38.25	lower width
	17	upper width
Main-topgallant	13	long
	17	lower width
	15.5	upper width
Foresail	16	long
	34	wide
Bonnet	3	long
	34	wide
Fore-topsail	19	long
	34	lower width
	15.5	upper width
Fore-topgallant	10.5	long
	15.5	lower width
	14.5	upper width
Spritsail[b]	13	long
	27	wide
Mizzen sail	34	long edge
	20.4	short edge
	20.4	short edge

[a]AGM, C. F. 134; AGS, Guerra Antigua, leg. 3149, no. 2.
[b]There would also be a spritsail topsail, but the documents give no hint as to its dimensions.

ribs on both sides of it, in this case 18. In other words, with an astilla muerta of 1 codo, as it was in the galleon with a 17 codo beam, the height of the astilla muerta at the master ribs would be ⅔ codo. The ribs on either side of it would each have an astilla muerta of ⅔ codo plus 1/18 of the remaining ⅓. Each successive pair of ribs toward the prow and the poop would be another 1/18 of the ⅓ codo higher, until the total height of 1 codo would be reached with the ribs at the fore and aft ends of the hull. The same amount of 1 codo was assigned as *joba* (increase) of the thickness in the ribs at the upper wales. Each rib at that point would be 1/18 codo thicker, to strengthen the hull. The concave part of the hull above the keel, called the *rasel,* measured 1.9 codos at the prow (*rasel en proa*) and three times that, or 5.67 codos, at the poop (*rasel en popa*). This proportional rise helped to direct the flow of water toward the rudder.

Regardless of the size of the ship, the sheer was the same. Starting from the midpoint of the ship, the line curved upward 1.75 codos to the prow and 2.25 codos to the poop. At the lower deck (cubierta), the curve was only .5 codo to the prow and 1 codo to the poop, following the general rule that the deck should be as flat as possible for efficient use of the artillery. This would have given a greater sheer to smaller ships than larger ones, and it is not certain that Arana followed the provisions of the 1618 ordinances in this respect. The upper deck (bridge or puente) was supposedly located 3 codos above the lower deck, regardless of the size of the ship. Two openings pierced this deck, one at the prow and one at the poop, each 1 codo square. The tiller (*caña*) fit through the opening at the poop, in reach of a man on the lower deck, who then moved the rudder to steer.[51] Another, thinner piece of wood called the whipstaff (*pinzote*) was attached to the tiller, so that the ship could be steered from the upper deck where there was a better view forward. In large ships, the whipstaff could be difficult to use, because of the great force of the water pressing on the rudder; nontheless, some very large ships continued to use them in the seventeenth century.[52] Though the 1618 Spanish regulations did not mention the whipstaff, each of Arana's six galleons came equipped with one. The compass box (*bitácora* or binnacle) would go outside the opening in the poop, "in the English style," and there would be a 1-codo opening from the deck to the gangboard (*travesaño*). The forecastle (*castillo*) and the aft-castle (alcázar) should each be 3 codos tall, with the tiller passing through an opening of 1 codo in the aft-castle at the base of the bows. Finally, an inside beam (*contracodaste*) reinforcing the sternpost should be at least .5 codo thick at the reinforcement of the keel, tapering to nothing as it moved upward to arrive at the opening (*limera*) made for the tiller. Like the other reinforcing beams, this would vary in thickness with the size of the ship.[53]

With these characteristics, the ships built by Arana were seaworthy and serviceable, representing a stage in the evolution of ship design. We can see the future direction that some theoreticians were promoting if we look at the dimensions in an anonymous treatise dating from about 1635.[54] The treatise is in the form of a dialogue between a Vizcayan and a native of Santander. One of the speakers, evidently representing the author, shows great contempt for the ship designs of nonseafaring academicians. Instead, the ideal ships mentioned by the speakers would have a floor equal to half the beam, a depth in the hold of .56 the beam, a length 3.7 times the beam, and a keel 3 times the beam. In other words, compared to Arana's ships, they would be longer in relation to the beam, as well as deeper and wider in the hold. Additional specifications called for a longer, lower forward rake to the stempost, and a more upright sternpost. The deck was to be curved upward only .5 codo at both prow and poop, and the curve at the top wales was to be 1 codo at the prow and 1.5 codos at the poop, compared to 1.75 and 2.25 codos in Arana's ships. All these specifications would have produced a longer, sleeker ship, although the additional depth in the hold could have caused problems in shallow waters. There is no question, however, that longer, narrower ships were the shape of the future. One galleon of 18.5 codos' beam made near Santander in 1668 would have a keel-to-beam ratio of 2.86 to 1 and a length-to-beam ratio of 3.57 to 1.[55] These measures were 13–15 percent higher than the same ratios in Arana's ships.

As ship design evolved, however, it was important not to let theory outrun experience. At the same time that Arana was building his six galleons, the famous *Nya Wassan* or *Vasa* was being built for the king of Sweden, according to measurements provided by the king himself. The completed ship had a length-to-beam ratio of 5.1 to 1, a depth-to-beam ratio of .41 to 1, excessive top hamper, and gunports too low to allow the necessary ballast in the hold, all of which made the *Vasa* dangerously unstable. She heeled over and sank in Stockholm harbor on her maiden voyage in August 1628, taking more than one hundred people with her. A board of inquiry found no one to blame, but it seems clear that poor design, royal or not, was the culprit.[56]

By early June 1627, Arana's ships were nearing completion, and everyone concerned was anxious that they sail as soon as possible. But as final preparations got under way, the terms of the contract caused a dispute that was to delay the completion for more than a year. The individuals involved included Martín de Vallecilla, captain-general of the squadron of Cantabria in the Armada del Mar Océano; Domingo Ochoa de Yrazagorria, the inspector whom Arana considered a personal enemy; and Martín de Arana himself. At issue were the responsibilities for providing certain of the ships' sails, the levy of troops and sailors for the ships, and even the version of the contract to which Arana was bound. Ochoa wrote to the Junta de Armadas on June 13, 1627, reporting that Vallecilla thought the ships should be moved from the shallow waters at Zorroza downriver to Portugalete to be rigged, since the job could be done there more quickly and safely. Arana evidently balked at moving the ships, because the terms of the document he signed did not require it. Although Arana had implicitly accepted the official contract of March 14, 1625, when he accepted the first payment for the ships, he had never actually signed it. Ochoa recommended a prompt investigation of the matter, so that work could proceed. The levy of sailors was particularly urgent, so they wouldn't take other jobs.[57]

Meanwhile Arana was pressing his own case. "Your Majesty must have found very little satisfaction in the faithfulness with which I serve you, since you have sent so many inspectors," he wrote the king from Zorroza. He referred to the arrival of General Vallecilla, Captain Francisco de Berroiz, and several other officials who were trying to judge how long it would take to ready the ships to sail. Time was short; provisions, artillery, bunting, and flags needed to be secured as soon as possible, and Arana claimed he had no responsibility to provide them. He complained that the rush of the final outfitting had doubled its cost; further expense came from building additional storage compartments and providing decorative painting and gilding for the ships.[58] There was no question that the crown was to provide artillery and provisions, and even then orders were going out to secure artillery from a variety of sources, including some Portuguese ships that had wrecked on the coast of France.[59] The bunting and flags were another matter, and Arana would not provide them until the king sent him a brief, but direct, order to do so. Later he could press his case that they were not his responsibility.

For a variety of reasons, the king decided by early August that the ships would not be ready in time for that year's fleets. Perhaps Arana had been too optimistic in setting a completion date, or had created too much irritation with his complaints. More likely, the crown simply found it inconvenient to provide the artillery and the money needed to finish the ships that year. The Junta de Armadas had warned the king in July that sufficient artillery would be very hard to come by and suggested that he postpone the ships' official entry into royal service.[60] When he learned this, Arana wrote an emotional letter to the king on August 7, saying that he grieved in his soul (*"siento en el alma"*) that the king had been disappointed in the good care and the desire for service that he had shown, especially since he had built "six such fine galleons that I promise God I think none better have ever entered in the armada."[61] Whoever had informed the king that the ships could not sail in 1627, Arana insisted, had made a manifest error that would be harmful to the crown, especially since the fine sailors available now would go off to serve in other ships. Arana made a special point that he had built all six galleons in thirteen months, claiming that through his efforts they were at the mouth of the sea in Portugalete, masts and yards raised, and with all the equipment, bunting, and flags they needed to sail. The last surely was an ironic comment on the disputed items he had been forced to provide. Despite his protests Arana had to face the inevitable. The ships would not sail in 1627, and his task now was to have the crown take delivery of them so they would no longer be his responsibility or his expense. He urged the king to move them from Portugalete, which was not a good port for wintering over and which was choked with fishing boats in the summer. Moreover, it had an entry for enemy vessels and almost no defenses. Arana was having the ships guarded with as many as fifty men, armed with artillery and muskets, but the best course would be to move them to Santander or even La Coruña at the northwest tip of Spain. It would be easy enough to find sailors and artillery for such a short voyage.[62]

The crown began the process of accepting the galleons, but slowly. The order seems to have been written in late August, but it was not sent. Arana decided to go to Madrid in early October to speed things along, leaving the ships in the charge of paid guards who were sworn before a notary to guard and defend them night and day.[63] Finally, on October 16, the crown directed Martín de Aróztegui, a member of the Council of War who happened to be on the north coast, to take delivery of the galleons. Should he already have left for Madrid, General Vallecilla was to accept them, and should Vallecilla already have left for La Coruña to join his fleet, the job was to fall to the inspector and the purveyor of armadas in Vizcaya—Domingo Ochoa de Yrazagorria and Aparicio de Recalde y Hormaeche (usually called Hormaeche).[64] As a subsequent inquiry proved, the crown officially took delivery on December 15, 1627. In February and early March 1628, Arana and the royal officials began to assemble the provisions and the remaining equipment needed for the six galleons, which remained in Portugalete despite Arana's plea to move them.

Late in March a more urgent matter arose on the north coast. A squadron of the Armada del Mar Océano had returned from a mission to the French coast in desperate shape. Many of the men were seriously ill and almost no supplies remained.[65] Several of the ships needed careening and refitting in Santander. The flagship of General don Francisco de Acevedo had a hull so badly damaged that she had been hauled up on land rather than risk being careened on the water. The supplies that Arana had assembled so painstakingly for his ships were needed urgently for the work in Santander, but when General don Martín de Vallecilla specifically requested them through the inspector Domingo Ochoa, Arana tried to stall. He sent two foremen, each with eighteen workers, to Santander with some hemp and nails to work on the general's flagship, but he resisted sending anything else.

It is easy to understand Arana's reluctance to release the equipment it had taken so much effort to acquire, and it is even more understandable that he would be reluctant to release them to Ochoa, whom he viewed as an enemy. Nonetheless, the equipment did not belong to him, or to the six galleons he had built. It was government property, even if Arana had not been reimbursed for all of it. A flurry of letters and reports in late March relates how the supplies were pried from his grasp. Since Ochoa could not get a full accounting from Arana, he questioned the master cord makers and anchor makers about how much cable, anchors, and rigging they were holding for Arana, and sent the report to Madrid. Altogether they claimed to have 20 large cables, more than 230 quintales of rigging from France, 50 quintales of hemp that was being worked into rope, more than 60 quintales of tow, and 12 anchors. Ochoa's ploy was effective. The Junta de Armadas had the king order Arana to release the supplies for use in Santander, even as he worked to finish outfitting the galleons he had built.[66]

Regardless of his disputes with the crown, Arana chose winter and early spring of 1627–28 to request favors from the king. In a series of letters he reviewed his service in building the six galleons so quickly, at a saving to the treasury and a loss to himself, claiming that he had put 8,000 ducados of his own money into the project. Currently he was engaged in gathering supplies on the north coast, without salary, because of his zeal to serve the crown. Despite his financial loss, he had already offered to build twelve more galleons on the same terms. In return for all this he asked to be given two properties in Vizcaya, the *patronazgos* of Santa María de Galdácano and La Magdalena de Arrigorriaga. Together they were worth 250 ducats in annual income and they could be held only by a Vizcayan who was a member of a military order. Arana further asked that his elder son Diego, who had shown a particular affection for the sea and for ship construction, be given a commission to raise one of the companies of infantry to serve on the six galleons. Although Arana did not say so, this commission would further his son's career in royal service and provide him an opportunity to advance as his father had done.[67] The king referred the matter to the Junta de Armadas for its recommendation. There was no hurry, as long as Arana continued to work zealously for the crown on his own initiative.

In the meantime Arana had been commissioned to buy supplies for the six galleons and had traveled along the north coast to San Sebastián and St. Jean de Luz in France securing them. He wrote the royal secretary Pedro de Coloma that he had traveled 68 leagues in five days (about 35 miles or 57 kilometers per day) buying supplies, not a small feat in the terrain of the north coast. In addition, he was already starting a new construction contract to build forty pinnaces (light vessels using sails and oars) for the crown, each one having 21 codos of keel.[68] Arana had put much of his own money into this job as well, since the crown had sent only one-third of the price in silver and the rest in common copper coins that were greatly reduced in value. In fact, 1627 had seen a state bankruptcy and the marketplace was still suffering from the monetary confusion in its wake.[69]

At the very least, Arana seems to have spread himself thin in his efforts to prove himself to the crown; the Junta de Armadas could be accused of having encouraged him in this, since the only marginal comments to his letters mention spurring him on to even greater efforts. Many of Arana's problems with royal officials seem to have come from an excess of zeal and an inability to compromise. He was very anxious to keep the credit for his services to the crown, and this may have made him uncooperative. This comes through very clearly in three sets of reports to the Junta de Armadas—those from Arana, those from the royal officials Ochoa and Hormaeche, and those from General Vallecilla—in April 1628.

General Martín de Vallecilla had become more than a bit exasperated with Arana over the business of supplies for the careenings and repairs in Santander. The ships there were old and in need of all the labor available, whereas Arana's ships were new and needed very little work before completion. When the crown authorized Vallecilla to take all the supplies he needed from Arana, he did so, removing 100 quintals of tar, some oakum and nails, and eighty caulkers to do the work. Promising to send the workers back as soon as possible, he left Arana with nothing, furthermore, he blamed Arana for the delays in starting the work in Santander. Evidently the general had lost confidence in Arana's ability to do anything but build ships. He wrote the royal secretary asking that his brother, Admiral Francisco de Vallecilla, who had been ordered to Santander to help in the repairs there, instead be sent to Bilbao to work with the inspector Ochoa in readying the six galleons for royal service. Although acknowledging that Arana was a "good person," Vallecilla said he lacked the experience to fit out a ship properly for war.[70]

There is no doubt that Arana was new to provisioning, however well he knew his way around the north coast. In the margin of one of Arana's reports, the Junta de Armadas made a note to tell him it was not necessary to account for every small item that he purchased, a sign that Arana was unfamiliar with standard procedures in military procurement.[71] Nonetheless, there was enough work to be done that the Junta continued to welcome Arana's services, even though they were not free of problems. Most serious was the running dispute about the extent of his responsibilities under the contract for the six galleons. Even as he worked to procure supplies, Arana reminded the royal secretary Pedro de Coloma that he was obligated only to supply the six galleons rigged and ready to sail; he did not have to provide spare equipment (*cosas de respeto*) as emergency replacements.[72]

In this dispute, the inspector Ochoa and the purveyor Hormaeche were caught in the middle. There is every indication in the documents that they acted fairly, even though their work was complicated by the dispute and by the closely related functions of all the parties involved. Arana was procuring ship fittings and supplies, they were supplying food and crews, and the money sent for Arana passed through their hands as a matter of official procedure. Consequently, Arana's claims on the crown were relayed by them to the government in Madrid, since he repeated them whenever he accepted payment for disputed items.

Arana won his point at the end of April, when the Junta de Armadas acknowledged that he was not obligated to provide spare equipment at his own expense. He was asked to provide it, but at the crown's expense.[73] More letters traveled back and forth between the north coast and Madrid, and by early May some of the conflicts about provisioning and the final preparation of the galleons were resolved. Arana continued to help, hiring the crew, preparing and provisioning the six galleons, and building the forty pinnaces. These last, he claimed, were costing him 300 ducados each to build, although the crown was paying him only 100.[74]

At the same time Arana was sending military supplies to Santander for the six nearly finished galleons, which would collect them when they arrived there from Portugalete. Fully loaded ships would have had difficulty sailing the shallow coastal waters between the two ports. Because the ships had been in the water in Portugalete for nearly a year by the spring of 1628, at least two of them needed a full careening to check for leaks, according to Admiral Francisco de Vallecilla, who had been directed to help with the six galleons as his brother had suggested. Careening was usually done by running cables from the masts to smaller ships and using the leverage thus created to pull the ship over on its side in the water, on top of a flat barge. It cost considerable time and money to do a full careening, or to "uncover the keel," as the phrase went. Arana preferred to do only a partial careening, without the use of a barge, exposing the side to about 1 codo from the keel, just far enough to avoid taking on water.[75] He argued rather unconvincingly that the inspector Ochoa and various experts agreed that the partial careening was sufficient, since the only places needing more caulking were above the water line. But his main concern, as always, was who would pay for the work. Once the crown took responsibility for it, Arana was only too happy to proceed with the full careening. Collecting for the work proved to be a problem, as he might have suspected; as he reported on his progress, he continued to complain that the 2,600 ducados sent for provisioning, hiring the crew, and making final preparations on the ships was about 10,000 ducados short of what was needed.[76]

Relations among the inspector Ochoa, Admiral Vallecilla, and Arana seem to have improved, however, due in large part to Ochoa's diplomacy. Although Arana continued to claim he was in charge of all of the work for the galleons, Ochoa managed to reconcile him somewhat to Vallecilla's presence by portraying the admiral as a sort of assistant to Arana in his enormous task. In return for Ochoa's acknowledgment of his superhuman efforts, Arana actually praised the inspector's work in levying the crew for the galleons, for which they were jointly responsible.[77] In early June, Ochoa and Hormaeche reported that they had finally paid Arana the balance of the

30,000 ducados owed him, plus the 2,600 ducados provided for the careening and preparation of the six galleons.

By mid-June one hundred men had been assigned to guard the ships, because of fears that English ships sent to aid rebels in La Rochelle might continue south to attack the galleons in Portugalete. For the moment, the six galleons were fairly safe behind the bar at Portugalete, but the sooner they could be armed, crewed, and provisioned, the sooner they could join the fleet in Santander. The Junta de Armadas on June 25 ordered artillery sent from Santander to the ships, because the armaments due from Andalusia had not yet arrived.[78] With the artillery in place, they could safely plan to sail to Santander.

Another flurry of letters in early July showed the quickened pace of the preparations. Arana wrote to report his progress and to remind the king again that his zeal and financial sacrifices in serving the crown had all been aimed at gaining official posts for his sons, so that they might follow their ancestors in royal service.[79] Yet, at the same time that he so bluntly requested favors from the crown, Arana may have been delaying sending to Santander the rest of the supplies he had collected, because he still had not been paid in full for them. Ochoa reported that the supplies had not arrived by July 10, nor had the artillery and ammunition the crown was sending from Cádiz.[80] The Junta could only urge Arana to hurry the provisions, including the reserve equipment for which the crown was paying an additional 7,000 ducados, plus 1,800 more for six large cables.[81] The five hundred sailors to crew the ships on the way to Santander and the one hundred soldiers who would guard the ships on that journey were ordered to report to Portugalete on July 30. There they would begin to draw rations in kind from the crown; payments in money would not go far enough, given the scarcity of foodstuffs in a town so small.[82]

The Junta de Armadas also ordered Admiral Vallecilla to inspect the six galleons, listing in detail for each ship the equipment on hand, any items missing, and whose responsibility it was to provide the rest. On the last day of July, Ochoa and Hormaeche carried out the inspection and inventory for Vallecilla. It is those inventories that have found their way to the James Ford Bell Library at the University of Minnesota (see appendix A).[83] The inspection documents do not give the dimensions or the tonnages of the ships. (Table 1, appendix C, calculates these figures from other sources.) They do, however, add to our knowledge of the hull characteristics of Spanish galleons and provide the only specific information we have on the sail plan and equipment on each of the ships built by Arana.

The *San Felipe,* although not the largest of the six, was clearly destined to be the capitana, since it carried the only elaborate poop lantern, which served as a symbol of authority as well as a light to follow on dark nights.[84] It also had the most gunports—thirty in all—which agrees with general prescriptions that a galleon of 500 toneladas needed twenty-eight pieces of artillery of various sizes. Typically, this would include four *medias cañones* (demi-cannons) firing 22-pound balls, another four firing 18-pound balls, ten *medias culebrinas* (demi-culverins) firing 10-pound balls, and ten *sacres* (sakers) firing 7-pound balls. In addition to at least twenty balls and three hundredweight of powder for each gun, many supplies had to be carried, from the wheeled carriage (*cureña*) and gun crib (*cuña*) used to set its angle for firing, to

Figure 17. Cartagena de Indias, ca. 1628–30, showing galleons in port. Note the three-course sail plan. Also note the fortifications enclosing the city proper, just left of center. (AGI, Mapas y Planos, Panamá 45. Courtesy of the Archivo General de Indias, Seville.)

rammers, copper spoons for the powder, fuse, and various specialized tools.[85] For comparison, the galleon *Encarnación* (1646), nearly identical in tonnage to Arana's *Begoña,* evidently carried only twenty-six guns.[86]

The full complement of artillery defined a ship's armament for battle readiness. On short coastal voyages in home waters, even a fighting galleon would be much less heavily armed. The six galleons bringing artillery from Cádiz to Santander for Arana's ships carried an average of just 18.5 guns each for their own use and an average of only 16.8 guns for each of Arana's ships.[87] Only when the ships were outfitted for official duty would they be given a full battery. The artillery, in short, was not an integral part of a ship's equipment. Rather, it was part of the equipment loaded for specific voyages, along with the food. There was never any doubt in Arana's contractual disputes with the royal bureaucracy that artillery was the sole responsibility of the crown. I will return to the question of artillery and its procurement in chapter 5, which deals with provisioning in general. It is interesting to note that the powder magazine on Spanish ships was called the "Rancho de Santa Barbara," for the saint who offered protection from thunderstorms, fires, and sudden death, a reminder that guns and ammunition could explode unexpectedly.[88] According to official regulations dating from 1552, the powder was to be kept in the prow below decks, although some illustrations locate the Rancho de Santa Barbara in the poop, below the cabins.[89]

For the most part, the equipment on the *San Felipe* and the largest ship, *Nuestra Señora de Begoña,* was identical. Both ships carried a full complement of sails (including reserves), with two for the foremast and mainmast, and one each for the bowsprit and the mizzen. There were also topgallants for the foremast and mainmast and a spritsail topsail for the bowsprit on all six

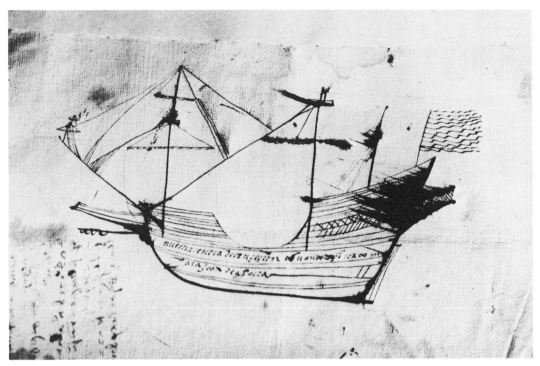

Figure 18. Guipúzcoan galleon, 1611, with spritsail topsail and topgallant. (Archivo Histórico Provincial de Guipúzcoa, Oñate, Partido de Vergara, leg. 2567. Reference courtesy of Selma Huxley Barkham. Photograph courtesy of Michael Barkham.)

ships. This is somewhat unexpected equipment for Spanish ships of the period, given that neither the 1618 regulations nor Arana's contract mentioned either topgallant or spritsail topsail (*sobrecebadera,*) and that most authors assume that Spanish ships did not use topgallants until the late seventeenth century. Nonetheless, their presence on Arana's ships demonstrates that Spain was moving in the direction of a multiple-sail plan much earlier. Although topgallants rarely appear in depictions of Spanish galleons of the period,[90] they are clearly visible on a map of the bay of Cartagena de Indias, given the tentative date of 1628.[91] (See figure 17.) Similarly, the spritsail topsail, useful in turning the prow upon entering and leaving ports, was characteristic of many nations' ships in the seventeenth century.[92] Though not always discernible in illustrations of the period, a spritsail topsail and even a spritsail topgallant appear on a rough sketch from 1611 of a Guipúzcoan galleon.[93] (See figures 18, 19, and 30.) The two largest ships Arana built also carried a davit (*dabiete*) to aid in raising the anchors, but the smaller galleons made do with capstans alone. All the ships evidently carried just one rudder, although a 1575 law had specified that a second rudder be carried in reserve on Indies voyages. On the other hand, each carried three pumps, one in reserve, although Indies legislation required only two.[94] By Arana's time the bilge seems to have been partitioned into two compartments so that sea water and ballast could not shift so easily. That made it necessary to have a pump on each side of the ship.

The smaller galleons had equipment proportional to their size. This is

Figure 19. French view of a Spanish galleon from the mid to late seventeenth century. Note particularly the spritsail topsail (sobrecebadera) and the mizzen topsail (sobremesana). (Jacques Guéroult du Pas, *Recüeil de veües de tous les differens bastimens de la mer Mediterranée y de l'ocean* [Paris, 1710]. Photograph courtesy of the James Ford Bell Library, University of Minnesota.

shown especially in their smaller cables and fewer gunports.[95] The inventories of Arana's galleons do not list the weight of their cables, much less the amount and weight of their rigging. A list of equipment for 400-tonelada galleons in the proposed Armada de Barlovento in 1609 called for about one quintal or hundredweight of cable and rigging for every tonelada, about half in cable and half in rigging, plus reserves.[96] An estimate written about 1635 called for just two-thirds of a hundredweight for every tonelada.[97] Based on the size of the cables, it would seem that Arana's galleons were closer to the lower estimate than to the higher. The sail plans for the four smaller galleons were nearly identical to those of the two largest ones, although there is some confusion in their lists of sails. Neither the *Tres Reyes* nor the *San Sebastián* has topsails listed for the foremast, although for the mainmast the list includes *gavias,* a word that could refer to topsails on both the main and the foremast.

The 1618 regulations had given very precise proportions for the masts, yards, and sails on warships, although we cannot necessarily assume that Arana's six galleons followed them. The regulations allowed for variations according to custom. (See appendix C, tables 3 and 4.) It is possible that the principal masts were made of several joined pieces, rather than a single timber.[98] The mainmast was to be as long as the keel plus 2 codos, with a circumference at the upper deck of as many palms (*palmos*) as half the beam in codos. In other words, in a ship with a beam of 17 codos, the mainmast should measure 8.5 palmos, (each approximately 8.2 inches) at the upper deck. The foremast should be 4 codos shorter than the mainmast, and five-sixths its circumference, tapering to the tip. The bowsprit should be 6 codos shorter than the mainmast, and 1 palmo thinner than the foremast at the opening in the upper deck, then tapering to the tip. The topmasts of the fore and mainmasts were proportionately shorter and thinner. The mizzen should be as thick as the main topmast and 3 codos longer, because it had to be seated on the lower deck. The rules took care to specify where each mast was to be fixed. The mainmast was to rest on the floor, lashed at the empty bows and at both decks. The foremast was to have its butt at half the lanzamiento of the stem post, lashed like the mainmast. Both fore and mainmast were to pierce the decks through holes that left some room for the mast to bend in the wind. The bowsprit was to rest on the lower deck, set so that it formed an angle of 45 degrees with that deck. It should be lashed to timbers at the cutwater (*tajamar*), so as not to place weight and strain on the unsupported beak.

The yards of both main and topmasts were also in proportion to one another, and to the overall dimensions of the ship. They were to have their full thickness in the middle, tapering toward the ends. The great length of the yards and bowsprit gave the ships their distinctive silhouettes. The relative lengths of masts and yards in the 1618 regulations were very similar to the proportions Tomé Cano had proposed in 1608, except that he suggested a much shorter bowsprit, only half the length of the mainmast. He favored the same long yards for warships that appear in the 1618 regulations, however, arguing that a warship could safely sail closer to the wind with more canvas than could a merchant ship.[99] In the matter of girth, the 1618 regulations specified masts and yards considerably thinner than standard practice required. They were 25–50 percent thinner than masts and yards for the proposed Armada de Barlovento in 1609.[100] Shipwrights might have ignored the 1618 rules in practice. A full set of new masts for the *San Felipe* in 1636 followed proportions closer to the thicker ones proposed for the Armada de Barlovento.[101] (See appendix C, table 5.)

Tomé Cano's prescriptions for the relative size and shape of the topsails of fore and mainmast are also very similar to the 1618 regulations. The lower sails on both fore and mainmast were rectangular, whereas their topsails were roughly trapezoidal, with the lower billowing edge wider than the upper edge attached to the yard. According to Cano, the lower sails should provide the main propulsion for the ship, with two-thirds of their total area for the principal part of each sail, and one-third for the removable bonnet attached to the lower edge.[102] This basic sail plan was already well established when Cano wrote, and García de Palacio in 1587 had given detailed instructions for constructing the sails, providing diagrams of how they were to be sewn together of vertical strips of canvas.[103] (See figure 20.)

By Arana's time the sail plan included not only topgallant sails, but other innovations as well, if we can trust the one available document that gives sail measurements on one of the ships he built.[104] (See appendix C, table 6.) The principal part of the mainsail was three-fourths of its length, not just two-thirds, as in García de Palacio and Cano's times. The mainsail would have accounted for about 24 percent of the total sail area, and the foresail for about 16 percent. The main topsail accounted for another 21 percent and the fore topsail for 13–18 percent. The spritsail and mizzen each added another 8–9 percent, and topgallants on the fore and mainmasts together made up the remaining 2–4 percent. As in the 1618 regulations, the lower sails were much wider than they were long, even with their bonnets attached. The trapezoidal topsails and topgallants had lengths and maximum widths that were more nearly equal. (Compare fig. 16 with table 6.)

The overall configurations of each ship would determine the arrangement of the hold and the size and quantity of equipment on board. Most large ships had two decks above the floor, with the hold divided into compartments for storage. The castles fore and aft provided quarters for officers and important

Figure 20. Sailmaking diagrams for a mainsail (papahigo) with its bonnet, and a topsail (vela de gavia). (Diego Garcia de Palacio, *Instrucción náutica para navegar [1587]*, fols. 104–104v, 106v–107.)

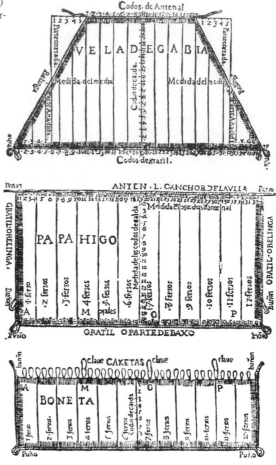

passengers. Ordinary seamen, apprentices, pages, and soldiers would have had to find places for themselves and their belongings somewhere on the crowded decks. (See chapter 6.)

The official inventory mentions little about the decoration of the ships, except to note that each included a painted image of its holy namesake, appropriately painted and gilded rear galleries, and a beakhead featuring a gilded figure of a crowned lion rampant. In addition, each ship carried at least one white linen flag painted with the royal coat of arms, and red bunting to be used during battle. This suggests a rather more austere image than legends of Spanish galleons have led us to believe, yet it seems very close to the truth. The ships were covered with tar and alquitrán to make the hulls more watertight and protect them against shipworms, which would have made them appear nearly all black. (See figure 21.) The few touches of color, especially red, the religious image, and a bit of carving and gilding would have stood out dramatically against the black hulls. These were working ships, not ceremonial barges, and it should not surprise us that they were austere. Even some of the color had a practical purpose. The traditional red paint and the red bunting strung along the wales and the lookout platforms served to hide the inevitable bloodstains during battle.[105]

Figure 21. Galleons sent to relieve Pernambuco, Brazil, in 1635. The ship in the lower left is presumably the capitana of Lope de Hoces y Córdoba, captain-general of the armada. Note the imposing poop lantern and the banner of the commander. The poop galleries, the bunting draped along the wales and the crow's nests, and the banner are red. The tarred hull appears black. (Archivo Museo del Viso del Marqués, painting by Juan de la Corte. Courtesy of the Museo Naval, Madrid.)

After making their official inventory of Arana's ships, Ochoa and Hormaeche questioned the *contramaestre* (master's assistant) of each one as to whether it was "masted, rigged, and outfitted in all perfection." Only when this was done were the ships officially certified ready to sail by Gaspar de Carasa, an infantry captain who was in charge of their removal to Santander as the representative of Admiral Vallecilla.[106] At dawn on August 2, 1628, the six galleons began the trip to Santander, with their crews, eighty-seven pieces of artillery, and one hundred soldiers aboard. This was even less artillery than had been planned and could provide just minimal protection from the enemies of Spain in the dangerous waters off the Cantabrian coast, but it was considered sufficient for the short voyage. Arana supplied crews at his own expense (as he was quick to point out) for six of the pinnaces he had built for the crown, to tow the galleons over the bar below Portugalete (see figure 22), and he proudly reported that the galleons proved to be "handsome, swift sailors."[107] The voyage was not entirely without incident, however. Five of the ships made it over the bar very well and continued on to Santander with Carasa. The *Begoña,* largest of the six, ran aground before reaching the bar because it had deviated from the narrow main channel as the tide began to go out.[108] The pilot major had some fifty large barrels of water emptied to lighten the load and moved some artillery to the larboard side of the ship to balance it against the bottom and the falling

Figure 22. Detail of a map of the ria of Bilbao in 1734, showing the town of Portugalete and the sandbar at the entrance to the open sea. The numbers in the channel indicate the water's depth (in feet) at high tide. By 1734, it was nearly impossible for large ships to use the channel, and the map forms part of the planning documents aimed at deepening it. (AGS, Mapas, Planos y Dibujos, III–18. Courtesy of the Archivo General de Simancas, Simancas, Valladolid.)

tide. With that the ship was "secured and as upright as if it were afloat," awaiting the turn of the tide. With the pinnaces, the crew and royal officials got the *Begoña* back in the main channel that afternoon, but it was not until high tide at five-thirty the next morning that she successfully crossed the bar, sailing on alone to Santander to join the others. In their haste to take advantage of the high tide, the departing galleons had left six anchors and their cables stuck in the mud, thoroughly embedded from the long mooring in Portugalete. They were to be sent on to Santander shortly, along with additional supplies.

The Junta, very pleased that the galleons had at last set sail, sent messages of praise and commendation to Arana and to the royal officials for their work and care.[109] Admiral Vallecilla reported to the crown that all the galleons had arrived in Santander by August 5, and that the small damage sustained by the

Begoña could easily be repaired. It is appropriate that in the same letter Vallecilla recommended that an old galleon in Santander named *Santiago* be sold out of royal service, for an assessed valuation of 5,000 ducados. In the hard life of armada galleons, Arana's *Santiago* would take its place.[110] Less than a month later the Dutch admiral Piet Heyn would capture the New Spain fleet at Matanzas, striking a terrific blow to the royal treasury and the armada—not to mention Spanish pride. The naval forces that Arana's six galleons would join in 1629 had a formidable task ahead of them.

With the galleons finished and safely delivered to Santander, Arana might have hoped for unmixed praise from Madrid; if so, he was disappointed. The king wrote him on July 30 that someone had said the galleons still were not ready. Though the king surely knew by the time the letter reached Arana that they were not only ready, but safely in Santander, Arana felt the need to respond, defending his honor and venting his hurt feelings. Since he had never said anything untrue to the king, it grieved him to his soul to think that such a thing could be believed. He had worked night and day, aided by his sons, using the money left by his ancestors, to get the ships ready. He had supplied everything required of him, and many things that were not, all because of his special love for the king, his sovereign. He swore that the pinnaces he had built, and his efforts to find crews for them, had cost him 6,000 ducados more than the 4,000 the king was paying for them, "from which I hope to receive great favor [from the crown]."[111] Even as we smile at Arana's self-serving moral outrage, it is impossible not to admire this proud and irascible man. It took his sort of pride and tenacity to benefit from dealings with the crown, and, although his six galleons were delivered, it would take much more of his time and effort to settle the accounts satisfactorily.

FOUR
Reckoning the Cost

The documents assembled to clear the crown's accounts with Martín de Arana provide considerable evidence about the cost of the galleons and the sources of supply for their construction materials and rigging. Although I have not found any comprehensive accounts for the galleons' construction, information about them is threaded through all the official records. The accounts filed by the paymaster for ship construction in Vizcaya showed the lump sums paid to Arana, but they were rarely broken down by individual items.[1] The best information available, ironically, comes from the records of Arana's disputes with the royal bureaucracy over the terms of the construction contract.

Costs that were borne without protest either by Arana or by the crown have left little trace in the official record. Arana's original contract with the crown allowed him 30 ducados for each tonelada, setting a maximum size of 2,400 toneladas for all six galleons, for a total of 72,000 ducados. About 22 percent of that could be spent abroad, for "masts, sail canvas, tar, and pitch."[2] Arana later gained permission to import some cable as well, but he almost certainly spent no more than the contract guidelines allowed, because any breach would have been mentioned in the official reports. Changes in the measurements Arana was ordered to follow brought the finished size of all the galleons to 2,658.4 toneladas, so the crown paid 79,752 ducados for the ships and the equipment Arana provided for them.

Labor cost is the greatest unknown component of the construction price. The ordinances of 1607 had included a wage scale for shipwrights, allowing 4.5 reales per day on the north coast, 5 in Lisbon, 8 in Seville, Cádiz, and Puerto de Santa María, and 10 in the smaller ports downriver from Seville.[3] Supervisors made more than that, and apprentices made less. The ordinances of 1618 repeated the 1607 wage scale but allowed only 4.25 reales per day on the north coast.[4] Wages for shipwrights in the New World were about double the highest rates in Spain.[5] Interestingly, skilled workers at royal sites in Spain also made about double what shipwrights did, or even more. Skilled workers at the Retiro Palace in 1633 were supposed to make 8–9 reales per day, but some evidently earned as much as 10, 12, 16, or even 20.[6] Whether or not the wage scale reflected the cost of living in various parts of Spain, it still made sense to build ships in Vizcaya. In Arana's accounts, labor and materials costs were often combined, so that carpenters' wages could be included along with the costs of the wood, and the caulkers' wages could be included along with the oakum, pitch, and tar they used. Because of this, I will defer an estimate of the overall cost of labor until later in the discussion.

One of the few cost estimates we have for shipbuilding in Arana's period analyzes the construction of eight galleons built for royal service in Vizcaya from a contract in 1617. For the average-sized galleon of 325 toneladas, Fernández Duro estimated the following costs:

> 189 codos of wood—1,633.6 ducados, or 31 percent
> Manufacture—600 ducados or 11 percent
> Nails and spikes—600 ducados or 11 percent
> Rigging, anchors, sails—2,500 ducados or 47 percent
> Total—5,333.6 ducados[7]

These figures are often cited, yet they are misleading in several respects. First of all, the entry for wood (*tabla y madera,* or planks and wood) is surely wrong. A ship of 325 toneladas would have used over 16,000 codos of wood. The line for manufacture may or may not have included all the labor charges, but it probably did not. The line for nails and spikes (*clavazón*) may have included labor, and the line for rigging, anchors, and sails almost definitely did. The most likely explanation for the figures is that they represented only a partial list of costs. With the total given, the ship would have cost just 16.4 ducados per tonelada, which is simply not believable in the Vizcaya of 1617. In 1588, a ship's hull alone supposedly cost 18–25 ducados per tonelada to build, according to one official estimate.[8]

Frederic Lane estimates that the cost of building a light galley in Venice rose 214 percent from 1580 to 1643, adding to the distress of the Venetian shipbuilding industry.[9] In Spain the cost undoubtedly rose also, though perhaps not as fast as we might expect. An estimate of the cost of building large ships in Flanders in 1625 came to 24–27 ducados per tonelada, in an area known for efficient ship construction.[10] Building similar ships in the Baltic in 1628 would have cost about 40 ducados per tonelada,[11] and galleons built in Havana in 1617–19 cost 47.3 ducados per tonelada.[12] Arana's contract price of 30 ducados per tonelada was probably a reasonable estimate of the basic costs of building a galleon in Vizcaya in the late 1620s, though additional expenses would raise the price. That can be examined further by looking at some of the elements that went into the construction.

Wood of all sorts was one of the most expensive and important elements for the seaworthiness of the ship. Different varieties of wood were required for various parts of the ship, with oak preferred for the hull planking and internal bracing, because of its strength, and pine preferred for much of the superstructure, because of its light weight. In general, the hull planking was thickest below the water line, becoming thinner at the upper levels of the hull.[13] The Spanish used walnut for cabinetry in the poop cabins, and preferred alder for the pumps and other sorts of wood for special purposes. Still, the bulk of the construction would have been of oak, with a smaller amount of pine. Some of the pine came from Flanders, although it probably did not originate there; Arana's contract specified masts, at least, of Prussian pine.[14] The oak all seems to have been supplied locally. A respected commentary on shipbuilding estimated that ships below 400 toneladas took 70 codos of wood per tonelada; those above 500 toneladas took 50 codos, and those in between took 60 codos.[15] Arana's ships would have required some 155,402 codos of wood of all kinds, using this scale, an average of 25,900 codos per ship. This would represent several thousand trees of moderate size.[16] Since the north coast had been producing ships for centuries by Arana's time, forest management was an important concern of government and private citizen alike.

The crown routinely regulated the cutting of trees all over the north coast, balancing military needs and conservation with the requirements of the local economies, not always to the satisfaction of local populations. With sixteenth-century increases in population, military needs, and the American trade, wood scarcity became a serious problem in many parts of the coast. It was particularly noticeable in Guipúzcoa, the Basque province whose capital is San Sebastián. Many memoranda on coastal defense during the reign of Charles I in the mid-sixteenth century already mentioned the problem.[17] By then masts were regularly purchased from northern Europe, although Spain still had sufficient supplies of other types of ship timber.[18]

As demand continued to press on supply, it was doubly important to manage the forests intelligently. Memoranda dealing with trees and reforestation abound in government archives, and it is clear that Philip II related the decline in northern shipbuilding to the scarcity of trees. Early in his reign, the king took an active interest in the northern forests, ordering his ministers to devise a conservation plan.[19] Beginning in the 1560s, a comprehensive royal effort evolved to replenish the forests within 2 leagues of the sea and to ensure supplies of wood for the shipbuilding industry. Cristóbal de Barros, the king's man on the north coast, supervised the plan, aided by representatives of the royal government (*corregidores*), registering forest acreage and taking a direct role in reforestation.[20]

The plan enjoyed a moderate success, even though Guipúzcoa and Asturias in the northwest resisted compliance on a variety of grounds.[21] Local officials realized that a lack of trees was not the principal cause of the decline in shipbuilding. Moreover, in livestock areas, or where there were other alternative uses for the land, the case for reforestation and naval needs seemed less than compelling. Vizcayan forests were probably the best cared for, despite their heavy use, because shipbuilding was such an important part of the economy.[22] The crown persisted in its conservation efforts, and royal officials on the north coast in the seventeenth century continued to have reforestation as one of their assigned duties, despite opposition from local citizens who were required to pay for part of the tree planting.[23] Though Spain continued to import masts from northern Europe, that was standard practice in most western European shipbuilding by the seventeenth century. The Dutch got their supplies from Norway and Germany. The English and the French augmented their dwindling forests with American timber, once they developed their own colonies, and governments everywhere tried to regulate their remaining forests as closely as possible.[24] In fact, Spain was fortunate to have as much wood available as it did, given the enormous strain that the empire put on scarce resources.

The only account available for Arana's purchases of wood is a partial list mentioning payments during the fall of 1626. All together the list involved forty lots of wood, averaging about 2,000 codos, each sold to Arana by a separate individual. From their names, all the suppliers seem to have been Spanish Basques, and there is no reason to think that any of this particular wood was imported.[25] The account does not include unit prices, but a detailed inventory of the wood used for a galleon built in San Sebastián in 1629 shows a range for various kinds of wood from 1 to 1.75 reales per codo.[26] The 25,769 codos purchased for the entire ship also fits within the formula used to estimate the wood on Arana's ships. In all, the 155,402 codos of wood I have estimated for Arana's ships would have cost about 242,742 reales, or 22,067 ducados, based on the proportions of variously priced wood used in the San Sebastián ship. In 1568, the wood for a set of small galleons or "galizabras" built in Vizcaya cost about .68 reales per codo, less than half what Arana had to pay. The sixty intervening years had seen much inflation, however, and the relative cost of wood may actually have fallen. In the 1568 ships, wood represented 30.1 percent of the total cost.[27] With the basic cost of Arana's ships at 79,752 ducados, wood accounted for 27.7 percent of the total. If we add the 6,000 ducados Arana spent of his own money to the basic cost, wood accounted for about 25.7 percent of the total. (See appendix C, table 7.) By the early seventeenth century, some ships for the Indies run were being built in the New World, in part because wood was abundant and fairly cheap near the ports of Havana and Cartagena.[28] Nonetheless, in the area serving the Zorroza yards in Bilbao, wood was still abundant enough to be competitively priced in the inflationary spiral of the early seventeenth century.

Iron construction materials and fittings played a large role in Arana's ships, even if their relative cost was considerably less than that of wood. The Vizcayan industry used the usual nails, tacks, and spikes of contemporary shipbuilding and also used iron treenails for attaching the planking to the hull. There were nearly a dozen separate types of nails mentioned in some of the careening and refitting accounts examined for this study, and they could be a significant part of the expense of that work.[29] There were also iron chains, belaying pins, rings, posts, locks, keys, grills, and various other fittings, as well as the anchors.[30] With few exceptions, iron was priced by weight. Unfortunately, there are no available accounts for the total iron used in the construction of Arana's ships, although there are some partial accounts for the anchors and various fittings. This would not have composed the bulk of the iron used, however, and would have accounted for no more than 5 percent of the basic cost of the ships.[31] On the "galizabras" built in Vizcaya in 1568, iron items of all sorts accounted for 17.4 percent of the total cost of the ship, but they may have been only 11.7 percent of the cost of several ships built in Vizcaya in 1616–19.[32] The Vizcayan iron industry, although it too was in decay in the seventeenth century, still provided a price advantage for ships built in the vicinity, and we know that the foundry supplying Arana was located quite close to the Zorroza yards. It seems reasonable to assume that iron items accounted for 10–20 percent of the cost of Arana's galleons, probably something close to 15 percent of the basic contract price. With 5 percent for anchors and fittings, that would mean about 917 quintales (100 pounds each) of nails and other fasteners on all six ships, at 100 reales the quintal. That is a reasonable estimate, considering that 12 quintales of nails alone, in addition to other iron fasteners, were to be carried by the six ships as reserve supplies on their first major voyage.[33]

Sails and rigging together constituted a major expense, larger in fact than the wood, but the sails were the lesser part of the cost. Sail canvas was imported, much of it from western France. The town of Olonne in Brittany is mentioned in several accounts, and probably gave its name to the Spanish word for sail canvas, *olona*.[34] The canvas, priced by the yard (vara), came in narrow strips, which were then sewn together in the proper shape and dimensions. Though neither the 1618 ordinances nor other official records provide us with precise figures for the sails on Arana's ships, they can be estimated. García de Palacio included sail diagrams in his 1587 treatise, and the sail plan continued to evolve thereafter. Based on the best estimate available for Arana's time, a full complement of sails for a galleon of 500 toneladas required about 4.5 varas (yards) of sail canvas per tonelada. Larger ships required 4 yards per tonelada, and those smaller than 400 toneladas required 5.[35] Using these parameters, the two full sets Arana supplied would have taken 23,515.4 yards. In the only account available, one set of sails for the average-sized *Tres Reyes*, which may have been missing one sail, measured 1,773 yards,[36] so twelve full sets would have required 21,276 yards. Generally speaking, hard-working sails used the heavy canvas called olonas. Topgallants, and probably mizzens, used lighter canvas called *pacages*, because both the latter sails were priced the same in the 1628 accounts for Arana's ships. The cost of sail canvas could vary considerably, especially since it was subject to wartime disruptions in supply. Olonas for Spain's American shipyards cost 3.5 reales per yard in 1612.[37] Pacages cost 3.5 reales in Bilbao in 1639, in the midst of war with France.[38] And in 1668, canvas for all types of sails ranged in price from 1.25 to 2.25 reales per yard.[39] The cost of the cloth was 81.46 percent of the total cost for the sails, with labor adding 6.11 percent, bolt ropes 7.19 percent, and thread 5.24 percent.[40] Using the figure of 2 reales in silver per yard, Arana's finished sails, including all materials and labor, would have cost about 5,248.7 ducados.

Far more expensive than the sails were the thousands of pounds of rigging and tackle needed to work them and to hold the masts and yards in place. In today's engine-driven ships, the machinery is below decks, concentrating the key parts of the vessel within the hull. In a sailing ship, the important machinery is above decks, in the rigging and sails that regulate the force of the wind. The quality of the cable and rigging was therefore of the utmost importance. (See figure 23.) Delivery inventories and later documents indicate that most of the cable on Arana's ships came from the towns of Calahorra, Aldea de Morillo, Alfaro, Rincón de Soto, and Aldea Nueva in the Calatayud area of Aragón.[41] This included the two heaviest categories—cables and mooring cables (*ayustes*)—and the lightest category—hawsers (*guindalesas*). Together Calatayud cables accounted for more than 93 percent of all the cables. Imported from France were all the laid ropes (*calabrotes*), which were roughly 30–40 percent as thick as the average cable.

One respected nautical treatise recommended .67 quintales of cables and rigging for every tonelada.[42] Official estimates for the proposed Armada de Barlovento in 1609 called for 1 quintal for every tonelada, but that was higher than standard practice.[43] Using the lower figure and the size of the cables, we can estimate that Arana's ships would have carried about 707.3 quintales of cables and 1,073.8 quintales of rigging (*jarcia*). Some of it was probably imported from France or Flanders, as it had been in the sixteenth century; if so, the price had to be paid in silver.[44] Based on a price of 12 ducados the quintal, Arana's cables and rigging together cost about 21,373.2 ducados.[45] In 1629 the price of all sorts of cables and rigging in Bilbao was 12.4 ducados the quintal.[46] It is likely that the cost included not only labor for their manufacture but also the pitch, tar, and labor for treating them to resist water. Together, the rigging, cables, and sails cost more than the wood for the hull.

Wood, iron, canvas, and rigging on the six galleons probably accounted for three-quarters of the total contract price. Additional oil, tar, pitch, and oakum for the caulking would not have taken more than another 5 percent, based on figures for other ship construction. Pulleys and other tackle would have added less than 1 percent.[47] The remainder—about 17.95 percent— would have had to suffice for the labor involved in hull construction. In various accounts for the late sixteenth and early seventeenth centuries, carpenters were paid 11–18 percent of the cost of construction, caulkers 3–5 percent, those who inserted treenails 1–2 percent, and helpers of various kinds a fraction of 1 percent.[48] The estimates for Arana's ships, though admittedly rough, fall well within probable limits.

The crown was responsible for outfitting the ship beyond the terms of Arana's contract, providing everything from such homely items as buckets and cooking supplies to the decoration on all the ships and the elaborate poop lantern on the *San Felipe*. The largest single expense involved gilding and painting, including painting the portrait of each vessel's namesake on the flat face of the stern. Juan de Meaza, the artist employed for all Arana's galleons, received 1,000 ducados for his work, including the gilding on the poop cabins, the beak, and the carved rampant lion that served as the figurehead of each ship. He received another 200 ducados for painting the royal coat of arms on eight linen flags, to be carried on the masthead of each ship. The two extra flags were presumably for the *San Felipe* and the *Begoña*. The poop lantern cost 131.2 ducados, most of it going for the copper, bronze, walnut trim, and glass that went into its manufacture. In comparison, six ordinary tin running lanterns cost 16 ducados in all. Other major expenses were 466.7 ducados for 604 yards of bunting for all the ships, at 8.5 reales per yard, and the 400 ducados the crown eventually allowed Arana for mending sails damaged by rats. Everything else was minor, except for the cost of the guards Arana had supplied before December 1627, for which the crown finally repaid him in part.[49]

In all, the crown reimbursed Arana 3,403.6 ducados for the items supplied by him outside of his contract obligations. In addition the crown paid for a long list of reserve supplies, including sail canvas, rigging, thread, planks, nails, tacks, lead sheathing, copper kettles, and a host of other items for

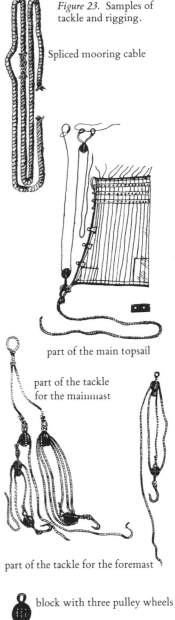

Figure 23. Samples of tackle and rigging.

Spliced mooring cable

part of the main topsail

part of the tackle for the mainmast

part of the tackle for the foremast

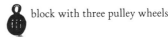 block with three pulley wheels

small block   sailmaker's palm

(Representation of the illustrations found in AGM, Marques de la Victoria, Diccionario [1756]. Drawings by Michael Etoll.)

emergency replacements during the first major voyage. Together these miscellaneous items cost 6,618.5 ducados, plus another 1,800 for six new cables, and 2,600 for careening and final preparations. Adding these additional costs to the basic contract price gives a total of 94,174.1 ducados for the six ships, rigged and ready to sail, but without artillery. Even without Arana's supposed contribution to the work, the ships had cost 35.4 ducados per tonelada. Adding the 6,000 ducados he claimed to have spent without reimbursement would bring the cost to 37.7 ducados. (See appendix C, table 7.)

With the galleons in royal hands, the long process of settling accounts began. Arana had already been paid the basic contract fee of 30 ducados per tonelada, or a total of 79,752 ducados for all six galleons, but that was not the end of the matter. Arana had provided much equipment under protest and later made claim for reimbursement. On the other side of the bargaining negotiations were the various officials of the crown, from the king himself and his officials in Madrid, to the inspector and purveyor in Bilbao and Admiral Francisco de Vallecilla in Santander with the ships. Each party to the negotiations had a slightly different point of view. To make matters more difficult, there was considerable confusion over which version of the contract was binding. Arana had signed a preliminary contract sometime before March 14, 1625, and he continued to claim that he was bound by its terms and no others. The king had signed the official contract dated March 14, 1625, and his ministers claimed that this was the only binding contract. Luckily, both sides were willing to compromise.

The new round of negotiations began with a report by Francisco de Vallecilla, who reinspected the galleons in Santander with the aid of the master's assistant (contramaestre) of each one. Late in September 1628 he sent a detailed list of items he had found missing from the ships and equipment he deemed below the standard for armada service. To complete the itemized list for each ship, Vallecilla had copies of the contracts as well as the delivery invoices written by Ochoa and Hormaeche to guide him. In general, he complained that the cables were shorter than they ought to be, and that many of them were thinner, and therefore weaker, than ships of that size required. For example, he thought some of the cables should be 90 *brazas* long instead of 70 (1 braza was 5.5 feet or 1.67 meters), and the ayustes (mooring cables) 120–130 brazas instead of 100.[50] Some of the anchors he thought were too light as well. Two of the *Begoña*'s four anchors weighed only 1,200–1,300 pounds; Vallecilla thought they all should have been at least 2,000 pounds. He blamed light weight for the breakage of two anchors and one mooring cable while the ship was in port. The standard seems to have been changing, however. A later galleon of 803 toneladas and 72 cannons would carry anchors of only 1,800–2,000 pounds.[51] Vallecilla also thought that a few of the bowsprits and one set of topmasts were too thin. As missing equipment for the six ships, Vallecilla listed braces (*gimelgas*) for the thin bowsprits, one mizzen sail per ship, various pulleys, some pump fittings, some of the wall planking and storage chests in the poop cabins, one ship's boat per galleon, the sails and rigging for the other ship's boat, and some of the bunting.[52] In general, Vallecilla's inspection was much more thorough than that reported in the delivery invoices (see appendix A); this was to be expected, since Vallecilla was an experienced mariner, whereas Ochoa and Hormaeche probably were not.

Arana had to respond to the report, but meanwhile he had some claims of his own to press. In late October, he presented the first of several partial accounts of monies he had spent on items not required by the version of the contract he acknowledged. In addition to the cost of guarding the galleons before the crown took delivery, his claims included various fittings for the gunports, locks and keys for storage areas, flags painted with the royal arms, and the running lanterns carried by each ship. His total bill for the equipment alone was 777,722 maravedís, or 2,073.9 ducados.[53]

Making his own claims against the crown strengthened Arana's position as he responded to Vallecilla's report in late November. The official record is arranged in parallel columns, with requirements based on the contract in the left-hand column and Arana's response in the right-hand column. In studying both, it becomes clear that the Junta de Armadas considered custom and good faith efforts as well as legal obligations. The contract required Arana to provide two sets of sails for each galleon, but did not specify the individual sails; Vallecilla had faulted him for providing only one mizzen each for five of the galleons. Arana responded that it was not customary to have more than one mizzen, "because it is a sail that does little work and lasts a long time," though he had weakened his own point by providing two mizzens for one of the ships.[54] In addition, he claimed reimbursement for the topgallant masts and sails, which were not mentioned in either contract.

All the rigging was to have come from Calatayud in Aragón, an area known for the quality of its hemp and the cable made from it, but the inventories showed some from San Macari and Cherba. San Macari is probably St. Macaire in the French Gironde; the identity of Cherba is not certain. Arana responded that he had gained permission for the San Macari cable from the royal secretary Clemente de Ochandiano, in a letter of June 25, 1627. The inventory item saying that four of the laid ropes (calabrotes) came from Cherba must have been a slip of the pen, he said, because it was not true. Arana did not respond at all to the issue of the size of the cables, stating only that he was providing the full number required. He took the same tack regarding the anchors, stating only that the six left behind in Portugalete could be claimed any time by the crown to make up the full complement.

Arana had no trouble answering the point that the galleons had only one boat (*batel*) instead of two (a batel and a *chalupa*). All the chalupas were in Portugalete, left behind by their captains because of the need to lighten the ships to pass the sandbar downriver. The boats did carry fewer oars than the contract required, a point that Arana could not contest. He defended his failure to provide bronze reinforcements for the pulley rollers on all the ships, although his version of the contract had specified them. He claimed that the bronze broke the lines—not a very likely excuse—and that, even though his contract had mentioned bronze, the version signed by the king had not. In other words, when it was in his interests, Arana could allow the validity of the contract he disputed. The other points raised by Vallecilla he answered easily, stating that he was providing wood and carpenters to finish the planking and missing fittings for the poop cabins.[55]

Part of Arana's response was a further statement of his claims for reimbursement; in the margin, the Junta indicated its initial response to those claims. Its members thought Arana should be paid for any additional cables he had provided, of course, and for any items not specified in the contract, such as compass boxes (bitácoras). On the other hand, they did not favor paying for the guards placed on the galleons before the crown accepted delivery, despite Arana's reminder that he had also spent 6,000 ducados of his own money, for which he was *not* claiming reimbursement.[56]

In mid-December Ochoa and Hormaeche received orders to collect the chalupas and anchors left in Portugalete.[57] The next week they were asked to make their independent judgments on the claims and counterclaims by Vallecilla and Arana within a fortnight, so that the matter might be resolved.[58] Their full report, sent to Martín de Aróztegui of the Junta on January 15, was remarkably detailed and fair-minded. Since they had not yet received the missing cables and anchors, Ochoa and Hormaeche assessed Arana for their value in the report. Using the same general approach for the rest of the list, they assessed Arana the value of any missing items. If he had substituted one piece of equipment for another of more or less equal function and value, they took it as fulfilling the contract. If the items substituted were of inferior value, they assigned the difference to Arana. Regarding the missing bronze pulley fittings, Ochoa and Hormaeche indirectly supported Arana's noncompliance by mentioning that they were not standard equipment in Vizcaya. Their value would have to be ascertained from elsewhere in Spain where bronze fittings were standard. They also deferred an assessment of the value of the missing planking and chests, and the reinforcements of various masts, since they did not know just how much work and material it would require. The tonnage figures for the six galleons exceeded the figure mentioned in the contract, but that had been due to official changes in the measurements, they agreed, and should not be charged to Arana.

The royal officials also supported Arana's claim that he was exempt from supplying a variety of equipment: bunting; the fancy poop lantern for the *San Felipe;* ordinary running lanterns; royal flags; locks, hooks and hinges for the poop chambers; buckets; and padlocks and other fittings for the hatch covers. In addition, they agreed that the artwork and decoration of each galleon was at the crown's expense.

The auditors took a neutral stance on Arana's claim to be repaid for guarding the galleons; they merely related the chronology of events. Arana had hired guards from the end of July 1627, because at that point the galleons were effectively completed. The crown had not ordered Ochoa and Hormaeche to inspect them until the end of October, and by the time they carried out the order it was mid-December. Then, finding them "well constructed and with the necessary fortification," they took the galleons under the protection of the crown, using as guards eighteen fugitive sailors who had been jailed in Portugalete. Even with their supervisors included, this was a far smaller contingent than the fifty or so men Arana had hired, but the royal officials refrained from comment on that point.[59]

Although the topgallants were not mentioned in either version of the contract, they were standard equipment on armada ships by then, so Ochoa and Hormaeche left the Junta to figure out whose responsibility they were. Arana claimed 11,000 reales for mending some of the sails damaged by rats after the galleons had come under royal protection. Ochoa and Hormaeche noted that since some of that cost was for additions to sails that Admiral de Vallecilla considered skimpy, the expense should be divided in some way. They had no doubts that the full careening of the *San Felipe* and *Los Tres*

Reyes was the crown's complete responsibility, since only partial careening was included under the terms by which Arana accepted 2,600 ducados for the final preparations of the six ships.

Regarding the cables, the royal officials confirmed Arana's claims about their origins. As for their length and thickness, the master cordwainers who made them swore under oath that cables 80–84 brazas long and 360–450 threads thick, and *ayustes* 120 brazas long and 504 threads thick, were perfectly suited to the galleons. They testified further that for forty years they had not made larger or longer cables for ships of those sizes. The royal officials were forced to conclude that Arana had fulfilled his obligation, even though it was true, as Vallecilla had said, that cables of 95–100 brazos and ayustes of 130 brazos and more were superior. They made a similar determination regarding the anchors. The master craftsman who made them declared that the orders came from the shipwrights, whose recommendations Arana had followed. If some of the anchors were light, it was not Arana's fault; Ochoa and Hormaeche concurred.

In all, their report vindicated Arana and supported his claims for reimbursement, except for those items on which they deferred judgment or passed the responsibility on to the Junta de Armadas. Vallecilla's complaints about the galleons were not entirely unfounded, however. The anchors and the cables do seem to have been lighter than was customary on the best armada ships, and that may indicate that the Vizcayan shipbuilding industry had sacrificed some of its legendary quality to cut costs. The change had undoubtedly taken place earlier—if we can believe the cordwainers, about forty years earlier—when the industry was already in trouble because of rising costs and uncertain supplies.

After Ochoa and Hormaeche filed their report, Martín de Aróztegui of the Junta de Armadas reviewed their findings, glossing each point with his corrections, additions, or concurrence. He revised the figures for missing and substituted cables on the basis of their weight, cutting by more than half the amount counted against Arana. On the other hand, he assigned a value for the missing woodwork against Arana, until and unless the work was completed in Santander. As for the guards Arana had placed on the ships, Aróztegui was inclined to pick up some of the cost, since much of the delay in the fall of 1627 had been caused by the king's illness, but he made no estimate of how much Arana should be repaid. The total cost of the guards had been considerable—some 300 reales per day, when the full contingent worked. Aróztegui recommended that the crown pay for the topgallants and for the full careening of the *San Felipe* and *Los Tres Reyes*. He judged that only one-third of the costs for sail repair should be paid to Arana, however, since the rest had gone to alter defects in the sails he had supplied. Similarly, even though the short weight of some of the anchors was not Arana's fault, Aróztegui recommended assessing him the value of the missing iron, "since the lack of weight was to the benefit of don Martín, although it was not his fault." For the rest, Aróztegui confirmed the findings of Ochoa and Hormaeche, and the matter went to the full Junta de Armadas.[60]

On March 17, Junta members made a major decision in Arana's favor, confirming the opinions of local and other royal officials that Arana was not obligated to pay for the items included in the official version of the contract without his knowledge or consent. That cleared the way for the final settlement of claims, though it by no means resolved all the outstanding issues. At the same meeting, the Junta, with four members in attendance, reviewed Aróztegui's report point by point. Although they confirmed every one, they reduced the amount Arana was assessed for bracing the masts and building the missing storage compartments. They also agreed not to assess him for the lack of bronze pulley reinforcements, "in consideration of his care and good service."[61] For the two troublesome points about providing the topgallant sails and mending various others, the Junta directed Aróztegui to seek outside opinions, which he did, from General don Francisco de Acevedo and Vincente de Anziondo. Both men agreed that since the topgallants were not mentioned in the contract, Arana was not obligated to provide them at his expense. Despite a protest from Pedro de Arce of the Junta, the other members voted to favor Arana's claims, and also to raise his reimbursement for mending the damaged sails.

Throughout this inquiry, the crown was not looking for fraud; it was simply trying to get full value for its money. In fact, while Arana was still working on the galleons, he had been questioned about any profits he was making in the purchase of materials. He answered that he might have got some advantage on the price of the anchors and nails, but that he had lost that and more in purchasing the rigging. Comment from Madrid was that it was "tolerable that he have some benefit in some part of the transactions," since the important thing was to complete the ships as expeditiously as possible.[62] Royal officials could easily have found sloppy figuring and some misrepresentation in the accounts Arana submitted, but they had to tread the fine line between attention to their accounting duties and the kind of niggling that would have discouraged willing subjects such as Arana from any further service to the crown.

The resolution of responsibility for some of the ironwork illustrates the crown's desire to be fair to Arana, but not at the king's expense. The crown had to provide artillery fittings, including the restraining rings attached to the deck where the guns would be located. When Arana presented his bill for the ironwork, however, it was not divided up to show what individual items had cost. Because iron work was generally priced by weight, he could not prove what he had spent for the restraining rings alone. While sympathizing with his difficulty, the Junta resolved the matter to the crown's advantage. Without documents to support him, Arana had little leverage. When he had proof of his expenses, as in the costs of painting and gilding for the six galleons, the Junta accepted his figures without complaint. After some deliberation, they even voted to accept the expense of guarding the galleons for three and a half months in 1627, disclaiming only one small amount from Arana's bill of 12,327 reales (1,120.6 ducados).[63]

By late May 1629 the inquiry was completed to the crown's satisfaction, though Arana had not been paid the approximately 44,000 reales (4,000 ducados) owed him to clear the accounts. The Junta noted "that don Martín has served well, with much zeal and satisfaction and harm to his finances, and thus it is just that he be paid punctually what is owed him, and that His Majesty order the Contador Mayor to pay him."[64] That was easier said than done. Even after the king issued a special decree authorizing reimbursement, the bills were not settled.[65] The royal paymasters had their own priorities, and, as loyal a servant as Arana was, there were more pressing bills to be paid than his.

Luckily, Arana had a potential solution. Of the forty pinnaces he had built for the crown to serve in Flanders, only five had been delivered, and all seem to have been too large for the job for which they were ordered. The thirty-five remaining were still in Arana's care, although the crown had already paid about 100 ducados each for them. Together they were worth nearly 38,500 reales, though Arana claimed he had spent much more than that in their construction, and the Junta thought they were worth somewhat less than that in 1629 because of weathering. Nonetheless, when Arana heard the crown planned to sell them, he recognized his chance. He offered to "buy" the pinnaces for what the crown had paid for them, making the purchase with the credit owed him for the balance on the six galleons. He would lose something on the deal, besides absorbing the costs he had spent on guarding the pinnaces, but there were advantages to both sides in his proposal.[66]

Arana made his offer in early June, but nothing was done until the end of the summer, again at his prodding. He reminded the Junta of his offer and, nearly at the same time, put in another request for royal preferment for his son Diego, who had already been made a gentleman of the military Order of Santiago. Clearly, Arana thought his bargaining position was strong in the summer of 1629, and he was not mistaken. With the Junta's support for his scheme, the matter was settled in September, with Arana taking charge of the unused pinnaces.[67] Even if he had merely made enough to satisfy his creditors, Arana had at least cleared accounts with the crown just over a year after the six galleons had sailed for Santander. Many other royal contractors would have envied that timetable.

In due course, he was repaid in favor and honor as well. On June 27, 1631, the king named don Martín de Arana Superintendent and Captain of War over the soldiers who resided in the city of Santander and three smaller towns on the north coast, in view of his service "in different tasks and particularly in the outfitting and construction of armadas, among others six galleons that sailed to bring the silver from the Indies. . . ."[68]

In 1632 Arana would sign another contract with the crown, this time for the construction of nine galleons for Indies service. Completing these and other ships and negotiating with the crown for payment would occupy him until his death in 1644, in the midst of another dispute with royal officials who, he complained, were driving him and his family to ruin. Yet, for all its aggravation, the partnership between Arana and the crown seems to have been mutually beneficial.

FIVE

Preparations for the Indies Fleet of 1629

The acquisition of ships was a necessary first step in keeping the lines of trade and empire open, but it was by no means the most important expense. Far more costly, both in money and in human effort, was the task of supplying the ships with artillery, officers, sailors, soldiers, and the food and equipment needed to sustain them and their vessels. Based on the figures presented in chapter 4, each of Arana's six galleons cost the crown about 15,696 ducados to build, rigged and ready to sail in 1628. In the same period, provisioning and operating a galleon on just one round-trip voyage to the Indies cost two to three times that much. The figures come from a detailed estimate of costs for four galleons outfitted and provisioned by the king in 1626.[1] The king did not own those particular ships, so rental fees were a large proportion of the total expense—about 25 percent. Artillery and gunners cost another 30 percent of the total, food 26 percent, and wages for the sailors and soldiers another 13 percent. Ship equipment, minor fees for loading, and miscellaneous expenses made up the balance. Since the king owned the galleons built by Martín de Arana, he would save a considerable amount in rental fees, but the cost of food, artillery, wages, and other expenses still brought the cost of a single round-trip voyage to the Indies to at least double the initial cost of the ships, with the total varying in proportion to the length of the voyage. There will be more to say about the prices of individual items of food and ship equipment later. For now, the total price tag emphasizes the central role that fleet provisioning played in royal policy.

Just as the crown used various means to acquire the ships it needed for the Indies run, so it used various means to supply those ships, employing its own officials or turning the job over to private individuals on contract. Merely deciding what means to choose in a given situation took an enormous effort

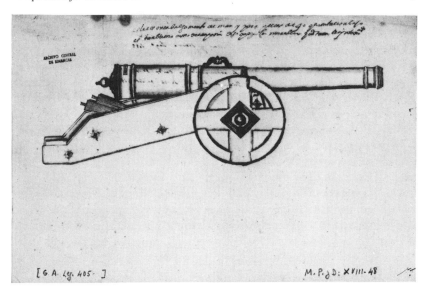

Figure 24. Gun carriage for use at sea, bearing guns up to 40 quintales (about 4,000 pounds), sketched in 1594. Its estimated cost is 30 ducados. (AGS, Mapas, Planos y Dibujos, XVIII-48, from Guerra Antigua, leg. 405. Courtesy of the Archivo General de Simancas, Simancas, Valladolid.)

on the part of the royal bureaucracy, in estimating costs and surveying the availability of food and supplies in different ports suitable for armada ships. The royal archives are filled with memoranda on those topics as each fleet prepared to sail. How much biscuit was available in Vizcaya? Where were the tackle and rigging promised from Cádiz? How soon could the artillery arrive in port? The impression gained from reading through hundreds of these reports is of the steady hum of a massive bureaucratic machine in motion, increasing speed as the time for departure came near, settling back to a steady rhythm thereafter, but never ceasing to function. Even winter months when the fleets were idle saw much provisioning activity, with food and other supplies being arranged, procured, and stored while the ships themselves underwent repairs.

Artillery, as we have seen, was the sole responsibility of the crown in Arana's contract, as in all the others noted for this study. Royal officials kept track of guns, ammmunition, and supplies at all times, both on board ships and in storage on land between voyages. Artillery had been commonly carried on Spanish ships since the late Middle Ages, definitely by the fifteenth century, and perhaps even earlier.[2] Nonetheless, the artillery on a given ship was not a permanent part of its equipment. Instead, it was logged on board for a given voyage and removed again as soon as the ship returned to port. This was true even of the war galleons of the Armada de la Guardia during the sixteenth and seventeenth centuries. (See figure 24.) An official called the *mayordomo de la artillería* of the Armada del Mar Océano registered and identified each gun in his care as precisely as possible, and equally carefully signed it out when it was delivered elsewhere. Guns from ships could be used interchangeably on land for the defense of city walls and ports, and vice versa. By keeping a close control over the available munitions, the crown could make do with a surprisingly small number of major artillery pieces, shifting them around as the need arose.[3] This small but flexible arsenal represented an important savings, given the high cost connected with the use of artillery. A planned military expedition to Africa in 1577–78 estimated the average cost of the ball, powder, and fuse for each artillery shot at 2.6 ducados—at a time when a soldier was paid 3 ducados a month.[4]

As mentioned in chapter 3, the crown had established norms for the armament of its warships, matching the number and size of the weaponry to the size of the vessels. A set of rules dating from 1552 listed the artillery and manning ratios for several sizes of ships, including the amount of powder and shot that should be provided for each gun.[5] As time went on, supplying those weapons and their equipment became an increasing problem. The Spanish crown made its own gunpowder and guns through most of the sixteenth century, tightening regulations and standards in the 1570s. Nonetheless, supply could not keep up with demand, and, despite its continuing legal monopoly of production, the crown let contracts to private manufacturers in the 1580s and beyond. In addition to royal arms factories such as that in Seville, dating from 1611,[6] the famous cannon foundry of Liérganes near Santander was established in 1622 on contract with a wealthy founder from Liége (Belgium). It continued to supply artillery to the crown through the period under study here. In addition, a private contractor took over gunpowder manufacture from the royal monopoly in 1633,[7] with the crown retaining close control over the quality and quantity of the factory's production. Detailed accounts from the Liérganes factory from 1628–1646 give a very clear idea of the calibers and weights of the munitions produced there, even if they tell us nothing about how and where it was distributed. Table 8 (appendix C) summarizes the information contained in those accounts.

Judging solely from the quantities produced, cannons of 24-, 16-, and 10-pound balls were clearly the most common weapons, though the range of gun sizes was much more varied than that. Not all the items mentioned in the documents included information about weight, but it would seem that there was a considerable range of acceptable weights within a given caliber. In other words, although officials noted that 10-pounders weighing 3,100 pounds (when the average was 3,300) and seven-pounders weighing 2,300 pounds (when the average was 2,377) were too light, standardization had not proceeded very far. The calibers and weights for the cannonballs showed a similarly wide range. Everything produced at Liérganes was made of iron; for bronze artillery, the crown used the foundries at Seville and elsewhere. Like the other items made of iron that have been mentioned before, the weaponry made at Liérganes was priced by weight, with one fee encompassing both materials and labor. For each hundredweight, guns cost 8 ducados, cannonballs cost 46–49.5 reales (or 4.2–4.5 ducados), and iron bombshells cost 5.45 ducados; presumably the prices reflected the different amounts of labor they required.

The completed munitions were delivered to royal officials for distribution where they were most needed, on land or sea. Officials assigned to the armadas that included Arana's galleons had to keep track of 380 separate categories of guns, ammunition, and other weaponry and supplies, as well as oversee the quality of items supplied by private contractors.[8] In addition to these locally assigned officials, a captain-general of artillery oversaw weaponry in the central government. The post was held in 1648 by the Marquis of Castrofuerte, who at one time or another served as general infantry commissioner, inspector-general of cavalry, and member of the Council of War and its Junta de Armadas.[9] The bureaucratic hierarchy associated with munitions kept governmental control over the private contractors who were brought in to help provide weaponry for Spain and its empire.

Provisioning nearly always involved a combination of royal officials and private entrepreneurs, and individuals working on contract were regular members of provisioning teams at least as early as Charles I's reign in the early sixteenth century. It is likely, in fact, that Charles relied on private contractors more than his successors did, simply because his developing bureaucracy could not match the demands of his vast empire. For a voyage Charles made to England in 1554, a *factor* (victualler) named Francisco Duarte, engaged by the House of Trade in Seville, made the arrangements for the royal fleet, hiring his own men to buy supplies in Seville and arrange for their delivery to ships in the fleet. Already the pattern of accountability was set in the victualler's accounts. He received large lump sums for the provisioning, and then later had to account for every penny spent and every measure of grain and other supplies delivered. To confirm his accounts, he required each ship's master to sign a receipt for whatever was delivered.[10]

When Charles returned to Spain from Flanders in 1556, he had already abdicated most of his power to his son Philip; he was coming home to retire from his responsibilities and, a few years later, to die. His homecoming fleet has assumed much romantic importance in the historical literature, yet even it was subject to strict standards of cost control and accountability. In all, the fleet would carry about two-thousand courtiers, members of the entourages of Charles and of his two sisters, widowed queens accompanying their brother on his last voyage. Food for nine-hundred soldiers was also part of the royal budget, but provisions for the ships themselves and their sailors were budgeted separately. Charles's ministers compared the costs of provisioning the fleet in various ways. By far the most expensive was to pay a daily *ración* from which each person would supply his own food for the voyage. As an alternative, Flemish ship masters offered to provision the ships more cheaply, but their offer was still 30 percent higher than the royal officials could do it themselves by buying food and supplies on the Flemish market. Assuming the same standard shipboard diet, paying the ración would have cost a total of 37.5 Castilian maravedís per day per person. Paying the Flemish ship masters to supply the royal entourage alone would cost 35.2 maravedís, whereas buying the supplies directly would cost only 24.4 maravedís. Since the soldiers would not be working, they could be fed less expensive food, bringing the average daily cost for the 2,900 persons in the royal party to 20 maravedís.[11] The choice was clear. Charles had driven Castile deeply into debt defending his inheritance, and he wisely chose to come home as economically as possible.

By the late sixteenth century provisioning for royal armadas was overseen by purveyors (proveedores) named to each fleet. For example, a "proveedor de la Armada de la Guardia" supervised provisioning for the escort squadron that sailed with the Indies fleets—the squadron in which Arana's ships would first sail. Each official filed detailed accounts for his part in provisioning the fleet.[12] Often, purveyors were responsible for overseeing shipbuilding and repairs in their districts, as well as provisioning, so lesser officials carried out the day-to-day tasks involved in supplying the fleets with food and equipment.

By Arana's time, the crown again relied heavily on private contractors for the actual provisioning, although royal officials continued to oversee the work. This was a mixed blessing, similar to the situation in shipbuilding by private contract, but it became the norm in the seventeenth century. In the sixteenth century royal commissioners (*comisarios*) had often generated ill will by interfering with normal marketing channels to supply the fleets. Private contractors certainly influenced the market, but they did so through their buying power rather than through coercion. Once a contract was signed, the contractor had a free hand to deliver the goods agreed upon, taking any profit he could generate in the process. Royal officials often helped to negotiate the supply contracts, but thereafter their role was only to inspect and either accept or reject what the contractor supplied.[13]

In 1625, the Junta de Armadas spent months discussing the best means to provide for the Armada del Mar Océano in Lisbon, since Portugal was then still joined to Spain under the Habsburg monarchs. The Junta decided that the only convenient approach was to find a private contractor. Although there were many good royal officials, not one of them could operate in Lisbon with the efficiency of a private party, especially one with sufficient wealth to advance money for supplies from his own pocket. Strains on royal finances were great, especially in the 1620s, years that saw several harvest failures and a serious industrial collapse. The royal government would suspend payments to its creditors in 1627 in another of the "bankruptcies" that forced creditors to accept devalued state bonds for their short-term loans. The problem was already serious in 1625, and the most trustworthy contractors were very wary of taking on more royal business. Top royal officials in Madrid and Lisbon finally induced Manuel Gomez y Acosta to take on the job, after a series of meetings that cannot have been very pleasant for Acosta.[14] He held out for a fairly high contract price for his efforts, 55 maravedís per man per day in silver, in recognition of the higher food prices in Lisbon. There was a bid of 54 maravedís from a Spanish contractor in Seville, but he was not prepared to deal quickly enough to suit the crown and he did not know Lisbon as well as Acosta, who was Portuguese. The contract with Acosta was nearly settled by the end of May, but by then the provisioning timetable was so far behind that royal officials in Lisbon had already been scrabbling for months getting what supplies they could, so that the fleet would not have to be canceled altogether. The Marquis of Hinojosa, who headed the provisioning effort, had to pawn his valuables to come up with the cash to buy supplies. By the end of June, time had effectively voided the contract for 1625 with Acosta, because the fleet had been supplied during the months of negotiations.[15] The Junta recommended supplying the fleet in Lisbon directly the next year as well, but by May 1626 Acosta had finally taken the contract, to run until 1631. Royal officials on the north coast, who would have to relay grain from Castile to Lisbon, were notified to give him every assistance.[16]

When Arana's ships first entered royal service in the Armada del Mar Océano, they were assigned to the Armada de la Guardia for the Indies. Horacio Levanto, a victualler in Cádiz on contract to the crown, provisioned them for their first Indies voyage in 1629. The account he later filed shows very clearly his place in the chain of command. The purveyor in Cádiz, with the consultation of the veedor general (inspector-general) of the fleet, gave

Levanto the official order to purchase the needed supplies and deliver them to the master or the master of rations of each ship. The royal *contador* (comptroller) in Cádiz kept the official accounts for the items supplied. Levanto was paid from Madrid by the *receptor general* (receiver-general) of royal income, and thereafter had to file a full account of his receipts and expenditures.[17] Later in the galleons' careers, their provisioning in Cádiz would involve another royal official, the *tenedor de bastimentos* (keeper of supplies) Bartolomé de Vega, who held the post from 1632 to 1636.[18] When they were supplied in Seville in the same period, their masters dealt with the tenedor de bastimentos Tomás Velázquez de la Cueva. Each of these men, and the purveyors in Seville and Cádiz, helped provision the galleons at various times, and each official filed accounts of his transactions.[19] This extraordinary wealth of documentation was the product of official accountability in the Habsburg bureaucracy. Not only does it provide a chronological survey of prices and supply areas, but it will allow us in subsequent chapters to trace the history of Arana's galleons in royal service. The layers of bureaucracy and the intermingling of public and private authority continued to characterize armada provisioning during the seventeenth century. It has striking similarities to the functioning of modern military procurement in many countries, another reminder of the sophisticated bureaucratic organization of imperial Spain.

In all the negotiations for ship provisioning, the key figure was the price of a ración, the daily supply of food and drink for those on board. Not surprisingly, the value of the ración rose in the period under study. At the end of Charles I's reign, it was officially worth about 37.5 maravedís, although, as we have seen, that was much higher than food could be purchased, at least in Flanders.[20] About seventy years later, Manuel Gomez y Acosta received 55 maravedís in silver for supplying the fleets in Lisbon, not an outrageous jump in price considering the rampant inflation of the late sixteenth and early seventeenth centuries.[21] Harvest volume in any given year could affect the contract prices negotiated by the crown, and the nominal cost could vary greatly depending upon whether the price was given in copper or silver currency. Horacio Levanto supplied the galleons built by Arana at a price per ración of 52 maravedís in silver in 1629, and in 1638 some food lost at sea was said to have cost 51 maravedís in silver, suggesting that prices held stable for about a decade.[22] On the other hand, the crown seemed to have paid 60–68 maravedís and up for rations purchased by royal officials.[23] An anonymous author writing in about 1635 confirmed this, noting that rations supplied by contractors cost only 52–62 maravedís, because (he said) they were of lower quality.[24] The author did not specify whether the prices he quoted were in silver or in copper vellón, but his remarks are still suggestive. It is possible that by using contractors, the crown could save money without looking too closely into the quality of the items supplied. We will examine the question of the prices and quality of rations later.

The use of a standard figure for the ración implied that there was a standard list of food supplied for armadas, as indeed there was. The basis of the calculation was the number of sailors and soldiers on each ship, and that, in turn, sprang from the size of the ship and the standard manning ratios prescribed by law and custom. It was imperative, in the cramped quarters on board, to provision as precisely as possible, particularly on warships. Each

Figure 25. Household equipment for use at sea. (Left to right, top to bottom): small barrels for salt pork, vinegar, rice, and other foodstuffs; jars for oil; tied bundle of dried salted cod; ham; cheeses; biscuits; fresh bread; scales; wooden tray for scales; measures (1 azumbre for water, 1 cuartillo for wine, 1/2 cuartillo, 1 cuartillo for vinegar, 2 oz. for oil); fire bucket; funnel for wine; funnel for vinegar; funnel for oil; pitchers for wine, water, vinegar; signal lantern; hand lantern; iron shovel; funnel for filling barrels; bucket for water; small tubs for wine and vinegar; bucket for alquitrán or tar; slop-bucket for the sick; bucket for bailing; water tub.

(Representation of the illustrations found in AGM, Marques de la Victoria, Diccionario [1756].
Drawings by Michael Etoll.)

man on a galleon on the Indies run required 850 kilograms of the ship's carrying capacity, assuming eight months' food and four months' water.[25] To plan for the voyage successfully, the weight and volume of each pipe of wine, each cask of vinegar or oil, in fact everything that the ship carried, needed to be known and planned for in advance, exactly as on a modern cargo aircraft's weight and balance forms[26] or an airliner's flight manifest. The Spanish crown had detailed the standard weights and sizes of nearly sixty containers and commonly carried items on the Indies run late in the reign of Charles I, about 1550.[27] (See figure 25.) Although the list was undoubtedly useful for all ships' masters, its primary purpose was to regulate the loading of merchant vessels. Merchants were notorious for overloading their vessels on the Indies run, and by prescribing the weight and sizes of common containers, the crown tried to assure the safety of the ships and the provisioning needs of those on board, while leaving the maximum possible space for trade goods.

Through the Habsburg period, the standard foodstuffs carried on board for mariners and soldiers included ordinary ships' biscuit or hardtack; water; wine or cider; salt pork or ham; dried beef; salted codfish; cheese; rice, broad beans, and chickpeas; olive oil; vinegar. These were the rationed items. In addition, some fresh items such as garlic, onions, and sometimes peppers, were allotted sparingly but not formally rationed.[28] Other special items were carried for the sick and wounded, as well as for the highest officials of the fleets. These included live chickens (and sometimes sheep, pigs, or cattle), eggs, raisins, almonds, sugar, and often white biscuit. More will be said about the daily rations of all these items and their nutritional content in chapter 7. For now it is sufficient to note that the basic items were the most important in terms of bulk and expense, and most of the energy of the official purveyors was devoted to locating, buying, hauling, and loading them on the fleet. The job took many months, generating a vast correspondence and voluminous accounts for every fleet that sailed.

The key to successful provisioning lay in knowing where to go to fill out the shopping list. Rarely could all the provisions for a fleet be found in the immediate locality of the port where the fleet was assembled. Instead, at times they had to be brought from all over Spain, and even from abroad. Andalusia was one of the richest agricultural areas of Spain, with fairly easy access to food supplies inland from its many ports.[29] Yet even Andalusia could have trouble outfitting a fleet. In 1513, for example, French raids damaged the local economy, and local officials and residents were less than enthusiastic about contributing to the provisioning of a fleet.[30] Other fleets had better luck in Andalusia in the early sixteenth century, with Cádiz, Málaga, and Seville serving as the major assembly points for fleets destined for both Europe and the Indies.[31]

Fleets bound for northern Europe would most logically assemble on the north coast of Spain, which had good harbors and supplies for shipbuilding and repair. But there were serious provisioning difficulties in northern Spain, isolated from the interior by high mountains and notoriously poor in bread grains and other staples. Most areas of the northern Spanish coast were habitual importers of basic foodstuffs for their own populations, and in wartime they often had to be allowed to import food even from enemy countries. Provisioning the armadas that assembled there for the regular wool and defense fleets to the Spanish Netherlands required great organization. For one important armada to Flanders in 1539–40, wheat was brought to the port of Laredo near Santander, where it was baked into the biscuit required. For that fleet the immediate area also provided some salted beef, but salt pork and fish, as well as many other items, had to be brought from Galicia on the extreme northwest coast.[32] For another armada to Flanders in 1553, biscuit had to be brought all the way from Málaga to Bilbao by sea.[33] Luís de Carvajal's 1557 armada, provisioned in Laredo, secured about 52 percent of the wheat it needed for biscuit from Castile, and the rest from foreign sources. About 51 percent of its wine came from northern Spain, 5 percent from Castile, 7 percent from Andalusia, and the remaining 37 percent from France.[34] Peace with France between 1559 and 1594 was a great boon for the fleets supplied on the north coast, giving them easy access to French imports.[35] Still, the flow of troops toward embarkation points had to be regulated carefully to ensure there was enough food for them along the way and in the port itself.[36]

The north coast continued to be the staging area for fleets sailing to northern Europe, with La Coruña taking a more active role by the mid-

seventeenth century.[37] Even so, local economic distress could force a temporary shift in operations to other areas that were better provisioned. For
example, the fleet supplied in Santander and La Coruña for Flanders in 1631
was urged to make its return voyage to Lisbon instead, because the whole
north coast was temporarily stripped of provisions and ship supplies.[38]

When Arana's ships were still several months from completion, he had
already begun scouring the north coast for five months' provisions, enough
to take the ships to Santander and beyond. Wheat was expected from
Guipúzcoa as early as mid-February 1628, and Arana had purchased 280
French hundredweights (at 110 pounds each) of dried cod and some bacon in
St. Jean de Luz, where he traveled to purchase other supplies. No sooner had
he sent it to Portugalete than most of it was preempted by the fleet in
Santander, which was nearly out of supplies and unable to buy any in the
neighborhood. As soon as Arana's wheat arrived, some if it, too, was sent on
to Santander.[39] This was doubly irritating to Arana; he had spent his and his
associates' money buying the supplies, thinking they would be for his ships.
His dilemma over foodstuffs was the same as that over ship equipment.
Although he was obliged to supply the six ships he had built, other officials
on the north coast had to supply the entire armada, and more urgent needs
for the supplies Arana gathered preempted him time and again.

Royal officials working on the provisioning of Arana's ships in Portugalete in 1628 had major problems finding enough wine. The previous harvest
in the nearby Rioja region of Navarre had been very poor, and money and
credit difficulties left the entire area short of supplies. Ochoa and Hormaeche
recommended that the 450 pipes (large barrels) of wine they needed be
brought from Andalusia, along with some olive oil, in the same ships
bringing the artillery for Arana's galleons. In the meantime they bought 62
pipes of Andalusian wine at what the Junta considered an exhorbitant price.
For their unauthorized purchase, they were sternly reprimanded and ordered to resell the wine.[40]

The flow of supplies started to return to Bilbao when the crisis in Santander had passed and Arana's ships had become the ones most in need of
immediate attention. Six hundred *fanegas* of wheat arrived from Santander
on May 11 and were immediately consigned to the bakers.[41] A further
shipment in mid-June ran into the start of the dry season, which slowed
down the milling process. Nonetheless, enough biscuit had been made by
early July for nearly 47,000 daily rations.[42] The total was 700 quintales of
biscuit, which would provide 46,666 rations at 1.5 pounds per daily ration.
All the other basic supplies were on hand as well. By the end of July 1628, the
five hundred sailors and one hundred soldiers hired for the trip to Santander
had arrived in Portugalete. Since the town did not have enough food to sell
them, they began to draw rations from the supplies Arana had laid in. Ochoa
had to buy twenty-four additional pipes of wine and could not resist telling
the king that it would have been preferable to keep the wine he had been
ordered to resell, rather than buying at the inflated market price in late July.[43]

The experience of Arana's ships seems to have been typical of armada
provisioning on the north coast. Because of the shortage of basic foodstuffs
there, most provisions for the fleets had to be shipped in, and ships with an
imminent departure date took precedence over those with more time to
spare. Nonetheless, after all the frantic buying expeditions and shifting of

supplies, somehow everything came together on time, the product of hard work and a few minor miracles. It would have been more efficient for the crown to stockpile and warehouse the supplies, since they were designed for long storage anyway, but the fact is that there was never enough cash on hand to do that. Private contractors such as Arana served a crucial function in advancing some of their own money to purchase supplies. In effect, they provided short-term credit to the crown, something that the actual suppliers of the food were unable or unwilling to do.

However great a strain provisioning the armadas could be, it still meant a great deal of business and employment to local economies. Merchants, ships' pilots, boatmen, stevedores, messengers, craftsmen and women, and warehouse owners were all happy to do business with the crown and its representatives, especially in cash. An international trading mecca such as Seville and its outports had a sprinkling of foreign names among the suppliers and some exotic items among the salt cod and ships' biscuit. An armada supplied in Seville in 1554 bought some "lienzo calicud" (linen from Calcutta) to make artillery cartridges and dealt with numerous resident foreigners for basic armada supplies, although the list of suppliers was overwhelmingly dominated by native Spaniards.[44] Women played a fairly small role among armada suppliers in Seville—only three in a list of about two hundred payments went to women in 1554—but women were prominent among suppliers of ships' biscuit on the north coast. Six of the sixteen biscuit makers in two towns near Santander in 1557 were women, some in business alone, others as partners or successors of their husbands.[45] And in Bilbao in 1568, women seem to have controlled biscuit production altogether, from hauling foreign wheat from the docks at San Sebastián, to warehousing, milling, and baking it in Bilbao. At least one of these women was a general ships' chandler as well, dealing in a wide range of supplies.[46] Overall, local suppliers of armadas dominated provisioning, which helped to spread employment and profits widely in the port towns, even while it complicated provisioning for those in charge of coordinating the arrival of supplies and the settling of accounts.

The costs of basic foodstuffs for armada fleets fluctuated along with general price curves in Spain, but they were also affected by the same pressures that influenced supplies. Because many of the ports frequented by the fleets were supplied by sea, the cost of provisions included transport costs as well. Moreover, under the pressure of time, officials supplying the fleets sometimes had to pay exhorbitant prices, because they could not wait for the market to go down. Indies fleets generally departed in spring and summer, before the harvests, and needed to be provisioned just when prices were at their seasonal high points for the year. One major source for Spanish prices from 1501 to 1650 is the classic study by Earl Hamilton, researched in the 1920s and published in 1934.[47] Many of the commodities tracked by Hamilton also appear on the provisioning lists, so the two series of prices can be compared. Unfortunately, Hamilton's sources did not include a few of the most important items of ship provisioning—biscuit and dried beef and pork in particular—probably because there was little demand for them among the resident population of Spain. (See appendix C, table 16.)

Ships' biscuit rose in price about fivefold in the course of less than a century, a rise that roughly paralleled that for wheat and bread grains in general.[48] The rapid rise in Andalusian grain prices after 1570 has often been

attributed to the notable rise in population there.[49] This was surely part of
the reason, but armada provisioning in Andalusia probably contributed as
well.[50] Not only did the need for ships' biscuit increase the demand for
wheat, but it also distorted the market. The bread needs of a rising resident
population would add fairly constant pressure to the demand for grain. The
need for ships' biscuit to supply a nonresident population for months beyond
the purchase of the grain would add great but intermittent pressure to that
demand. It would have the same effect on the market as if thousands of
people suddenly moved to town, demanding to be fed, and then just as
suddenly moved away again. Thus, even though Andalusia was agricultur-
ally much better able to supply the fleets than was the north coast, armada
provisioning could create supply difficulties there as well.

Wine prices varied enormously because of the wide range of quality
available. The wine bought for the table of the captain-general of an Indies
fleet in 1562 cost 1.5 to 2 times more than the ordinary wine bought for
everyone else. Since the latter sort represented the vast majority of wines
purchased for the fleets, the average price paid for armada provisioning may
have been lower than the general average of wine prices in Seville in the mid-
sixteenth century.[51] There are too few data to generalize about wine prices in
the seventeenth century, but it is possible that supplies for the armada were
getting more difficult to procure, and therefore more expensive.[52] Another
possibility is that fraud in the procurement of armada supplies falsely inflated
prices. That is possible, but it does not seem likely, given the many layers of
bureaucracy through which the accounts had to travel. As we have seen,
officials in Madrid promptly reprimanded their subordinates on the north
coast for paying a higher price for wine than they thought justified. On the
whole, it seems more likely that high prices were caused by suppliers
charging what the market would bear; with the rigid timetable needed to
coordinate the fleets, it was a sellers' market.

Salt pork (*tocino*) was the most common meat supplied to armadas, although dried strips (*tasajos*) of beef or pork, salted beef, and ham could also
appear on supply lists. In the mid-sixteenth century, Flanders supplied much
of the salt pork sent with the fleets. The price rose by about 2.5 times
between 1562 and 1626 in Seville—a modest increase given the inflation of
the period—and fleet prices tended to run higher than those in the general
market.[53]

The fish ration for European voyages showed considerable variety, but on
the long voyages across the Atlantic, there was no good substitute for lean
fish, salted and dried—especially the ubiquitous cod, staple of so many
European diets. Because of the different sizes and qualities of dried fish
purchased for the armadas, it is difficult to track its price over time. The
available data indicate that it stayed remarkably stable in the late sixteenth
and early seventeenth centuries, probably because coastal areas were well
supplied with fresh fish, and residents of small towns all along the south
coast made their living from preserving the catch by drying and salting.[54]

The cheese supplied for armadas rarely amounted to even a tenth the
supply of salt pork.[55] Much more important on Indies voyages were rice and
dried legumes, especially chickpeas and broad beans (*habas*). Rice rose just
2.5 times in price between the mid-sixteenth century and 1626; chickpeas
and broad beans rose fivefold.[56] It would be interesting to know if armada

suppliers attempted to save money by substituting rice for legumes as the price rose, because they occupied the same dietary niche in armada provisioning. There is no evidence of this, however. Instead, the precise composition of shipboard provisions varied according to what was available in a given port. Rice was undoubtedly more plentiful on the east coast of Spain, near the rice fields of Valencia, but few Indies ships would ever have been provisioned there.

Olive oil and vinegar, staple products of Andalusia, rose less than 2.5 times on the Seville market between the mid-sixteenth century and 1626; elsewhere in Spain they could cost much more.[57] Garlic, always carried but not formally rationed, was negligible in cost, though it, too, doubled in price between 1554 and 1626. Other items of diet on armada ships were not generally rationed. The additional foods carried for important persons on board and for the sick were minor considerations compared to the bulk and total expense of the basic rations, although they often fetched a higher unit price.[58]

In the Indies nearly everything supplied to the fleets cost more and was harder to procure. To lower the cost, armada suppliers frequently used local American products to supplement the standard rations; for example, *casabe* was added to supplies of biscuit and *tortuga* (tortoise) to supplies of meat.[59]

The high price of foodstuffs in the Indies may have encouraged fraud of a special sort. In a memorandum to the king about careening and supplies in 1613, Diego Ramírez mentioned that armada ships habitually received provisions for 80–90 days for the return voyage from Havana, the last port of call in the Indies. This should have allowed a considerable reserve for bad weather and spoilage, since the actual return voyage was usually much shorter. Yet ships arriving from Havana rarely reached their first Spanish port with more than 3 or 4 days' food left, and some ships had to be resupplied just to make the voyage up the Guadalquivir River to Seville. Ramírez suspected that the extra food was actually staying in Havana, to be resold later at a profit.[60] There is some confusion in Ramírez's report, as armada ships generally returned to Cádiz, not Seville, but if he was right, this fraud would have meant the crown was paying over and over again for the same supplies, at inflated prices.

It is difficult to trace variations in the general provisioning pattern over time. Many fleet accounts include a detailed spread sheet (*mapa de bastimentos*) listing all the ships in the fleet, the number of persons drawing rations, and the total amounts of every commodity supplied. Unfortunately, rarely do we know if these figures include only the amount of newly purchased items or the total amount loaded on the fleet. Most of the fleets were supposed to carry more provisions than they actually needed, to ensure against overly long voyages or mishaps at sea. The leftover provisions were then transferred to other ships and would often appear separately from the currently acquired supplies. At other times an account might include only those supplies acquired to date. Other supplies would be added later, although there is no guarantee that we have the later accounts. That explains why some provisioning lists are missing such ordinary items of supply as wine, although we can safely assume that wine was added later.[61] Of fifteen detailed accounts analyzed for the proportions of various foods supplied, only two or three were indisputably complete, and they show no clear pattern of variation.[62] The same sort of difficulties arise if we try to analyze the provisions of any particular ship. Indies ships sailed in convoy for most of the sixteenth and seventeenth centuries, and all the vessels of the same fleet were provisioned together. Although a great deal of care went into supplying precise amounts of food for each ship, the fleet as a whole carried those provisions. One ship might have all of the cheese and almost none of the cider, for example, simply because it had space available when the cheese was loaded. Thus, although most ships must have carried their own supplies of daily rations such as biscuit, less essential items would be exchanged back and forth among members of the fleet as it sailed.

The first full provisioning of Arana's six galleons is a good example of the misleading impression given by the list of supplies on a single ship. Judging only from the amount of provisions carried, we might guess that the *Santiago* and the *San Sebastián* were much larger ships than the *San Felipe* and the *Begoña,* although that was clearly not so. Instead, it seems that the *Santiago* and the *San Sebastián* carried most of the reserve provisions, serving as a storehouse for the rest of the Armada de la Guardia. Looking at the provisions carried by all six ships together gives a much clearer idea of how well they were provisioned. First of all they carried enough biscuit to sustain five hundred men for 214.6 days.[63] That would have taken the fleet across the Atlantic as well as providing for its needs during a long winter layover in Cartagena de Indias. There was enough wine for 191.4 days, and nearly twice as much water as wine. Salt pork, the only meat provided, was enough for 46.1 days' rations. The salted fish carried could feed the men for another 40.5 days, and the cheese for another 4.7 days. Altogether, then, the animal protein carried could sustain five hundred men for 79.8 days, about double the time it generally took to make the voyage from Cádiz to the Caribbean Islands.[64] In addition, there were enough broad beans, chickpeas, and rice to feed five hundred men for 273 days, and enough oil and vinegar for 177.2 days.[65] Since oil and vinegar were served only on fish days, about three or four days a week, there was enough oil and vinegar for nearly a year.[66] The pattern that emerges from this analysis is that Arana's galleons carried ample provisions for the voyage across the Atlantic, and enough of the items that were scarce in the Indies to get them through a winter layover. Meat and fresh food of all kinds were available once they arrived in the Indies, to supplement the dried meat, fish, and legumes they carried.

The attention to precise food rations had its complement in the provision of cooking, measuring, and eating utensils, spare equipment for the ships, and supplies to carry out any repairs that became necessary. Like food, these items were calculated carefully for each ship in an armada, and their prices, like food prices, rose during the sixteenth and seventeenth centuries. Firewood and charcoal had to be provided for cooking, except for those days when the sea was too rough to risk building fires in the cookstoves. Illumination for officers and crew at night, and to indicate the location of each ship in the fleet, came from a wide variety of sources. There were small wax candles for the officers and large ones (*hachotes*) of 1.5 to 2 pounds each for religious services on board and for some of the poop lanterns. The price of the hachotes more than trebled between 1562 and 1626, from 198 to 600 reales the quintal in Seville.[67] Tallow candles just doubled in price during the same period, although they were more expensive in the Indies than in

Andalusia.[68] Lanterns (*linternas*) and lamps (*lampiones*) varied so much in size, shape, and material that it is impossible to know how much they changed in price. In the 1620s and 1630s they could cost anywhere from 2 to 28 reales each.[69] Similarly, in 1626 alone, large running lanterns varied in price from 40 reales for the lantern of a small galleon, to 775 or even 1,000 reales for a large gilded lantern such as the one carried by the capitana of a squadron or fleet.[70] The lantern on Arana's *San Felipe,* we should recall, cost 1,433.2 reales.[71]

Containers purchased for food and supplies also showed considerable variety in size, shape, and materials. There were at least four traditional sizes of barrel, several sizes of small cask, six sizes of wooden box, and so on, each traditionally used for a separate purpose.[72] The very large barrels called pipes, for water and wine, were about 27.5 arrobas in capacity, and the *botas,* also used for wine, were about 30 arrobas. Stiff baskets of willow reeds (*mimbre*) and flexible baskets and panniers of esparto or other grasses all had their traditional uses as well and came in traditional sizes. As random and chaotic as the long list of containers and sizes might seem, the capacities and weights of each of them were well known and helped the individuals who had to keep track of the crucial allotment of daily rations.

The most expensive household items on board were probably the copper cauldrons weighing 40–45 pounds each and used for cooking or for melting tar for repairs. The copper, imported and priced by weight, showed an increase of nearly sixfold on the north coast between 1540 and 1628, from 1.2 to 7 reales the pound. The price had risen to 9 reales in 1639.[73] Far less expensive but equally important were the sets of measures of wood and tin, and the scales used to dispense daily rations. Each ship carried several sets of measures and at least one scale with counterweights, the measures costing 2 to 4 reales a set in Seville in 1626, and the scale about 50 reales.[74] Hatchets, funnels, brooms, plates and cups, ladles and other utensils, jugs and jars, and a long list of other items completed the household equipment. As extensive as the list appears, it was really the bare minimum needed for shipboard life, a spartan version of normal life on land.

By the time Arana's ships were provisioned for their first Indies voyage in 1629, Spain was approaching the end of a century and a half of inflation. The prices of nearly everything supplied to the armadas had risen greatly, with ordinary problems of supply in peacetime exacerbated by wars and piracy. A twelve years' truce with the rebellious provinces of the Netherlands had expired in 1621, and renewed warfare there became part of the generalized conflict known as the Thirty Years' War. Disruption of the Indies fleets naturally formed part of the Dutch strategy against Spain, with its most spectacular success in the capture of the New Spain fleet at Matanzas in 1628. The loss of that treasure and the fear that a broad attack on the colonies lay ahead would alter the rhythm of fleet provisioning for several years, leading to less frequent but larger fleets.[75] During the years in which Arana's galleons sailed for the crown, these changes undoubtedly made an already difficult task even more so.

By the time of the Matanzas disaster in 1628, Dutch attacks had been a problem for several years. Spanish intelligence reports from Antwerp had reported large fleets sailing in the direction of the Spanish colonies as early as

1623, and in 1624 a Dutch fleet attacked the major port of Lima-Callao on the northwest coast of South America, an area that had long been considered safe because of its remoteness from Europe. Although that attack was successfully beaten off by local forces, it was clear that even the most remote colonies were no longer safe from seaborne enemies, pirates, and interlopers. It was not sufficient to protect the convoys back and forth across the Atlantic, but the resources of the crown had to be stretched ever further in mission to find and engage enemy ships all over the empire. The regular Armada de la Guardia, which usually accompanied the Tierra Firme fleet to South America, carried orders in 1625 to sail also around the Cape of Good Hope to the Mar del Sur (eastern South Pacific) in pursuit of the Dutch.[76] In 1626 a contingent of four galleons continued the pursuit off Puerto Rico.[77]

Even the increased defensive needs of the empire were not supposed to alter the rhythm of the convoys. Pierre Chaunu, and most other scholars who discuss the Indies trade, write of the two-year cycle that characterized it during the sixteenth and seventeenth centuries. The average turnaround time for the two merchant fleets—to New Spain and Tierra Firme—was about 14–15 months, although, as Chaunu so cogently points out, there were rarely average fleets, just slow ones and fast ones. The two-year cycle of preparation, sailing, loading, unloading, and waiting time usually involved 16.5 months in ports and only 5.5 months of effective navigation. Thus, in ordinary times, there were two sets of fleets functioning at once, one that wintered over in the Indies, and one that wintered over in Spain, sailing on their separate trajectories from spring to early fall, the safest time for the crossing. Merchants in Seville, the monopoly port for the trade, had to maintain long credit lines to reap the profits from their investment in ships and trade goods. The arrival of the annual returns in silver were crucial to the continuation of their business, and even a brief delay could send shock waves through the business community, not only in Seville, but in other major financial capitals in Europe.[78]

What is often ignored in the emphasis on the two-year cycle for the fleets as a whole, is that the royal contingent of galleons followed a different rhythm. The ships of the Armada de la Guardia served as military escorts for the various merchant fleets and carried public and private silver and other treasures on the return voyages, as mentioned in chapter 1. Appropriately, they were generally the strongest and best-armed ships available. Despite its close identification with the merchant fleets, however, the Armada de la Guardia ideally had a one-year rather than a two-year cycle. It was supposed to make the round trip to the Indies and back in one sailing season, returning to Spain with the royal treasure, wintering over and undergoing any repairs in Iberian ports. Most of the sailors and soldiers it carried were allowed to go home for the winter, which, not incidentally, saved the crown the expense of feeding them. In more than a quarter-century before Arana's galleons first sailed, the Armada de la Guardia barely missed a beat in its steady yearly rhythm. Commanded by a captain-general, the ships usually sailed with the outgoing Tierra Firme fleet some time between early March and mid-May, and returned to Spain in the fall, as we have noted before. A few fleets left as early as January or February and others returned as late as December, but most stayed within the safer spring-to-fall sailing timetable. No Indies voyage was without considerable risk, yet the yearly rhythm of the Armada de la Guardia could be quite predictable for long stretches. There was great continuity in the ships used, indicating very rapid careening schedules for those that sailed year after year, and great continuity in the commanders as well. Don Gerónimo de Portugal y Córdoba sailed as captain-general every year from 1608 to 1613.[79] Don Lope Díaz Armendariz, the Marquis of Cadereyta, served as captain-general every year but one from 1615 through 1620, and alternated with other commanders for several years thereafter.[80]

Storms and other disasters might alter the ideal of a one-year cycle for the galleons of the Armada de la Guardia, but, even in the years after 1621 when the Dutch threat loomed in the Indies, the pattern still held. The 1621 Armada de la Guardia, under the leadership of the admiral Tomás de Larráspuru, left Spain with the outgoing fleet in early May and returned with sixty-one ships of the previous year's fleet in early November.[81] In 1621, Captain-General Juan Flores de Rabanal accompanied the New Spain fleet to the Mexican coast, while his admiral and the Armada de la Guardia went with the Tierra Firme fleet to mainland South America, then returned safely through Havana to Spain. The 1622 armada was not so lucky. Under its captain-general the Marquis of Cadereyta, the fleet was battered by severe storms both coming and going. After the fleet left Havana very late in the sailing season (mid-October), a storm sank three of its galleons, forcing Cadereyta to return to Havana for the winter. Because of its unexpected sojourn in Havana and extraordinary damage to its provisions from storms and rodents, the fleet was low on food when it left for home the following spring. More storms and rodent infestation on the return voyage made the situation very serious by the time the fleet finally arrived in early June 1623.[82] The drama of the 1622 fleet and its Armada de la Guardia were chronicled at the time, so it happens that we know a good deal about its difficulties, and about the sunken treasure ships left behind by the storms. In all, nine of the twenty-three ships that left Havana for Spain never made it home; what is more surprising is that fourteen of them did.[83] Luckily, such disasters were rare, or the carrera could never have lasted as long as it did.

Nonetheless, bad luck often came in batches, especially when it related to the weather and enemy movements. There were new disasters in 1623. The Armada de la Guardia under don Antonio de Oquendo as captain-general had to winter over in Havana following shipwrecks on his attempted return home.[84] Because of intelligence reports of Dutch plans to attack the colonies, most of the 1624 Armada de la Guardia sailed alone to the Indies, crossing the Atlantic dangerously early in February or March, and arriving in Cartagena de Indias before May. While Captain-General Tomás de Larráspuru went in pursuit of the Dutch with seven galleons, another three crossed the Atlantic with the main Tierra Firme fleet as usual, traveling from Cádiz to Cartagena de Indias in about a month and a half. The Armadas de la Guardia of both 1623 and 1624 returned to Spain in 1624, Oquendo's 1623 contingent in late May, and all ten of Larráspuru's galleons in mid-October, reestablishing the one-year cycle. Though the whole Indies trade was involved in war with the Dutch by then, the Armada de la Guardia of 1625, 1626, and 1627 still held to a one-year cycle, each one leaving between early April and early May and returning by mid to late November. As long as the armada left mainland Iberia by mid-May, it could expect to return safely before the onset of winter storms, with another year's treasure for the crown and profits for merchants trading with the Indies.

Unforeseen disasters could alter the timetable, and the capture of the New Spain fleet at Matanzas in 1628 was perhaps the worst disaster that ever befell the carrera de las Indias. In the long run, natural disasters such as the fierce hurricanes in the Caribbean did more harm to the carrera than all of Spain's enemies combined. In the short run after Matanzas that was small consolation, because regular fleet planning and provisioning were thrown into chaos, at the very time that the Spanish economy as a whole was in serious difficulty. Upon hearing the grim news about Matanzas as he arrived in Havana to join the New Spain fleet for the voyage home, Tomás de Larráspuru kept the Armada de la Guardia there over the winter, rather than risk further losses.[85] He returned to Spain in the spring of 1629, accompanying the Tierra Firme fleet under Captain-General don Luis de Velasco.[86]

It is hardly surprising that the Matanzas loss upset the one-year rhythm of the Armada de la Guardia. Matanzas and continued depredations by enemies in the Indies also forced a major restructuring of the carrera de las Indias as a whole, beginning in about 1631.[87] Since the late sixteenth century the two merchant fleets had usually left Spain separately, as we have seen, with the Tierra Firme fleet and the Armada de la Guardia sailing in late spring, and the New Spain fleet sailing in mid-summer. At the end of the summer, the Armada de la Guardia would meet the two fleets from the previous year in Havana, then all would travel home together, arriving by late fall. The restructuring that took place after 1631 had both fleets traveling together on the outbound as well as the homeward bound voyage, largely for safety. What is usually missed in examinations of this restructuring is that, from 1629 until 1636, the time that we will be following Arana's six galleons on the Indies run, the Armada de la Guardia was forced into a two-year cycle, regularly wintering over in the Indies, whereas before such layovers had been rare and unwelcome expedients. Don Antonio de Oquendo (see figure 26) had to face charges for having wintered over with the Armada de la Guardia in 1623. Although absolved of all blame for that and for the loss of two ships in a storm, he was stripped of his offices in the carrera de las Indias for four years and fined 12,000 ducados.[88]

The temporary loss of the one-year rhythm was an important change for royal officials who readied the Armada de la Guardia in Cádiz. More ships were needed, ideally twice as many, so that every year's merchant fleets would be properly defended. Provisioning each armada for a possible winter layover as well as for the actual voyage raised the costs and added to the pressures on supplies of food and equipment. A certain number of ships from each fleet always had to be repaired during the winter. To do these repairs in the Indies greatly increased the cost and the difficulty involved. The ships had to take their own supplies with them, as well as much of their own food, because the small ports in the Indies could not handle the job. The more time that ships spent in America's tropical ports, the more damage they incurred from the dreaded shipworms and from rotting hulls, rigging, and sails. On the positive side, the fleets and the colonies themselves were better defended with the Armada de la Guardia staying over the winter. This was no small advantage, because the Spaniards fully realized how vulnerable they were in the dangerous waters of the Caribbean. If the enemy took only Cartagena

Figure 26. Don Antonio de Oquendo, ca. 1626, with the red sash and baton of a captain-general. (Courtesy of the Museo Naval, Madrid.)

and Portobelo, the lifeline of the Spanish empire would be cut. Havana would then easily fall into enemy hands, and all would be lost.

The need for increased defenses in the Caribbean had been obvious for decades, but it took the loss at Matanzas to precipitate the temporary change to a two-year rhythm for the Armada de la Guardia, and even that was not consciously planned. It evolved during the course of provisioning the 1629 fleet, the first in which Martín de Arana's six galleons would sail. Fleet provisioning was not easy at the best of times, and 1629 was arguably the worst of times. With the loss of the New Spain fleet, and the delay of the Tierra Firme fleet, Spain was short of men, ships, and money, the basic ingredients of any fleet. The Junta de Armadas began planning for the 1629 fleets in the fall of 1628 to have them ready in time for the spring sailing. Although the Matanzas loss came on September 8, authorities in Spain did not hear of it until several months later. Meanwhile, planning went on for the new fleets, to be financed by the treasure that the returning fleets would bring. In October, the Junta counted thirty-three likely ships, including Arana's six new galleons, in the Armada del Mar Océano, from which the Armada de la Guardia would be selected. The thirty-three ships averaged 444.3 toneladas; Arana's six alone averaged 442.8. The list of budgeted items for the fleet was quite extensive, from the cost of careening the ships in port and the salaries of all the officials employed to outfit and provision them, to the costs of those provisions and other supplies.[89] The average cost to outfit each of the twenty-six ships owned by the crown was estimated at 28,267.4 ducados, or 59.6 ducados per ton. In other words, to run Arana's ships for a year cost nearly twice as much as Arana had been paid to build them, and they did not require repairs, being new. The cost of food was

Figure 27. Cádiz and the gateway to the Atlantic in 1614. The letters B and C mark the bay and city of Cádiz. The area between Puente de suazo (H) and the town of Puerto Real (I) was La Carraca, an important refitting point for Spain's Atlantic fleet. Other towns indicated are Puerto de Santa María (M), Rota (O), and Sanlúcar de Barrameda (P). (Manuscript of Nicolás de Cardona, *Descripciones geographicas, e hydrographicas de muchas tierras y mares del norte, y sur, en las Indias* [Madrid, 1632]. Courtesy of the Biblioteca Nacional, Madrid.)

particularly high in 1628, due to harvest failures in 1627 and the monetary dislocations that followed the devaluation of 1627.

As the fall wore one, royal officials in Madrid, Seville, and Cádiz began to grow anxious about the delay of the fleets. (See figure 27.) Don Antonio de Oquendo had gone to wait for them off the Azores as usual, but several Junta members suggested that he be recalled if the fleets still had not arrived by the end of December, on the assumption that they were probably wintering over in the Indies. Letters from the House of Trade in Seville were openly worried about the fleet by early December.

On December 7 a royal official in the Algarve in southern Portugal received the devastating news about Matanzas from a frigate that sailed in from Cartagena.[90] Anguished officials in Seville wrote to don Fernando de Vargas in Cádiz to have the reports confirmed, "since we esteem the care which you always take to bring us good news of the ships," almost apologizing for asking him to confirm the worst.[91] At the same time, Spanish officials in the Netherlands sent their own reports of the disaster to Madrid.[92] Yet even before every detail could be sorted out, royal officials from Madrid to Cádiz and the merchant and financial communities in Seville were already planning what to do next. For the merchants, the "blow was so terrible that one cannot bear to think about it," but they still had to begin preparations for the next fleet.[93] Most of the best ships were already spoken for or still in the Indies, and without Arana's new galleons, the Armada de la Guardia would have been a sorry sight in 1629.[94]

Nonetheless, the king's first thought was to send another fleet to join the Tierra Firme fleet and the Armada de la Guardia to bring home the rest of the silver. In late December, even before he was sure of the details of Matanzas, the king ordered his officials to prepare twenty-two large galleons for the purpose.[95] The Junta de Armadas accordingly began discussing a plan to send don Antonio de Oquendo with the Armada del Mar Océano in January, or by mid-March at the latest, risking the fleet in the rigors of the Atlantic winter to avoid the financial abyss that loomed ahead.[96] But how was this possible without the treasure? The crown lived from year to year on credit and the expectation of the incoming fleets. Without the fleets, neither the crown nor its potential creditors had any ready cash. The situation was desperate, but everyone knew that it could not get any better until the fleets returned to their regular schedule. Hardly pausing to register their dismay over Matanzas, and rarely mentioning it on paper again, the royal bureaucracy turned to the task at hand, the same task that was at hand every winter—preparing the fleets for the coming year.

By the end of December, don Antonio de Oquendo had been ordered to take the Armada del Mar Océano from Lisbon to Cádiz, which would be the staging area for the new Indies fleets. In the extraordinary situation of 1629, the Armada del Mar Océano would supply most of the ships for the Indies run, although it usually had its own job to do in patroling the Atlantic between Spain and the Azores. Don Fadrique de Toledo y Osorio, Marquis of Villanueva de Baldueza and captain-general of the Armada del Mar Océano in 1629, was already involved in the fleet's careening and outfitting.[97] Oquendo would take over the day-to-day supervision of the work and serve as admiral of the fleet behind don Fadrique. Although still technically under sentence from his 1623 voyage, Oquendo had petitioned to be reinstated. In the crisis of 1628-29, the crown was pleased to oblige him. Oquendo already had begun issuing orders and making suggestions to the king and the Junta de Armadas in Madrid before he left Lisbon. He advised sending the sailors and soldiers home for the winter and replacing them with fresh ones, paid six months' advance wages to leave with their families and to provide the clothes needed for the voyage. Wood and other supplies should be assembled at the Puente de Zuazo in Cádiz for the extensive careening needed on some of the ships. Oquendo had twenty-nine ships with him in Lisbon, including Arana's six new galleons, but even they needed minor repairs by then and may already have been with the fleet on patrol off the Azores.[98] Oquendo arrived in Cádiz on January 23, with seventeen ships and three dispatch boats. Another three ships and one dispatch boat had deviated from course three days before and, with the prevailing northeast winds, were having trouble coming into port. One of the ships, in fact, would wreck near Chipiona, down the coast from Cádiz, and have to jettison its artillery. Even a trip as short as from Lisbon to Cádiz was perilous in the winter.

On the morning the ships were to arrive, Sebastián de Oleaga, who would serve as purveyor for the careening and repair of the fleet, went down to the shore to arrange the coming months of labor with the shipwrights and boatmen who lived there. He had already assembled the materials that would be needed to careen the twenty-two ships and four dispatch boats planned for the armada.[99] Oleaga, with Oquendo and Francisco Beltrán de Manurga, the comptroller, formed the Junta del Apresto (outfitting committee) to oversee the careening, repairs, and provisioning. Because of the importance of the fleet and the difficulties in finding money to outfit it, the king sent don Juan de Castro y Castilla from his Council of Finance to Cádiz, to serve as a sort of superintendent of the preparations. After forty-seven years of royal service, Oleaga was in no mood to be supervised. He wrote back that he was "hurt and disheartened by this demonstration of a lack of confidence" in him. If the king were dissatisfied with his work, he would gladly let Castro handle the whole thing. A personal note from the king assured Oleaga of his support, but this minor flap serves to remind us that the bureaucracy had traditions and a sense of hierarchy that could not easily be shunted aside, even in a time of emergency. The Junta de Armadas was well aware of this, sometimes much more sensitive than the king to the important role played by the bureaucracy in naval affairs.[100] As time went on, Castro proved his worth, to Oleaga and to the whole enterprise, spending much of his time in Seville dealing with bankers and officials of the House of Trade and the royal mint, and therefore freeing Oleaga and Oquendo for the vital work in Cádiz.

By late January, the House of Trade was clamoring to know the names of the eight "galeones de la plata." Because the previous year's remittances from the Indies had not arrived, it was increasingly obvious that the merchant fleets would not sail in 1629. If that happened, there would be no Armada de la Guardia either, technically speaking, only galleons to carry treasure. The few merchants with enough goods to send in 1629 were expecting to send them on the galleons.[101] (When galleons sailed without a merchant fleet and legally carried merchandise, they were sometimes dubbed a "galiflota," meaning galleons acting in place of a merchant flota.) Oquendo had a list drawn up of the twenty-two galleons most apt for the voyage, a list that included the four largest ones built by Arana (the two smallest ones were listed among those remaining behind).[102] Although the list would be changed several times, it was necessary to begin selecting the ships as early as possible, so that officers, crews, and careening and provisioning schedules could be planned as accurately as possible.

In late January, the Junta de Armadas presented nominations to the king for captain-general and admiral of the "galeones de la plata," to serve behind Toledo and Oquendo. The king chose don Francisco de Acevedo as captain-general of the squadron and Roque Centeno as the admiral, both of whom had distinguished service records in the carrera and came highly recommended by the Junta de Armadas.[103] Personal considerations intervened to change the list of officers, however. As late as December 1628 don Martín de Vallecilla had been the Almirante General of the Armada del Mar Océano, behind don Fadrique de Toledo. When Oquendo was abruptly returned to active service as admiral, he displaced Vallecilla, who had been serving in his stead. Vallecilla was furious and wrote complaining about this treatment to don Fernando Girón of the Council of War, asking that his letter be passed along to the king.[104] Vallecilla was a loyal and experienced commander, important enough to bypass ordinary procedures. When the 1629 fleet sailed, he would be captain-general of the "galeones de la plata"; neither

Acevedo nor Centeno accompanied him, a change that precipitated a personal financial crisis for the latter.

Roque Centeno had served the crown for forty-five years by 1629 and had sailed as captain-general of the Tierra Firme fleet in 1627. Since then, however, although he was technically in charge of the section of the Armada del Mar Océano that was in Cádiz, he served without salary while awaiting a definite posting. During the fleet preparations in Cádiz he lent invaluable service to the crown. Royal officials later reported that he was almost constantly with the ships, sometimes even spending the night on board during their outfitting—all without salary. His family's finances went from bad to worse, and he finally reached the end of his resources. Evidently no one had been aware of his plight but the Duke of Medina-Sidonia, who urged Centeno to stay in Cádiz to continue his vital work, rather than going to Madrid to plead his case. When the 1629 fleet sailed without him, he could take no more, writing Medina-Sidonia that "with pure truth I say to Your Excellency that I do not have bread to give [my six children]." The Junta de Armadas was stunned and embarrassed when its members realized the oversight that had driven such a dedicated man to penury and immediately saw to it that Centeno received a retroactive post in the careening in Cádiz, with back salary from January 1629. In addition, he was assigned to the 1630 fleet, and the king provided pensions, stipends, and preferment for his children, even for one son who was still in school. As the Junta remarked to the king, "It is convenient that it be seen that Your Majesty takes account of the children of those who serve him, because it inspires others."[105] It is commonly thought that the zeal for royal service in Spain had greatly declined in the seventeenth century, yet in the crisis of 1629, there were still men like Roque Centeno. Although he expected that his work would be recognized and rewarded, that did not diminish the sacrifices that he and his family made while he served the crown.

To provision the fleet, the crown turned again to Horacio Levanto, who had served as victualler of the Indies fleets since 1627. Royal officials knew they could save money by buying supplies themselves, but that usually required cash, and in 1629 there was very little cash at hand. The proveedor Sebastián de Oleaga conferred with General Martín de Vallecilla, Roque Centeno, and others, then advised the king that there was no real alternative to paying Levanto the arrears of his previous contracts and asking his help again. Since he had enough personal resources to pay cash for his purchases, he was an efficient and successful victualler. Levanto accepted a contract price of 52 maravedís per ration, plus a 5 percent premium for the vellón (copper currency) that he would have to convert to silver.[106] The harvests in 1628 had been good, after widespread failures in the previous year, so the food would cost less than the estimated price. In fact, a later audit of Levanto's accounts showed that he actually paid only 49.4 maravedís per ration for the food he purchased, evidently in part because he dealt in cash and received quantity discounts for biscuit and wine. To see Levanto making such a large profit galled royal officials in Madrid, but they had no choice. Even in "a year as abundant as this one," provisioning was impossible without cash. The crown had no credit after Matanzas, until the next fleet arrived, and was almost never able to get credit for provisioning in any case.[107] Given this, "the retention of [Levanto] was of the utmost importance" to the crown and its fleets.[108] Levanto's contract was to provide for 4,830 sailors and soldiers for eight months, assuming they would serve on twenty-two galleons and four dispatch boats.[109] It is clear from this that the armada was supposed to make the round trip in one sailing season. Even before Levanto took the contract in early February, however, the king had increased the fleet to twenty-eight galleons and four dispatch boats, including eight galleons and two dispatch boats for the treasure.[110] There would also be three *urcas* (hulks) to carry food and provisions that would not fit elsewhere.

In this expanded fleet all six of the galleons built by Arana had a place, the two smallest in the main armada and the four largest among the eight "galeones de la plata." When the fleet finally sailed, all six were among the silver galleons. Altogether, the crown owned twenty-one of the thirty-five ships and rented the remaining fourteen from their owners. The average size of the twenty-eight principal ships in the fleet was 541.9 toneladas, with the smaller dispatch boats averaging 140 toneladas each. The crown planned for 2,916 sailors (including artillerymen) and 3,862 soldiers on thirty-two ships, using as guidelines the standard manning ratios of 16 sailors and 26 soldiers per 100 toneladas (18 and 28 for the capitana real and the almiranta real). The men who would travel on the urcas raised the total to over 7,000 men on thirty-five ships. Their food alone for the eight months would cost the crown 2,569,411.7 reales.[111] The expenses of careening, repairs, and refitting (*proveeduría*) came under the proveedor Sebastián de Oleaga, who estimated the cost at 3,179,698 reales. Arana's six galleons accounted for only 10 percent of that amount (319,893.5 reales), an average of 53,315.6 reales for each ship. Half to two-thirds of the expense was for careening and recaulking, and the rest was for replacing equipment and sails. On all six of the ships, the shrouds staying the mainmast were to be moved to the foremast and replaced by stronger ones on the mainmast, suggesting again that Arana had supplied less than ideal original equipment, either through his own fault, or because his best supplies had been taken for use elsewhere. Otherwise the ships were in better shape than their counterparts, simply because they were nearly new. In addition to careening and repairs, Oleaga's budget was to cover all the miscellaneous equipment that the ships needed, from buckets to painted linen flags, lanterns, and candles—an array estimated to cost 13,000 reales for each ordinary galleon in the fleet.[112]

The care taken in careening Spanish vessels for the Indies was justly famous. One French observer in the late sixteenth century described the procedure: They began by flaming the hulls to melt the old tarred coating. Then they removed the old caulking and hammered in five fresh layers of oakum before retarring the hull and attaching two layers of cloth covered with alquitrán from the water line to the keel. As a final barrier against shipworms, a layer of parchment-thin lead sheeting was added, attached with so many large-headed nails that the lead was nearly covered. Another layer of alquitrán finished the work.[113] It is small wonder that the work took so long and cost so much.

Oquendo, as admiral of the Armada del Mar Océano, supervised the expenses that came under the captain-general's authority (*capitanía general*) during the 1629 preparations, which included wages, living stipends for soldiers and sailors lodged in the vicinity, hospital expenses for the sick, couriers, and salaries for officials overseeing the work and handling the accounts that had to be kept of all income and expenditures. The total cost for the capitanía general was budgeted at 3,441,130 reales. Artillery accounts formed the third part of the budget for the preparations. A spread sheet included with Oquendo's accounts detailed all the artillery and supplies warehoused in Cádiz, including broken equipment that could be repaired, and the amount of artillery each ship would need. The artillery accounts also included costs for two *pontones* (mudscows or dredges), two pinnaces, and one *falua* (barge). These were the workhorses of the crown's operation in Cádiz Bay, hauling ships over by their masts to be careened, ferrying artillery and other heavy items back and forth, dredging for equipment dropped accidentally into the bay, and doing a hundred other jobs. All the boats in question needed repairs before the work could begin, but that would be less expensive than hiring local boats and boatmen for the work. The total costs in the artillery accounts were estimated at 244,687 reales, making a grand total of 6,865,515 reales for the complete preparations. That was about 436.3 reales or 39.7 ducados per tonelada for the thirty-two main ships in the planned armada.

With Levanto providing the food, and Oquendo, Oleaga, and their associates supervising the preparations, there were still two unmet needs— men and money—that were to dominate correspondence back and forth among Cádiz, Madrid, and Seville until the fleet finally sailed.[114] In early March the fleet still lacked 1,184 sailors and 730 soldiers, prompting orders for another levy in Vizcaya and the rest of the Cantabrian coast, as well as an additional sweep in Andalusia. All royal officials in both areas were expected to do whatever they could to assist the levy, but there was no mention of impressment, even with time so short. The great need was for money, so that the new enlistees could be given several months' pay in advance.[115] The king was determined that the fleet leave before mid-May, "because, if not, all will be lost,"[116] Letters of exchange payable in Seville arrived just in time to keep the preparations going without a pause in late April, and the safe arrival, at long last, of the Tierra Firme fleet and the Armada de la Guardia from 1628 eased the situation somewhat. Larráspuru had written from Havana in January that he was nearly ready to make the trip home, but his letter arrived in Spain just a few weeks before he did. Consequently, most of the preparations for the 1629 fleet were finished before it was clear that there would be money to pay for them.[117] The men who arrived with Larráspuru were signed up again, before they had a chance to drift away, but it was nearly impossible to get the House of Trade to release any of the newly arrived treasure before all the paperwork was in order.[118] The final loading of the "galeones de la plata" was nearly finished by early May, and the king made sure that they carried the usual mercury for silver refining in the Indies, as well as papal bulls to be sold there for the benefit of the Santa Cruzada, a branch of ecclesiastical income given to the Spanish crown by the popes in Rome.[119]

Despite the frantic preparations, there was still much to be done before departure, and the May 15 deadline approached too fast. On May 14, the Junta de Armadas received word from don Fadrique de Toledo that only twenty of the galleons were loading supplies; the other eight were still being refitted. He also requested more crew and money before departing, though already 698,608 ducados had been spent on the preparations and provisions. To say that the Junta de Armadas and the king were disappointed with their captain-general is putting it mildly. He had delayed going to Cádiz to supervise the preparations until the end of April, and then he sent a letter "of such lukewarmness that it left the Junta disconsolate and dispirited."[120] He did not even bother to estimate when the fleet might leave or to suggest how things might be moved along more quickly. Don Fadrique does not seem to have held much enthusiasm for his assignment, perhaps because his ordinary post with the Armada del Mar Océano would not have taken him to the Indies, and he was reluctant to go.[121] Nonetheless, he viewed the situation in Cádiz as a professional military man and simply knew that nothing could have been done to have the fleet ready to sail by mid-May, regardless of the consequences. His "lukewarmness" and his continued requests for money, supplies, and crew said as much without his having to question the king's orders openly.

By May 20, with the unrealistic deadline past, the Junta de Armadas acknowledged that the fleet would not be able to reach the New World in time to return before winter. Further arrangements had to be made to tide it over during the *invernada* or winter layover. Unavoidably, this raised another set of logistical difficulties. There were thirty-five ships in the fleet, with more than seven-thousand men. Not only would they have to be fed for another four months, but the ships would have to carry materials for careening and repairs during the winter layover. There was no question but that the fleet would have to carry much of its own food—Havana and Cartagena were too small to be able to feed an additional seven-thousand men over the winter. Horacio Levanto began to make provisions for the fleet to carry as much extra wine, oil, and other staples as possible.[122] The little space left on board the ships would be used up by a part of these extra supplies, and there could no longer be any question of the galleons carrying trade goods for the merchant community. Only Horacio Levanto, as a condition of his contract, would be able to send a certain amount of merchandise, a fact that greatly irritated the Consulado (merchant association) in Seville.

Money was still scarce, despite the arrival of the 1628 Tierra Firme fleet. As of May 22, there was available in Seville and Cádiz only half the 122,632 ducados needed for departure and for purchases of winter provisions in the Indies. The Junta de Armadas set a new departure date of June 8–10 at the latest, complaining to the captain-general that the fleet was consuming in port what would have sustained it at sea had the departure been more timely.[123] The continuing difficulties in signing on crew were closely tied to the lack of funds and belied the Junta's insistence that the fleet leave immediately. Don Fadrique put in an urgent request at the end of May for money to pay the soldiers and sailors the advance wages owed them, lest they disband and leave the fleet stranded. The king had asked his ministers "with more claims to honor than self-interest" to forego their salaries so that the men could be paid, but he had also asked the men to accept fewer payments than they expected. Don Fadrique wrote on behalf of the men who would serve with him, saying that they needed the full payment, because, in addition to leaving some money with their families, they needed to buy clothes to wear and plates to eat from during the voyage, not to mention what they would have to spend in the Indies. Indeed, some new recruits arrived in Cádiz practically naked, he reported; they had to have clothing or they would sicken and die on the voyage.[124] To these ragged men, whether peasants or fishermen and sailors, the advance wages were a powerful incentive to enlist—perhaps the only incentive. Those who were less in need tended to avoid levies for the armadas, which helps to explain the chronic difficulties in finding crew and infantry for them.

At last, by the end of June don Fadrique requested pilots for the fleet, signaling his near-readiness to sail. He awaited only additional money, which don Juan de Castro, "whose diligence in this collection has been incredible," still could not get released from the bankers and businessmen in Seville.[125] Neither the Junta de Armadas nor the king himself could get them to relent, although the Council of the Indies did send funds for Spanish governors in the Indies. The Junta de Armadas ordered Oleaga and Castro to provide suitable clothing for the new recruits and authorized the arms warehouse in Cádiz to release the weapons they would need. By then the Junta had grown exasperated with don Fadrique's endless series of requests. All they cared for by early July was that he leave as soon as possible. Bluntly they informed him that no more money would be forthcoming and that he should not wait for it. Furthermore, he should not write another letter until he was under sail, when ample orders would be sent to him. Any further correspondence before then would be "neither opened nor answered." Still, the Junta urged the king to send his captain-general a few lines of encouragement in his own hand, lest he balk yet again and risk harming the operation with further delays.[126]

While the ships were waiting for their pilots and more recruits for their crews, the final loading proceeded. Horacio Levanto, as we know, had permission to load 5,000 ducados worth of merchandise and 20,000 ducados worth of food and supplies on his own account, but the House of Trade tried to block this, irritated that no other trade goods could sail to the Indies in the fleet that year. It took the combined protests of all the royal officials in Cádiz to force them to back off. As Levanto defined it, he was doing a public service. If no new supplies went to the Indies, those who had goods warehoused there would be able to sell them at excessive prices, though they had not "earned" their profits by moving the goods in such a difficult year. He, on the other hand, had gone all over Andalusia gathering food and supplies for the armada and providing for all, "even the least apprentice seaman." He had earned his profits, and the money he made would be used to provision the fleets in the Indies for the return voyage. The Junta de Armadas had no choice but to agree, even though Levanto stood to make a windfall selling his wares, some of them to the crown. In fact, one of the few restrictions on his cargo was that the food could not be sold on the open market until the armada's needs had been met.[127]

After all the delays, the fleet was finally ready to sail in early August, but the crews were still dangerously short-handed, since some of the men had "absented themselves," after accepting advance wages. They could be caught and punished later; the immediate problem was how to replace them. On Tuesday morning, August 7, don Juan de Castro y Castilla met on board one of the ships with the officers of the armada, revealing the king's orders that they could impress men in the locality should all else fail. Trusted men

left for the targeted towns in small teams, and the next day the sweep began.
Castro himself arrived in Sanlúcar de Barrameda at midnight on Tuesday and
early the next morning visited the Duke of Medina-Sidonia, the principal
aristocrat in the area, to inform him of the impressment. Medina-Sidonia
was being bled by his barber at the time. Hearing of the urgent need for
crew, he volunteered himself and his entire household, if necessary, to man
the sails. More usefully, he dismissed the barber, called three of his best
retainers, and sent them to conduct the sweep. Within a few hours they had
rounded up no fewer than ninety-six persons, seventy-eight of whom Castro
found to be very apt for armada service. As Castro returned to Cádiz to
prepare for their arrival, the duke sent the men after him in several small
boats, putting up the money not only for the boats, but also for the advance
wages paid to the men. The men Medina-Sidonia collected were so good that
they were all assigned to the two flagships of the fleet. Medina-Sidonia's
recruiting efforts for the 1629 fleet had already been noteworthy, but this
final effort deserved special thanks from the king.

On the day of San Lorenzo, August 10, the armada was at last ready to sail,
awaiting favorable weather. Following custom, the bishop of Cádiz ordered
public prayers in all the churches and convents of the city, asking God's
blessing for a safe voyage.[128] That the fleet was ready to sail at all was already
something of a miracle, given the losses at Matanzas the previous year. Yet,
with barely a break in the rhythm, the Indies run had continued. The most
important changes in the armada of 1629 were in its character and timing.
The thirty-six ships sent out (an extra dispatch boat had been added to the
list) formed a much smaller fleet than usual, but it was made up entirely of
warships and their support vessels, carrying large crews and contingents of
infantry in anticipation of meeting the Dutch.

The thirty-six ships had taken six months to prepare, not a bad pace,
considering that many of them had needed major repairs and that every *real*
had to be justified and diverted from less urgent undertakings. The bill for
the eight "galeones de la plata" alone came to about 230,000 ducados,
including food and supplies.[129] The treasury was exhausted, royal officials
were exhausted, even the king's pontoons and barges were exhausted. The
latter, after six months of steady hauling and careening, could not transport
another cannon without major overhauls themselves.[130] But the job was not
over yet. The 1629 fleet had not been able to carry much more than basic
supplies for eight months, even with three extra hulks accompanying them.
No sooner had the 1629 fleet finally left Cádiz on August 14 than preparations began for another small fleet to take an additional four months'
supplies for the ships and the 7,000 men on board. The shipping capacity
needed was estimated at 2,480 toneladas, counting 1,400 pounds of supplies
for a tonelada of shipping. That meant five ships of 500 toneladas each, or the
equivalent. Although the king had the tonnage available in Cádiz, some of
his ships were not well suited for carrying cargo, and they all needed repairs.
Much better would be to rent several of the German hulks that were in
Cádiz, since they were much better designed for cargo. Altogether, the
foods, supplies, preparation, and transport costs were estimated at 1,355,540
reales.[131] That would include not only food and wages for the men, but
wood and supplies needed for careening. Native wood in the Indies could

undoubtedly be found, but there would be no time to cut and cure it properly.[132]

Horacio Levanto would provide the rest of the food, as he had contracted. The money would have to come from a motley collection of sources. Because the total cost of the 1629 fleet and its resupply mission was so large, and because the main fleet carried cash to purchase supplies in the Indies, the king was anxious to have a royal accountant travel with the resupply fleet. The choice naturally fell to Francisco Beltrán de Manurga, the comptroller who had kept accounts for the earlier preparations. Evidently, he did not want to go, protesting that his work in Cádiz was too important and that he still had mountains of paperwork to file. Not only did his protest fall on deaf ears, but he was placed under house arrest while the resupply fleet was being prepared. The comptroller's plight was a bit of comic relief in the whole desperate situation in 1629. When don Juan de Castro asked that Beltrán at least be allowed to go back and forth to his office to continue work on the resupply mission, Madrid responded that the house arrest was a necessary warning to his fellows. He could leave his house to go by a direct route to mass on holy days, but for his work, the office was in effect moved to his home. Oleaga and others who needed to see him had to go there to do their business, because "there resides the office of the comptroller."[133]

With its captive comptroller, the resupply preparations continued, but the whole operation was difficult to arrange. The plan was for the resupply fleet to leave by early or mid-December at the latest—alone—because joining the regular 1630 fleets in spring would be too late. The resupply ships would go directly to Cartagena de Indias, in the hope of finding don Fadrique and the fleet still there. If not, they would have to track him around the Caribbean.[134] The crown took no chances that the supplies would be misdirected. In addition to choosing officers for the resupply fleet who had proven themselves to be brave and loyal servants of the crown, the government in Madrid issued precise orders for the disposition of the supplies. If don Fadrique could not be found, or if he did not need the supplies, they should be given to royal officials in the Indies, who were to sell the food and send the money, along with the careening supplies, back to Spain.[135] The man chosen as admiral, Captain Francisco Díaz Pimienta, had seventeen years' experience in the carrera and may have owned at least one ship that regularly sailed to the Indies in those years.[136]

As usual the major difficulties were finding enough money and crew members. Some of the crew could come from the north coast, but, with the 1630 fleets already forming, the resupply mission would be competing with them for the few available men. Some of the money was pledged from the private owners of bond income from tax revenues, but, because many taxes were in arrears, it was not forthcoming.[137] Cash was so short, and the crown had so little credit left, that even Horacio Levanto demanded to be paid for the wine, oil, and vinegar he had bought on his own account; he had not dared to oblige himself yet for any biscuit.[138] As late as December 21, the resupply was still in Cádiz, waiting for money. Preparing two galleons to accompany the resupply hulks would cost a great deal of money—40,000 ducados—and for a time it was thought that they might wait for the regular 1630 fleets to leave. That was deemed to be too late to do any good, and, after all the frantic preparations, it is probable that the resupply mission never sailed at all. Chaunu makes no mention of it in his extensive listings of the Indies fleets.[139] Don Fadrique de Toledo had been authorized to cut rations of bread and wine should he run low, and, one way or another, he brought his fleet home to Spain about the first of August, just a year after he had left, bringing Arana's six galleons with him. That story will be pursued later. For now it is sufficient to note that they made their first round trip to the Indies in 1629–30 with don Fadrique de Toledo y Osorio, wintering over in the Indies by plan rather than by accident, and surviving without being resupplied from Spain.

In the meantime the regular 1630 fleet underwent its preparations and supply in Cádiz. This time, royal officials planned from the beginning for a possible winter layover. The Armada de la Guardia would carry food for all its men only for the eight months of actual sailing. Should a winter layover become necessary, the fleet would provide for just thirty men per ship during those five months, dismissing the rest to live on the local economy.[140] That would make the timetable of a two-year cycle for the Armada de la Guardia practical and possible, even though it put increased strain on the markets of the Indies. Already by October 1629, officials had come up with formulas for supplying the Armada de la Guardia on the new cycle. The ships would carry wine, oil, vinegar, salt, and a combination of rice and chickpeas for eight months, or 240 days. They would carry biscuit for only 153 days, enough for the sailing time from Spain, through the winter layover and the trip to Havana. In Havana, they would buy fresh biscuit for the return home. Firewood and water for the three months allowed for the outgoing voyage completed the list. In all these supplies, according to custom, an extra 13 percent was included to allow for waste and spoilage.[141] The generous timetable allowed for voyages, and the extra for waste and spoilage, help to explain how the 1629 fleet could have made it through twelve months on only eight months' rations. Subsequent fleets would be expected to do the same.

During the desperate months that followed the losses at Matanzas, the royal bureaucracy began to restructure the supply and organization of the Indies fleets, especially the Armada de la Guardia. When the 1629 fleet missed its departure deadline, plans evolved to supply a winter layover. Plans for the 1630 fleets, on the other hand, included a possible winter layover from the start, in case enemy activity caused a delay in the transport of treasure. The two subsequent fleets that included Arana's galleons all took a winter layover in the Indies, even when they left well in advance of mid-May.[142] Although the one-year cycle of the Armada de la Guardia remained the ideal, the bureaucracy had to face the reality that fleets would often need more supplies than they customarily carried. Despite the common assumption that the centralized Spanish bureaucracy was sluggish and unimaginative, it proved to be surprisingly responsive and efficient in the midst of the crisis of 1629 and in subsequent years. With the chronic shortage of ready cash and the overextension of Spanish forces around the globe, the successful provisioning of each year's Indies fleets would continue to be a minor miracle, eased along by a bureaucracy imbued with that delicate blend of dedication and self-interest that defined state service.

SIX

Officers and Men

The bureaucratic hierarchy that supervised the fleets in port accompanied them even at sea. When royal fleets set out for the Indies in the early seventeenth century, they carried an official inspector (veedor) and a chief notary (*escribano mayor*). Some carried a paymaster (pagador), a comptroller (contador), and a purveyor (proveedor) as well.[1] Their collective responsibility was to keep track of all the men and equipment in the fleet, seeing that laws were obeyed and duties done, and recording receipts and expenditures for later audit by the crown.

In the Indies fleets of 1618–1620, the paymaster had a special charge to see that all private silver and gold shipments were registered and taxed.[2] Judging from the widespread reports of smuggling, the paymasters faced an extremely difficult task. Also in 1618–1620, the purveyors oversaw the provisioning and crewing of the fleet not only in Spain, but also in the Indies. Their duties included striving to cut costs, buying needed supplies at public auction from the lowest bidder, and seeing that there were regular musters of the men to make sure that the crown paid only those wages that were due. The purveyors also collected duties on merchandise sold in the Indies and saw that passengers on the fleet paid their taxes.[3] Because there were no merchant vessels and no passengers in the fleet of galleons that sailed in 1629, and Horacio Levanto had contracted to resupply the ships in the Indies, it is probable that neither paymaster nor purveyor accompanied the fleet that year. In such a case, the inspector, comptroller, and chief notary would have shared the duties of guarding the king's interests, with the inspector bearing the main responsibility.[4] Although essentially bureaucratic, these jobs were not exempt from the perils of the voyage. The general inspector of the Armada del Mar Océano in 1637 evidently drowned on duty.[5] The great reluctance of the comptroller Francisco Beltrán de Manurga to accompany the planned resupply mission in 1629, discussed in the previous chapter, may have been prompted by his fear of joining a fleet that was highly likely to encounter the enemy.[6] This should remind us once again that the 1629 fleet was an exception to the norm, responding to the crisis in shipping precipitated by heightened Dutch activity in the Caribbean.

The regular fleet officers, crews, and soldiers held responsibility for meeting the Dutch challenge in the New World. Organized in a strictly defined hierarchy, the individuals in the fleet functioned as a small seagoing republic, with the captain-general as its absolute ruler. In 1629, don Fadrique de Toledo y Osorio held that office in the Armada del Mar Océano, and sailed a large contingent of that fleet to the Indies.[7] Despite the extraordinary nature of the 1629 fleet, however, the chain of command and the qualities and duties of the officers and men remained unchanged. The captains-general from 1609 on were appointed by the king from nomination lists prepared by the Junta de Guerra de Indias, composed of four members each from the Council of War and the Council of the Indies. Although the president of the Council of the Indies chaired the sessions, we can assume that representatives from the Council of War had priority in setting the agenda. The Junta ordinarily met Tuesday and Thursday mornings, but the president could convene it at any time he deemed necessary. If the person chosen as captain-general were in Madrid, he swore his oath of office before the Council of the Indies; otherwise he swore it in Seville before the officials of the House of Trade. The ceremony had evidently been more elaborate at one time, with the man chosen keeping religious vigil, then presenting himself richly dressed before the king. From his sovereign, the new captain-general would accept a ring symbolizing honor, a sword symbolizing power, and a royal standard symbolizing his rank at the head of the fleet. In return he would swear to defend the Catholic faith, the honor and justice of the king, and the well-being of the kingdom to the death.[8] Once the captain-general had been chosen, the fleet was publicly announced, accompanied by fife and drums and calling for sailors and soldiers to sign up for the voyage.[9]

Experience and character weighed most heavily in the Junta's nominations for captains-general and in the king's final selections, as befitted a matter of such importance. Some nonscholarly works have portrayed captains-general as a group as venal or incompetent, or both, without presenting anything resembling proof of such assertions.[10] Undoubtedly, there were lapses in the system, and by the late seventeenth century successful candidates would be required to advance money to the crown upon taking up their posts. That is not the same as buying the office, however, and the system itself was designed to select the best men for the job. In the period we are studying, it seems to have succeeded in that goal more often than not.

One of the best descriptions of the ideal captain-general comes from Juan Escalante's *Itinerario* of 1575. In a fictional dialogue, the pilot described his captain-general as

> "a very good man, of good family and well born, a native of Seville, a good Christian and experienced on the sea, since he has made other voyages on this same course to the same destination. He is discreet and very fair and evenhanded in dispensing justice, well-intentioned and understanding, vigilant and careful of everything in his charge, affable and of a proper age, neither old nor young.

Along with being very brave, forceful, and skillful with weapons, he is also slim and fit, because he can jump agilely into any ship's boat when the need presents itself of visiting any other ship in the fleet, no matter how rough the sea and wind. He is not covetous nor greedy nor avaricious, but generous, sharing whatever he has with the soldiers and officers of the fleet, and all are content with him. He is determined in all his duties and careful that punishments due are given, and very diligent in pursuing any opportunity for battle with the enemy. He has good judgment and is circumspect in all his duties. He is sober and temperate in eating and drinking, and very disinterested in the use of his charge and command, because he has no business interests of his own, contenting himself with the ordinary salary of his office, although it is not as much as he merits. In all the fleet, [the officers] are very content to have such a good captain-general . . . and they pray that God protects the king for many years for appointing such a man to the job."[11]

Perhaps no real captain-general could match Escalante's ideal, but distinguished commanders such as don Fadrique de Toledo y Osorio came closer than most.

It is not difficult to see why captains-general were often compared to absolute rulers, since their charge included executive, judicial, administrative, and even spiritual functions in the floating republic they ruled. Before setting sail, the captain-general was to inspect the entire fleet, seeing that ships, equipment, crews, provisions, and munitions were fit for the voyage and for any battle that presented itself. He was also to warn the officers on each ship not to permit concubinage, blasphemy, excessive gaming, or any other public sin to go unpunished, allowing nothing that would offend God and invite his wrath. Further, he should urge all on board to confess their sins and take communion before embarking, so that they would be in the state of grace should death overtake them on the voyage.[12]

Six hours before sailing on a favorable tide, the captain-general should order an artillery shot fired, alerting all who would accompany the fleet to embark. He himself would sail in the vanguard of the fleet, in the ship designated the capitana, which carried the royal standard as well as his own banner. On general instructions from the royal authorities, the captain-general, his admiral, and his chief pilot determined the course. During the voyage, other ships in the fleet were to follow the capitana's flags during the daytime, and its large poop lantern at night, with strict penalties for the officers of any ship that outran the capitana or strayed from the fleet. At sea the captain-general arranged with the inspector and chief notary for regular musters of the men and inspections of the provisions and armaments. In addition, the captain-general judged any civil or criminal quarrels that arose in the fleet, with the right to put serious offenders in bonds or retain them for punishment by local authorities upon arrival. In ordinary fleets with civilian passengers, the captain-general had particular responsibility to see that women, children, the old, the weak, and the sick received proper care. Emphasizing the ceaseless vigilance that should define the head of the fleet, Escalante urged captains-general to stay awake during the night and sleep only during the day, when there was less danger of accidents or enemy ambush. Those who did so set an example for all. One Francisco de Mendoza as captain-general habitually spent the night sitting at the foot of the mainmast wrapped in his large cape, and by his vigilance saved his entire fleet from running aground.[13]

Once in the Indies, the captain-general took effective command of any port he visited, with responsibility for its defense, even supervising local civil and military authorities as long as the fleet remained there.[14] When two fleets came together, each with its own captain-general, a legally defined hierarchy of command determined precedence, with the Armada del Mar Océano at the top of the list and merchant fleets at the bottom. When two fleets of equal rank arrived at the same port, the captain-general of the first to arrive took precedence, and the captain-general of the second fleet became his admiral for any subsequent joint voyage.

Captains-general were forbidden by a 1568 law to trade for themselves or for anyone else in the Indies, to avoid conflicts of interest. The harsh penalties for those who disobeyed included the loss of the goods, plus half the culprit's estate in Spain, and his barring from any further post of honor.[15] Nonetheless, many contemporaries commented on the widespread flouting of this law at various times.[16] The commentators provide no evidence that the abuse was widespread, and we should not automatically take their word that a few notorious cases defined the norm. It is unlikely that a captain-general such as don Fadrique de Toledo y Osorio, with extensive property in Spain and high social position, would have engaged in forbidden trade, and the same doubts must attach to other commanders of similar wealth and prestige. It is possible that detailed research into the legal actions brought against various commanders will yield evidence on this point, but in its absence, at least we should give captains-general as a whole the benefit of the doubt, especially when they commanded war fleets rather than merchant fleets.

The second in command on any large fleet, royal or merchant, was the admiral (almirante), chosen and sworn to office by the same process that selected the captain-general. Both titles referred to functions of command rather than to rank. An individual who had sailed as captain-general of the New Spain fleet, for example, might later sail as admiral of the Armada del Mar Océano. In other words, appointment as admiral of a more important fleet marked a promotion for someone who had previously served as captain-general of a lesser fleet. By 1629 don Martín de Vallecilla had already served as captain-general of both the squadron of Vizcaya (part of the Armada del Mar Océano) and the armada and fleet of Tierra Firme.[17] In 1629 he held the rank of general, and, after serving briefly as admiral of the entire fleet under don Fadrique de Toledo y Osorio, he became captain-general of the Armada de la Guardia sailing with it. The personal qualities desired in an admiral and his duties differed little from those of the captain-general, and both positions required the posting of bonds to guarantee faithful performance.[18] Escalante de Mendoza stressed the nautical skill of the best admirals, who ideally would have spent their lives at sea, passing through all the offices in the chain of command.[19] Intimate knowledge of ships and their equipment and crews would serve an admiral well, since he was often delegated to carry out many of the inspection duties technically falling to the captain-general. One set of instructions specifically ordered the admiral to make the detailed inspections of ships and their equipment before the fleet sailed. During his stint as admiral of the Armada del Mar Océano, Martín de Vallecilla had inspected the six galleons built by Martín de Arana. The admiral was also to see that the best sailors and gunners served on the flagships of the fleet—the capitana of the captain-general and his own ship, the almiranta.

As the fleet left port, the admiral arranged the sailing order behind the capitana, visiting the ships in his launch and sending them on their way in close order. Ideally, he followed the fleet in the almiranta, remaining in the rear guard for the duration of the voyage, although in practice this was not always done. From his position, the admiral would daily count the ships in the fleet, always alert that they stay close together and that corsairs and enemy intruders be promptly identified and driven off. Twice a day he was to make contact with all the ships, receiving fresh orders from the captain-general and spreading the next day's password—usually a saint's name—among the fleet.[20] If any ship fell behind, the admiral was to visit it by launch and offer assistance to get it back on course, if necessary warning the captain-general to halt the fleet and send further assistance to the straggler. Approaching any port, the admiral needed to watch for enemy vessels and keep his own fleet in close order and ready for battle. If the captain-general did not take up residence in port, the admiral did so in his stead, to supervise the unloading of merchant vessels.[21] This would not have applied in 1629, when there were no merchant fleets, but it followed the principle that the admiral was the captain-general's surrogate in many command duties of the fleet.

Just as the captain-general had overall command of the fleet, a captain (*capitán*) commanded each of the ships within it, autonomous up to the point that fleet decisions were involved. Whether captains in the Armada del Mar Océano should have jurisdiction only over the ship and its crew (*capitanes de mar* or sea captains) or over the ship and all on board (*capitanes de mar y guerra*), including the infantry, was still a major debate in Spain in 1629. (The Dutch, the English, and other European powers had already adopted a joint command.) The problem was that the land forces had their own organization and traditions, much stronger in Spain than those of the seaborne forces, and indeed dating from the reconquest of the peninsula from the Muslims. Despite the undoubted naval power of Habsburg Spain, the dominance of central Castile in the government reinforced its self-image as a land-based empire, and this greatly complicated the creation of a joint command for armada ships. Spaniards had been debating the issue for almost fifty years. From 1607 on, many royal seaborne forces had a joint command—notably the Mediterranean galleys, the Portuguese fleets, and the armada of Flanders. Furthermore, don Fadrique de Toledo y Osorio had been using such capitanes de mar y guerra in the Armada del Mar Océano for seven or eight years by 1629.[22] Nonetheless, the debate was by no means finished, and the need to provide captains for the six galleons built by don Martín de Arana revived the familiar battle between soldier and sailor. Arana had obligated himself to propose captains for the ships, but at the last minute he excused himself, asking to devote his attention instead to the crew levy. This put the nominations back into the hands of the Council of War. To clarify the definition of the role of captain, the king ordered the Council and its Junta de Armadas to discuss again and vote upon a proposal made by the distinguished naval commander don Diego Brochero in 1625, when he held the title of Grand Prior of the Order of San Juan.

Brochero's proposal, strongly supported by the king's chief minister, the Count-Duke of Olivares, called for the general appointment of joint commanders of mar y guerra to avoid shipboard conflicts between the officers of land and sea forces, and to end the status distinctions that held soldiers in much higher esteem than sailors, mirroring their positions in Spanish society. Because many considered the life of a sailor vile, they were treated with scorn. Even if they rose to command a ship, as many undoubtedly did, Brochero thought they would lack the necessary confidence for effective leadership, because they had been treated as inferiors all their working lives. The best sailors, he charged, switched to soldiering to further their careers, or sailed with fishing and merchant fleets rather than with armadas, because they were treated better in the absence of soldiers. To lure sailors from Cantabria to royal armadas, they had to be promised a winter return to their homes after the sailing season, and this led to extra expense and delay as new levies gathered the men again in the spring.[23] The continued distinction between land and sea commands was thus indirectly responsible for the shortage of mariners, especially in the royal armadas. Joining the commands of sea and land would raise the sailors to equal status with the soldiers, end the mutual recriminations among commanders, and make much more efficient use of the men on board. In Brochero's proposal, all would be listed together as soldiers and sailors—or as soldiers only, if they chose. In his mind, there was no doubt that the dual commands had hurt Spanish military performance in the past, and that a joint command would go far toward improving it.

Brochero was a navy man, and the infantry commanders on the Council of War saw the situation much differently. Their greatest fear was that joint commands, instead of raising the sailor in status, would lower the soldier. Because any single commander would have to be a seaman first and an infantry commander second, the soldiers would fall to the lowest positions in his command, if only because their work was intermittent, whereas that of the sailors was continual. A more general but similar point was that the requirements of sea and land commands were so different that few persons would have the needed experience and skill to be effective in a joint command. There would also be problems when the joint commander accompanied the infantry for land actions, thus leaving the sailors without leadership, and in many other instances in which the time-consuming duties of each command could not be done by one person. Don Juan de Velasco Castañeda doubted that the example of the English and the Dutch was useful for Spain. They were seafaring peoples, unlike Spaniards, and it was natural for them to consider all on board ship as part of the same command. Moreover, even they had separate commands when they embarked an army, and, in a sense, the armadas of Spain always embarked an army. That was the real reason for the persistence of the dual commands, according to Velasco. Several members of the Council of War shared these misgivings about a joint command, even when they recognized its value. The Marquis of Cadereyta, who had commanded several Indies fleets, provided a reasoned statement that many could support: a joint command should be the goal, but in the absence of appropriate commanders, the dual command should persist.

Some members were unwilling to support joint commands in any circumstances, basing their arguments largely on tradition and on the status distinctions between soldiers and sailors. Don Fernando Girón feared that noblemen would no longer seek the coveted reputation of having served in the infantry, if sailors held equal distinction with soldiers. The Marquis of Montesclaros, president of the Council of Finance, clearly shared in the prejudice against sailors, seeing them as lazy louts, without honor. How could a commander continue to treat his soldiers with the "courtesy and decency due them," he asked, while at the same time using force to drive reluctant sailors from their hiding places to take up their duties? With a dual command, the soldiers had their own duties, though honor led them to help in hoisting anchors and sails, and even to repair rigging, when the need arose. Without that need, no soldier would be pleased to see himself dressed like a sailor or seated on the ground sewing sails, or stirring a cauldron of tar, as sailors commonly did. Montesclaros had little use for the argument that Spain's enemies made good use of joint commands, since he had little use for their methods of naval warfare, preferring the old style of grappling and boarding to the new style of artillery battles, which he considered cowardly. Montesclaros represented the extreme position against the general use of joint commands, a position that had been outmoded for decades.

Eventually, all resistance to joint commands was vanquished by their clear advantages and the support of military men who had used them, such as don Fadrique de Toledo y Osorio. The real problems during the transition were to find enough men who had the necessary experience to exercise a joint command over land and sea forces and to overcome the natural antagonism between mariners and soldiers. The anonymous author of the "Diálogo" written in about 1635 complained that the post often went to career soldiers who knew little of the sea. In his plea for the king to appoint mariners rather than soldiers as capitanes de mar y guerra, the author showed no more understanding for the soldier's value than Montesclaros had shown for the sailor's.[24] Yet the transition continued, and when ideal appointees could not be found for a single command, strict delineations of duties tried to lessen conflicts between the separate commanders of land and sea forces.

For the fleet of 1629, at least, there was a considerable pool of able and experienced men from whom to choose. The Junta de Guerra de Indias voted on forty-one nominations, nine of whom received the vote of all eight members of the group. From the ranked list presented, the king chose the capitanes de mar y guerra needed for the eight silver galleons, which included the six built by don Martín de Arana. Although the king chose only four names from among the nine unanimously recommended, all his choices had distinguished service records and experience with both land and sea commands. Several had already served as capitán de mar y guerra in the Armada del Mar Océano, the Armada de la Guardia, or the Armada del Mar del Sur (southeastern Pacific). On balance, they came more from backgrounds as soldiers than as sailors, even though three of the top four candidates were clearly naval commanders as well. One had even served as an admiral at one point in his career. All but one of the men chosen held the title of captain; the exception was a nobleman, a gentleman of the Order of Santiago who had risen rapidly in infantry commands as his brother's subordinate and had also served as a capitán de mar y guerra in the Armada del Mar del Sur.[25]

It is clear from the nomination procedure for the chief officers of the fleet of 1629 that a military career in Habsburg Spain offered advancement for meritorious service—on land, at sea, or both. One of the opponents of joint commands, denying that sailors were held back by prejudice, had pointed to the careers of several distinguished commanders who had begun as common sailors and had risen to become captains, admirals, and even captains-general. It was no accident, however, that the men he mentioned were from the north coast, where seafaring was an ancient and honored tradition. Families such as the Oquendos and the Vallecillas would continue to add luster to that tradition in the seventeenth century. Nonetheless, for most Spaniards who aspired to military command, a more likely rise through the ranks began with infantry service, as many of the nominees for the 1629 captaincies exemplified.[26]

Perhaps the most impressive career among the men encountered for this study was that of Roque Centeno, the admiral originally chosen for the 1629 fleet. He had served the crown since 1585 on land and sea, beginning as a soldier and ending as captain-general on the Indies fleets. In more than fifty years of service, he participated in every major theater of war, displaying conspicuous bravery in countless infantry and naval battles. In the process, he also acquired such a thorough knowledge of ships and the sea that his expert supervision of careenings and repairs became legendary. He was also distinguished as a naval commander, consulted along with don Fadrique de Toledo y Osorio and very few others when the royal government debated naval matters.[27] Surely such a career was unusual, if not unique, but it suggested that the ideal of officers equally versed in naval and land commands was possible, as well as highly desirable.

The duties of the sea captain included the supervision of everything having to do with the ship and its crew, including their rations of food and drink. In battle, he was to direct the gunners, generally below decks, and see that any damage to the hull was promptly repaired. A capitán de mar y guerra had all these duties plus commanding the infantry, which will be discussed later.[28] Of course, the sea captain's role was largely supervisory; other officers gave the actual orders. In general, he saw that the ship ran smoothly and kept peace among the crew, adjudicating disputes, punishing minor offenders, and referring major ones to the captain-general of the fleet, if there was one. The sea captain was to be like the father or uncle to the young pages and apprentice seamen on his ship, punishing their transgressions gently and in general dealing with them as with boys—which many of them were. With the grown men in the crew, however, his discipline was expected to be harsh if necessary.[29]

Viewed in one way, the sea captain, like the captain-general and the admiral, was more a bureaucratic supernumerary than an integral part of the life of an individual ship. In traditional Cantabrian practice, from which much of Spain's Atlantic naval organization sprang, the natural commander of a ship was the master (*maestre*). The Andalusian voyages of discovery in the early sixteenth century evidently followed the same pattern.[30] Indeed, on many merchant ships of the sixteenth and even the seventeenth century, the master was in sole command.[31] Escalante de Mendoza's 1575 *Itinerario* did not even mention sea captains, and Chaunu states flatly that ships' masters on the Indies run commanded the ships, and that the captains present on warships commanded only the infantry.[32] That is misleading, however. By the late sixteenth century, sea captains were normal on Indies ships above a certain size, in both merchant fleets and armadas. García de Palacio's 1587 treatise dealt with them at some length.[33] With a sea captain present, the master became the second in command, with responsibility for sailing the vessel, in consultation with the pilot, who actually fixed the course. Upon the illness, absence, or death of the sea captain of a warship, the master would take his place.[34] He also had authority over the pilot and was supposed to be experienced in charting a course and using the standard navigational instruments. Just as a master could serve as sea captain in the latter's absence, so he was supposed to be able to serve as pilot if necessary, according to Escalante de Mendoza in 1575. The fictional master in Escalante's dialogue was a "very good man, a good Christian and skillful mariner, native of the town of Palos, . . . truthful, [and worthy] of all credit and confidence."[35]

In addition to the master's nautical responsibilities, he also had more purely administrative duties involving the provisioning and loading of the ship, the care and distribution of food, drink, and supplies, and the maintenance of the ship itself. On merchant ships, the master was also responsible for registering all the trade goods that came aboard and for making an accounting to their owners at the end of the voyage. It helped that masters in Seville belonged to the same guild of seafarers (*Universidad y Cofradía de Mareantes*) as merchants, captains, pilots, and owners of ships involved in the Indies trade.[36] A master's administrative duties often overshadowed his nautical responsibilities, and in Mediterranean mercantile tradition, they were much the more important part of his job. Extrapolating from the Mediterranean tradition, C. H. Haring mistakenly attributes the same administrative character to masters on the Indies run.[37] Instead, the Indies fleets long followed Cantabrian traditions, in which the master was a mariner first and the ship's business manager second. It is important to keep these distinctions in mind to better understand the changes that were occurring in the master's role in the seventeenth century.

In the analogy of Escalante in 1575, the master ruled the ship like the queen bee in a hive. His nautical duties came first—seeing to the careening and outfitting of the ship, checking all its equipment for soundness, especially the rudder and the pumps, inspecting the caulking, and seeing that there was sufficient crew, rigging, sails, and equipment of all sorts for a safe voyage. In his description of eleven duties of the master, Escalante mentions merchandise and purely administrative matters in only two of them.[38] Yet in the Indies fleets, exact planning and provisioning loomed so large that the master's detailed responsibilities began to concern his administrative duties more than his nautical ones. This was especially true of merchant vessels, but it also applied to armada ships. In one list of instructions for masters in the Indies fleets, nearly all thirty-five points dealt with cargo, provisions, passengers, royal documents carried, regulations about loading and unloading, and the need to have all transactions duly notarized.[39] The laws about masters in the Indies fleets also emphasized their administrative functions, dealing primarily with conditions of the 10,000-ducat bond they had to post to guarantee the proper performance of their duties.[40] In reading such documents, it is easy to forget that the master was supposed to be a mariner first of all, and was traditionally chosen from the ranks of career sailors who had already held lower posts in the nautical chain of command.

During the seventeenth century, the master's administrative functions inexorably took over from the nautical ones. As early as 1619, Juan de Hevia

Bolaños, writing about commerce to the Indies, described the job of master of a merchant ship as vile, likening it to the keeper of an inn or tavern. The innkeeper had a certain authority over all those who frequented his inn, but it was authority lacking any basis other than the need to keep public order.[41] Hevia did admit that masters on warships were part of the military and therefore different in some ways from the masters he described. Nonetheless, with his analysis of Indies commerce, we can see the Mediterranean tradition of the master's functions and status overtaking the Cantabrian tradition. By 1672, when Josephe de Veitia Linaje wrote his important analysis of laws pertaining to the Indies trade, the master no longer had to be a skilled mariner, as long as he took two pilots with him. Furthermore, Veitia mentioned that masters had long since ceased to submit journals of their voyages to the chief cosmographer in Seville. Had such journals still been required, they would have come from the pilots.[42]

As they lost their nautical expertise, so the masters lost their place in the nautical chain of command, and some of the respect formerly accorded them. The capitanes de mar y guerra tended to come from among those who had begun their careers as soldiers rather than as sailors, as we have seen. Eventually, the traditional second in command to the infantry captain—the *alférez* or lieutenant—came to replace the master as second in command to the capitán de mar y guerra.[43] This was a logical development, springing from the increasing administrative burdens on the masters and the subsequent diminution of their nautical functions. Already at the time of the 1629 armada, the masters had largely administrative duties, although they still held their posts of second in command without challenge. In this period, the master's functions on armada ships would sometimes be split, with a separate master of rations performing the administrative functions of the job.[44] Other times, the same individual would carry out both functions. The anonymous author of the "Diálogo" written in about 1635 mentioned the master and the master of rations as one and the same person on galleons, with essentially administrative functions. In general, the master was responsible to the sea captain for the proper conservation and distribution of the rations and ship's supplies, and to the infantry captain for the conservation and distribution of the munitions on board.[45]

Whether or not he also served as master of rations, a master was usually identified with a particular ship, until death or some other extraordinary event dissolved the partnership. The Chaunus used the names of both masters and owners to verify the identities of the thousands of merchant vessels they investigated in the Indies fleets, and the same method is useful for checking the identities of armada ships as well. Because most large Spanish ships were named after relatively few religious figures, and because the crown often owned two ships with the same name one after another, the names of their masters can help to identify individual ships unequivocally. The six galleons built by don Martín de Arana and owned by the crown had the same names as private vessels in the Indies fleets at the same time. Their royal ownership and the names of their masters, as well as their size and class, can help to distinguish them from those other vessels. Unfortunately, the Chaunus' tables list those six ships, and many others, with the name of the master of silver (maestre de plata), who kept track of the treasure on a ship during a particular voyage, rather than with the name of its permanent master.[46] The confusion is heightened by the grouping together of laws pertaining to both sorts of masters.[47] Nonetheless they were separate offices, generally, though not always, assigned to separate persons. Veitia Linaje remarked that the two jobs were "ever committed to several persons," though a law of 1609 provided that, when a private ship carried silver for the crown, the owner or master of it could function as master of silver, with the approval of the House of Trade and the merchants of Seville.[48] I will discuss the masters of silver later, with other officials outside the nautical chain of command. For now it is sufficient to note that only the masters, sometimes serving as masters of rations as well, were identified with particular ships.

The pilot was third in the nautical chain of command on an Indies ship, behind the sea captain and the master, with primary responsibility for setting the course and navigating the ship. In a fleet, the chief pilot (*piloto mayor*) set the course for all, as well as exercising a supervisory control over all the other ships' pilots in the fleet. Nonetheless, each ocean pilot was supposed to be capable, on his own, of setting the course and bringing the ship safely to its destination. Before the Indies fleets ever reached the open sea, they often needed two other sorts of pilots, those who guided vessels down the Guadalquivir River from Seville to Sanlúcar de Barrameda, and those who guided the ships over the bar at Sanlúcar. The skills of the river pilot were highly specific and limited to his locality. The river bottom could change from day to day, and no matter how much experience an ocean pilot possessed, he needed a river pilot on board for that part of the journey.

Once downriver, a bar pilot would come on board, collaborating with the ocean pilot, as Escalante described in 1575. The ocean pilot would order all but one of the anchors raised fully, and the last one raised until it was just ready to leave the bottom. Then, with the masts and yards in place, and the sails raised but not unfurled, he would order two apprentice seamen to climb the foremast and stand ready on the yard. When the bar pilot said it was time to move, the ocean pilot would order the last anchor raised and call out to the two men aloft: "Ease the rope of the foresail, in the name of the Holy Trinity, Father, and Son, and Holy Spirit, three persons and one true God only. Be with us and guard and guide and accompany us, and give us a good and safe voyage, and carry and return us safely to our homes."[49] After the sail fell into place, the ocean pilot ordered all on board to say an Ave Maria to the Most Holy Virgin Mary to protect them on their way. At that point, he would officially turn control of the ship over to the bar pilot. So that nothing would disturb him, all on board were to remain silent, each one in his place, until the ship had passed the shallows and was safely in the middle of the channel. Only then would the ocean pilot come fully into his own responsibilities for guiding the ship to the Indies. In the case of the 1629 armada, the galleons avoided the river passage by being outfitted in Cádiz, a protected sandy bay in which the ocean pilots could maneuver without aid. They could also manage in a port with a clean sandy beach, such as Málaga, but any time a port featured a river flowing to the sea, they could rarely do without the services of a local bar pilot.

At sea, the pilot needed five principal skills: (1) to set and read a compass in all its variations; (2) to set a course and tack the ship to follow it, while charting its progress, and to take the altitude of the sun with the astrolabe and that of the North Star with the forestaff (*ballestilla*), using the tables available for the daily declination of the sun; (3) to know the weather and the winds, and the changes that occurred in them with the phases of the moon; (4) to know how the sails should be disposed to respond to wind and course variations; and (5) to know the characteristics of the lands to which he sailed, including the proper course to follow to arrive there and the compass locations of the ports.[50] According to the anonymous author of the "Diálogo" written in about 1635, each pilot was to carry with him four compass needles, fixed and well conditioned with the lodestone; six hourglasses (*ampolletas*), each of one-half hour; a sailing chart for the voyage, marked with compass points; an astrolabe weighing over ten pounds; a forestaff with three scales marked for the sun and stars; 150 brazas (825 feet) of sounding line, fine and thin and well-tarred; and three lead weights (*escandallos*) of six, ten, and fifteen pounds each.[51] A list in 1587 mentioned also a wooden quadrant, a copper lantern, and two clocks of the sort made in Lisbon.[52] The calculation of one's position, based on estimates of speed, direction sailed, and time elapsed since the last known or estimated position, is generally called "dead reckoning." Because the instruments to measure the variables were far from ideal, a pilot had to make reasoned or intuitive adjustments to the measurements he took. Observations of latitude using the astrolabe or forestaff could supplement the information on speed, direction, and time, but a pilot who was a skilled dead reckoner, as Columbus reputedly had been, was able to chart his course well beyond the accuracy of his instruments.

If the sea captain needed to be vigilant during the voyage, the pilot needed to be even more so, watching day and night for changes in weather and sea currents that could affect the ship and the disposition of the sails. When in difficulty, a wise pilot would consult the sea captain, the master, and other good sailors on board, although he was not obliged to take their advice. The pilot had general responsibility to see that the helmsman followed the course set, that the sailors stood their watches with vigilance, and that the caulker inspected the pumps once during each watch and reported their condition.[53] Many of the pilots in the Indies fleets took assistants with them, both as apprentices and as helpers in the continual task of monitoring wind and seas. One author urged that there be two pilots on all galleons of the royal armadas, as there were on some ships of the Armada de la Guardia and on the capitana and the almiranta of each fleet.[54] That was difficult to put into practice, however, given the chronic shortage of pilots. At one point in the early seventeenth century, Philip III even considered using pilots from the Spanish Netherlands for the Indies run, although the law excluded foreigners in most cases.[55] The crown often had lists made of all pilots in a given area, such as the list made on the north coast in 1575, so that they could be more easily found when the need arose.[56] Nonetheless, there was usually a shortage of fully qualified men for a given job, because their skills were specific to the route traveled. It was much easier to reassign ships from European to Indies duty than it was to reassign pilots. In the absence of a second pilot, or even an assistant, the pilot on a ship would have to rely on the helmsmen for the observations crucial to accurate and safe navigation.

The job of chief pilot (piloto mayor) was pivotal to the safety of any fleet, and those so named enjoyed high personal status and royal favor for their children.[57] To a certain extent, the chief pilot made up for the shortage of a second pilot on individual ships, and his skills compensated for the lack of experienced and fully trained pilots on some of them. The chief pilot set the course and the sails on the capitana, and an alert but inexperienced pilot following behind could keep his ship on the same course without great difficulty. There were undoubtedly many of these "pilotos de fanal y bandera" who safely directed their ships across the Atlantic simply by following the poop lantern (*fanal*) and flag (*bandera*) of the capitana.[58] Because the Indies fleets were enjoined by law to stay together, in effect letting their slowest members set the speed, the convoy system protected the ships under the control of apprentice pilots or those with little independent experience.

Pilots for the Indies run were generally appointed by the captains-general of each fleet, in consultation with the chief pilot, from lists of eligible men compiled by the House of Trade.[59] Until the mid-seventeenth century, the captain-general also named the chief pilots, with the approval of the king through the appropriate government body—the Council of War, the Council of the Indies, or the Junta de Guerra de Indias, depending on the period. From the mid-seventeenth century, chief pilots were chosen by a process of nomination and approval similar to the one that chose the captains-general and admirals.[60] The selection of the best-qualified men for the job was of the utmost importance, and any pilot who lost an armada ship through deceit or wrongdoing earned the death penalty. A loss through carelessness or negligence earned appropriate penalties as well, although punishment was optional on merchant ships.[61] Even years of experience could not guarantee a faultless record. The veteran pilot Francisco Zapata came up on charges when he lost the capitana of a Portuguese fleet in 1640.[62]

Pilot training relied on apprenticeship more than on formal instruction, and many contemporary Spanish authors discussed the points of weakness in the system. Pedro de Medina, in introducing his pioneering work on navigation in 1545, complained that there were few proper teachers and textbooks from which pilots could learn.[63] Martín Cortés, in his book on navigation in 1551, complained about the quality of aspiring pilots.[64] García de Palacio in 1587 said that many held the office who were not properly trained for it or who lacked the ideal combination of personal qualities and skills to be good pilots.[65] The anonymous author of the "Diálogo" written in about 1635 used language so similar to García's that he might simply have paraphrased his distinguished precursor.[66] The most reasoned critique of the system came from Pedro Porter y Casanate, who wrote in 1634 to suggest ways to improve pilot training, dedicating his work to don Fadrique de Toledo y Osorio, with whom he had sailed.[67] Since not all pilots were scientists, or needed to be, he suggested their training be divided into theoretical and practical segments. By then, most pilots used the 1581 book of Rodrigo Zamorano for basic navigational techniques.[68] Porter approved of this as a first step, though he pointed to errors in some of Zamorano's rules and urged that his solar declination tables be brought up to date, because the positions of celestial bodies constantly shifted. Other standard treatises also contained errors, which Porter proved by taking his own measurements in Cartagena de Indias in 1632. Once they had mastered the techniques in Zamorano and other treatises, the candidates should work with experienced pilots for further instruction before being examined. The use of two pilots on each ship would make such training easier and would avoid the potential danger when a new pilot first had a ship in his care. Because of the shortage of pilots, some were even given ships before they had been formally examined and licensed. Others were recommended by chief pilots who chose men for character, even though they might not be fully trained. Porter urged an end to these abuses and recommended the standardization of celestial measurements, charting, and recording practices, to improve navigation.[69]

In pointing to the gap between ideals and reality in pilots' training, Porter served the crown and, not incidentally, laid his claim to be appointed one of the royal officers dealing with navigation. Yet we should be careful not to judge the skill of pilots in general by these critiques of lapses in the system. Historians of an earlier generation often took the Spanish critiques at face value, leaving a general impression that Spanish pilots and navigational training and techniques were seriously defective.[70] Although such ideas still creep into many popular works, the best modern works on navigation history recognize the Spanish contributions to that field.[71] As H. A. Morton observed,

> Portuguese and Spanish supremacy in early exploration was as much a result of their pilots' training schools as it was a cause of them. The navigational systems of both countries were admired and copied by the English, French, and Dutch. Nearly all the early books on navigation were published in Spain, a country which produced naval officers of the highest quality—contrary to much popular belief in the Anglo-Saxon countries. Spain's training schools were successful, and, by the seventeenth century, their navigators were thoroughly versed in the several sciences of mathematics. Much of the entire maritime system of Spain was copied, albeit in modified form, by sixteenth-century England and, by the end of that century, the English had caught up.[72]

Despite the strains produced by a shortage of pilots for the pressing demands of Spain's fleets, the system functioned well enough in the early seventeenth century.

For the 1629 fleet, the House of Trade provided a list of examined and licensed pilots for don Fadrique de Toledo y Osorio, on the king's orders. Don Fadrique often preferred men from Sanlúcar de Barrameda, choosing several of them for the silver galleons.[73] The men on the list had all gone through the standard examination and licensing process specified by law.[74] First, a candidate would petition the House of Trade to examine him, citing his years of experience as a sailor, helmsman, and pilot's assistant, and listing the places for which he was qualified to chart a course, such as New Spain, Santo Domingo, Puerto Rico, Havana, and so on. Generally speaking, Indies pilots were usually qualified for New Spain and the Caribbean, or for Tierra Firme and the Caribbean, but not for both.

In the papers documenting the pilots' examinations, witnesses testified that the applicant was a native of Spain over twenty-five years old, and not a drunk, nor a blasphemer, nor a gambler. Stating when and in what context they had observed him, they also testified to his experience and skill as a navigator and to his knowledge of mathematics and navigational techniques and instruments. The testimony usually finished with a formulaic assertion that the applicant was a good and diligent mariner, worthy of confidence, whom the witness would trust with his own ship, if he had one. Applicants for pilots' licenses in the late 1620s and 1630s, at least those noted for this study, each had fifteen to twenty years' experience on the Indies run by the time they applied. In the course of that time, they had risen through the ranks from pages or apprentice seamen to serve as sailors and officers in the nautical chain of command. All had served as pilots' assistants (*ayudantes de piloto*), and several had also been principal pilots for short missions on small ships, usually in the Caribbean during winter layovers.

Another set of witnesses testified about the candidate's legitimate birth and status as a good Christian, free from Jewish or Moorish ancestry and from punishment by the Holy Office of the Inquisition. The testimony, entered by a notary at the House of Trade in Seville, could take several weeks or months to collect, depending upon when the witnesses could appear. An applicant could apply at any time, but it was most usual for the pilots' examinations to occur from the late summer to the early spring—in other words, outside the standard Atlantic sailing season. Besides arranging for witnesses' testimony, the applicant needed to prove that he had attended lectures on cosmography for two months, which constituted the only formal academic training that he had to receive. The lectures, delivered by the chief cosmographer of the House of Trade, were traditionally scheduled every afternoon starting at three in the winter and five in the summer, presumably lasting until sunset. Although there was no fee for either the classes or the examination, it became customary by the end of the sixteenth century for successful candidates to give the lecturer two or three ducats "for gloves and hens."[75] In the late 1620s and 1630s the chief cosmographer was the learned *licenciado* Antonio Moreno, widely praised for his knowledge and experience, who also held the job of chief pilot of the House of Trade.[76] Once the candidate completed the course of lectures, the chief cosmographer certified his attendance and set a day soon thereafter for the formal examination, inviting all available pilots licensed for the same voyages to attend. Indeed, the law obliged them to do so, or pay a fine of six reales. On the day of the examination the doorkeeper would admit them to the Hall of Government (*Sala de Gobierno*) in the House of Trade. Sometimes foreign visitors would attend an examination as well, once the fame of the nautical school in Seville had spread.

The number of licensed pilots attending the examination varied depending upon who was in town; six was the legal minimum, and eight to ten was a normal attendance. Together they composed the three most difficult questions they could think of for the candidate to answer. Based on his performance they voted by secret ballot, in favor of (with broad beans) or opposed to (with black balls) his candidacy. The chief pilot announced the results of the ballot in the presence of all, a favorable vote clearing the way for swearing in and registering the new pilot. In the name of the Holy Trinity, the pilot swore he would neither give nor sell nor otherwise alienate his sailing charts or his instruments to any foreigner. Furthermore, he swore not even to tell foreigners the particulars of the currents and bottoms of the Indies ports, nor how to set a course for them, nor how to enter and leave them safely. Because of such precautions, very few sailing directions to the Indies have made their way to Spanish archives, and mariners sailing for other nations considered it a great prize to capture such *derroteros* or navigational directions. It is not clear how the concern for secrecy fit with allowing foreign visitors at the examinations. Perhaps they were admitted only before or after the actual questioning. Duly sworn to secrecy for the protection of the empire, a new pilot entered the honored company of those licensed for the Indies. Pilots' assistants were supposed to be fully examined as well, but the shortage of pilots often reduced this requirement to a last-minute verbal examination by experienced pilots.[77]

On board, the pilot was followed in the nautical chain of command by the minor officials. Chief among them was the contramaestre, the master's primary helper, as his title indicates, but with duties also related to the general charges given to the captain and pilot. In Spain the office dated from before Columbus's time. The closest equivalent in English is boatswain, but to avoid confusion, I will use the Spanish term. In port the contramaestre was to see that all the ship's cables were moored properly and to assist in the careening and refitting of the ship.[78] Not only should he be a good sailor and a tireless worker, but he should also be able to read and write, since he was delegated to carry out the master's function of recording everything that came on board. His special charge before sailing was to oversee the loading of the ship and the proper stowage of everything on board. In a merchant ship, this included putting the heaviest and least valuable items farthest below and the more valuable and lighter items higher up, to protect them from excessive water damage, and to keep the center of gravity of the ship low for stability. On merchant and war vessels alike, he had to know how to adjust the quantity and disposition of the ballast in accordance with the cargo and the characteristics of the ship—a crucial job, since even a good ship would handle poorly if the contramaestre failed at his work.[79]

At sea the contramaestre's most important charge was the maintenance of the sails and rigging, seeing that they were kept out of the wet and in good order, along with other supplies for the maintenance, repair, and smooth running of the ship. He was to take particular care with the cables, making sure that the ones attached to anchors did not get cut during the voyage, and protecting them from mice and rats as well as from the weather. During the voyage, he should climb to the topmasts twice daily to inspect the rigging, checking for wear and frays, seeing that the pulleys and other tackle functioned well, and having them cleaned and treated with tallow. The contramaestre also had important responsibilities over those on board. In the master's absence, only the captain and the pilot were not under his orders. In other words, he was fourth in command on the ship, with direct command over all the sailors, apprentices, and pages. In his housekeeping duties he generally took his orders from the master; for his supervision of the crew, he generally took his orders from the pilot. His habitual post was at the foot of the mainmast, where he could hear the orders of the captain and the pilot well, and could relay them to the crew, with his characteristic whistle (*pito*) and verbal commands. He would also salute the capitana and the almiranta with his whistle if his ship came to windward of those vessels.

Before nightfall, he was to order an inspection of all the rigging, taking particular care with the lines on the topmasts and yards, and fixing extra lines on them so that if the wind made it necessary to lower the yards during the night, they could be hauled down from the deck. He also set the sails for the night, on the pilot's direction, and stationed sailors where various lines were stayed on deck, so that if a crisis arose during the night, they could act without delay. It was particularly important that all the lines be in their proper places, so that a well-trained sailor could handle them even in the dark. Before going to sleep at night, the contramaestre was to see that the cooking fire was extinguished with water, that all unnecessary candles were blown out, that there was no water in the pump box, that the ship's boats were well secured, and that the grates on the hatchways were closed. Upon approaching land, the contramaestre was to keep two anchors secured and at the ready, in case they had to be dropped suddenly.

In short, the contramaestre was the workhorse among the officers. If he carried out his multiple tasks well, he could hope to rise to master and beyond. Ideally he should be a man of honor and good repute, a native of Spain with something to lose and neither old nor too young, because his job required discretion and diligence. Above all he should be an experienced mariner, "very measured in his eating habits and much more so in his drinking habits," so that his authority over the crew would be unquestioned.[80] The captain-general named the contramaestre on the capitana, and on galleons in a war fleet; in a merchant fleet, the choice generally lay with the master.

Assisting the contramaestre in all his tasks was the guardian (*guardián*), often described as the fifth-ranking person on board, but in fact he had no claim to authority except to relay the contramaestre's orders. He was to help in the inspection and repair of sails and rigging at sea and in the disposition and conservation of cables and other mooring lines in port. On board at night, he was to doublecheck that the cooking fire was out and that all lanterns and candles had been prepared and placed where they were needed. Besides relaying orders to the crew in general, the guardian was responsible for keeping order among the apprentices and pages. García de Palacio thought he should be somewhat rigorous in that task, so that his charges, "like boys and disorderly persons," would fear him and thus keep out of trouble.[81] The guardian's only independent authority was over the ship's boat, going with a crew of apprentices at the oars to fetch cargo, water, and firewood from land. The cleaning, refitting, and repair of the boat fell to the guardian as well. During loading, the guardian carried out the contramaestre's orders for stowage in the hold, and he remained responsible during the voyage for seeing that the holds and the ship in general were as clean as possible. The sea captain of a warship, or the master of a merchant ship, usually named the guardian, choosing from among the most experienced sailors. Although they were not formally part of the chain of command, the best guardians could become contramaestres in time.[82]

The dispenser (*despensero*) served as a kind of major-domo for the master, in charge of preserving and dispensing the stores of food, wine, water, and all else that had to be carefully rationed. He was responsible for the material and even the spiritual well-being of everyone on board, just as the contramaestre was responsible for the well-being of the ship on which they sailed. In that sense, the dispenser held a command function parallel to that of the contramaestre. The dispenser had charge of the keys to all the locked storage spaces on the ship, with delegated responsibility for the care of everything loaded on board. He also had keys to the grates and hatchways leading to the hold, and no one could open them except in his presence. To preserve the stores in the hold, the dispenser exercised special vigilance regarding light and fire on board, seeing that no one but himself took lights into the closed storerooms or below decks, and then only inside a lantern.[83] A shipboard fire was one of the worst things that could happen at sea.

Although none of the treatises on Spanish shipboard life mentions who did the cooking for the crew, in the sixteenth century the dispenser probably had responsibility for food preparation. The closest English translation of *despensero*—steward—suggests the same conclusion. His officially defined responsibility was to measure the food allotted to each man carefully, with the standard measures that were part of the ship's equipment. Since the weekly diet involved dried meat or dried fish with legume stews, many of the ingredients had to be soaked overnight before cooking. This the dispenser directed the pages to do just before going to sleep. The following day, he would have the fire lit and tended and the day's food cooked, unless a storm or battle prevented it. Then the men received cheese instead, with their usual ration of biscuit and wine. Mealtimes on board and their nutritional content will be discussed in the next chapter. Because of his primary responsibility for the crew's basic rations, the ideal dispenser should be sensible, patient, prudent, calm, temperate in eating and drinking, and able to keep accurate accounts of the rations, firewood, and water supplies consumed. He was to see that any provisions about to go bad were used up first, to reduce the amount of waste. If it became necessary to cut back on the daily ration because of a shortage of provisions, the dispenser was the one to do it, with the approval of the captains of both sea and land forces on board.

Although the dispenser could be responsible for water as well as food rations, there was often a special official, called the *alguacil de agua,* for that job, which could be highly contentious if the water supply ran low. When dispatching his duty, he stood at the opening of the hatch seeing that water was distributed in just measure to all the men. Apprentice seamen would assist him when necessary.[84] In a war fleet, both dispenser and alguacil were named by the captain-general for the capitana. On other ships in the fleet, the captain probably named the alguacil and the master named the dispenser, as was the practice in merchant fleets.[85] The alguacil de agua needed to be a good sailor, because it was expected that he would step into the role of guardian, should that official die or fail in his duty.

Other officers and officials on board had equally specific duties that set them apart from common seamen, although they were not part of the nautical chain of command. Perhaps the most important official of this type was the master of silver (maestre de plata), assigned to the Armada de la Guardia to register all the public and private treasure taken aboard ship, and to see that the proper duties had been paid on it. Present from the late sixteenth century on, at first this official was named by the captain-general of the fleet, then by the House of Trade, and after 1615 by the Council of the Indies, with royal approval.[86] The master of silver identified each shipment as specifically as possible, including the registration number and other unique information marked on each bar of silver, and the precise description of ornaments and jewelry. The registers were later submitted to the House of Trade in Seville, where many survive today.[87] Each master of silver posted a bond of 25,000 ducats to guarantee the proper execution of his duties. His underwriters each assumed part of the bond, and it was not unusual for one man to have as many as a dozen or so underwriters (*fiadores*). Because of the shortage of cash in Seville in 1629, several of the proposed masters of silver for the fleet had trouble finding underwriters with sufficient liquid assets to guarantee their bond. The royal attorney (*fiscal*) who reviewed the bonds of the proposed masters of silver demanded additional underwriters in several cases, claiming that some of the men on the original list could not have produced the cash if called upon to do so.[88]

Masters of silver earned fees for the treasure in their care, up to about 1 percent of its value. This could be quite lucrative in a wealthy fleet, but by the 1630s the registered treasure receipts had entered a decline. Masters of silver on the smaller galleons of the Armada de la Guardia in 1633 complained that only their counterparts on the capitana and almiranta could make a profit, because everyone preferred to use those larger, stronger ships. After taxes on their fees and the expenses for assistants and for building proper containers for the treasure they carried, masters of silver on the smaller ships had no profit left.[89] Diminishing returns would have provided an incentive for some masters of silver to collaborate with smugglers. A law of 1640 seems to indicate that such fraud was on the rise—it set harsh penalties for carrying unregistered treasure: a loss of all possessions, perpetual exclusion from the Indies trade, and exile from the kingdom for four years. Should the culprit break his exile, he would be sent to serve in the North African garrisons of Larache or Mamora.[90]

Those masters of silver who faithfully carried out their duties could be useful extensions of royal authority on the voyage and in the Indies, because they were outside the nautical chain of command and had custody of royal funds. In the fleets of 1618–1620, the crown placed masters of silver in a supervisory capacity over the ship's master, although that was not part of their normal duties. One list of instructions for those years ordered a master of silver to oversee all expenses in the Indies and spend as little as possible of royal money. During careenings and repairs, he was to keep track of all materials and to watch for fraud by the contramaestre, guardian, and dispenser, as well as by the master. He was also to keep a copy of the lists of persons on board and check to see that provisions and munitions were justly distributed and registered.[91] In effect, at least for the fleets of 1618–1620, the master of silver on a given ship was the assistant of the veedor (inspector) of the fleet, both representing the king's financial interests.

The notary (escribano) performed a similar oversight function on board. At first named by the masters on merchant ships, the notary later became a crown appointee to preserve his independence. By the seventeenth century, notaries were chosen by royal officials in Seville and were directly responsible to the House of Trade. No master could dismiss the notary on his ship, and, if one died, any replacement appointed by the master had to meet with the approval of all on board. Like the notaries on land in Spain and elsewhere in continental Europe, the notary's primary duty was to register and witness all transactions, thus guaranteeing their legality. It was a position of honor on both merchant and armada ships, given to a person of confidence and ability.[92] The notary recorded everything loaded on board and noted any damages to the ship or its cargo during the voyage, giving as precise information as possible. That was particularly important on a merchant ship, because insurance claims could depend upon detailed information about the loss.

In a general sense, the notary was the legal guardian of all on board, certifying among other things that crew members and soldiers received their just rations. Every day he presided over the distribution of water, wine, and provisions, calling the name of each man entitled to receive rations, and monitoring the removal of provisions from below decks. He was to be present, along with the ship's cooper (*tonelero*) and a representative of the sea captain at the opening of every pipe of wine or vinegar, to certify any waste. This would be entered on the accounts of the master, who had ultimate responsibility for waste above a certain percentage. The notary monitored the decisions of the sea captain, the master, and the dispenser regarding the use of provisions about to go bad, and obtained permission from the fleet's inspector to dispose of thoroughly ruined food, "so that the bad odor does not affect the men." The items thrown overboard would first be weighed and their disposal duly noted in his ledgers.[93]

The notary also kept the pay books for sailors and soldiers, ensuring that they received all the wages due them, and that anyone who died or failed to attend the periodic musters was striken from the rolls. When someone on board fell ill, the notary drew up the person's will. After a death, he made an inventory of the deceased's belongings, in the presence of the chaplain, and saw that the property was distributed according to law. Arriving on land, the notary took his registers to the offices of the inspector and comptroller of the fleet, and helped the ship's master present his own paperwork for the voyage.[94] The shipboard notary thus had functions similar to his counterpart on land, recording and certifying what happened in his presence, but because he also watched over the administration of the ship and everything on board, he had more extensive powers than those of a land-based notary.

The office of chaplain (*capellán*) became common on warships in the late sixteenth century. The captain-general appointed chaplains for the ships in his command, after they had been examined by the chaplain on the capitana, called the *capellán mayor,* who continued to supervise them. By the seventeenth century, the chaplain of a 500-tonelada galleon appeared just after the pilot and before the contramaestre on the roster of the ship, presumably enjoying status between the two.[95] Whether assigned to the ship in general or to a company of soldiers on board, the chaplain had particular responsibility for the sick men in his charge, visiting them twice a day and seeing that the surgeon also visited them to give them their medicines and order the special food carried for them (called dietas). A brother of the order of St. John of God often traveled on the principal galleons of the Armada de la Guardia as a nurse, and, in the Armada del Mar Océano, the chaplain had the only key to the medicine chest and one of the two keys to the dieta chest.[96] The chaplain held responsibility to see that the sick actually received that food and that an apprentice seaman fed those who were unable to feed themselves. At the end of the voyage, he had to file a sworn report *in verbo sacerdotis* that the dietas had been used only for the sick. When anyone became gravely ill, the chaplain saw that he made a will, and stayed with those in imminent danger of death until the end. Evidently, not all chaplains were paid to say mass or daily prayers or to administer the sacraments. Those who were would say mass each day, weather permitting, and chant the Salve Regina every afternoon and the Ave Maria every night. During battle, the chaplain was to be at the opening of the hatchway below decks with the surgeon, receiving and comforting the wounded, taking their confessions, and giving the last rites to those who could not be saved.[97]

The ship's surgeon teamed with the chaplain to care for the sick and wounded on board. Royal decrees from the late sixteenth century called for well-trained medical officers on all the ships of the royal armadas, ideally a doctor (*médico*) accompanied by a surgeon (*cirujano*) and a pharmacist (*boticario*), although it is doubtful that this was ever fully carried out. Galleons in the seventeenth century might have a surgeon assisted by a barber, but it was common to have barber-surgeons alone on merchant ships, and even on some galleons.[98] According to the anonymous author of the "Diálogo" written in about 1635, a ship's surgeon should know Latin and be able to serve as both physician and surgeon. He should have all the tools needed to do surgery and to amputate limbs; the medicines he used were part of the standard ship's supplies. On a personal level, the ideal surgeon should be a good Christian, charitable, diligent, hard-working, clean, and well groomed. On board he should visit the sick twice a day, administering the appropriate medicines and telling the chaplain what special foods to give each patient. If he had no barber to help him, he should get whatever help he needed to do any necessary bleeding himself. A barber acting as the ship's medical officer could also shave the men on board for a fee of two reales each, to help him buy and maintain his tools.[99]

General maintenance and repairs to the ship and its equipment fell to the various workmen carried on board—a carpenter, a caulker, sometimes a cooper, and so on—known collectively as the *maestranza*. The carpenter and the caulker, especially, needed to be good mariners and generally came from the ranks of the sailors on board. Their ability to mend anything on board relied more on their experience of the sea than it did on their artisanal skills. Nonetheless, the carpenter had to be able to set the curve for constructing a ship's boat, or even a ship, should the need arise, just as any good river carpenter could do. He should also know something about turning wood, be able to make pulleys and other fittings, and come prepared with a large assortment of his own tools. The small jobs he could do himself. For the larger ones he could ask for help from the crew. During battle, he was to stay below decks, repairing any holes made by enemy artillery.[100] The caulker, too, needed his own tools; he had particular responsibility for checking the pumps and the seams in the hull and decks to see that they were watertight. The pressure of heavy seas could make even a well-constructed ship lose its caulking. Twice a day during his watches, the caulker was to inspect the pumps, reporting their condition to the captain and the pilot. He could direct the apprentice seamen in their idle moments to pick apart old cables to make the oakum he needed. Otherwise, he did all the caulking work himself and remained fully responsible for it. Like the carpenter, the caulker stayed below decks during battle, repairing damage from artillery fire. Both the carpenter and the caulker could earn extra money for work in the careening and repairs of their ships on land, but if they were salaried at the time, they could collect only half the daily wage paid to local workmen.[101]

A diver (*buzo*), carried on the capitana and almiranta of each fleet, inspected and repaired leaks below the water line on any ship in the fleet. The job required a good sailor who was also a good swimmer. Using a thin-bladed knife, he tested the seams, then caulked leaks and patched holes, using oakum for the former and thin lead sheets and scupper nails (*estoperoles*) for the latter. During battle the diver stayed below decks, helping the carpenter and the caulker to fill holes made by enemy shot. Once the ships disengaged, he went over the side to finish the job.[102] The trumpeter (*trompeta*), another specialized mariner, served only on warships. During battle, he stood on the afterdeck near the poop lantern, playing loudly and continuously to animate his shipmates and strike terror among the enemy. In calmer times, he played once each morning and afternoon and provided festive flourishes at official ceremonies. There had evidently been as many as six trumpeters on each galleon in the sixteenth century, but seventeenth-century ships had just one.[103]

All the officers and officials mentioned thus far belonged to the general category of ship's crew (*gente de mar* or mariners), from the sea captain to the diver, yet each had specialized duties that did not usually involve the direct handling of the ship and its equipment. That fell to the sailors: common seamen (*marineros*), apprentices (*grumetes*), and pages (*pajes*). In a crisis, all on board might lend a hand to the lines and cables, because their lives depended upon it, but in normal times the actual number of hands operating the ship was smaller than we might think. General manning ratios, such as those briefly discussed in chapter 2, can be quite misleading, unless we are sure just who is included—the sailors alone; all the mariners, including the gunners; or everyone on board. One rule of thumb in the late sixteenth century called for 1 man for every tonelada of warship.[104] A Hispano-Portuguese expedition to Africa in 1577–78 planned for 1.5 men per tonelada.[105] Both these figures surely included everyone on board. Official rules in 1550 for ships going to the Indies called for 1 man for every 5.6 toneladas of a 360-tonelada ship, including all the mariners, though actual manning ratios diverged considerably from the rules.[106] Other Spanish ships in the sixteenth century might carry 1 man for every 5 toneladas, as did a Cantabrian vessel sent for Mediterranean grain in 1528, or 1 man for every 7.14 toneladas, as did a Vizcayan warship armed in 1582.[107]

In providing for crews and infantry on the galleons of the 1629 Indies fleet, the Junta de Guerra de Indias used a formula of 1 mariner for each 6.25 toneladas and 1 infantry man for each 3.8 toneladas.[108] Those rates still obtained for ordinary galleons in the 1633 ordinances for the Armada del Mar Océano, but the capitana and almiranta, as well as the smallest ships, had to carry 1 mariner for each 5.6 toneladas and 1 infantryman for each 3.6 toneladas, similar to the figures set in a royal decree in 1631.[109] The anonymous author of the "Diálogo" written in about 1635 recommended 1 mariner for each 5 toneladas and 1 infantryman for each 4 toneladas.[110] It is clear that these ratios included all the sailors and soldiers, with their officers. In practice, these recommended ratios seldom set an absolute standard, although some ships might come very close to it. Olesa Muñido mentions one 500-tonelada galleon in the seventeenth century that carried 1 mariner for each 4.9 toneladas and 1 infantryman for each 4.2 toneladas.[111] On the other hand, a list of thirteen galleons that sailed for the crown between 1600 and 1665 carried an average of 1 mariner for each 6.4 toneladas and 1 infantryman for each 2.3 toneladas. For nine merchant ships in the same period, the respective figures were 8.3 and 3.5 toneladas. In 1700 a list of fourteen galleons carried an average of 1 mariner for each 3.24 toneladas and 1 infantryman for each 3.79 toneladas.[112] Not surprisingly, galleons generally carried more men than the merchant ships, and short voyages within Europe during

wartime often served to transport troops to one of Spain's European possessions, greatly inflating the ratio of infantryman.

The proportions of officers and men among the mariners appear quite
clearly in two lists for the Armada de la Guardia to the Indies, one from 1601
and the other from 1613, and each comprising six galleons. (See appendix C,
Table 9.) There are relatively more officials and common seamen in the 1613
list, but far fewer pages, although the number of pages was quite high on
both lists. So many things could have affected the pool of available men in
any given year that it is difficult to draw any conclusions about the state of
maritime recruitment in Spain, based on these two examples. It seems that
shortages of qualified mariners were chronic from the late sixteenth century
on, yet the potential causes of those shortages must remain speculative.
Some authors have blamed low pay; others point to government policies and
the low status of mariners. Almost unmentioned is the population crisis in
central Spain from the late sixteenth century on. What is clear is that most
fleets had trouble raising the full complement of crew recommended by law,
and that the compositions of crews could vary from year to year, even on
fleets raised for similar purposes.[113] To remedy the lack of available mariners
for the armadas, the crown instituted a mandatory registration plan in a
royal decree of October 31, 1625, probably published in January 1626, a more
formal version of the periodic censuses of mariners carried out in the sixteenth century.[114] The registration, called a *matrícula,* aimed to list all men in
Spain with seafaring experience, even on small fishing boats. Benefits such as
tax exemption awaited those who voluntarily registered and served, and
penalties awaited those who tried to avoid the registrars. The notary of each
town council had to make the list and keep it up to date, seeking the advice of
local persons who knew the sea and local mariners. With personal information about each man's home town, marital status, and experience on the sea,
these matrículas could provide a fascinating picture of seafaring in Spain, if
they still exist in sufficient quantity. Evidently, one copy stayed in the
locality and another was sent to the Council of War in Madrid.[115]

The ideal mariners went to sea as children and learned their craft by
practical experience and apprenticeship. Some might specialize in fishing and
coastal trade, rarely straying from the sight of land or from well-charted
waters. Others might sail the open sea, where even regularly traveled routes
offered danger and sudden death to the unwary. Among Spaniards, the
Vizcayans long held first place as the most skilled mariners; an old Italian
saying was that all mariners should be Vizcayans, and all merchants should
be Florentines. In the late sixteenth century, Escalante de Mendoza praised
the Vizcayans' skill at coastal chart sailing and in defending their ships from
enemies; he also gave high marks to mariners from the Triana district of
Seville. He preferred the Portuguese, however, for voyages on the open sea
and in difficult gulfs and coastal waters, in large part for what he defined as
their ability to suffer hard work and hunger without complaint.[116]

Escalante's remarks point up the hardships attending a life at sea, even in
the late sixteenth century. Things had not changed much since the days of
Anacharsis, born six hundred years before Christ, who said, "There are
three kinds of human beings: the living, the dead, and those who sail the
sea."[117] Common seamen for the Indies armadas had to be between twenty
and fifty years old, and free from patronage ties to officials at the House of

Trade. Supposedly limited to natives of Spain, a seaman's post might go to a foreigner in exceptional circumstances. On a return voyage from the Indies, even captured prisoners might serve as seamen, if the fleet were short-handed, although this must have been rare.[118] For García de Palacio, a good seaman should be modest and respectable, with experience of everything on board, particularly the helm. He should be able to make and attach any rigging and sail, lower stowage into the hold, use the ship's boat, attach cables to anchors, attach the topmasts, rig the parrel (*racamento*) for raising and lowering the yards, stay and release all the lines, and attach and detach the bonnets on the main and foresails. Sewing the sails and tarring the rigging and cables also formed part of his duties. In addition to these basic requirements, the best mariners also learned how to chart the ship's progress and take sightings with the quadrant, the astrolabe, and the forestaff, and could judge the effects of the moon and the tides. Such knowledge could make a bright and diligent seaman into a pilot eventually, and in the short term it would gain him a pay supplement.[119] Ambitious soldiers could benefit from learning navigation as well, since that could help them rise to the rank of capitán de mar y guerra. The soldier and adventurer Alonso de Contreras did just that during several expeditions against pirates in the Mediterranean. As he related it, "During these voyages I scarcely slept; for I went mad on navigation, and was always instructing myself in the company of the pilots, watching them making charts, and getting to know about the lands which we passed, with their ports and capes, which I marked down."[120]

Every seaman, and many officials as well, stood watch in shifts round the clock. The crucial thing was to stay alert, watchful, and—above all—awake. The entire ship could be lost or saved in dangerous waters, according to how well the men stood watch; anyone who fell asleep merited severe punishment and a lowered repute among his fellows. To stay awake, the men on watch were well advised to remain standing, looking toward the prow of the ship—the direction of danger from shallows or obstructions—and to windward—the direction of storms overtaking the ship. Anything unusual should be reported to the pilot or contramaestre immediately.

In battle, the worthy mariner should bravely attend to the tasks assigned him and resist surrender as long as he was able to fight. That would earn him the respect of everyone, even the enemy, but "if he surrendered like a chicken," he would forfeit all esteem.[121] The seaman's constant companion should be his knife, useful in a hundred tasks, and crucial for cutting lines and cables to save the ship during a sudden storm. Unfortunately, the seaman's knife must also have made it easier for minor quarrels on board to turn into deadly confrontations.

The master of the ship generally chose the sailors, with the approval of the captain. Levies could also be carried out by individuals on contract to the crown, as we have seen. In formal recruiting, each sailor received several months' wages in advance, thus binding him to serve his term; for Indies voyages, a term was usually two years. The law defined the rights and duties of masters and sailors quite carefully for merchant ships, and made the master responsible for the prompt payment of the sailors' wages.[122] Sailors' rights seem to have been more restricted on armada ships, and no legal remedies could force the crown to pay the wages due. Sailors who accepted advance pay and then failed to show up for embarcation committed fraud, making them liable to imprisonment and seizure of their goods, at least to the value of the money they had accepted. The roundup of sailors and infantrymen who failed to appear for the armada typically began within weeks after its departure, with commissioned bounty hunters carrying out the arrests.[123]

Apprentice seamen (*grumetes*), equal to about two-thirds the number of seamen, served from about age sixteen or eighteen to about age twenty. They needed youth and agility to carry out their duties, but beyond age twenty, Escalante observed, men attended lazily to apprentices' duties and worked more diligently as seamen.[124] Apprentices traditionally manned the oars in the ship's boat and held responsibility for caring for it, mooring it properly, and making any repairs necessary to the oarlocks and other equipment. Whenever the boat went on an errand, whether to ferry an officer between ships in the fleet, or to fetch water and supplies on land, the apprentices provided the power, commanded by the guardian. Their second major responsibility was to attend to the rigging of the sails whenever ordered to do so, by anyone from the sea captain on down to any common seaman. Often this involved climbing aloft to the topsails or even the topgallants, lengthening or shortening them as ordered, when the lines manipulated from the deck could not accomplish the adjustment alone. An experienced apprentice would know all the parts of the rigging by name and be able to follow verbal commands by the pilot and the master, even in the dark. An inexperienced one would still be "learning the ropes." All were apprentices in some sense, acquiring the knowledge and techniques that would make them fully qualified seamen. Part of that knowledge involved knowing how to work the pump, as well as mastering the dozens of knots and hitches pertinent to separate parts of the rigging. "Those who do not know all this," García de Palacio wrote, "with practice and fear of the lash will learn, if the guardian is diligent."[125]

Every apprentice had to carry a knife at all times and wear strong ratlines around his waist, to use for making repairs in the lines aloft. Anyone found without his knife could be punished and docked in pay by the guardian. Besides their regular duties, apprentices could be assigned to special tasks. One had responsibility for keeping a light in the compass box, supplying oil and twists of rope (if it used an oil lamp) or tallow candles (if it used a lantern). Another lit the poop lantern every night. And finally, the captain, master, and pilot could each have an apprentice and a page assigned to him as a personal servant for the length of the voyage.

Occupying the lowest ranks in the hierarchy on board were the pages (*pajes*). On Spanish ships they came in two distinct sorts. The first might be relatives of the captain or his principal officers, or the sons of family friends. They would act as personal servants of their patrons during the voyage, attending to their needs, even cooking their food. Officers' pages of high social standing would likely come from the same social group as their patrons. Quite different were the pages in the nautical chain of command. Generally about twelve to sixteen years old, many were orphans or even fugitives from their families, choosing a life at sea because they had a natural inclination toward it, or because they had no other choice. It was their lot to perform all the menial tasks on board, and to take orders from everyone else in matters regarding the running of the ship. They scrubbed the decks and the area between decks twice a day, morning and evening, and assisted the dispenser in preparing the meals. It is probable that pages often did what cooking was required, tending the giant cauldron when meals were prepared communally. At mealtimes, the pages set up the table (when one was used) and served the food, taking their own meals when everyone else had finished, then removing the table and cleaning the area. Pages also lent a hand to raise and lower the sails, beginning the learning process that might carry them upward in the nautical hierarchy. In their spare time, they twisted cord and rope, always carrying a supply of replacement cords in their belts to give to sailors who needed them. Morning and evening, pages chanted the traditional prayers loudly enough for all to hear, their youth and innocence presumably adding value to their supplications.

Their most important nautical job involved tending the watchglass (*ampolleta*) or sandclock, turning it as soon as it ran out every half hour, and thus helping the pilot plot the course by knowing the time. Before going to sleep, they also set out the lanterns that might be needed during the night, seeing that each had candles. Although ordinary pages took orders from virtually everyone else on board, only the officers could punish them, even if an offense had been against a seaman or apprentice. This provided a certain amount of protection against arbitrary punishment, but how well pages actually fared depended very heavily upon the character of the officers. During battle, pages had the dangerous job of carrying lighted cord to the infantry to fire their guns, maintaining a supply of smoldering cord in large earthen jars on deck. This left the pages exposed to enemy fire with no means to defend themselves, not even a knife. Despite their youth, they could easily meet death on an Indies voyage.[126]

The gunners (*artilleros*) on a galleon occupied an intermediate place between the sailors and the soldiers. Chosen from among the skilled seamen, the gunners held a privileged position on board, earning 2 ducats per month more than common seamen. After 1576, a chief gunner (*artillero mayor*) appointed in Seville provided training for potential armada gunners. Each had to be at least twenty years old, to have made a voyage to the Indies, and to attend artillery practice with the chief gunner. He had to know how to make and use incendiary devices and gunpowder, and he would be examined before an official judge by four or five experienced gunners. On an armada ship, the gunners could constitute as much as 30 percent of the mariners, several times as many as sailed on a merchant ship.[127] On the galleons of the Armada de la Guardia in 1601 and 1613, however, gunners accounted for just 24.2 and 22.1 percent, respectively, of the mariners. (See appendix C, table 9.)

Their most important tasks involved caring for the artillery, from the moment it came on board until it was unloaded for temporary storage at the end of the voyage. The guns could range considerably in size and type as mentioned in chapters 3 and 5, each one requiring its own quality of powder and shot. The gunners needed to keep the supplies for each gun at hand, taking care not to mix the supplies for one gun with those for another. As soon as the guns were in place on board, the gunners greased the axles on their carriages, attached removable plugs to the muzzles, and arranged each size of shot in a separate shot locker in a central place. With each gun in position, the gunner assigned to it would tack a strip of linen or sail canvas to the hull above it, labeled with the gun's caliber in ink or red ochre.[128] On a galleon, a gunner usually had responsibility for six or seven guns, but the range on Spanish ships in general could run from three to ten guns for each gunner. During battle, apprentices and pages, and sometimes even soldiers or seamen, would help the gunners by fetching supplies and loading the pieces in between shots.[129]

The gunners' functions on galleons so closely approached those of the infantry that it is difficult to remember that they were sailors first of all. Castro even calls them "soldados especiales," though they clearly formed part of the mariners.[130] The anonymous author of the "Diálogo" written in about 1635 criticized some gunners for claiming exemption from sailors' duties. Even though their positions as gunners raised them above the level of their fellows, he said, they remained part of the nautical chain of command, required not only to help with the sails in time of need, but also to stand regular watches, help moor the ship in port, and lend a hand at all times without being asked. The best gunners could hope to rise to guardian, contramaestre, master, captain, and even beyond, as the careers of numerous armada officers testified.[131]

A master gunner (*condestable*) commanded the gunners, and needed to have the qualities of a contramaestre, or even experience in that post, to do his job well. On land he would see that all the guns assigned to his ship had sufficient ammunition and other supplies, working with the master in correcting any deficiencies. As the guns came on board, the master gunner directed their positioning, in general putting open-chambered pieces above decks and closed-chambered ones below decks. He had to know everything his men knew about each gun in order to supervise their work. At sea the master gunner divided the gunners into two watches, without exempting anyone. Those who knew how to steer the ship he assigned to the helm during their watches, which generally put them in charge of the helm from the evening prayer until sunrise. Others would stand watch at the firebox near the cooking stove, with powder horn at their belt, seeing that there were always two lit and four unlit match staffs (*botafuegos*) available, insurance against a sudden need to use the artillery during the night. The master gunner should ensure that his men stayed on deck to sleep, wrapped in their large capes (*capotes*), rather than seeking shelter below decks. As sailors, they needed to be at hand to man the rigging and sails during the night.[132]

The master gunner assigned specific guns to each of his men, so that they would learn the characteristics of each one and care for it properly. During battle, the master gunner supervised his gunners and any sailors and infantrymen assigned to help them. If the fighting took place only on one side of the ship, he would have those on the opposite side help, so that no one stayed idle. The master gunner also kept his men from firing until they had a target in range and saw that they cooled the guns with vinegar after every three shots. If the enemy ship was close alongside, his men were ordered to try to sink it by ripping holes in the side with crowbars or other tools and by launching firebombs and incendiary grenades into the enemy ship. At first the master gunner came from among his men, receiving a small salary supplement for supervisory duties. Eventually the important responsibilities of the post made it part of the command structure.[133]

The six galleons built by don Martín de Arana had from eighteen to twenty gunners on the smallest two ships, and thirty to thirty-three on the largest two. The gunners' names appeared in the crew books for each galleon, with their presence or absence noted for each of the musters during a voyage. Usually there was one muster just before departure from Cádiz, a second at the first main port of call in the New World, and others at intervals of about two months during the winter layover. In the months before the return voyage home, musters came at least once a month, to verify that the men were still present and earning their pay. For the Armada de la Guardia, the last six of the usual eleven musters occurred in Havana, the staging area for the homeward voyage. Each muster had its identifying letter in the crew book. The letter F by a man's name in one book, for example, meant that he had been present at the muster in Havana on October 9, 1634.[134] Those who had signed on at the beginning of the voyage and who remained until the end would have a long string of letters with their names. Those who missed various musters, or who arrived later on a particular ship, for whatever reason, would be missing various letters, and would not receive pay for those periods. The numbers of effective gunners and other crew members fluctuated, falling when men disappeared or were in hospital and thus temporarily off the rolls, and rising when the men returned or new men signed on. On the galleon *San Felipe,* one of the two largest built by Arana, twenty-eight gunners began the 1634 trip to the Indies, and thirty-three gunners returned about fifteen months later. In the interval, one of the original gunners jumped ship in Cartagena de Indias, four died in hospital, four others fled, two spent time in hospital and returned, and five transferred to other ships. Ten of the original twenty-eight served the full voyage without incident, and new men signed on to replace those who had left.[135]

Although sailors and gunners were expected to participate in battle, the infantry formed the specialized fighting arm on a galleon. In general, each galleon carried an infantry company of 100 men or more, with its own officers. This was much smaller than a typical land-based company which could have 200–250 men.[136] As long as the voyage lasted, infantry units fell under the jurisdiction of the captain-general of the fleet and the sea captain of the ship that carried them. Ideally, however, infantry units received all orders from their own officers, beginning with the infantry captain who had embarked with them. Cordial, or at least correct, relations between the sea captain and the infantry captain could smooth many potential conflicts on board; an open clash between the two captains could be disastrous.

From the late sixteenth century, an infantry regiment existed especially to serve on the Armada de la Guardia, with its own officers and troop spirit. Although it was more efficient than organizing the infantry afresh for every fleet, the existence of this regiment probably emphasized the separateness of land and sea forces and their mutual antagonism. The debate over joint capitanes de mar y guerra at least addressed this problem, even if it did not solve it. In 1634 the galleon regiment was disbanded and incorporated into the garrison at Cádiz, losing its separate identity. Authors have noted that the old soldiers of the disbanded regiment drifted away.[137] This may be viewed as a setback for military organization, but it can also be viewed as a victory for the principle of joint command over sea and land forces on board. Without their own leaders, the infantry companies embarked could more easily take orders from an unfamiliar capitán de mar y guerra. Even so, the land forces had little to do during the voyage, unless enemy action loomed. They tended to fall into the habits of passengers rather than workers, viewing the sailors as hired help and lounging around the deck getting in the way. Some authors argue that their very presence posed a danger to ship discipline, and that soldiers often took justice into their own hands, to assure that they got their full rations of food and drink.[138]

One can assume that the sailors returned the soldiers' contempt in full measure, relying on their knowledge of the ship to gain an advantage. The massive yard of the mizzen mast on the afterdeck was supposedly called the "matasoldados," for its tendency to sweep unwary loungers from its path as the ship changed directions. Men of generous spirit on both sides of the gap between the two cultures surely accepted one another's presence with grace, cooperating effectively for the good of the ship. But in the cramped conditions of a voyage that took several months, only the enforced discipline of the command structure kept minor irritations from becoming full-scale battles.

An officer called the governor (*gobernador*) headed all the infantry companies in a fleet, subordinate to the captain-general and the admiral but occupying first place among the officers of the infantry regiment, or combined companies, of the fleet. The governor had third choice of the ships in the fleet, with his chosen vessel receiving the designation of *gobierno,* next in importance after the capitana and the almiranta.[139] For the 1629 fleet, the king chose as governor don Cristóbal Mexía de Bocanegra, a man with thirty years' continuous service in Flanders, France, Spain, and the carrera de las Indias. He had served previously as governor in an Indies fleet under Captain-General Tomás de Larráspuru.[140] On the 1629 voyage, he would sail in one of the eight "galcones de la plata," serving as its capitán de mar y guerra as well as infantry governor of the fleet. The king chose the other seven capitanes de mar y guerra from a separate list of nominations.

Whoever commanded the infantry on a given ship—their own captain or a capitán de mar y guerra—had general responsibility for their discipline and their welfare, making sure they had sufficient provisions, arms, and supplies to do their job. During battle, he stationed his men around the ship, with the best ones in the prow, camouflaged by bunting. Other groups had battle stations in the waist, the aft castle, and the poop, each with its own squadron leader (*cabo*). If there were enough men, one-third might be kept in reserve to replace the dead and wounded. With an enemy ship alongside, the soldiers would be arranged in two ranks, one firing from the side of the ship while the other retreated to reload. Half those firing at any given time were to aim at the rigging of the enemy vessel and the other half at the gunports. Two men would be sent below to help with the artillery, and another two would supervise a detail of soldiers at the powder magazine (*pañol de pólvora*), filling flasks and cartridges and delivering them to the mouth of the hatch for whoever needed them. They would also fill containers with salt water to put out burning fuses and soak old capes in water to extinguish fires. If possible, the captain would order sand thrown around the deck, so that grenades and combustible balls heaved by the enemy would not explode. To prepare for boarding an enemy ship, the captain would name an assault group, one-third with harquebuses, one-third with lances (*chuzos*), and one-third with sword and shield.[141]

An alférez (lieutenant) served as second in command of the infantry, with special responsibility for assigning space on board for the soldiers' belongings and for keeping order among them. On land, the lieutenant's main responsibility was to protect and display the company flag, especially during battle, defending it with his life.[142] At sea, the flag was generally stored out of sight, and one expert urged that it remain so, even during battle, presumably because it served no useful purpose during a naval battle.[143] Like other officials, the lieutenant had to have underwriters subscribe to a bond guaranteeing the proper performance of his duty.[144] As the "father and protector" of the soldiers, he settled small disputes and supervised the distribution of the harquebuses, muskets, and other weapons carried on the galleon. All weapons formed part of the ship's supplies, under the control of the master, and had to be signed out from him. Only the biggest and best men received muskets; their large size and caliber made them "the most furious arm invented [and the one that] most offends the enemy."[145] The soldiers were charged a bond for the arms, to ensure they would be returned. In addition to the normal powder ration, recruits received half a month's extra ration so they could practice. Every afternoon, or at other convenient intervals, the lieutenant ordered the infantry guard on duty to fire their guns, as a check on the competence of both men and weapons.

A sergeant (*sargento*) cared for the physical well-being of the soldiers, seeing that each received a fair ration of undamaged provisions by stationing an observer at the opening of the hatchway when the day's rations were weighed. On land, the sergeant made sure that proper supplies were bought and loaded on board, pressing the master in his duties, if need be. On land or sea, the sergeant accompanied the master, the notary, and the ship's cooper during the opening of any pipe of wine, checking the amount of waste, which was then recorded against the master's account. When a soldier fell ill, the sergeant had responsibility for putting him in hospital, if on land, or for asking the surgeon and chaplain to visit him, if on board ship. He arranged for those in danger of dying to make a will and receive the sacraments, and inventoried the goods of any man who died. Thereafter he saw to the disposition of the dead man's belongings, with the knowledge of his captain, the lieutenant, and the chaplain.

The sergeant's most important military responsibility involved assigning soldiers as guards, in four-hour shifts. During the daytime, one should stay with the company flag (evidently on the poop), one at the door of the captain's chamber, one at the gangway (if the ship was in port), and one at the cooking fire. At night the sergeant substituted a guard on the forecastle for the one at the cooking fire, and added another guard on the poop near the mizzen to tend the lantern. From time to time he was to visit his men on duty, urging them to vigilance and care. At other times, having assigned the guard, he would station himself midships aft of the mainmast—the "plaza de armas"—with sword in hand, instructing the recruits.

An infantry company on a galleon had several squadrons within it, each one with about twenty-five men and a squadron leader (*cabo de escuadra*). Ideally each cabo would know the names and personal histories of all his men and would inspect their weapons to see they were cleaned and ready to use. He would personally post his men at their duty stations, removing the guard from the cooking fire at night once he was sure it was out. Most important, the squadron leader should treat all his mean equally, neither exempting nor favoring anyone through affection or familial ties, because that would prevent him from learning the discipline needed to make him a good soldier.

The common soldiers, who had to be at least eighteen years old to sign up, had mainly to obey orders given them without question or deviation. On guard, a soldier watched for enemy ships, just as a sailor watched for changes in the wind and sea, notifying the pilot and his superior officers if he saw any evidence of the enemy. Above all, he must remain awake on guard, marching back and forth at his post, and not sitting down, "because it gives occasion to sleep, which is the worst crime that can be committed in the military, punishable by death."[146] Completing the infantry roster, each company generally had a fife player (*pífano*) and two drummers (*tambores*), to inspire the men during battle and attend at ceremonial occasions. On land, they arose at the break of day and awakened the company with their instruments. At sea they accompanied the sergeant and played as the afternoon guards were placed at their posts.

Infantry books similar to the ones for mariners kept track of the men in each company and the wages due to each one.[147] Although this study did not involve any systematic examination of the muster books, the ones analyzed in detail seem to show considerably more instability among the infantry companies than among the mariners. In one company of more than two hundred men in 1634–35, only 24 percent served the whole term in the same company, with no interruptions. Sickness and other excused absences kept another 28 percent off the rolls at one time or another, 8 percent died, 19 percent went to serve on other ships, and 2 percent joined the ship in the Indies from other infantry companies. Of the remainder who left the company, 4 percent remained in known locations in the Indies, and 15 percent simply disappeared, whereabouts unknown.[148] The movement to other ships was not typical; in this case it was a planned transfer of men to a dispatch boat upon arrival in the Indies. The 15 percent who disappeared are more interesting.

Desertions among the soldiery presented a problem for Spanish authorities. Many men who had been denied legal immigration licenses to the Indies simply sailed across the Atlantic as soldiers, then deserted at the first opportunity. This "clandestine immigration," as the Chaunus call it, often required the collusion of infantry officers on board, who collected a fee for their compliance.[149] One author remarked that poor men in the Indies might sign on as soldiers for the return voyage, though they had never fired a gun in their lives, bribing the lieutenant or the sergeant with part of their promised pay for taking them on.[150] It is difficult to know how widespread this abuse might have been. The author gives no citation, and in the few lists analyzed for this study, no new recruits joined the ship in the Indies. Illegal migrants in either direction would not have affected the efficiency of the ship, unless they knew nothing about their jobs. Those who were neither sailors nor soldiers would probably have been safer trying to hide their ignorance as soldiers. A brave man with a quick wit might be able to masquerade as a soldier long enough to become one. A seaman or apprentice who knew nothing of the sea would have less hope of escaping detection and might very well fall to his death the first time he was ordered aloft.

The scale of wages earned by the mariners and infantrymen on Spanish ships generally ran parallel to the hierarchy of command, based on experience and the level of responsibility of the post. (See appendix C, tables 10, 11, and 12.) In 1634–35, the captain-general on the galleons of the Armada de la Guardia probably earned some 5,500 reales per month; his admiral probably earned about half that. The captain-general and admiral of a merchant fleet earned somewhat less. Capitanes de mar y guerra on individual galleons collected a salary only 1.8 times higher than each separate captain earned—a saving for the crown as well as an increase in the efficiency of the command. Only one master served on each of the galleons built by don Martín de Arana during their voyages in the Armada de la Guardia, combining the functions of master and master of rations. According to the crew books, however, each master collected only one salary, unlike the increase enjoyed by the capitán de mar y guerra for holding a joint post. In the crew books I examined, the pilot earned about the same as the master, but salaries could vary. Indies pilots might be paid by the voyage, for example, and a 350 ducado salary would work out to 256.7 reales a month for a 15-month voyage, or 220 reales for a 17.5 month voyage.[151] This encouraged the pilot to chart the most direct route. Chief pilots might make 1.5 or two times as much as an ordinary pilot. A master's wages were about 5.7 times higher in 1634–35 than in the time of Columbus (around 1500), and an ordinary pilot's wages were about 4.9 times higher. If we can trust Olesa Muñido's figures for the mid-sixteenth century, that meant an average rise of about 3.5 percent a year for the entire period.[152]

The contramaestre enjoyed slightly more than a threefold increase in wages in the same period, which suggests a widening gap among officers in salary as well as status. Somewhat surprisingly, the diver in the Armada de la Guardia earned as much as the contramaestre in 1634–35, yet this does not upset the generally hierarchical order of importance and rewards on armada ships. The discomfort and danger of the work, as well as the skill and courage required to perform it, raised the diver's worth to equal importance with the contramaestre, although he was no higher than an ordinary seaman in the nautical chain of command. The guardian (assistant to the contramaestre) and the master gunner earned the same salary for parallel supervisory functions. Below them were the minor administrative and artisanal offices, including the gunners, all earning the same wage and each responsible for specialized tasks, though not for command functions. The medical officer occupied a somewhat anomalous position, earning only slightly more than common seamen, yet clearly set apart from them in status as well as function.

Common seamen in 1634–35 earned a base salary roughly 1.5 times higher than that of apprentices and double that of pages, the same proportions that existed in the sixteenth century. Particularly good sailors and those with navigational skills often earned a supplement (*ventaja*) on their pay.[153] Unlike the officers, however, ordinary seaman earned wages that were only twice as high in 1634–35 as they had been in about 1500. The hierarchy of command had widened the gap between officers and men in the course of the sixteenth century, a gap that expressed itself in the wage scale as well as in the generally low status of common seaman. Whether they had enjoyed higher relative status in the days when their wages compared more favorably to those of their superiors is an open question. It is possible, however, that the increasingly sophisticated needs of the Spanish fleets, as well as the availability of sailors for most of the sixteenth century, influenced changes in the hierarchy of wages and importance among the mariners. Officers' wages rose about as fast as inflation, in recognition of the skills needed to command; sailors' wages kept pace through the middle third of the century.[154] Then in the late sixteenth and seventeenth centuries, the government relied on coercion and poverty rather than wage inducements to produce men for armadas.[155] By the seventeenth century, the depressed wages of sailors exacerbated the problem of finding crews for the transatlantic run. Overall, to estimate the costs of running a ship in the Armada de la Guardia, royal officials assumed an average of 6 ducados (66 reales) per month for each man among the mariners.[156] The common seamen, apprentices, and pages at the lower end of the wage hierarchy bore the brunt of keeping the costs of imperial defense as low as possible.

Wages of the infantrymen showed a similar pattern, and royal officials also used an average of 6 ducados (66 reales) per man per month to estimate their wage costs. (See appendix C, table 13.)[157] Status and importance governed the wage hierarchy among the infantrymen also. A *maestre de campo* was often appointed to form a new regiment, but captains-general ordinarily held supreme command over them in battle. The governor of the regiment in 1634–35 served as head of all the infantry on the fleet as well as capitán de mar y guerra on the gobierno. He earned only somewhat more than an ordinary capitán de mar y guerra, however, though twice as much as an infantry captain alone. The wages for simple infantry captains declined sharply from 1578 to 1634–35, judging from the examples presented here, a phenomenon that may reflect the increasing importance of capitanes de mar y guerra and the subsequent displacement of simple captains.[158] The sergeant, with his primarily administrative role, earned the same pay as an ordinary squadron leader, and less than a squadron leader on the capitana.

Soldiers receiving supplements on their pay for superior skill and experience (*soldados aventajados*) could receive more than 1.5 times as much pay as recruits. Sometimes the weapons they handled served to distinguish among their levels of skill. Those assigned muskets (*mosqueteros*) generally earned more than those assigned harquebuses (*arcabuceros*).[159] The fife and drum players earned as much as the highest paid soldier, presumably because of their role in animating the troops and the danger they faced in battle, but the standard bearer (*abanderado*) earned no more than an ordinary soldier.

The average wages of all types of soldiers were higher than those of the various types of sailors. A full ration did not come with their pay, however. Each soldier had to pay for rations, gunpowder, fuse, and medical care from his salary, a deduction that amounted to 28 reales a month, according to one author, though this may have been only an average figure.[160] Thus, the total of wages and benefits rewarded common seamen more than all but the most skilled soldiers. Although this did nothing to support the soldiers' opinion that they were superior to the sailors, it was logical and just. The sailors bore most of the burden for handling the ship during the voyage. The soldiers, during a lucky and uneventful Atlantic crossing, were little more than passengers.

The bureaucratic and military hierarchy described here provided order and continuity in the floating republics that were the Atlantic fleets. This was important at any time, but even more so during the critical decades of the 1620s and 1630s. In more human terms, the standard of correct behavior that hierarchy enforced helped to mitigate the often difficult conditions of life at sea.

SEVEN
Shipboard Life

The limited space on any ship, especially those crossing the Atlantic, required that human beings on board be distributed and stowed as efficiently as the cargo. Since ships in the carrera de las Indias varied so much in size and appointments, it is difficult to generalize about how the internal space was used, but we have some specific information for warships—galleons such as the ones built by Martín de Arana. The hold, called the *bodega* in Spanish, carried ballast of rocks or sand immediately above the reinforcing timber of the keel and below the floor. The heaviest barrels of provisions that would be least damaged by water occupied the lowest parts of the hold and served as additional ballast. The lower deck, or *primera cubierta,* which the 1618 regulations specified to be 8.5 codos (about 15.6 feet) above the floor, marked the upper limits of the hold. The upper deck, called the puente (bridge) or the *cubierta alta,* was about 3 codos (5.5 feet) above the lower deck.[1] It was on these two decks, and the superstructures erected on the upper deck fore and aft, that the human cargo of the ship found their lodgings.

The sea captain lodged in the main cabin, so-called, on the aft end of the upper deck, sharing it with the infantry captains on board and having as much space to himself as each one of them had. In other words, a capitán de mar y guerra, filling the dual role, could have the whole cabin to himself. A sea captain sailing with, for example, two companies of infantry, would have only one-third the cabin to himself. Besides personal belongings, the cabin would hold various ship's supplies, most notably a box of hatchets for use in battle, which ordinarily remained beneath the sea captain's bed. The master on a merchant ship had lodgings in the so-called *camarote* above the main cabin, but on a warship he lodged at what one author calls the opening of the "astilla," which would seem to mean near the entrance to the hold on the first deck. The pilot on a warship occupied the camarote, sharing it with his assistant, if he had one.[2]

Few of the minor officers enjoyed defined places to lodge themselves and their belongings. Presumably they simply slept among the mariners. It was their duty stations that were defined clearly; for example, the contramaestre at the foot of the mainmast and the guardian on the prow castle, listening for orders from the captain and the pilot and relaying them to the crew.[3] The master gunner lodged in the Rancho de Santa Barbara, which held artillery supplies, located on the lower deck between the mizzenmast and the poop. The gunners lodged with him. Unlike the rest of the lower deck on a warship, the Rancho was closed off with planking, so that no one could enter the area or sleep there without the master gunner's permission. The chaplain had a privileged position, far above the wages paid to him, lodging under the covered part of the upper deck called the quarterdeck (alcázar), between the mainmast and the main cabin. Alternatively, he might lodge in the Rancho de Santa Barbara with the gunners, or with the soldiers if he was an infantry chaplain. The surgeon lodged near his boxes of medicines, which ordinarily were close to the opening of the hatch on the lower deck.[4]

Seamen lodged in the forward parts of the quarterdeck, if the ship had one, or on the lower deck from the mainmast to the poop, wherever they could find space. Apprentice seamen lodged between the seamen and the prow castle, and pages presumably had what was left over, usually on the deck.[5] In such close quarters, custom and regulations avoided disputes over space allocation. As mentioned above, all the captains of sea and infantry shared the main cabin, unless, of course, a general or admiral came on board, outranking them. Then the captains of whatever stripe had to find lodging under the quarterdeck. If a capitán de mar y guerra commanded the ship, his infantry company lodged on the port side of the lower deck, near the locker for the ship's flags and banners. If another company sailed on the same galleon, it had to lodge on the starboard side, even if its captain had seniority over the capitán de mar y guerra. Don Fadrique de Toledo y Osorio evidently established this order of preference to settle conflicts when he commanded the squadron of Cantabria after 1607.[6]

After nightfall, the captain traditionally ordered his men to go below decks to turn in, except those on watch, although grown men did not always react well to being ordered to bed like children. On a voyage to Puerto Rico in 1619, the capitán de mar y guerra Alonso de Contreras found his order to go below challenged before he even left port, an ill omen for the rest of the voyage. To deal with the problem, he first co-opted the natural leader of the undisciplined recruits as his sergeant. Then the next night, when his order to go below again met resistance, he took his sword and laid open the head of one of the bravest men in the company. Having learned the meaning of military discipline, all the other men "in a moment were in their rancho, like so many sheep."[7]

On merchant ships of the carrera, an average of 17 to 20 paying passengers might buy space in private or shared cabins or in general open areas on the ship. Cabins could be above decks or in two levels of rentable space below decks, some near the mainmast, others near the poop, depending on the ship. Documentary evidence suggests that the order of preference on a typical ship was first, port and starboard cabins immediately below the poop; next, the main cabin, always on the starboard side above the poop; then cabins amidships; and finally, lower-level cabins in the stern.[8] The size of the cabins could vary considerably, from less than 5 feet square on up, although they would usually have a standard height of 5.5 to 5.75 feet—roughly the 3 codos separating the decks. Passengers went through various formalities and preparations in Seville, with its bustling port activities and exotic merchandise from around the world hinting at the excitement of the voyage to come. The opening scene of Lope de Vega's "El arenal de Sevilla" captures some of the flavor that Seville must have had in the sixteenth and early seventeenth centuries.

> The most praiseworthy thing,
> is to see leaving from these ships
> of so many nations,
> the things they unload,
> their comings and goings,
> and their return later
> with as many other things as they embarked.
> For knives, mercery, and Rouen cloth,
> the Frenchman carries away oil.
> The German brings linen, fustian, and *llantes;*
> He loads wine from Alanis.
> The Vizcayan brings iron, wood, girders, ordnance, pine,
> The New World colonist brings ambergris, pearls, gold, silver,
> Campeche wood, hides.
> Everything in this port means money.[9]

The romance must have begun to fade even before the voyage began, however. Because of silting of the Guadalquivir, many passengers had to travel from Seville to Sanlúcar or Cádiz to embark, either by small boat or barge, or by wagon, a trip that could take four or five days.[10] While the fleet made final preparations, the nervous traveler had ample time to reconsider his plans, or at least to make a will. Royal officials traveling to the Indies to take up new assignments for the crown could not afford second thoughts, but for many of them, the mere notion of a sea journey was alien. Although our primary concern is with the royal ships of the Armada de la Guardia, it is worth looking at the experiences of some of these reluctant mariners, because they remind us that most Spaniards had no direct knowledge of the sea, even though they were part of the first great global empire. Their perception of life on board ship drives home this point very clearly and, not incidentally, provides us with some of the only information we have about the day-to-day routine in the carrera de las Indias.

Eugenio de Salazar wrote one of the most famous reports of an Indies voyage, and also one of the funniest. Born in Madrid in about 1530, this well-educated royal official served in a wide variety of judicial, fiscal, and administrative posts in his long career, finishing as an auditor (*oidor*) of the Council of the Indies in the early seventeenth century. His literary talents found expression in verse as well as prose, but it is his hilarious burlesque of life at sea that preserves his fame. Setting out with his wife and two children to take up a post in Santo Domingo (Española) in 1573, he wrote his classic landlubber's lament for the entertainment of a friend back home. Because Salazar's letter is one of the only pieces of evidence we have about shipboard life on the

Indies run, and because it is so well written, many modern writers have borrowed heavily from him. Unfortunately, not all of them keep in mind the purpose of the letter, taking Salazar too seriously on some points and not seriously enough on others. As a talented writer, he deliberately exaggerated some of the unpleasant parts of the trip for comic effect, but at the same time his well-trained mind found endless fascination in observing and analyzing the strange floating world in which he found himself. For all his exaggeration, Salazar clearly admired the men who sailed Spain's imperial fleets. When he wrote about the working life of the crews and the intricacies of sailing an Atlantic ship, he demonstrated that he was an admiring as well as intelligent observer, much more aware of the complexities involved in seafaring than most other passengers who sailed to the Indies.[11]

To Salazar, the ship and its crew were no less strange than they would be to us, who view them from a distance of several centuries. His whole tone was that of the observer of a foreign culture, trying to understand it by analogy to more familiar surroundings. The ship itself he likened to a city, with its central plaza in the waist, its fountain the pump that sucked up the foul waters from the bilge, "steaming like hell and stinking like the devil."[12] The hold beneath the hatches served as lodgings in this strange town, and most of the inhabitants lived underground in smelly, cramped quarters, while above ground there were strange trees bearing even stranger fruit. The double meaning of the word *arboles* as both trees and masts is typical of Salazar's rich use of language. At night the guiding light of the city was enclosed with the compass in the binnacle, a box Salazar likened to the container for a gentleman's chamber pot. He defined the municipal officials of this floating city—the captain and crew—with only a few touches of humor, neatly capturing the essence of each job. The householders, however, represented by his fellow passengers, he dismissed as unfriendly and no more charitable than bijagos—particularly mean and voracious fish.[13]

Their ill humor is not difficult to understand. From the moment they came on board, these land-bound Spaniards found themselves stuffed into cramped and airless cabins and afflicted by one of the worst possible introductions to life at sea—seasickness. According to Fernández Duro, it was a "tribute that very few of those who sail for the first time fail to pay to the sea, and which others continue to pay, though they sail repeatedly."[14] Even birds got sick, though they were used to balancing on moving tree branches. The physician Luis Llobera de Ávila, who accompanied Charles I on many of his travels, wrote a treatise on seasickness, unwillingly researched in his own violent experience with the malady. "A person calmly looking at the beauty of the view and vaguely noticing the unfamiliar motion of the ship can suddenly be attacked by an ill-feeling he cannot define, turning him sickly pale, with a bitter taste in his mouth, an agitated pulse, thumping temples, weak legs, and a variety of other alarming symptoms. Often, forgetting all considerations and appearances, including those of decency, he falls to the ground as if he were going to expire."[15] Or, as Salazar described it,

> The force of the sea did such violence to our stomachs and heads, that, parents and children, old and young, we turned the color of corpses, and we commenced to give up our souls (for that is the meaning of being seasick—*almadiar*) [a play on words], and to say "baac, baac," and after that "bor, bor, bor, bor," together spewing from our mouths all that had entered therein that day and the preceding

one, in their turn some cold and sticky phlegm; others burning and bitter choler, and some, earthy and heavy black bile. In this manner we continued without seeing sun nor moon, nor did we open our eyes, nor change our clothing from when we entered the cabin, nor even move, until the third day at sea.[16]

Anyone who has ever been seasick can recognize the accuracy of these descriptions and the very real discomfort they represent. Everyone had a favorite remedy, most of them wisely based on eating little in the days before embarking and simply letting the affliction run its course. Escalante de Mendoza advised staying upright on the deck, looking at the sea, rather than going below to lie down, and, once the stomach was cleaned out and the worst past, building up one's strength with stewed chicken and strong chicken broth.[17] But, ultimately, as Spanish mariners knew, the only sure remedy was the shade of a mud brick wall—in other words, a return to land, which many of the passengers must have longed for before their voyage had even begun.[18]

The wealthy gentleman described in Mateo Alemán's picaresque novel, *Guzmán de Alfarache,* embodied the ideal life on board ship, with servants to attend his every need, a fluffy wool mattress for his bed, and storage boxes so clean that there was not anywhere in them—nor, presumably, on him—a flea or any other vermin.[19] The reality can rarely, if ever, have been like that. On galleys in the Mediterranean and galleons in the Atlantic, no one could escape vermin. They thrived in the warm climates of the Mediterranean and the Caribbean, feeding off the captive humans on board ships. As one observer noted of Mediterranean voyages,

> It is a privilege of the galley that all the fleas that jump on the planks, and all the lice that grow in the seams, and all the bedbugs that are in the crevices, be common to all, and be distributed among all, and be maintained by all; and if anyone appeals from this privilege, presuming himself to be very clean and neat, from then on I prophesy that if he put his hand to his neck, and down his back, he will find more lice in his doublet than he has coins in his purse.[20]

Fleas seem to have been most common when there were cattle or women aboard, probably because they preferred to reside in the warm hides of the cattle or the voluminous skirts of women passengers. Lice and bedbugs seem to have been less discriminating. They got into the stuffing of mattresses and the seams of clothing, and the only way to get rid of them was to submerge—not a very practical remedy.[21] Interestingly enough, it is possible that galley oarsmen were less bothered by personal vermin than crews and passengers on the Indies run, because they generally wore little clothing and put in to shore often enough to wash it as regularly as once a week.[22] Passengers on the Indies run could do little about personal vermin except complain. Sanitary facilities were minimal, but even if the cabins had been scrubbed daily, flea and louse infestations are not that easy to eradicate. Better personal hygiene might have helped, but even that is debatable, given the cramped lodgings on board.

Another indignity was the lack of proper toilet facilities. Columbus's ships had seats humorously named *jardines* (gardens) hanging over the rails fore and aft, but male as well as female passengers on later voyages were generally too modest or fearful to use such an arrangement. Instead, so we are told, they settled for slop pails or the bilge.[23] If the latter is true, it undoubtedly contributed to the unpleasantness of the bilgewater on passenger ships. The bilge was the space beneath the floor of the hold that eventually collected all the loose liquid on the ship, including seepage from the ocean. Ships' bilges always smelled bad, because of a lack of ventilation and the variety of their contents. In warm climates, they could become so mephitic as to be actually poisonous. Many witnesses reported that sailors who opened the hatchway to the bilge passed out instantly, pitching forward to a hideous death. Other reports, particularly in extremely hot weather, mention the difficulty of pumping out the bilgewater; even diluted with sea water, it made the crew sick as it rose up the pump shaft into the air. Some fumes could turn all the metal fittings on the ship black, even those that were not directly exposed to the air.[24]

Compared to personal vermin and the quality of sanitary facilities, other pests on board might seem mere nuisances, but many of them could be quite dangerous. Scorpions and centipedes came aboard with loads of wood in the tropics. Although they preferred to hunt insects on board, they also stung unwary humans who came their way, especially sailors going barefoot, as many of them did. Much more important were cockroaches and rodents, however. Both could bite humans from time to time, but their real danger was the damage they did to provisions and supplies. Like everything else, this was worst in the tropics. Stories presumably dating from the late eighteenth century tell of powder magazines blowing up in Havana because roaches had eaten through the wax and tallow on cartridges stored there, setting off the fulminate of mercury.[25] Everyone agrees that mice and rats were good sailors, often coming aboard a vessel in the shipyards before it was even finished. Salazar calls rats the big-game animals on ships, noting that they behaved like the dangerous wild boar when cornered, turning to attack their pursuers.[26]

For the most part, rats caused more nuisance than real harm, though cables and sails had continually to be protected from their gnawing teeth. On some voyages, however, serious rat infestations threatened the very lives of the people on board. The most famous was the disaster-prone Indies fleet returning in 1622, which suffered hurricanes in the Caribbean as well as a rodent plague. More than one thousand rats were killed on one ship while it was still in Havana; once at sea, the crew discovered that there were several thousand more, and that they had eaten tons of food and ruined much of the fresh water. They gnawed through jars, sacks, boxes, stoppers, and casks. They fell into barrels of fresh water and drowned. They invaded the chicken coops, killing the helpless fowl and eating them. Crew and passengers eventually destroyed more than three thousand more rats before they got home, some of which served as food for those more hungry than squeamish. Only a fortuitous rainfall and their arrival in the Azores saved the passengers from real starvation.[27]

The mariners shared the discomforts of the passengers, and in most cases fared worse. Nonetheless, to them the sea was not an alien environment, although it was often a hostile one. The very elements of the universe, as defined by seventeenth-century minds—earth, wind, fire, and water—worked against them, since each one could endanger their ship and their lives.[28] It is no wonder that many of the popular sayings of Spanish mariners contain a strong sense of human frailty and impotence in the face of the

arbitrary power of the sea. "Against fortune there is no skill that can
compete," they might observe in the aftermath of a storm.[29] Or "Against
adversities and inclement weather, one's only shield is patience."[30] And, of
course, there were dozens of variations on the theme that "he who goes to
sea learns how to pray."[31] That seems odd at first, because many contemporaries viewed sailors as notorious swearers, blasphemers, and undisciplined
louts, known for their irreligion and lack of respect. In the late sixteenth
century, Philip II ruled that everyone had to confess and take communion
before setting sail. Official fleet regulations called on the captain-general to
enforce rules against offenses to God such as swearing. Although the rules
were observed on some fleets, on others the sailors' ordinary language had
nothing but "blasphemies and oaths that they themselves don't understand."[32] Yet, in real adversity, even the most impious sailors "learned to
pray," when they had no other options.

Most of the time, however, their fate was at least partly in human hands,
and they knew it. Mooring the ship securely guarded investments as well as
lives.[33] The captain who overloaded his ship was lost.[34] Real mariners had
nothing but contempt for the fairweather sailors who pretended to be
experts, then collapsed in a crisis, or who claimed superior skills to a pilot
who had the misfortune to lose his ship. "In good weather, there is no lack of
pilots," the saying went, or, regarding the clarity of hindsight, "When the
ship is lost, all are pilots."[35] Anyone could sail under ideal conditions.
"With friendly waves and a following breeze, Sancho Panza could master
the seas"[36]—but the real sailor's skills proved themselves in adversity.

The mariners knew that only they could control the ship, and that the
soldiers on warships and the passengers on merchant ships were like so much
cargo, if not active nuisances. To the passengers, as well as the soldiers,
sailors were a different breed of human being, alien and largely incomprehensible. It must have been particularly galling to some of the aristocratic
passengers to realize that their fate rested in such coarse hands. Cervantes
called them "heathen and inurbane persons, who know no other language
than that used on the ships; in good weather they are diligent; in squalls,
they are lazy; and in real tempests, many give orders and few obey them;
their God is their sea-chest and their lodging place, and their favorite amuse-
ment is to watch the passengers being seasick."[37] Yet a more sensitive
observer such as Salazar learned to appreciate both the disciplined skills and
the hard work of the sailors, as well as the necessarily specialized language
and traditions on board. He wrote wryly that, although the pilot was really
just the lieutenant of the real commander—the wind—

> I have not seen a gentleman as well served nor have I seen knaves who serve as
> well and so well merit their wages as these sailors. Because if the pilot says, "Hey,
> you at the prow," you will see them instantly come running to him like so many
> conjured demons; and their eyes are fixed on him and their mouths hang open
> awaiting his commands, and he, with great authority, orders them to [do a dozen
> different and complicated tasks]. And when the pilot has provided these orders, it
> is something to see the diligence and quickness of the sailors in carrying them out,
> because instantly you will see some on the crossbeam of the topsail; others,
> climbing by the ratlines on the shrouds; other gentlemen on the spars, others
> clinging to the masthead; others with the topmasts; others clamped on and
> holding the step of the mast to its cap; others grasping the sheets, hauling and

tallying the sail; and others clambering and chasing from one place to another by the rigging, some high and others low, so that they seem to be cats chasing through the trees or spirits of those who fell from heaven and remained in the air.[38]

Salazar's obvious fascination with this performance and with the rich and precise nautical vocabulary sets him apart from most other observers of the mariners' skills and their world.

The varied and extremely heavy work involved in handling the sails and rigging required all possible coordination among the sailors. For this reason, Spanish crews, like all other seafarers we know about, used rhythmic chants as they heaved and hauled on the rigging, pushed the capstan bars raising the anchor, and did dozens of other jobs. Each sort of task had its own rhythm, relating the force of the men to the resistance of the material. One was a steady marching beat, used to coordinate the footsteps of sailors walking around and around the capstan or the length of the deck to haul up anchors and do other similar tasks. Another was a regular and slower rhythm for tasks that involved standing in one place and hauling on lines hand over hand. A third sort called for a two-part rhythm, coordinating preparation time and action time, for heavy jobs that required standing in one place and hauling with both arms at once, then getting into position for the next pull. This last would have been used for raising heavy sails and their yards. *Salomar* meant to sing or chant these various rhythms, and most often the contramaestre, the guardian, or an old sailor set the rhythm, either making up words as he went along or chanting what he had heard all his life. The sailors answered in chorus, or kept silent, according to the situation. We know that the ship on which Salazar and his family sailed used these chants, because he transcribed one with a two-part rhythm, which seems to have been in a mixture of several dialects.[39] On warships the contramaestre's whistle supposedly replaced the familiar and traditional chanting, but there is no question that the sailors preferred the human voice to a whistle.[40] With work so hard that "the devil himself would not be a sailor," the men needed all the human encouragement they could get.[41]

An ordinary day at sea had its own steady rhythm, punctuated by changes in the watch and prayers chanted by the pages as they turned the watchglass. None of the contemporary documents discusses the divisions of the watch in detail. Most scholars have assumed there were three watches, each presided over by one of the first three officers of the ship: four to midnight, the captain's watch; midnight to eight in the morning, the pilot's watch; and eight to four, the master's watch. In midocean, the contramaestre might sometimes stand in for the captain, and the guardian for the pilot, but on most voyages the pilot and his assistant were in charge of the night watch throughout the voyage.[42] Nearly all the mariners on board had two four-hour watches each day, although Morison thinks that the afternoon watch was split into two-hour segments so that the midnight to four shift would rotate among the crew.[43] The day began with a page chanting the morning prayer: "Blessed be the light, and the Holy True Cross; and the Lord of Truth, and the Holy Trinity; Blessed be the soul, and the Lord who rules it for us; Blessed be the day, and the Lord who sends it to us."[44] Then the page said a "Pater Noster" and an "Ave Maria," followed by the morning prayer: "Amen. God give us good days, good voyage, good passage to the ship, sir captain and master and good company, amen; So let there be, let there be a good voyage; may God grant many good days to your graces, gentlemen, from poop to prow."[45] Hearing these words of God for the first time in what he had thought was a house of the devil, Eugenio de Salazar felt some comfort.

At each half-hour turning of the watchglass, the page on duty called out a verse, with words specific to each of the eight turnings in the four-hour shift. At the first turning, he would say, "Good is what's past, and better what comes; one glass is past and the second is filling; more will be filled if God be willing; to keep the right time makes the voyage fine."[46] Fernández Duro provides an interesting variation of ritual, and mentions that the page first turned the glass, then sounded the hour with the bell of the watchglass, before running toward the prow to recite his verse: "One glass is past, and the second is filling; more will be filled if God be willing; to God we ask that we make a good voyage; and we ask the Mother of God, our advocate, to free us from waterspouts and storms."[47] At the end of the verse, the page would shout, "Hey, you at the prow, be alert and guard well," to see if the watchmen were awake. They would prove they were by shouting back a response, and perhaps someone would order the page to say a Pater Noster or some other prayer.[48]

When the watch changed after the eighth glass ran out, the page called the next watch to duty. At midnight, when the pilot's watch began, he would say, "To your watch, to your watch, sir mariners on duty; to your watch, to your watch, at the right time for sir pilot's guard, for the hour is here; arise, arise, arise."[49]

At nightfall after the evening meal, those on board heard the Buenas Noches of the page bringing light to the compass box for the night: "Amen, and God give us good night; good voyage, good passage for the ship, sir captain and master and good company."[50] Then two pages recited the evening prayers: Pater Noster, Ave Maria, Credo, and Salve Regina. Once finished, the pages on duty went to care for the watchglass, which presumably had been running as usual while the prayers were being said, and recited the nightly blessing:

> Blessed be the hour God came to earth,
> Holy Mary who gave him birth,
> And Saint John who saw his worth.
> The guard is posted,
> The watchglass filling,
> We'll have a good voyage,
> If God be willing.[51]

Clearly, daily ritual and religion played an important part in the life of the ship, however casually the crew might have treated it. Religious ceremony also provided welcome breaks in the daily routine. Every Saturday night on the ship that carried Eugenio de Salazar and his family to the Indies, the master called all on board together and led longer services that replaced the regular nightly prayer. "Are we all here?" he would ask. "God be with us," the company would respond. Then all joined together in singing the Salve Regina. As Salazar described it,

In our song we did not proceed by thirds, fifths, or octaves, but by singing at the same time all eight tones and many other half and quarter-tones. That is because the mariners are friends of division and divide the four winds into thirty-two, so they also divide the eight tones of music into another thirty-two diverse, perverse, resonant, and very dissonant ones. The result is that we made this chanting of the "Salve" and litany into a tempestuous hurricane of music, and if God and his Glorious Mother and the saints to whom we pray looked to our pitch and our voices, and not to our hearts and spirits, it would do us no good to ask their mercy, with such dissonant howls as we offer them.[52]

The service continued with a recitation of the Credo; then a page acting as acolyte led his fellows in an Ave Maria and the regular nightly prayers.

On special occasions, there might be quite elaborate religious ceremonies in a fleet, particularly on the capitana and the almiranta. After surviving a thirty-six-hour hurricane, one ship returning from the Indies in 1622 held a service of contrition dedicated to Our Lady of Carmen, patroness of mariners. Everyone on board attended, with an image of the Virgin, adorned with what finery they could salvage, presiding over the gathering from a portable altar on the poop. The Jesuit chronicler of this voyage led the service, including in his chronicle the long litany to the Virgin recited by those on board, with Latin phrases chanted by the priest answered by Latin responses from his floating congregation.[53]

For Holy Week, among other great festivals of the church year, crew and passengers participated more fully in the events, although Holy Week would have been rather early for voyages across the Atlantic. One description of the events noted,

Since there were religious in the fleet, most of the people confessed, and on Holy Thursday, with silks and other things that had been brought along, each ship decked itself out in the manner of a monument, displaying images and crosses, and on many ships there were a large number of penitents attending the persons who carried the images. Holy Saturday, at the time of the "Gloria," the capitana first and afterwards the other ships made much rejoicing and fired all their heavy and light artillery, so much that it was quite something to see. Easter Sunday, in the morning, all the ships, led by the almiranta, went to salute the capitana, which displayed its many flags and banners, and they saluted her with much artillery. The capitana returned the salute of the almiranta with seven or eight pieces of heavy artillery and with music and trumpets and other instruments, returning the salutes of the other ships with music alone.[54]

The extra expense of such festivities had to be accounted for when the fleet returned home, but the excitement alone must have been worth every maravedí to the participants.[55]

Death, a frequent enough occurrence on long voyages, merited more solemn ceremonial attention. Senior officers might have a farewell salute fired and music played in their honor. A character in one of Cervantes's tales saw a black standard on the topmast of a nearby ship and, coming closer, "heard played on the ship hoarse clarions and trumpets, clear signals either that the general was dead or some other principal person on the ship."[56] Ordinary funeral services were simpler. Unless the ship was very near land, the dead were usually either weighted with stones or wrapped in a shroud of ruined sail canvas and lowered into the sea at night, after a brief funeral

service, with those on board saying a prayer of Buen Viaje. As the sailors'
refrain went, "The dead belong to the sea, when the land is far away."[57]

With a good voyage, there would not be many such breaks in the normal
routine, and boredom would settle around the ship like another kind of
shroud. Eugenio de Salazar, used to an active and mentally stimulating life,
felt the idleness of his sea journey keenly. What struck him most was the
sameness of travel by sea.

> Travel on land with a good mount and some money in your pocket can be quite
> pleasant; you go a while through a plain, then you climb a mountain, you
> descend from there to a valley, you pass a cool river, you traverse a meadow full of
> diverse cattle, you raise your eyes and see diverse birds flying through the air, you
> encounter diverse people on the road, from whom you ask for news from diverse
> parts; you overtake two Franciscan friars with their pilgrims' staffs in their hands
> and their skirts tucked in their girdles, traveling on a humble little ass, and they
> salute you with a "Deo gratias"; . . . You will not lack an agreeable encounter
> with a buxom farm girl, who goes toward town fragrant with pennyroyal and
> sweet marjoram, . . . nor will you fail to meet a whore . . . seated on a mule, with
> her pimp on foot behind her. You will meet a peasant who sells you a beautiful
> hare, . . . and a hunter from whom you buy a pair of good partridges. If one day
> you come to a village with nothing much to eat, tomorrow you will see yourself
> in a city that is copiously and sumptuously provisioned. If one day you dine at an
> inn with a rogue of an innkeeper . . . who sells you cat for hare, goat for lamb,
> dried horse meat for beef, and sour vinegar for pure wine; at night you will sup at
> the house of a different sort of host who serves bread for bread and wine for wine.
> If today you pass the night in the house of a hostess who is old, dirty, quarrel-
> some, wretched, and covetous, tomorrow you will . . . fall in with a hostess who
> is young, clean and cheerful, gracious, generous, of good appearance and much
> piety. . . . But at sea there is no hope that the road, nor the lodgings, nor the host
> will improve; Each day everything can only get worse and more annoying with
> the increasing irritations of the voyage and the lack of ship's stores as they
> continue decreasing and becoming more offensive.[58]

Except for the unwelcome excitement of an unfamiliar sail in the fleet—
possible pirates looking for a chance to attack—or bad weather, those on
board had to look to themselves for amusements. They might organize
choral singing accompanied by guitars, evoking memories of home with
popular regional songs; at sea, as on land, music played an important part in
Spanish life. They might present amateur theatricals or stage dances on deck
at night, by lantern light. The anticipation of a major religious ceremony
could keep boredom at bay for weeks, with crew and passengers alike
making their own banners to carry in the processions, using whatever scraps
of finery they could spare. Among the more mundane pastimes, we are told,
were races among the live animals brought on board for food, or cock fights
among the birds ultimately destined for the pot. The sailors often fished and
swam when the ship was becalmed, which could often happen in Caribbean
waters.[59] Various games also had their following, and on many ships, games
of chance were not only pastimes but obsessions, especially among the
soldiers and sailors. The latest game from Germany or Rome, the classic
games of Catalonia or Burgundy, and every new fad added excitement to the
dead times on board. Civilian passengers on the Indies fleets repeatedly
warned their friends and relatives back home not to get involved in the
crew's gaming, since many of them were accomplished cheats, and the play

could turn deadly serious. Some ships' officers tried to prohibit cards and dice altogether, but there was always something to bet on, if you were so inclined.[60] One way or another, the time passed.

In this atmosphere of boredom and dreary routine, enlivened for the crew by hard work, mealtimes came as welcome diversions, even though the quality of the food was seldom up to the standards of land-based passengers. The greatest difficulty was simply keeping the food and drink on board in a wholesome condition. The only thing that benefited from a sea voyage was wine from Jerez, presumably because it was fortified. For the rest, "From poop to prow, everything that goes on board a ship deteriorates."[61]

Water was as much a problem as food. A persistent folk idea held that water got "seasick" just as humans did, turning from clear to cloudy and beginning to stink after just a few days at sea—perhaps the result of recently filled casks conditioning themselves.[62] Supposedly the water cleared of its own accord in time, but eventually it went bad, as bacteria had a chance to grow. Nonetheless, there was usually quite a sufficient supply of once-fresh water carried on Indies voyages, even if it became increasingly unpalatable. Hamilton found only one fleet of the Armada de la Guardia in which water was rationed, that of 1631, when each man received one-half gallon daily.[63] The ill-fated 1622 return voyage suffered real privation because of water spilled and ruined in the famous rat infestation. When a sudden rainstorm appeared, those on board caught the rainwater in sheets, tablecloths, sails, and awnings, channeling it into containers.[64] This was evidently a classic method of water collection on Spanish ships, particularly on the so-called Manila galleons that crossed the Pacific. They reportedly could be identified at some distance, because the awnings and other parts of the water collection system gave the rigging such a distinctive look.[65]

On the war galleons of the Armada de la Guardia, the water supply was carried in very large pipes (barrels), each 3 codos or 5.5 feet tall, and each holding six pipes' worth of water (4,125 pounds). The rule regarding these enormous *pipotes* appeared in 1613 and in the 1618 regulations on shipbuilding.[66] Compared to earlier practices, larger barrels were more efficient and also served as additional ballast, being partially buried and steadied in the rocks or sand beneath the floor. Once the water had been used, sea water replaced it, with the barrels continuing to serve as ballast. Their size and the thickness of the staves supposedly made them less subject than smaller barrels to damage caused by the motion of the ship. An added advantage was that during the wintering over, sails could be stored in them as protection against rats.

Ship's biscuit, the key element of the diet on board, undoubtedly resisted spoilage better than ordinary bread, but not entirely. Put on board as close as possible to the actual departure of the fleet, biscuit traveled in sealed boxes or casks to protect it from the damp. Some instructions to the masters specified that biscuit storage lockers should even be sheathed in tin, and caulked, lined, and bound with metal.[67] Inevitably, however, the biscuit softened with the humidity on board, and began to ferment and spoil. Eventually a variety of vermin infested it, taking up residence inside the decaying loaves. The crews on Columbus's fourth voyage supposedly ate their meals only after dark, so they could not see what they were eating.[68] Such problems of spoilage affected virtually every ship that sailed, as long as provisions had to be carried for some time. Rats, roaches, grubs, mites, and weevils all contributed to the damage, which increased the longer the biscuit had to last.[69] Indies fleets often carried enough biscuit for the round trip, because it was so scarce and costly in the New World. That meant that toward the end of the voyage the crew might be served some biscuit that was at least fifteen months old. If provisions ran low, the broken bits (called *mazamorra*) left in the storage lockers would be made into a sort of stew, along with whatever else was available, usually water, oil, and garlic. Evidently, galley oarsmen ate mazamorra more than they ate whole biscuit.[70] Others were better supplied, though occasionally everyone who traveled by sea had the opportunity to try it.[71] When rations ran dangerously low on the 1622 return voyage, the passengers were happy to have that.[72]

The fish carried by the Armada de la Guardia was usually cod, cleaned, split open, and flattened out, then dried and salted. The finished product, stacked and tied in large bundles, kept fairly well, though the humidity and heat in the hold could cause it to spoil as well. Ideally, the cod would be kept in the open air from about the first of May on, to keep it wholesome longer, but that was not always possible.[73] Hams and salt pork, the former generally for privileged officers, seem to have been carried in the open air as well at times. On the ill-fated 1622 voyage from the Indies, sharks began following one ship in the Caribbean. Evidently, haunches and slabs of meat hung from the railings of the poop corridors came within range of the sharks as the ship pitched violently during a storm. Having tasted ham and salt pork, the sharks were willing to taste whatever else might come their way, and the terrified sailors could well imagine what would happen to them if they fell overboard.[74] Indies ships usually carried hens in coops on deck, they and their eggs reserved for the principal officers and the sick. As the sailor's complaint put it, "To him who doesn't work, a hen; to him who works, a sardine." A more extreme version of the same refrain had the workers eating bread and the nonworkers eating salmon and pheasant.[75] It is easier to rhyme sardine (*sardina*) than cod (*bacallao*), though the latter was surely the standard fish on Atlantic voyages. At times live sheep, cattle, and pigs might travel on board in addition to hens. In the generally peaceful two decades after 1600, even war galleons habitually carried live animals to enhance the shipboard diet. Tortoises appear frequently in the Havana accounts of the Armada de la Guardia in the 1630s, although the animals may have been slaughtered and their meat dried before the fleet sailed. The sailors evidently stewed it with garlic and compared its taste with the finest veal at home.[76] Like every other living thing on board, the livestock ate biscuit, or mazamorra.

Wealthy passengers might bring much of their own food, or at least supplementary items. Some documents mention passengers who brought lemons to combat seasickness, and many undoubtedly carried treats such as honey, figs, oranges, pomegranates, and assorted sweets for the long voyage.[77] Some brought a few hens, if they had permission. For the most part, however, passengers on merchant ships shared in the regular rations provided for the crew, paying the ship's master for their meals.

Interestingly enough, none of the dozens of provisioning accounts analyzed for this study, nor any of the descriptions of shipboard life, mentions how the food was prepared or who prepared it. On some ships, the obvious choice would have been the dispenser, as noted in chapter 6. He measured the rations for all food and drink and supervised the pages in setting up for meals, building the cooking fire, cleaning up afterward, and soaking dried provisions overnight for subsequent cooking.[78] It is probable that he also supervised the pages in stewing the dried legumes, salted meat, and fish of the standard ship diet, to be discussed in detail later. As the saying went, "Salted fish is good stewed and bad baked."[79] Nonetheless, there is no proof as to who did the cooking. On sixteenth-century merchant ships, the master provided paying passengers with water, salt, firewood, and access to a cookstove, where they did their own cooking. The standard cookstove on Spanish ships was the *fogón*, a rectangular metal box, three-sided and open on top, with an enclosed bottom lined with sand. A wood fire was built on the sand, protected from the wind by the three side pieces. Large cauldrons with legs could stand by themselves over the fire; other pots could be suspended by hooks from a bar running from side to side across the width of the stove. One author mentions a group of Dominican monks who brought their own fogón aboard, with servants to cook their meals.[80]

On warships, rules for the distribution to each man of his daily ration— seemingly uncooked—raise additional questions. The extreme danger of fire on wooden ships would increase with the number of cookstoves. Regulations repeatedly laid down rules for the use of lanterns, stoves, candles, and every other bit of fire on board, for obvious reasons.[81] In the late sixteenth century, the meals undoubtedly were prepared and served communally, because we have detailed descriptions of mealtimes. By the seventeenth century, it is possible that sailors and soldiers on warships cooked for themselves, pooling their rations with trusted comrades and taking turns tending the pot. Yet the galleons built by don Martín de Arana each carried only two fogones, which would work out to about one hundred men per stove. It is difficult to know how they can all have cooked and eaten in the course of a day, especially because the provisions—salt pork or dried fish and a mixture of rice and legumes—required long, slow cooking. A law of 1621, the same one that outlawed livestock on warships, also said there should not be as many cookstoves and other comforts on board any longer, which suggests that the ship's standard equipment had been augmented by private stoves brought on board.[82] It is clear from the documents surrounding the provisioning of the 1629 Indies fleet that the sailors had to buy some sort of eating equipment, although such items also figured in considerable abundance in the ships' supplies.[83] In the absence of more precise information, we can only guess at what the cooking arrangements might have been. It was obviously more important to specify how the rations were to be distributed equitably than how to cook them.

Mealtimes on board are somewhat less a mystery, though we do not know how many times a day they occurred. If the biscuit ration were distributed first thing in the morning, with the water ration, a few bites of one and a few sips of the other would have been breakfast. In the late sixteenth century on merchant ships, there were clearly two main meals, one at midday and one in the evening. The ideal gentleman in Mateo Aleman's *Guzmán de Alfarache* dined on the poop, with attentive servants to fill his plate, bringing him "silver serving pieces and more clean drinking vessels than you could imagine." After the meal, they presented him with cunningly carved toothpicks, vying with one another for his favor.[84] The average Indies traveler would have marveled at a scene of such decorum and cleanliness. As García de Palacio described a typical meal for the crew on a merchant vessel, the dispenser had the pages set up a trestle table lengthwise in the waist of the ship, where all the men could fit who were not on watch. He then had them distribute the food in piles that would each serve four men, pouring them wine as they ate.[85]

Eugenio de Salazar cast his discerning eye on the same scene and came up with a much livelier description. About noon the pages brought from below decks a suspicious-looking bundle that they called tablecloths,

> as clean and white and damasklike as pieces of filthy dark-colored fustian. Then they heaped on this table some small mountains of ruined biscuit, so that the tablecloths with the biscuits on them looked like heaps of cow dung in a farmer's field. Then they put three or four large wooden plates on the table, filled with stringy beef joints, dressed with some partly cooked tendons. They called these plates *saleres*, and for this reason they didn't put on salt cellars. Once the table was thus finished off, the page called all to table. "Table, table, sir captain and master and good company, table ready; meat ready; water as usual for sir captain and master and good company. Long live the King of Castile by land and sea. Who says to him war, off with his head; who won't say amen, gets nothing to drink. The table is set in good time, those who don't come won't eat." At the Amen, all the mariners came, sitting on the deck at the table, with the master's assistant (contramaestre) at the head and the master gunner on his right. One sailor stuck his legs away from the table, another had his feet forward; this one squatting; that one reclining, and sitting in many other ways as well. And without waiting for grace to be said, these Knights of the Round Table took out their knives large and small of diverse fashions, some made to kill pigs, others to flay lambs, and others to cut purses; and they grabbed in their hands the poor bones, separating them from their nerves and sinews, as if all their lives they had been practicing anatomy studies in Guadalupe or Valencia; and in the time it took to say a Credo, they left the bones as smooth and clean as ivory. . . . A page came by with a container of liquid in his hand and with his cup served them wine that was less, and worse, and more baptized [diluted] than they wanted. And thus dining with the first course last and the last course first and the middle course throughout, they finished their meal without finishing their hunger.[86]

The captain, master, pilot, and notary ate apart at their own table, no doubt enjoying a somewhat better meal. The passengers all ate at the same time, too, "because in this city it is necessary to cook and eat at the same hour as our neighbors. If not, you find yourself without light and without a ray of love in the stove," eating a cold meal in the dark. The passengers nicknamed the stove the Isle of Pots, because there were so many separate things cooking there, and Salazar marveled at seeing so many meals cooked, so many tables, and so many diners. All talked at meals about the food they would like to be eating instead: white grapes from Guadalajara, berries from Illescas, turnips from Somosierra, escarole and heart of thistle from Medina del Campo—naming what they missed the most. "And you could die of thirst in the middle of the ocean, because they give you water by the ounce, as in a pharmacy, after too much dried beef and salted things, since Lady Sea will not suffer or conserve meat or fish that is not dressed in her salt." Everything else went rotten and stinking, even the water. Salazar complained that you had to lose your sense of taste and smell and vision even to get it down.[87] It is no wonder that only ten days out, some travelers began to dream of the simple pleasures of fresh roasted meat and cool, fresh water from the village fountain.[88] We can sympathize with the complaints of these captive diners. The food obviously offended most of the bodily senses, even at the best of times. Even so, the quantity and nutritional quality of the shipboard diet deserve more attention than they usually receive.

The standard diet for sailors and soldiers on board sailing ships changed little during the Habsburg centuries. The most important parts of the daily ration were the allotments of biscuit (generally 1.5 pounds per man per day) and wine (half an *azumbre* or about two pints). Together they accounted for the bulk of the calories and much of the cost. (See appendix C, Tables 14, 15.) When the ships picked up supplies on the north coast of Spain, cider might be substituted for some or all of the wine, in which case the daily ration was twice that for wine. The Spanish carried beer only when they provisioned in their Netherlands provinces, rationing it like cider rather than like wine.[89] To the basic allotment of bread and drink was added a standard weekly pattern of food. In the mid-sixteenth century, provisioning for European voyages usually allowed four meat days each week (Sunday, Monday, Tuesday, and Thursday), with a daily ration of half a pound of salt beef or pork, or one pound of fresh meat, when it was available. During battles or days with seas too rough to allow cooking, each man received six ounces of cheese, half at the midday meal and half at night. It seems from various accounts that one cheese day per week could be expected in the general meat-day allowance. Three fish days (Wednesday, Friday, and Saturday) rounded out the week, with a ration of either a half pound of dried fish, six sardines, or their equivalent daily. A mixture (*menestra*) of rice and legumes—broad beans, chickpeas, peas—accompanied the fish ration, and, in some accounts, it accompanied the meat and cheese rations as well, although it is not clear how the menestra might have been eaten on days too rough to light the cooking fires. Three *celemines* (about fourteen liters) of menestra sufficed for one hundred men, according to an account in 1553.[90] Oil and vinegar also came with the fish ration.

Nonrationed foods, though part of the shipboard diet, do not appear at all in many accounts; in others they are mentioned but not itemized. These included onions, garlic, fresh fruits, and fresh vegetables. One account that gave precise figures allowed a daily average of one-third of an onion and one clove of garlic daily for each person.[91] That same account allowed forty meat days and twenty fish days in the two months of provisions carried, with menestra served only on fish days, and beer in place of wine. The food provided for soldiers on land varied little from their diet at sea, although it would have been supplemented by seasonal fresh foods.[92] This basic diet for European voyages in the sixteenth century could vary depending upon the length and trajectory of the voyage, the season of the year, and even the judgment of the commander of the fleet. In 1557 Luis de Carvajal, captain-general of a fleet from Spain to Flanders, allowed one pint of wine and two pints of cider each day for his men; the French wine was used before the wine from Navarre, since it did not keep as well at sea. Moreover, because Lent would begin during the voyage, Carvajal ordered all the meat days to come first, so that the fish days could be used during Lent. The three or four days each week when legumes were served would continue to be spread through-out the voyage, however.[93]

The dietaries for Spanish galley fleets in the Mediterranean were similar, though by no means identical, to those of sailing ships. The extreme differences in station among those on board—from officers and free soldiers and sailors to criminals sentenced to the oars—had its reflection in different dietaries. Mediterranean voyages were likely to include more rice as part of the menestra, and, because they touched port more often, they had more fresh than salted meat, although the oarsmen ate only legume stews with their twenty-six-ounce ration of biscuit much of the time.[94] One sixteenth-century author claimed that all the oarsmen got with their biscuit was white "wine" from the river (that is, water), thick and stinking, with lentil or rice stew, and a tiny bit of vinegar and oil, the vinegar not just for taste, but because traditional wisdom thought it to be invigorating. According to this author, although they got a pound of meat on Easter, they ate meat only two other times in the year.[95] If true, that was far less than the ideal. Luis Ortiz wrote in 1558 that "in season"—presumably the battle season—the oarsmen should get eleven ounces of fresh meat with their menestra three days each week, and menestra alone the other four days, with some fruit.[96]

Conditions on the Atlantic run followed the same basic diet as that for the European fleets, but with more dried and salted meat and fish than the fresh varieties. The early voyages of Columbus had shown the value of dried and salted provisions, and the list of items carried by Magellan in his voyage around the world provides an extensive catalog of foods that kept well at sea.[97] Most of the fleets of the Armada de la Guardia provisioned exclusively with dried and salted items, along with standard daily rations of 1.5 pounds of biscuit and two pints of wine. The fleet of 1560 allowed half a pound of either salted meat or fish, and 3.8 ounces of menestra, in addition to the standard biscuit and wine allotment.[98] Popular treatments of the treasure fleets are incorrect on many points dealing with diet, betraying their unfamiliarity with the wealth of archival materials on shipboard provisions.[99] Hamilton's scholarly treatment asserts that rations stayed constant through the middle of the seventeenth century, but by Arana's time the recommended rations featured smaller portions than Hamilton found for the mid-sixteenth century.[100] The anonymous author of the "Diálogo" written in about 1635 mentioned only six ounces of salted meat or fish for the basic ration, or twelve ounces of fresh beef, when it was available. He estimated twenty-two meat days and eight fish days each month. The six ounces of cheese that served as the main course during storms or battles would seem to have replaced meat days. Two ounces of menestra accompanied every main course except the fresh beef, though again, it is not clear how the menestra could be prepared during storms or battles.[101]

Official rations on the Indies runs from 1647 to 1651 are virtually identical to the menus given by the "Diálogo," although they mentioned the possibility of twelve ounces of pigs' feet or nine ounces of dried beef on meat days.[102] The detailed figures in the document reveal that the provisioners planned for nineteen meat days in the month, nine fish days, and three cheese days. Later in the seventeenth century, estimated provisions might allow for only 1 pound of biscuit each day, rather than the standard 1.5 pounds, but it is not clear if this marked a general trend of reduced basic rations or merely indicated unusual years.[103]

Unrationed items undoubtedly supplemented official rations on Indies fleets as well as European ones. Spices and condiments always accompanied the basic provisions—cinnamon, cloves, mustard, parsley, pepper, and saffron, to mention a few. Onions often figured among the provisions for the treasure fleets in the sixteenth and seventeenth centuries, and Hamilton found garlic listed in all but three of the years he examined between 1503 and 1660, with instructions to the master to see that it lasted the whole voyage.[104] In addition, passengers as well as sailors and soldiers could supplement their diet, if they had the money and the foresight to bring extra provisions on the voyage. Fresh fruits and vegetables would have been likely choices, even though they could not last the whole voyage. Lemons were thought to prevent seasickness, and in 1577 one recent immigrant to the Indies wrote to his nephew in Spain to bring four to six dozen lemons with him should he make the trip, packing them in crocks with layers of sand.[105] The cost of fruits, vegetables, and condiments was negligible compared to the cost of rationed items, particularly in Andalusia, where the Indies fleets provisioned for their voyages.[106] That may explain why so little attention was paid them in official budgets for the fleets. Unfortunately, what that means is that most writers have assumed that only the rationed items were carried, and they have analyzed the shipboard diets accordingly. It is wiser to remember that the official rations were often supplemented by unrationed items, even when we cannot know the amount of those items in the daily diets.

Very few authors have analyzed the standard diet in any detail, and even the best serious studies need to be reexamined in the light of ongoing medical research about food and nutrition.[107] For detailed analysis I have used a diet that can be considered typical of the fleets of the Armada de la Guardia in the early seventeenth century, featuring six ounces of either salt pork, dried fish, or cheese, and two ounces of menestra—half rice and half chickpeas—each day, plus the usual amount of biscuit and wine, with oil and vinegar on fish days and oil on cheese days. (See appendix C, table 14.) The first problem that confronts any such analysis is how to relate the items carried on seventeenth century ships to modern analyses of the nutritional content of foods.[108]

Ship's biscuit, the most important item in the diet for food energy, has no obvious equivalent in modern printed sources. We know, however, that it was made of more or less clean whole wheat flour, which was leavened and allowed to rise somewhat before baking. When it was done, the bread was cooked again in a moderate oven to dry out, making it keep longer than ordinary bread. It is from this process that it got its name—biscuit, from *biscotto,* or twice-cooked.[109] Contemporary authors complained that it was hard as a rock and about as appetizing, nothing like the bread they enjoyed on land.[110] Although contemporaries might have preferred fine white bread, the whole wheat biscuit clearly had more nutritive value. To analyze the nutritional content of ship's biscuit, I used the information for modern unenriched whole wheat bread, made with water. Its weight raises another problem. Biscuit had most of its water driven off in the baking process, so that the 1.5 pound daily ration of biscuit must have had considerably more calories and nutrients than the equivalent weight of whole wheat bread. We should be aware, therefore, that the calorie count and nutritional values given in table 14 for biscuit represent a minimum. No author dealing with shipboard diets takes this into account, as far as I know, although Dr. James Lind, an eighteenth-century British naval physician, did mention it in passing.[111]

The wines distributed as part of the daily ration raise other problems, because their alcohol content varied. Wine purchased in Galicia in northwest Spain might be quite low in alcohol, and therefore in calories, whereas wines from the Jerez region south of Seville—sherries, in other words—would be much higher. Hamilton and Sánchez-Albornoz, for the provisioning accounts they analyzed, assumed an alcohol content of 15 percent for the wines. Similarly, I have chosen to take the average between light and heavy wines from the standard tables, which works out to about 15.5 percent alcohol.

In the analysis in table 14, tocino—bacon or salt pork—represents the meat ration, and I have arbitrarily chosen to use the figures for salt pork, although one could argue for either choice. There is not a great deal of difference between the two in nutritional value, though salt pork has more calories and less protein than bacon.[112] The slabs of tocino purchased for ship provisions in Spain could vary in size. I found a range from twenty-one to nearly thirty-three pounds in various accounts.[113] For the fish ration, I used analyses for dried and lightly salted cod, probably a close equivalent to the seventeenth-century item. Various sorts of hard cheeses would have served for the ships' emergency rations, originating from as nearby as Seville or as far away as Flanders. I have used the modern figures for hard, whole-milk cheese to represent this component of the diet, though the figures would vary somewhat for each type of cheese carried. Modern unenriched rice and chickpeas approximate the shipboard rations fairly closely, and I have assumed as well that the olive oil carried on Spanish ships had the same nutritional content as modern olive oil. On the other hand, the vinegar carried on board was almost surely soured wine, rather than the cider or distilled vinegars in modern food tables. However we count it, vinegar added very little to the nutritional content of the diet.

As imperfect as these equivalents may be, they can still provide a fair approximation of the energy and nutritional value of the shipboard diet. In food energy, the shipboard diet provided amply for Spanish soldiers and sailors in the Armada de la Guardia, with 4,130 calories on meat days, 3,743 on fish days (not counting vinegar), and 3,609 calories on cheese days. The figures for every diet variation come well above the estimated energy needs for a moderately active adult man weighing about 143 pounds. It would even suffice for a very active man, and the sailors on duty in the seventeenth century surely consumed as much energy as the unskilled laborers and forestry workers labeled as very active in the late twentieth century.[114] However unappetizing the shipboard meals may have been, they were undoubtedly much higher in calories than the ordinary diet of the peasantry on land, particularly in poorer areas with an uncertain grain harvest.[115] One study of diets in southcentral France in the mid-eighteenth century found almost none that reached 2,000 calories a day, and some that fell considerably lower.[116] Authors who have written on Spanish shipboard diets agree that their caloric content was generous, but they usually deplore what they consider an unbalanced reliance on carbohydrate calories and an insufficient protein content. Earl J. Hamilton, writing in 1929, seems to have counted the biscuit solely as a carbohydrate.[117] Yet modern research has revealed the value of complex vegetable proteins, especially when they are eaten in the proper combinations. Spooner, writing much more recently, calls the diet on Spanish galleys in 1599–1600 "not too unbalanced," but it is not clear whether or not he considered vegetable as well as animal proteins. As presented, the galley diet he analyzed contained 12.58 percent proteins, 21.76 percent fats, and 65.66 percent carbohydrates. Spooner thought diets that contained at least 15 percent protein and no more than 50 percent carbohydrates were preferable, although modern research finds diets with 10–15 percent protein adequate.[118] The ship diets that included both whole wheat biscuit and legumes at the same meal would have provided complete vegetable proteins as well as substantial calories and nutrients, because legumes supplied the essential amino acids missing from wheat and rice.[119]

Counting vegetable as well as animal protein, any one of the three ship diets analyzed in table 14 far exceeded the recommended daily allowances that the Food and Agriculture Organization of the United Nations proposed in 1974.[120] These allowances strike a balance between the minimum allowances needed to avoid deficiency diseases and the much higher standards established for wealthy countries in the twentieth century, which would be too high for useful comparison with seventeenth-century data.[121] Without question the shipboard diets got the majority of their energy calories from carbohydrates, but not as large a majority as earlier authors claimed. Using modern nutritional information and caloric equivalents for the major food groups, and figuring a monthly average based on nineteen meat, nine fish, and three cheese days each month, reveals the following rather surprising conclusions. The Spanish shipboard diet had about 15 percent of its calories in protein, 31 percent in fats, and 54 percent in carbohydrates, using the standard of four calories per gram for proteins and carbohydrates and nine calories per gram for fats and oils. That was much more balanced than the eighteenth-century French peasant diets analyzed by Bernard, and also better balanced than the galley diet Spooner analyzed.[122] Moreover, it would be quite acceptable by modern standards of good nutrition. In modern analyses, the shipboard diet would be considered high in calories, but the strenuous work done by the sailors required high calories. Had they not been provided by carbohydrates, they would have come from other parts of the diet such as protein, which has more important functions in the body than simply providing energy.[123]

Clearly, the shipboard diet had enough calories and overall balance to keep Spanish soldiers and sailors well fed. That was the crown's aim, of course, but royal provisioners also cared about the cost of ships' rations. The overall price of the rations changed as the market prices for food changed, and we might suspect that provisioners stinted on provisions to keep the costs as low as possible. Interestingly enough, that does not seem to have been the case. If we figure the costs of the standard diets listed in table 14 for 1626 in Seville, a year in which there are confirmed prices for all the items on the list, we find that salt pork was over twice as expensive as dried fish and measurably more expensive than cheese. (See appendix C, table 15.) Yet meat days outnumbered fish days by more than two to one, and in fact there were more meat days in 1626 than there had been in the mid-sixteenth century. It would seem that the crown placed more importance on the good nutrition of its sailors and soldiers than on saving money.

Just how effective were their diet choices? Looking at the range of nutrients that human beings require for good health, it is somewhat surprising to find that the ship diets covered them rather well—surprising because most scholars have emphasized the disadvantages of shipboard meals. Without minimizing these disadvantages, not the least of which was the unappetizing and boring nature of the food, we should still recognize its merits. Of all the principal recommended nutrients, only three fell below the standard recommended allowances set in 1974: retinol (vitamin A), riboflavin (vitamin B2), and ascorbic acid (vitamin C). Retinol, richly supplied in eggs and dairy products, as well as in certain fruits and vegetables, was almost completely absent from every item of the official shipboard ration except cheese.[124] Although not as serious as other dietary lacks, retinol deficiency could have led to night blindness among those who lived solely on the official rations. In this context it is worth remembering the care taken to teach all seamen to "know the ropes" of the ship, so that they could handle them even on a dark night. The evidence from their diet would suggest that Spanish sailors suffered from a chronic retinol deficiency, if they lived on sea rations alone for long stretches of time. Riboflavin levels in the official rations fell just below recommended daily allowances, but probably not low enough to produce symptoms of deficiency disease. The recommended daily allowances are generally set much higher than the minimum levels necessary to prevent the symptoms of deficiency.[125]

Much more serious was the near total lack of ascorbic acid, present in large amounts in citrus fruits as well as in some other fruits and vegetables. As any educated person knows, the deficiency of ascorbic acid or vitamin C leads to scurvy, one of the worst diseases that plagued seafarers in the centuries following European expansion around the globe. It accompanied Vasco da Gama's 1498 voyage to India and Magellan's 1519–21 trip around the world, but it was not completely understood, let alone vanquished, until the twentieth century. As we know now, as little as ten milligrams of ascorbic acid daily—the amount in about half an ounce of orange juice—can prevent scurvy.[126] Less than that hampers the body's ability to produce collagen, the essential material that renews the connective tissues literally holding the body together. It also aids in the absorption of iron and calcium and in the management of stress. Without new collagen, the lining of blood capillaries loosens and blood escapes into neighboring tissue. The outward symptoms of this progressive breakdown include dark spots all over the body—actually hundreds of small hemorrhages—swollen joints, as blood seeps into the joint cavities, and swollen and bleeding gums, resulting in the inability to eat and the loss of teeth. Wounds fail to heal, and healed wounds and bone breaks many years old can open up again. With these horrifying physical symptoms come lassitude and an inability to withstand mental stress. In crews affected by scurvy, men whose legs would not hold them up any longer dropped like flies. Rest and care might make them feel better for a time, but any exertion, even the simple act of standing upright, could result in sudden death from internal hemorrhages and heart failure.[127]

Mariners had only limited means of understanding and combating this debilitating and often fatal disease. They knew that it struck during long sea voyages, and in the winter on land, especially in northern climes. They knew that fresh provisions had something to do with preventing its occurrence. And experience with peoples around the globe taught them a series of local remedies for it. What they could not do was prevent it, because they did not understand its nature. Magellan knew in a general way that fresh food prevented scurvy. He even carried a few antiscorbutics such as garlic and preserved quince among his provisions, but hardly enough to prevent scurvy on such a long voyage, even had he known their properties.[128] Antonio Pigafetta's diary of the voyage records symptoms of scurvy, when the expedition sailed for three months and twenty days across the Pacific Ocean without fresh food.[129] Only their arrival in what would be named the Philippine Islands saved them from complete disaster.

The first detailed description of the disease came from reports of the expedition of Sebastián Vizcaíno, from western Mexico up the California coast in 1602–03. Leaving Acapulco in May 1602, the men carried provisions for a year, expecting to supplement them with fresh food along the way, because they would seldom be far from land. They found friendly local Indians and fresh fish and fowl in abundance, but a shortage of water and trees in the dry, barren land of Baja California. As they moved north during fall and winter, scurvy set in. Experience told them they were safe in warm climates near land, with fresh food, so they were not prepared for scurvy in the coastal waters of Mexico and California, even in winter. Luckily they made it back to the Mexican coast in time, and were given a miraculous cure for their illness in the local *xocojuistle* fruit near Mazatlán. Forty-eight of the original two hundred on the expedition died, a relatively light toll compared to the wholesale devastation on other scurvy-plagued voyages.[130] A British expedition around the world in 1740–44 lost 1,051 men of the 1,955 who embarked, many of them from scurvy. Ironically, they first suffered from the disease as they left the same Mexican coast that Vizcaíno's expedition had explored a century and a half before. Like those earlier men, the British were not prepared for scurvy in warm climes, although they should have been familiar with it from home, because many northern Europeans suffered from scurvy in the winter.

It was the shock of those losses that inspired the English naval doctor James Lind to carry out controlled experiments on the cure and prevention of scurvy. He concluded quite correctly that oranges and lemons were the best preventives and cures for scurvy, rejecting most of the other proposed remedies.[131] Unfortunately, competing theories and Lind's lack of prestige in the medical profession meant that the British admiralty did not adopt his recommendations until half a century later, in 1795. It would take fifty more years before British merchant fleets did the same. In another of the ironies of the fight against scurvy, Captain James Cook usually gets the credit for finding a cure for scurvy on English ships, although he actually argued against the adoption of Lind's recommendations, favoring alternate remedies that were less expensive, and less effective, such as sauerkraut.[132] Benefiting from past experience and current theory, many late eighteenth-century expeditions carried provisions to combat scurvy. A Spanish voyage on the California coast in 1773–75 took two jars each of lemon syrup

and xocojuistle syrup, and—no doubt because of Cook's example—the
Spanish Malaspina expedition that left in 1789 took a special diet of sauerkraut, bacon, vinegar, wine, and grog.[133] Given the state of medical knowledge at the time, however, scurvy could not be eradicated. Neither Lind, nor
Cook, nor the learned medical men who wrote about it, understood the
nature of the disease; most of them attributed it in some way to dampness,
cold, and the quality of the air on board ships.[134]

   This discussion of scurvy is rather far afield from our main concern of the
dietary deficiencies of the Indies run, because it was rarely a problem to
Spanish voyages crossing the Atlantic. The symptoms of scurvy do not
usually appear until the sixth week of a diet totally lacking in ascorbic acid,
and the regular Atlantic run to the Spanish empire was rarely even that long
on the open sea between the Canary Islands and the Caribbean islands. With
any fresh vegetables and fruits at all in the early part of the voyage—and we
know that onions and garlic at least were carried—scurvy symptoms would
not have had a chance to develop.

   There is another reason that scurvy was not a problem on the Spanish
Atlantic fleets: it was not a problem in Spain. Spanish soldiers reportedly
called it "the Dutch disease," presumably because the Dutch they encountered suffered from it in the winter, but perhaps because they themselves
suffered from it as well, when they spent too much time in Holland.[135] Many
of the peoples of northern Europe in early modern times could be called
prescorbutic, because of the lack of citrus fruits and other antiscorbutics in
their diets. Every probable source for the word "scurvy" is either northern
or eastern European. People from the warm areas of Iberia and the Mediterranean almost certainly did not know scurvy until they began long sea
voyages. When the Portuguese first encountered the disease on Vasco da
Gama's voyage around Africa, they called it the "sickness from Luanda,"
because, as far as they knew, that west African port was where it came
from.[136] The ubiquitous presence of citrus fruits, onions, peppers, and garlic
in Mediterranean cuisine protected the Spanish population on every social
level from scurvy, even in the winter. In fact, the poor probably ate more
fruit and vegetables than the rich, finding them cheap and abundant, particularly in the south. Because of this, Spanish sailors were undoubtedly more
resistant than northern Europeans to scurvy and other vitamin deficiencies
aboard ship. Although it is generally assumed that ascorbic acid cannot be
stored in the body, modern research has shown that "the body has some
capacity for storing the vitamin, mainly in the liver. If the dietary supply of
the vitamin is cut off suddenly, this store can meet the needs for a short time,
usually for about two months, but if the previous diet has been rich in the
vitamin, for as long as six months."[137]

   In other words, although the symptoms of scurvy can appear in about six
weeks, Spaniards and other Mediterraneans would have been able to resist
them longer, even if their shipboard diet had included no ascorbic acid.
According to a Spanish physician who studied the diseases of mariners,
"Spanish mariners among all Europeans have the least propensity to scurvy,
which is only seen on very long voyages to our possessions in the Pacific . . .
."[138] On Magellan's voyage, many on board became ill during the three
months and twenty days they spent without fresh food. The astounding
thing is that they did not *all* become ill. Antonio Pigafetta mentioned that,

with all the diverse ailments that we now know to be related to scurvy, "very few remained healthy. However, thanks be to the Lord, I had no sickness."[139] Pigafetta was an Italian from Vicenza, Magellan was Portuguese, and the expedition as a whole was Spanish. Very likely the lifelong eating habits of the men in the expedition had helped them withstand the privations of their Pacific crossing.

It is very difficult to study the land diet of Spaniards in any detail. Much of the information we have comes from reports by foreigners traveling through Spain, whose perceptions were colored by their resistance to unfamiliar-tasting food. The common thread running through many of these accounts was the frugality of the Spanish peasant diet, and the lack of "butcher's meat" in the countryside.[140] Rural Spaniards did have fowl and game, however, and the occasional lamb, pig, or cow, and many had fish, although the casual traveler might have encountered little but chicken and eggs in wayside inns. Urban populations were more regularly supplied with "butcher's meat," which impressed the travelers, but we should not take their comments too seriously. Several accounts by Spanish travelers show a considerable variety and abundance of foods in the countryside, and a standard diet that varied little over the centuries. One ambassadorial party traveling from Navarre to Seville in 1352 made daily meals of "a plate of salad, meat and spices, and fruit," with bread and wine on the side. Because they traveled in summer, the fruit included cherries and other seasonal specialties. They bought fish often, as well as chickens, eggs, and kid, supplementing their main dishes with turnips, honey, mustard, onions, peppers, garlic, and nuts.[141] For a royal embassy this was not a luxurious diet, but it was surely balanced and satisfying.

Little had changed when the seventeenth-century physician Juan Sorapán de Rieros noted that the ordinary Spanish diet included "chicken, mutton, bread, some greens and fruits, and wine," which he pronounced healthful enough, provided that everything was eaten in moderation.[142] The royal household itself could have been included in his description.[143] One suspects that Sorapán wrote primarily of privileged groups in society, but careful attempts to analyze the diet of ordinary Spaniards differ little.[144] Writing as a traditionally schooled physician, Sorapán analyzed the properties of various foods by relying on ancient writers such as Galen and Hippocrates. The originality of his approach was in using popular sayings and refrains to guide the layman's approach to nutrition and disease. For example, according to traditional folk wisdom, fish and meat should never be eaten at the same meal, because this shortened one's life.[145] In general, such refrains praised all the standard elements of Spanish diet, and Sorapán used his erudition to show the medical wisdom that lay behind them. He was particularly enthusiastic about the healthful properties of chicken and especially eggs, which he praised as universally available, of excellent sustenance, good for rich and poor, for the healthy and the sick alike.[146] Fish he considered less healthful, but worthy of note since it was eaten so frequently—about half the time, counting all the fish days in the ecclesiastical calendar. Since fish were cold and wet, Sorapán categorized them as phlegmatic foods, following the standard doctrine of humors.[147] To neutralize their cold, phlegmatic effects, fish should be cooked with aromatic and "warm" complements such as pepper, cloves, parsley, garlic, onion, oregano, laurel, wine, vinegar, lemons, and oranges. Even though the fish carried on board ships was dried and salted, it presumably needed the same treatment—hence, the vinegar issued on fish days and the presence of onions and garlic. Sorapán provided instructions for preparing several dozen different kinds of fish commonly eaten in Spain, often including citrus fruits in the recipes.[148] Cheese, like fish and meat, had healthful properties, if eaten with the proper caution. Although in small quantities it contributed to good health, cheese gave little sustenance and caused kidney stones, according to the ancients. Sorapán guessed that their warnings referred only to aged cheese, because he found fresh or cream cheese to be innocuous. Nonetheless, he recommended eating only small quantities. "The cheese given out by a miser is healthful."[149]

The most interesting parts of Sorapán's treatise for our purpose are discussions of vegetables and fruits in general. The popular refrain "Comer verdura, y echar mala ventura"—eating greens is good for you—directly contradicted Galen's warnings about their harmful effects, and Sorapán had to go to considerable lengths to reconcile the two points of view. In cataloging the good and bad qualities of common Spanish greens and recommending ways to neutralize their bad qualities, Sorapán provided a lengthy list of nutritious vegetables eaten by Spaniards: lettuce, escarole, several kinds of cabbage, saltwort (*acelgas*), wild amaranth, borage, purslane, sorrel, watercress, common cress, parsley, mint, rocket, mustard, thistle, asparagus, radishes, carrots, onions, colewort, garlic, and mushrooms. Many of these, he remarked in passing, were favored by the poor, undoubtedly because they could be gathered freely in the countryside.[150] When the famous seventeenth-century adventurer Alonso de Contreras set out to do penance for the good of his soul, he lived on charitable contributions of oil, bread, and garlic, plus the many edible plants he found in the hills near Ágreda in northcentral Spain.[151]

Sorapán showed a similar breadth of knowledge about the fruits of Spain, among which he included nuts and items we usually classify as vegetables, such as eggplant and cucumbers. He discussed the merits of many varieties of apples, the pears of Granada, melons, squashes, figs, grapes, cherries, all sorts of peaches and apricots, pomegranates, quince, plums, dates, olives, capers, citrons, oranges, lemons, limes, and many kinds of nuts. Each region had its characteristic fruits, from the apples of Asturias to the olives and oranges of the south and east.[152] The citrus of Vizcaya had already become famous in the Middle Ages, used locally and even exported to less favored climates.[153] Although Sorapán scarcely mentioned them, legumes also flourished in Spain: chickpeas, broad beans, lentils, vetches, and peas, among others.[154] Some were eaten fresh, and others could be dried for long storage—the staple of the shipboard menestras. When we add cultivated grains to the wild and domesticated plants of Spain, we have strong testimony to the variety and nutritional wealth of a country that is usually considered poor.

Traditional wisdom judged the value in the various parts of a menestra, as it judged other foods mentioned by Sorapán. Broad beans and chickpeas were considered to give more sustenance than rice, for example. We know they all provide about the same calories, but that rice has only one-fourth the protein of most legumes and less than one-seventh the thiamine (vitamin B1). Spaniards in the seventeenth century knew that feeding galley oarsmen rice alone was bad for their health. We know that thiamine deficiency causes beriberi.[155] Tradition told them that a menestra was the best food to carry on ships to supplement biscuit, dried meat, and fish; we know about the complex vegetable proteins in such menestras. Ancient physicians told them to eat vinegar, citrus, onions, and garlic with their fish; modern nutritional analysis tells us why that kept them in good health. As we define things, it has nothing to do with the phlegmatic nature of fish and the need for "warm" foods to neutralize its effects, but we should not be too quick to dismiss ancient ideas. By whatever process of reasoning, Spanish folk wisdom and ancient physicians defined a very balanced and healthful diet. One of the most favored Spanish regions for nutritional variety was Andalusia in the south, the home of many of the mariners in the Indies fleets. If the rural poor could not afford all the meat they wanted or the fancy sweets for which the region was famous, they still had a wide range of food choices in the countryside during normal times. In dearth or famine they suffered, perhaps even more than their counterparts in the cities. Nonetheless we should not underestimate the value of their normal diet in building sound bodies. And the shipboard diet, though low in certain key nutrients, was more than adequate in calories, overall balance, and most of the vitamins and minerals necessary for good health.

However healthy Spanish soldiers and sailors might have been from their previous diets, and however well fed on board, they still encountered illness and accident on the Atlantic run. Some of the common shipboard ailments included seasickness, constipation, dysentery, and various fevers, and there was always the danger of men and equipment falling from the rigging and of artillery pieces exploding.[156] As we saw in chapter 6, surgeons or barber-surgeons commonly traveled with the Spanish galleons of the Armada de la Guardia from the end of the sixteenth century on, although Mediterranean galleys and small sailing ships still did without.[157] In the absence of a proper medical officer, the contramaestre often served instead, giving rise to the mariners' saying that "the ship's doctor doesn't know how to cure on land," and that "the hands of the contramaestre are salves for one's pain."[158] Given the state of formal medical knowledge at the time, a talented amateur might have been a perfectly adequate substitute. A ship's surgeon supplied his own medical instruments in the seventeenth century, which could include a sizable assortment of saws, knives, scissors, pliers, hammers, and probes.[159] The medicines and equipment for preparing them figured as part of the standard equipment of the ship; long before separate medical officers formed part of the crew, Spanish ships carried a full assortment of pharmaceuticals.[160] Surgeons or whoever acted as a ship's medical officer learned to be adept at amputating limbs damaged in accidents or battle, and in treating and binding wounds. Their success rates were probably not impressive, particularly when dealing with ailments that were not self-limiting, because most of the remedies available lacked what we would consider therapeutic value.

The contents of the shipboard medicine chest varied little, whether one looks at a list from the mid-sixteenth century or one from the late seventeenth century. In the dozens of such lists examined for this study, the items were nearly always the same, with Latin names enhancing rather simple concoctions under the general headings of syrups, salves, lectuaries, plasters, oils, waters, powders, confections, and drugs, together with the spoons, syringes, balance scales, and weights used in dispensing them.[161] No fewer than seventy-seven items figure in one list from 1650, and many of the lists examined had a similarly wide range of specific compounds. Their cost might mount quite high in the list of ship's equipment. The medical supplies for one galleon in 1650 cost 901 silver reales, about eight times the monthly wages paid to a surgeon and over thirteen times the monthly wages of a barber-surgeon.[162] That list included lemon syrup, an unusual item that may have been carried for treating scurvy, but there is no indication of its purpose. Without a complete chemical analysis of the items carried, it is difficult to judge how effective they might have been in treating the injured and the sick, yet we should guard against judging centuries-old medicine by our own standards. The intent was to provide high-quality medical care on the royal fleets, with everything recommended by the doctors and surgeons, so that, as the king's ordinances said in 1633, "the people who serve me will not suffer a lack of anything necessary [for their medical care.]"[163]

Contemporary medical practice, following the ancients, found the source of many ailments in an imbalance of humors in the body. Cures involved restoring the balance of humors that signified good health, which could often be done by diet as well as by medicines.[164] Spanish ships in the Armada de la Guardia carried a special set of foods for the sick, which in some cases served to supplement the diet of the high officers and gentlemen on board as well. As mentioned before, in a typical list of provisions, these special foods (called dietas) included white biscuit, sugar, almonds, and raisins, plus eggs, live hens, and sheep, often carried in considerable amounts. For the 1629 fleet in which Arana's six galleons first sailed to the Indies, the dietas included 1,500 pounds each of white sugar and almonds, 1,260 pounds of raisins, 6 sheep, 351 hens, and 4,619 eggs—and that was when the plans called for just 3,000 men in the fleet, not the 7,000 who finally sailed.[165] Eggs could have been preserved by keeping them in cold sea water during the voyage, as Sorapán recommended.[166] The live animals would usually come aboard after everything else was loaded, some at Sanlúcar de Barrameda, others in the Canary Islands on the outward voyage or in Havana for the return voyage. Although the "principal persons" on board undoubtedly shared in the rations of fresh meat, it is not clear to what extent they were supposed to share in the other items of dietas carried for the "cure and regalement" of the sick, as the phrase often had it.[167] The ordinances of 1633 for the Armada del Mar Océano called for foods for the sick to be carried in a box with two keys, held by the master and the chaplain, and the chaplain's duties, as mentioned in chapter 6, included certifying on his word as a priest that the dietas had been used only for the sick.[168]

To a modern eye, the list of dietas might seem rather odd. The value of fresh meat and eggs on long voyages is obvious to us, though we might ignore their supposed medical uses. The special qualities of sugar, raisins, and nuts might escape our attention altogether. In the seventeenth century, however, chickens and eggs, in addition to their acknowledged nutritional value, served as the basis of numerous remedies for everything from sties to dysentery.[169] And sugar, raisins, and nuts were thought to have powerful curative properties, as well as being the sort of delicate food that would benefit the sick. Sorapán discussed various potions of dried fruit and nuts mixed with wine in his treatise on seventeenth-century medicine, which followed standard medical practice.[170]

Where diet, medicines, and the surgeons' skills failed, hospitals took over. Writers who considered the health and well-being of Spanish mariners urged the creation of hospitals in all major ports in the Indies, as well as in Spanish ports on the north, south, and southeast coasts.[171] Spanish soldiers paid for the cost of their medical care, whether on land or sea. One planned expedition in 1577–78 charged each Spanish soldier 1 real per month for medical care, but noted that the Italian and German contingents in the expedition had no such arrangement, and presumably no formal medical care.[172] The crown bore the cost for sailors' medical care. Given the chronic shortages of funds in the treasury in the seventeenth century, mariners' hospitals generally suffered from a lack of equipment and personnel; nonetheless, they existed. There were at least two mariners' hospitals in Bilbao in 1613.[173] Medical care for mariners on the north coast came under the jurisdiction of the proveedor de armadas—Fernando de la Rivaherrera in the 1620s. Whatever his faults as an absentee official, he took a great interest in the welfare of sailors and their families, urging the crown to found a hospital in Santander in 1623, and arguing in general for better hospital care and other benefits for the men in his charge.[174] At about the same time, plans went forward for another hospital in San Sebastián, though it took many years to secure the money to make it permanent.[175] There was still no hospital in Santander in February 1628, when the Armada del Mar Océano arrived in port with many sick men aboard after a tour of duty off the French coast. With no hospital, General Martín de Vallecilla, the admiral of the armada, had to put together makeshift accommodations for his men by requisitioning beds and food from the local inhabitants.[176]

Such improvised remedies could not succeed in the Indies, because the small permanent populations of the coastal towns were incapable of providing medical care for all the crews and passengers of the arriving fleets. Already by the late sixteenth century, hospitals served the poor and sick in many of the major New World ports, with others along the major inland routes traveled by new immigrants.[177] Whether supported by institutional or private charity or by the crown, these hospitals provided at least some comfort for the sick. The Indies fleets kept a close accounting of the sick crewmen and soldiers sent to hospitals in Cartagena de Indias, Portobelo, Veracruz, and Havana, because each man received a monetary payment in lieu of daily rations when he missed musters because of illness. In 1634 this amounted to 3 reales a day for several officers being cared for in a private home.[178] When typhus or the fevers of the Caribbean struck the fleets on top of the ordinary casualties from accidents and minor ailments, a fleet might leave sick crewmen behind in every port it touched.[179]

The hospital in Portobelo seems to have functioned in some houses rented by the crown.[180] In less than three weeks in July 1622, the proveedor of armadas and major-domo of the hospital spent over 9,000 reales just on food for the patients in his care. An ordinary day's purchases included fresh bread, white biscuit, fish, oranges and lemons, eggs, oil, vinegar, chickpeas, wild amaranth, rosemary, saffron, pepper, cloves, cinnamon, cumin, and cilantro, plus expenses for firewood and the wages of a cook and his assistant. Other days would feature fresh meat rather than fish, and the almonds, raisins, and sugar of the shipboard dietas also played their part. Lemons and oranges appeared among virtually every day's purchases, along with bananas, quinces, and other fruits. Interestingly enough, wine rarely figured in the accounts. Expenses for bedding and for plates, spoons, jugs, and pots helped raise the cost. The food items were moderately priced, even if higher than those in Spain, and the major-domo bought everything he needed from the residents of Portobelo. With the exception of a few items such as bananas, the foods were familiar to anyone raised in Spain, evidence that Spanish colonists in the New World reproduced the generally healthful diet of their homeland.[181]

It is difficult to determine the overall death rate among crews and soldiers on the Indies fleets, or among the paying passengers they carried. Some authors have simply asserted that it was "appalling," but without offering any specifics.[182] To the developed world of the twentieth century, the death rates common in Europe as a whole in the sixteenth and seventeenth centuries seem appalling. Illnesses that hardly pose a threat to wealthy societies in the twentieth century were regularly life-threatening if not fatal then, to princes as well as paupers. In the two pay books analyzed in chapter 6, four out of twenty-eight gunners on one ship died on the round-trip voyage in 1634–35, a death rate of 14.3 percent.[183] That was about four times the death rate one might expect in the general population of Europe at the time, and higher still than the age-specific death rates for adult males. When we consider the hazards faced by gunners in the Armada de la Guardia, their high death rate is hardly surprising. Soldiers in one large company on that same fleet in 1634–35 lost 8 percent of their number to death, over twice the rate one would expect in the general European population, and much higher than the age-specific rate.[184] Again, considering their occupation and the hazards of sea travel, that is not a surprising figure. A thorough study of the pay books for sailors and soldiers in the Indies fleets could shed much more light on the matter, but that has not been attempted here. Given the admittedly limited nature of the evidence at hand, we would have to judge the death rates of sailors and soldiers on the Indies fleets as lying somewhere between those of the general European population in normal times and the truly appalling rates that could occur during epidemics or open warfare.

Death from disease was an enormously greater hazard to soldiers and sailors than deaths in battle, particularly during the seventeenth century. The history of the Thirty Years' War in central Europe is a horrific chronicle of plagues and pestilence as much as it is a story of dramatic military encounters. On the Indies fleets as well, the hazards from disease and shipwreck were undoubtedly more important statistically than losses from naval warfare. Nonetheless, in the 1620s and 1630s, the likelihood of battle greatly increased from earlier decades. It was in these crucial years that Spain fought for the preservation of its New World empire against the ever-present threat of invaders from Holland, England, and France. The six galleons built by don Martín de Arana for the Spanish crown played a major role in this struggle, as members of the Armada de la Guardia. The remainder of our story will deal with the several Indies fleets between 1629 and 1635 in which Arana's six galleons played a part, and with the later history of one of the six—the *San Felipe*—that had an even more dramatic role to play.

EIGHT

The Struggle for the Indies, 1629–1635

The "galiflota" of 1629, a war fleet of thirty-five ships, represented a tremendous effort in a year without merchant fleets. Royal ministers scarcely questioned that it had to be sent, despite the chilling losses at Matanzas in 1628. Fortunately the total receipts of treasure and trade in 1628–29 were quite respectable, once the Tierra Firme fleet returned home safely. There is no doubt, however, that the late 1620s and early 1630s marked a slump in the Indies trade, although not as serious a slump as Chaunu claims.[1] At that crucial juncture, the crown determined that war fleets had to sail in defense of the empire, whether or not the averías on trade could finance them. In the period when Martín de Arana's galleons served in the Armada de la Guardia—roughly from 1629 to 1635—the crown would continue this extraordinary response to the challenge to its empire. Although the cost was high, the results, as we shall see, would repay that expense.

The fleet of galleons in 1629, however unusual it was in some respects, continued the tradition of the Indies run (described in chapter 1) that had been evolving for over a century. Once the "galiflota" left the safety of Cádiz Bay in mid-August, it probably headed briefly down the African coast, then out toward the Canary Islands, following the traditional path of many fleets before it. The voyage from Cádiz to the Canaries could be as short as four days or as long as fourteen, depending on the winds and currents and on whether a ship sailed alone or in convoy. Even a merchant fleet could make it in eight days, if all went well.[2] At sea the commander of the 1629 fleet, don Fadrique de Toledo, opened his sealed orders, as generations of commanders had done before him.[3] In addition to delivering supplies for the reinforcement of Cartagena de Indias and combating any Dutch fleets

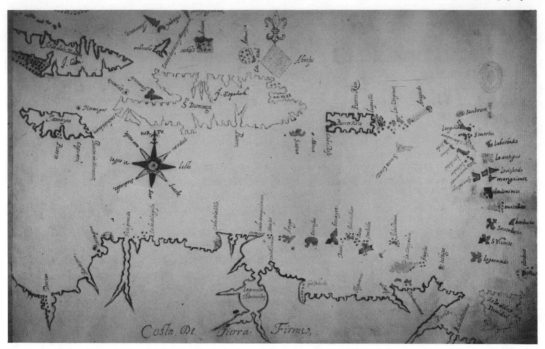

Figure 28. Stylized map of the Caribbean Islands. The mainland of northern South America (Tierra Firme) appears at the lower part of the map, with Jamaica, Española, Puerto Rico, and Cuba to the north. East of Puerto Rico and slightly south are the small islands of San Cristóbal and Nieves, the destination of the 1629 armada under the command of Fadrique de Toledo. They were listed as uninhabited on this map, which dates from about 1615. Manuscript of Nicolás de Cardona, *Descripciones geographicas, e hydrographicas de muchas tierras y mares del norte, y sur, en las Indias* [Madrid, 1632]. Courtesy of the Biblioteca Nacional, Madrid.)

encountered, the armada of 1629 had a new charge—to dislodge interlopers from the Lesser Antilles.[4] Don Fadrique's officers began to plan their strategy, studying what few charts they had of the Lesser Antilles. (See figure 28.) Spaniards had shown little interest in those islands, in part because they had less to offer than the main Spanish bases, and in part because the fierce Caribs who inhabited many of the islands rarely permitted visitors to stay long without attacking them. These islands, then, formed the southern outer fringes of the Spanish empire in the Caribbean, claimed but only tenuously held.

Spain had no serious challenges to its dominance of the Atlantic until the late sixteenth century. Even when European pirates and interlopers arrived, their early efforts were aimed almost entirely at forcing their way into the trade monopoly with colonial ports and preying on Spanish merchant vessels. Fernández Duro compared these early pirates to frigate birds, predators that steal fish from the pelican because they lack the skill to fish for themselves.[5] This unflattering, if accurate, picture began to change in the early seventeenth century, when French, Dutch, and English interlopers began to set up permanent factories for trade and even began to found settlements. One of their main activities was growing tobacco, which sold for outrageous prices in Europe in the early seventeenth century.[6] The peace treaties between Spain and its neighbors between 1598 and 1609 acknowledged

Spanish control over those parts of the empire that were effectively occupied and controlled, but everything else was fair game, at least according to everyone outside Spain. The point was not worth violating the treaties, however, and officially sponsored challenges to Spain's ownership of those areas outside the main bases of the empire were suspended during the peace. Once the Thirty Years' War began in 1618, other Europeans began to make increasing incursions into the Caribbean.[7] It was these resident interlopers whom don Fadrique and his fleet had orders to evict.

Linked to the foreign settlements, but more serious, were reports of a concerted Dutch effort to wreck the empire and its trade altogether. In Barcelona in late July 1629, Philip IV had received word that Dutch fleets planned to attack both the Spanish West Indies and the Portuguese East Indies. Some said they had joined with the English and the French. If that were true, it was the realization of the king's worst nightmares. The reports mentioned a fleet of one hundred Dutch ships with ten thousand men, twenty-four English ships with three thousand men, and sixteen French ships with two thousand men. Each contingent had a particular assignment, from the capture of one of the Terceras (Azores Islands) to the conquest of bases all over the Caribbean.[8] If they succeeded, it would be the end of the empire. As outlandish as such reports may seem, they were easy to believe in the atmosphere of crisis that developed after Matanzas.

Off the Canaries, don Fadrique de Toledo's armada had its first test. A Spanish traveler whose father was governor of the island of Gran Canaria reported meeting and saluting don Fadrique's ship on August 22 off Tenerife, accepting messages and trumpet salutes in return. Military secrecy was evidently not as tight as it might have been, because the young man was told where the armada was heading in the Caribbean. Four days later, some six leagues from Gran Canaria, he saw six Dutch ships within speaking distance of the armada. From another report, it seems that there were eight or ten Dutch ships altogether. Evidently, part of the Spanish fleet pursued them for two days, then fought a day-long battle. Reports of the battle disagree on several points, but they agree that seven enemy ships surrendered to the Spanish, an encouraging beginning to their mission.[9] A letter from Sebastián de Oleaga, purveyor of the Spanish armada, mentioned witnesses to the battle off the island of Tenerife who reported seven ships captured and three escaped, from an original ten, rather than eight, ships.[10] Unfortunately, the men captured would provide no intelligence of other Dutch fleet movements, although some reports said that fifty Dutch sails had been seen off the Canaries in the previous two months. The governor's son reported that his father was armed at all times, expecting to be ordered off at any moment to fight for the crown, and many other important people in the islands were following his example.[11] Such was the tense atmosphere in the Canaries, as the armada continued its mission.

The actions of the Indies fleet of 1629 thereafter found various chroniclers, but rarely do they agree on the details or even the broad strokes of the picture. One account had the fleet continuing south to the Guinea coast of West Africa near the Cape Verde Islands, where it encountered and captured two Dutch ships. Under threat of torture, the prisoners supposedly revealed that the Dutch were fortifying San Cristóbal Island in the Antilles. Don Fadrique then sent some of his men ahead in the captured Dutch ships to pretend they were the reinforcements, throwing the Dutch off guard and allowing the main force of the armada to strike. This account then had don Fadrique winning a major battle against eighty-six Dutch ships, sinking eight and defeating forty-six more, while losing only five of his own vessels.[12] This entire story seems to be a fabrication, illustrating more than anything else the Spanish need to score a victory against the Dutch in 1629.

The reality was rather more prosaic, if still impressive, although the captured enemies were French and English rather than Dutch. The most trustworthy accounts relate that the armada first made its way to the Caribbean leeward island of Nieves, southeast of Puerto Rico. There, permanent English settlers had forged an uneasy partnership with corsairs who had the ships and ammunition that the English lacked.[13] With don Martín de Vallecilla and four galleons in the vanguard, the Spanish surprised ten corsair ships in port on September 17. Two of the smaller corsairs escaped through the shallows despite a barrage from the armada guns. The others were pursued into deeper water and captured by units of the Spanish fleet. An official report later mentioned that only seven ships loaded with tobacco were captured and that only nine were surprised in the harbor.[14] The tenth may have been too small to mention. One near disaster occurred when Captain Tiburcio Redín impetuously sailed his galleon *Jesús María* too close to shore, trying to get within cannon range of the island's small fort. He ran aground within range not only of the fort's two cannons but also of its harquebuses. Luckily, don Antonio de Oquendo arrived in time to help, anchoring his ship and landing his men for an overland attack, something the defenders did not expect. After losing twenty-two men to the Spanish assault, the defenders gave up and fled into the forest, abandoning the fort and its weaponry.

The following day the English occupants of the island surrendered themselves and their possessions to the Spanish, realizing that further resistance would only get them killed. Don Fadrique had the fort dismantled and the tobacco warehouses and other buildings burned. Then he had the *Jesús María* refloated, loaded the prisoners on his ships, and, after consulting the senior officers in the fleet, headed toward the island of San Cristóbal, another center of illicit tobacco cultivation and corsairs. San Cristóbal had both English and French settlers, the English in the south and the French in the north. From their prisoners, the Spanish learned that the English end of the island had a well-situated fort called Charles, which dominated the harbor with twenty-two iron guns, nine mortars, and sixteen hundred men. The French had two other forts, one called Basse Terre nine miles from the English fort, with eleven guns, and the other called Richelieu on the other side of the north coast, in a site inaccessible to large ships.

One author mentions that the French government had sent a large fleet under the Sieur de Cahuzac to defend the island from an expected Spanish attack. Instead, that worthy commander had evidently gone off on a private marauding expedition in the Gulf of Mexico.[15] Nonetheless, at San Cristóbal the Spanish could be fairly certain that the inhabitants had been warned of their arrival, and they reconnoitered carefully, circling the island as dense smoke from the tobacco warehouses cast a blue curtain over their approach. Near the rocky coast where Richelieu stood, a furious storm suddenly caught the fleet, but the skill of the commanders pulled them through with

Figure 29. "The Recapture of San Cristóbal Island in the Caribbean, 1629" by Félix Castelo. The captain-general of the 1629 fleet, don Fadrique de Toledo y Osorio, appears in the right foreground. (Courtesy of the Prado Museum, Madrid.)

no more damage than a few broken masts and torn sails. Finding a safe haven at last, the Spanish dropped anchors, lowered boats, and took an assault party ashore, probably near the Charles fort, though that is not clear from the sources. (See figure 29.) A system of well-manned trenches defended the fort, and the Spanish fired artillery at the trenches to prepare their advance. Luck was on their side: one of the first volleys killed the governor of the fort. The defenders soon became demoralized and fled the trenches to the palm groves inland. As the Spanish companies continued their advance on the fort, a spokesman for the defenders advanced with a white flag and surrendered to don Fadrique. The rest of the operation was no longer in doubt. The other two forts surrendered without a fight, including Richelieu with 14 cannons. All told, the Spanish captured 129 cannons, 42 mortars, 1,350 muskets and harquebuses with abundant ammunition, and between 2,000 and 3,000 men on the two islands—all in seventeen days.

With noteworthy leniency, don Fadrique put the captives aboard six of the ships captured on Nieves and sent them back to Europe. He kept the best ship and six hundred men as hostages to guarantee repayment for the food he had supplied for the voyage. The only thing they offered in exchange for their lives was a promise never to return to the islands claimed by Spain. As it happened, their promise had little value, and many returned almost immediately to begin again. In the short run, the mission was successful, however. The settlements were at least temporarily destroyed, and don Fadrique had provided a sorely needed success for Spanish military might in the Caribbean. More important was the treasure that his fleet would bring safely back to Spain, although that would not happen until the following year. From San Cristóbal the fleet sailed for Cartagena on October 4, arriving at the end of the month. From Cartagena don Martín de Vallecilla and the silver galleons sailed on to Portobelo to collect the treasure accumulated in the uncertain situation of the previous year.[16] That assignment was a reminder that don Fadrique de Toledo and don Antonio de Oquendo were on loan, with their ships, from the Armada del Mar Océano in 1629. The silver galleons under Vallecilla, which included at least four of Arana's six galleons, had the prime responsibility for carrying treasure back to Spain; in an ordinary year, as the Armada de la Guardia they would have been the main Spanish military presence in the Caribbean.

In 1629, the Spanish war fleet of thirty-five ships stayed the winter in Cartagena. The city boasted fairly good fortifications, the product of nearly a century of Spanish settlement. The tempo of defense works had speeded up in 1625 under the energetic governor don Francisco de Murga, and one of don Fadrique de Toledo's instructions for the 1629 fleet was to carry more artillery and ammunition to the city. Don Francisco sent a lengthy report to the crown in 1630 detailing the work he had done and hoped to accomplish for Cartagena's defense.[17] The handsome map of the city and its harbor from the same period, mentioned in chapter 3, may very well picture some of the galleons in the 1629 fleet. They certainly have the proper shape and rigging, including full sets of topgallant sails.[18] From Cartagena, don Fadrique de Toledo wrote to Veracruz in February asking about enemy ship movements, sending two copies of his letter by separate dispatch boats, a standard precaution against mishaps. He was anxious to reach Havana, where his ships could be careened and readied for the homeward voyage. Even though they had been partially careened and worked on often, shipworms caused more damage every day, and a full careening could not be done in Cartagena, because of the risk of storms and the lack of shipwrights. The city also lacked sufficient food for the several thousand men in the fleet. More had to be sent from New Spain, and the humid climate easily corrupted what supplies they still had.[19]

Eventually the fleet was able to move on to Havana, but not in time for extensive repairs. Caution had kept don Fadrique in Cartagena until he was sure that the area was not infested with enemy vessels. By then his fleet carried two years' treasure, and the memory of Matanzas was still painfully fresh. On June 5, 1630, don Fadrique wrote to the crown from Havana, saying that he had all the treasure assembled and ready to bring to Spain, but he and his officers nonetheless agreed that the risk was too great. They decided to leave some of the treasure safely in Havana, dividing the risk with the 1630 fleet of don Tomás de Larráspuru. According to his orders, don Fadrique left behind a squadron of eight large ships and one dispatch boat to serve as Larráspuru's escort. Merchant vessels previously stranded in the Indies without escort returned with the fleet, except for eight ships considered unfit for the crossing.[20]

The voyage home passed uneventfully, contrary to expectations generated in the previous several years. Don Fadrique brought the fleet into Cádiz Bay on August 2, after waiting for a tide high enough to carry Vallecilla's silver galleons over the bar at Sanlúcar. He had not lost a single ship on the voyage, arriving back in Spain just under a year after he had set sail. The return had been slower than expected because the merchant ships with him were so heavily laden that, as he put it, he practically had to carry them in his arms.[21] Given the hazards of the Indies run even in ordinary years, the successful 1629–30 round trip was a remarkable achievement. Everyone greeted the fleet's safe arrival "with such joy and gladness that there is no pen that can describe the scene." The House of Trade wrote a glowing letter of praise to don Fadrique, as prayers and services of thanksgiving spread outward in waves from Cádiz to the court in Madrid and beyond.[22]

The treasure brought back by the armada in 1630 reached impressive proportions—more than 5 million pesos of 8 reales each, which worked out to over 3.5 million ducados.[23] About one-quarter of that belonged to the crown, and taxes on private treasure shifted more in the direction of the royal coffers. An unexpected bonus was the late arrival of a second load of treasure at the end of the year. The orders of the Armada de la Guardia sent out in April under don Tomás de Larráspuru had originally allowed for a possible winter layover, though royal officials urged the commander to try to manage without one.[24] In the summertime heat of the Caribbean, many of Larráspuru's men fell sick, but otherwise things went so well that he risked a return voyage late in the season. On the way home he proved his reputation for luck as well as skill by using an unaccustomed route through the Caribbean Islands, outwitting a Dutch squadron lying in wait for him.[25] Although not expected until March, he arrived safely home in December with another 5 million ducados, about one-third of which belonged to the crown.[26]

The averías designed to pay for ordinary escort fleets hardly began to cover the costs of the armadas of 1629 and 1630, especially with the expenses of wintering over and added repairs to the ships. Partial accounts from don Martín de Vallecilla for the Armada de la Guardia alone added 30,000 ducados to the total spent by the crown, most of which it hoped to recover from the merchant community.[27] All together, the king had spent a total of 1.5 million ducados on the wintering over, counting expenses for the ships under don Fadrique de Toledo, don Martín de Vallecilla, and don Hernán Gómez de Sandoval, captain-general of the New Spain fleet that had been in the Indies since 1628. To cover these and other expenses, the king asked the merchant community to pay averías totaling 31.33 percent of the value of their shipments.[28] With their trade at a virtual standstill, and the military achievements of 1629–30 of dubious benefit to them, the merchants of Seville protested these exactions as vigorously as they could. Eventually, a compromise gained them some concessions from the crown in return for their money, but the extraordinary cost of the 1629–30 fleets was a harbinger of things to come.[29]

For the next several years at least, the crown would press as hard as possible to supply large fleets for the Indies run. The aim was military—to drive interlopers and enemy powers from the empires of the united crowns of Spain and Portugal in the New World—but the crown could validly claim that the merchant community would benefit from military success as well. For that reason, they would be asked to foot the bill, although their trade showed no immediate signs of revival. In the strains of the struggle for the Indies in the 1630s, the aims of the crown and of the merchants would diverge considerably from one another. The crown favored an all-out military push, claiming this would protect the Indies trade. The merchants seemed to have lost faith that the trade could be defended at all. Instead of relying on expensive fleets that were extremely difficult to outfit and provision, many of them would have preferred a return to the days of individual sailings across the Atlantic, with swift galizabras carrying the treasure, as they had often done in the days of Philip II. The dilemma for the crown was that expenses for the needed military presence in the New World had to come from somewhere, and commerce was the only candidate.[30] So, in the crucial period of the early 1630s, the same pattern unfolded year after year: royal officials would plan large fleets, merchants would protest their poverty, and eventually the fleets would sail, financed by expensive loans and repaid by enormous averías and crown subsidies for the balance.

The increasing military demands of the 1630s strained human as well as material resources. No sooner had don Fadrique de Toledo's fleet returned from the Indies than he received further orders from the crown to report to Lisbon and rejoin the Armada del Mar Océano, which he commanded. Despite the "ordinary and common desire for land after so much sea" and their need for rest, his men were asked to stay in service and sail to Lisbon as well. The chronic shortage of experienced mariners was even worse in 1630.[31] Nonetheless, with money and supplies from the crown, don Fadrique reported, it would be done, and he ordered don Antonio de Oquendo to proceed to Lisbon from Cádiz as soon as possible.[32] General Martín de Vallecilla, badly in need of rest and medical care from his "great age, some old wounds, and the labors of forty-five years of continuous voyaging," was nonetheless ordered to stay in Cádiz preparing the ships for Lisbon. His petition for some time to go to his northern home, which he had not seen for some years, and to seek medical care, met a chilly response from royal officials in Madrid. One member of the Junta de Armadas, although acknowledging the service of General Vallecilla over the years, noted that the king had rewarded him for that service. Because no one else was available to supervise the refitting of the twenty-two galleons needed for the coming year, he could not be spared. If he needed a doctor, he could find one in Cádiz or Seville. Other members of the Junta showed more compassion, but the consensus was that Vallecilla had to stay in Cádiz unless he found a substitute, in which case he could have two months off, and no more. That was not overly generous: Vallecilla had neither official post nor salary in Cádiz.[33]

Don Antonio de Oquendo went to Lisbon about a month after returning from the Indies, taking seven ships and a dispatch boat with him. The other ships pertaining to the Armada del Mar Océano were to follow as soon as they were fit and crewed.[34] Don Fadrique de Toledo surveyed the ships in Cádiz along with Juan de Castro y Castilla for the king's council and Sebastián de Oleaga, the purveyor of the armada. Their list included four of the galleons built by Martín de Arana, all of which had served in the silver fleet under General Vallecilla that had just returned: *Begoña, San Felipe, San Juan Baptista,* and *Los Tres Reyes.*[35] They and the other ships fit to serve still needed repairs, either in Cádiz or in Lisbon, though don Fadrique was not disposed to supervise the work. Instead, after decades of loyal service, he drifted into disobedience to the crown and its unreasonable demands. His own private drama would end with his disgrace and death in prison a few years later (see chapter 9), but in the meantime, the fleet he had brought safely home in 1630 prepared for another mission. The other two galleons built by Arana— *Santiago* and *San Sebastián*—had not fared as well as the four mentioned on don Fadrique's list. Eventually judged too small for the Armada de la Guardia, they seem to have served with the contingent from the Armada del Mar Océano in the 1629–30 fleet, and the extended layover in Caribbean ports had done them no good.[36] After repairs, the *Santiago* joined a group of eight galleons going to Flanders with General Francisco de Rivera in 1632.[37] The *San Sebastián* was only a few toneladas smaller than the *Santiago,* but there seems to have been something wrong with it from the start. It had to undergo extensive repairs after the 1630 return voyage from the Indies, and it was probably the fairly new galleon *San Sebastián* that was sold before July 1632 "for not being appropriate for warfare." Bought by Nicolás de Massibradi, the Ragusan shipowner who held extensive contracts with the Spanish crown, it was destined to serve in its new owner's Italian squadron.[38]

In Lisbon preparations went ahead in the fall of 1630 to bring the Armada del Mar Océano back into fighting shape. Oquendo estimated that preparing twenty-three galleons and one dispatch boat would cost nearly half a million ducados, including careening, repairs, artillery, and wages for the sailors and soldiers already signed on. Food also needed to be provided for the men— more than 5,100 of them—on shore and for the coming campaign season. Horacio Levanto, the man who had supplied the 1629–30 Indies fleet, also held the contract for the Lisbon supplies, much of which he had to transport from Andalusia. The most immediate need was for 24,000 fanegas of wheat to be baked into biscuit, and that was just the beginning.[39]

As Oquendo prepared the fleet in Lisbon in the fall of 1630, events in the New World had taken an alarming turn. There were reports of enemy ships near Jamaica in the heart of the Caribbean sea routes. Much worse, the Dutch had established a foothold in Pernambuco in northeast Brazil. This attack on the Portuguese possessions in the New World also threatened the lifeline of communications and treasure receipts from Tierra Firme.[40] The Spanish needed to make a strong response, just as they had in 1625, when they had ousted the Dutch from Bahia, taken the year before. In 1625 the Spanish hero had been don Fadrique de Toledo; in 1631 it was to be don Antonio de Oquendo.[41]

The Portuguese governor of Pernambuco had burned his ships to keep them out of enemy hands, which meant that Oquendo could expect no help from local forces once he arrived. Scraping together a relief fleet of twenty-six ships and nearly five thousand men in Lisbon, Oquendo left for Brazil in early May 1631, making a brave show as they sailed out of Lisbon harbor. The fleet carried as its admirals don Francisco de Vallecilla, Martín's brother, and Nicolás de Massibradi, both of them devoted to Oquendo. The Junta de Armadas began planning a resupply mission to follow behind, but, as it happened, the fleet was home before the resupply was needed.[42] It took two months to reach Bahia with supplies and reinforcements for its defense. Then Oquendo reorganized the relief plans for Pernambuco and Paraíba and escorted the sugar ships heading for Lisbon into safe waters, with no hindrance from the Dutch. On August 18, the Dutch left Pernambuco looking for the Spanish fleet. When they found it, the Dutch admiral Pater took only sixteen of his thirty-three ships with him, judging only eight of Oquendo's ships battleworthy. Oquendo would have agreed with him, but he used what he had skillfully.

The battle raged for eight hours on September 12 without letup. The two flagships grappled and men fought hand to hand until the sand on deck was wet with blood. The Dutch flagship caught fire and exploded, and its commander died in the water. Vallecilla and his ship met the same fate. On the Spanish capitana, of the ten close comrades who had come to fight with Oquendo, eight were killed and two gravely wounded. In all, the Dutch had lost three ships and around two thousand men. The Spanish had lost one ship to fire, another to the Dutch, and nearly six hundred men, half of them on the capitana. In the next days, Oquendo landed troops and munitions on the coast to relieve Pernambuco—his main mission accomplished. The Dutch kept in sight but refused to engage again and, as Oquendo's fleet headed for home, contented themselves with attacking one of the ships in the rear guard. It escaped, but so badly damaged that it soon sank, in view of but beyond help from the armada. Thereafter Oquendo ordered the fleet to stay together regardless of provocation, and even stripped two men of their commands when they disobeyed him and pursued an intruder. The fleet returned in triumph to Lisbon in late November. They had done no more than loosen the Dutch grip on Brazil, but the victory could be savored nonetheless.

The celebrations would be short-lived. Oquendo's fleet had been an extraordinary effort, but the regular fleets for the year still needed to return safely before 1631 could be deemed a successful year. They were already late by the time Oquendo returned from Brazil, and it soon became clear that they must have been delayed in the Indies. Just what had happened was not known in Spain until the following March. The New Spain fleet under Admiral Manuel Serrano had left Veracruz very late in the season on October 14, carrying in addition to treasure and goods the body of its Captain-General Miguel de Echazarreta, who had died in the Indies. The fleet encountered one of the region's dreaded fall storms, losing the almiranta with all its treasure in Campeche, along with two merchant ships. Another ship sank one league from Tabasco. The remainder of the fleet returned to Veracruz for the winter. Meanwhile General Tomás de Larráspuru and the 1631 Armada de la Guardia waited for them in Havana, finally sending a dispatch boat to Spain at the end of December with news that they still had not arrived. The dispatch reached Sanlúcar in mid-February; the uncertain fate of the New Spain fleet gave rise to woeful speculation that the entire fleet was lost. The reality was bad enough. Larráspuru came home in April 1632 with the Tierra Firme treasure and the only two ships from the New Spain fleet still able to make the crossing. Private individuals lost 5 million pesos, according to the merchant consulado in Seville. The king's share of about 1 million had shrunk with the expenses of wintering over, and the balance passed entirely to creditors.[43]

It would be hard to exaggerate the gloom that settled in because of the 1631–32 losses. The king's chief minister Olivares himself said the monarchy could fall at one blow, that the king risked his crown because of the disaster. Pessimism spread through the court, with bitter satires of the monarchy circulating through the streets of Madrid in the next several years. The Indies trade was in deep depression in 1632, damaged by the 1631 losses as well as by fears of the Dutch in Brazil and the added expense of defending the Portuguese possessions. Spanish merchants considered going out of business rather than face continual threats to their livelihood from uncertain trade and royal confiscations. Licenses to foreigners to engage in the Indies trade in Seville and Cádiz plummeted in value.[44] In their fear, Spanish authorities already half suspected that the Portuguese were collaborating with the Dutch and would hand all Tierra Firme over to them soon. Even as Oquendo sailed against the Dutch in 1631, the king issued a decree ordering his governors in the Indies to expel foreigners from the Castilian possessions in the New World. The foreigners, of course, included Portuguese, particularly numerous on the islands of Puerto Rico and Cuba. Evidently, the order was not carried out anywhere, but it helped to deepen the mutual suspicion between the Spanish and Portuguese.[45]

Rumors and intelligence reports in 1632 had the Dutch mounting an attack on the Castilian Indies from Brazil, joined by a new fleet sent from Holland.[46] Because of this, the crown determined to send another large fleet for defense, mortgaging the treasure receipts in advance.[47] The king ordered at least twenty-six large ships and four dispatch boats prepared for the 1632 Indies armada, for a total of nearly 15,000 toneladas.[48] Yet it was not easy for the naval establishment to respond to repeated royal orders for large armadas. Many ships had been lost in recent years, and the ones remaining were older on the average than they had been before 1631 or would be after 1636.[49] The early 1630s thus presented a crisis in shipping along with everything else, and only the continued possibility of embargoes and contracts for foreign shipping brought the fleets near their desired strength. Even with merchant fleets unlikely for 1632, it would be hard to scrape together enough tonnage for a decent armada. In 1631 and early 1632 royal officials scoured the coast, but by February they had been able to locate only eighty-one likely ships in all Spanish ports, nineteen of which the king chose for his 1632 fleet, including several of the six built by Arana.[50] Don Antonio de Oquendo, who had become a member of the Council of War in 1630, reported the distressing news that of all the ships in Cádiz, only the *San Felipe* built by Arana was currently fit to carry silver.[51] If Larráspuru returned in time, some of his ships might serve as well.

General don Lope de Hoces y Córdoba, in charge of refitting armada ships in Cádiz, complained of particularly acute shortages of men and money for the work, though the infantry for the fleet was up to strength.[52] Through the winter of 1631–32 the costs continued to rise for the careening in Cádiz, in part because the ships that had sailed in 1629–30 needed so much work.

Even new ships such as the galleons built by Martín de Arana had needed
new rigging after their damaging stay in the Indies. The little good equipment they still carried had been taken from them to supply the ships sent on
to Lisbon and for Oquendo's emergency trip to Brazil in 1631. In addition,
the king had ordered extra fortifications on the ships for 1632, so that they
might stay at sea much longer than usual in search of the Dutch. An
unusually hot summer in Cádiz had opened up seams in many of the careened
ships, leaving their interiors unprotected when the winter rains began. In
all, the refitting costs for the 1632 fleet would be astronomical. The purveyor
don Francisco Beltrán de Manurga—restored to grace after his refusal to
accompany the 1629 fleet—had to justify his accounts in Madrid before a
largely incredulous Junta de Armadas.[53] Although one can appreciate the
need for cost-effectiveness in supplying the fleets, this incident reminds us
once again of the difficulties the naval establishment faced in working for the
crown. Grand plans for impressive fleets were rarely matched by a willingness to spend the money needed to carry out those plans. The difficulties over
unrealistic timetables and scarce funds that plagued the 1629 fleet continued
to characterize the fleets through the early 1630s.

The king wanted the 1632 armada to leave in April to reinforce the fleets
still in the Indies—clearly an impossible task. May was no better, unless don
Fadrique de Toledo could send four Portuguese ships from Lisbon. The Junta
de Guerra de Indias favored a September departure, avoiding the Dutch but
risking a winter crossing. None of the plans lacked difficulties. The Portuguese might resist sending their ships; a winter crossing was always dangerous; some silver had to be fetched before September. As debate raged in the
king's various councils and juntas during March, they still did not know
when, or if, Larráspuru would make it back with the Tierra Firme treasure
from 1631. At least there was a certain flexibility in timing, because no
merchant fleets would sail to Tierra Firme or Honduras that year, at the
request of the House of Trade. The major problem, as always, was money.
The king had asked the merchants for their averías in advance—set at an
outrageous 40 percent. That would kill what little trade remained, according to many of the king's councilors. The burden of their advice was that the
1632 fleet had to be on the king's account.[54] In Cádiz, don Lope de Hoces
continued refitting the nineteen ships that were to be the core of the fleet, a
list that included five of the galleons built by Martín de Arana—all but the
San Sebastián. The five were part of the ten designated as the silver fleet, to be
reinforced by four Portuguese galleons.[55] By mid-March Hoces could report
that the silver galleons were as strong "as if they had to make a voyage
around the world," a good thing because his recent intelligence confirmed
that the Dutch planned a major assault on the Spanish empire.[56]

Through April and May Hoces worked to finish the ships in Cádiz and
supply them with crews and companies of infantry, all the while pestering
the crown for needed funds and fighting his own exhaustion and ill health.
Oquendo arrived in Cádiz on April 21 from Madrid, preparing to take
command of the 1632 fleet.[57] By then the mood had lightened somewhat,
due to the long-awaited arrival a week before of Tomás de Larráspuru with
the Armada de la Guardia and the remains of the New Spain fleet from 1631.
Nearly all the registered treasure was earmarked for creditors of the crown,
who had advanced money for the fleets. Understandably, many private

individuals tried to avoid royal confiscations of their incoming treasure by concealing it. They were met by a fraud investigation team commissioned the previous December, which began two months of inquiries as soon as the fleet arrived.[58] In such an atmosphere, the merchants protested strongly against having to put together a New Spain fleet to sail with the galleons. Eventually, they made their point; the galleons under Oquendo would sail alone.[59] Luckily, Larráspuru's arrival with the silver made it less urgent for Oquendo's fleet to leave immediately. The galleons often carried mercury on the outbound voyage, because it was a crucial part of silver refining in the New World. Once the mercury arrived in Cádiz, special containers had to be built to protect it from dampness, and that could take considerable time. Altogether, some 198 toneladas of mercury would be sent in 1632, both to New Spain and to Tierra Firme for transshipment to Peru. Although Oquendo was none too pleased with the extra trouble caused by the mercury, after several years of uncertain fleets the New World mines were desperate for it.[60] The fleet also carried muskets and harquebuses, gathered from all over Andalusia, for transshipment to Peru.[61]

Final preparations continued through June and into July, with officials gathering crew, supplies, and infantry. Due to a major restructuring of Spain's military forces at the same time, the infantry companies on board were each supposed to contain 250 men, rather than the 100 or so that were traditional. Although don Fadrique de Toledo in Lisbon and don Antonio de Oquendo in Cádiz vigorously opposed the change, they had no choice but to carry it out, putting junior officers rather than captains in charge of contingents of the same company that had to travel on separate ships.[62] Still short of crew, the fleet left for the Indies on July 26–27, with eleven galleons from Spain, three (instead of four) from Portugal, one *urca de guerra,* three dispatch boats, and two tartans. They carried 4,100 men more or less, including 1,211 sailors, 2,449 soldiers, and more than 400 gunners. The total cost of the refitting was a very high 24.8 ducados per tonelada, including all the extra fortifications ordered by the king.[63] We might recall that Arana's ships had cost only 10 ducados more than that to build. With advance pay for the soldiers and sailors, food, and supplies, the cost came to over 716,000 ducados.[64] Averías of 22.5 percent on the returning fleets in 1633 would pay less than 20 percent of the total cost.[65] Even before the successful departure of the 1632 fleet, the royal bureaucracy had already begun planning for the next year. The Count-Duke of Olivares referred the king's order for a 15,000-tonelada fleet for 1633 to the Junta de Armadas on July 16, and they considered it on the 27th, the day the 1632 fleet left Cádiz for the New World.[66] Right at the start of their planning for 1633, ships purchased by royal agents in northern Europe figured in the fleet's roster, a necessary expedient as long as the crisis in Spanish shipping tonnage lasted.[67]

The irony of the 1632 fleet, prepared in anticipation of a major Dutch offensive, is that it saw no action that has left a trace in the records. The galleons wintered over in Cartagena, ready for a Dutch attack that never came. In fact, the entire round trip passed almost uneventfully, except for an unusual amount of sickness. This first became apparent in a report written from Cartagena de Indias in December by Martín de Velasco Brievela, the king's general comptroller for the fleet. In his letter he reported ''a great quantity of sick men,'' especially those on the three Portuguese galleons.

They alone had 55 dead and 140 more in hospital in Cartagena. Although no specific illness was mentioned, the men might have carried the disease from home. It was not unusual for Asian and African diseases to enter Lisbon and Seville with the fleets.

With more men falling sick every day, the immediate problem for Velasco was the cost, because he had to pay 4 reales per day for each man hospitalized. Although the Junta de Armadas did not question the need to pay for their care, it urged Velasco to pay no more than 3 reales per day, still more than it would have cost in Spain.[68] When the fleet returned home, the men who fell ill on the return voyage entered the hospital in Cádiz, which was run by the religious order of St. John of God. Even the monks complained of the cost of caring for so many sick, asking in vain for the alms they were paid to be raised to 3.5 reales from 2.5.[69] Altogether, the wintering over of Oquendo's fleet cost 523,000 ducados, plus another 50,000 for provisions sent from New Spain, probably to Cartagena.[70] The averías on trade that year, even set at 23.5 percent, would pay only about 20 percent of the total cost.[71]

On the return voyage, the fleet followed a nearly ideal timetable, leaving Cartagena on March 11, 1633, and arriving in Havana on April 2. After depositing the treasure, Oquendo set sail again to find and escort the New Spain fleet. General Martín de Vallecilla set out from Veracruz once he knew Oquendo was waiting, bringing with him the New Spain fleet that had left Spain in 1631. With favorable winds, they all entered Havana safely on May 9. After distributing the treasure among the galleons, the combined fleets sailed for home on May 26, arriving in Cádiz and Sanlúcar by mid-July.[72]

From one point of view, it was a miracle in those years to have had such an uneventful voyage. From another point of view, it was a terrible waste of money to have sent a war fleet that found no war. All five of the galleons built by Martín de Arana that served in the Indies fleets of 1632–33 carried treasure on the way home, the *San Felipe* acting as almiranta of the Armada de la Guardia. The silver registers for each ship still survive in the Archive of the Indies in Seville, each in a separate sewn book, running from nearly five hundred folio pages to over eight hundred. The maestres de plata are clearly identified as follows: *San Felipe,* Pedro de Olavarria; *Santiago,* Lucas de Berroa; *Los Tres Reyes,* Domingo de Oxirando (deceased and replaced by Martín de Yturrain); *Begoña,* Pedro de Medina; *San Juan Baptista,* Miguel de Solina.[73] The maestres of the ships were other men entirely, most of whom had been with them since they left the astillero in Bilbao, and who stayed with them voyage after voyage.

The 1633 fleet, surmounting the usual problems of a lack of men, money, and time, had already set out months before Arana's galleons had returned from their 1632–33 voyage. The commander assigned to the 1633 fleet, don Gerónimo de Sandoval, had to withdraw because of ill health. The navy as a whole suffered an even worse blow at the same time with the death of Tomás de Larráspuru. Larráspuru was one of the most successful commanders the Indies fleets had ever seen, justly famed for bringing his fleets home safely by avoiding enemy ambush time after time. Most recently he had done this in 1629, 1630, and 1632, and the treasure he escorted home kept the empire functioning. After decades of narrow escapes at sea, he had died in the small town of Azcoitia in Guipúzcoa, where he was born fewer than fifty years earlier.[74]

The difficulties in finding crew and officers were not helped by the crown's delay in paying the sailors and soldiers it already had. In Lisbon don Fadrique de Toledo exceeded his orders by ignoring a new lower pay scale when he distributed wages. He made no attempt to deny doing this, which he felt justified by circumstances. The men sent to Brazil with Oquendo in 1631 had been rougher types than the usual soldiers, as they had to be on such a dangerous mission. Unpaid, they posed a real threat to civil peace in Lisbon. Disturbances had already arisen between them and the townspeople, and worse could be expected if don Fadrique had tried to institute the new pay scale. This dispute, which widened the gulf between him and the crown, indicates the difficulties facing armada officials in the early 1630s.[75]

The 1633 fleets marked a certain restoration of the usual pattern of the Indies run, because they included merchant contingents for both New Spain and Tierra Firme, as well as the Armada de la Guardia. All were to leave together, and, to save time, goods were loaded on ships in Seville and Cádiz simultaneously. The logistics presented enormous problems, as the loading depended on the arrival of fleets from northern Europe and the Levant with trade goods, as well as on the usual difficulties of careening, refitting, and supplying the ships on time. Despite all these uncontrollable elements, the fleets were ready to sail by early May.[76] Before they even left, however, disaster struck: a violent spring storm destroyed eleven ships in Cádiz Bay on May 6 and 7.[77] With this inauspicious beginning, the 1633 combined fleets sailed for the Indies on May 12, under the distinguished command of the Marquis of Cadereyta as captain-general and don Carlos de Ibarra as admiral. Don Luis Fernández de Córdoba served as captain-general of the Tierra Firme fleet, and don Lope de Hoces y Córdoba as captain-general of the armada y flota of New Spain.[78] Each of the captains-general had many years' experience on the Indies run, and the crown was determined that they use the voyage for expelling interlopers and corsairs from the Caribbean, as well as guarding their fleets from the Dutch.

When they set sail, the combined fleets had fifty-five ships, including four Swedish hulks embargoed in Sanlúcar. Twenty-four of them were warships, specially prepared for the voyage. The Tierra Firme fleet split off, and the rest reached the island of San Bartolomé on June 22 after a very swift voyage, surprising six corsair vessels in the harbor and capturing one of them. Two days later, when they reached their major target on the island of San Martín, the enemy was waiting. Their fort was strong, defended by Dutch regular soldiers and several dozen black slaves. Don Lope de Hoces and the infantry commander don Luis de Rojas landed a party to cut through the jungle and attack from the rear of the fort. Sixteen men died from heat, thirst, and overwork in the eight days it took to accomplish their task, as the galleons exchanged fire with the fort on the port side. On July 1, the fort surrendered. Cadereyta accepted the governor's sword and gave him and his men nothing in return but safe conduct to leave with the clothes on their backs. He let the fort stand, assigning 250 men and ammunition to its defense, and sailed on to New Spain.[79] The New Spain fleet would winter over as usual on the Mexican coast, but the Tierra Firme fleet, escorted by the Armada de la Guardia, aimed at returning to Spain in one sailing season. Ibarra and the Armada de la Guardia went to Portobelo on August 25 and returned six days later to Cartagena de Indias, where the Marquis of Cadereyta waited for them. The fleets left Cartagena on September 16, arrived in Havana on December 17, then sailed on to Cádiz by February 15 of the new year, after a successful encounter with six enemy ships.[80] It was never advisable to sail the Caribbean or the Atlantic after August or before March, but this time, at least, luck was on their side. Trade benefited from Cadereyta's successful voyage, even if merchants had to pay 28 percent in averías as their share of the cost of the fleet.[81]

By the time Cadereyta returned in February 1634, planning was already well advanced for the 1634 fleets. With the Dutch menace continuing in the New World, the royal government in Madrid was nearly as interested in recapturing Brazil as were the Portuguese, yet there were continued difficulties in coordinating an approach.[82] As late as November 1633, tentative plans called for eight galleons to sail in a war fleet to Brazil, because the king had determined to retake Pernambuco in 1634. Four of the galleons had been built by Martín de Arana in 1625–28: *San Felipe, Begoña, Los Tres Reyes,* and *Santiago.* Technically, they and the other four galleons planned for Brazil were part of the thirty-three galleons of the Armada del Mar Océano, which had been supplying many of the ships for the Armada de la Guardia in recent years. The avería administration in Seville simply did not have access to enough strong ships in those years to protect the Indies fleets. With an expedition to Brazil as well in 1634, the Armada del Mar Océano would have few resources left to protect the coasts of the Iberian peninsula—its primary task.[83]

On February 12, 1634, just three days before Cadereyta's fleet arrived back in Cádiz, don Antonio de Oquendo chose the silver galleons for the coming spring. His list included the four galleons built by Arana that had been destined for Brazil, even the small *Santiago.* Oquendo noted that it did not sail particularly well and should be replaced if another ship could be found. Failing that, the *Santiago* and its three companions would carry silver on yet another voyage.[84] The large-scale plans for Brazil had to be abandoned, given the overwhelming opinion of the Junta de Armadas that it was impossible to have large fleets for both Brazil and the Armada de la Guardia in a year with "a notorious lack of ships and men." Galleons from the Armada del Mar Océano would go for the silver. Any mission to Brazil would have to be formed from Portuguese ships.[85] Faced with conflicting priorities, the government in Madrid had chosen a Spanish, rather than a Portuguese, solution, driving the wedge further between the two parts of the united monarchy. It must be said in Madrid's defense that the Portuguese had not been too enthusiastic about the plan to retake Pernambuco, because their own warships would be occupied with the fleet to India at about the same time.[86]

The start of actual careening for the fleet of 1634 had been delayed by the choice of the silver galleons, but it began in earnest with the new year. Admiral Gaspar de Carasa supervised the work in Cádiz, using his ingenuity to conserve materials and money for the crown. Standard practice called for collecting artillery, rigging, and sails from returning voyages and distributing them for use in one fleet while another underwent careening. The ordinances of 1633 repeated the rules for this, even to such specifics as picking apart the old cables to make oakum for caulking.[87] As soon as *San Felipe, Begoña,* and their smaller companions had arrived back in Cádiz in 1633, their masters had turned in substantial quantities of old sails and rigging to

Bartolomé de Vega, the *tenedor de bastimentos* or warehouser of crown equipment in Cádiz. Even tattered canvas had to be registered in the warehouser's accounts as he took it in, just as he registered the other sails he distributed. Some would be used for covering storage boxes for biscuit, powder, and even other sails, to protect them from rats. This conservation of materials not only saved money but made the most efficient use of the equipment, because ships being careened in port had no immediate use for much of their equipment, especially the artillery.[88] These accounts for the redistribution of ship equipment, as well as the provisioning accounts for the various voyages made by the ships under discussion, identify the ships' masters very clearly. Cristóbal de Garnica had served with the *San Felipe* since it first sailed in 1629, and continued with the ship through the 1634–35 voyage. The same was true of Pedro de Cardona on the *Santiago* and Domingo de Bareno on *Los Tres Reyes*. *Begoña* had sailed to the Indies in 1629 with Rafael Angel Quartín, but by 1633–34, Cristóbal de Molina had taken over as her master. Similarly, Juan Baptista López served as *San Juan Baptista*'s first master, but he had been succeeded by Juan de Acevedo sometime before 1634. Until it left royal service, *San Sebastián* had sailed with Juan de Susunaga.[89] Despite a certain amount of turnover, the tendency was for masters to be identified with their ships, whereas masters of silver were identified only with a particular voyage.

The available caulkers were distributed between Seville, where the merchant ships were careened, and Cádiz, where the same was done for the warships. Their wages, and those of other workers, constituted much of the total cost of the careening. Royal officials were forever trying to devise ways to protect the hull from shipworms as long as possible, thus avoiding frequent careening. Not only were careenings costly, but they meant that something like one-third of the useful life of a ship was spent undergoing repairs. This was particularly damaging given the shortage of ships in the early 1630s relative to the demands on Spain's fleets. In 1633 the Marquis of Oropesa proposed three methods for delaying frequent careenings: additional planking over lead sheathing and tarred canvas; double planking alone; and a new recipe for the tar and grease used to cover the hull. The Junta de Armadas relayed them to several naval experts for their opinions and ordered the three methods tried on three separate ships.[90] It is not clear what the results were, but it is unlikely that anything would have lasted the eight or ten years Oropesa claimed. In the conditions of the Indies run, frequent careening seems to have been unavoidable. As closely as the crown monitored costs for the fleets, a major improvement in shipworm protection would not have been ignored.

The immediate cost of the 1634 fleets fell on the crown and the Portuguese bankers who contracted to take over the avería administration. The king excused the House of Trade from participation, because of the continued slump in Indies commerce. Royal ministers thought that as many as twenty galleons might be needed to fetch the silver and fight the Dutch, and there was no way that Indies merchants could come up with sufficient funds for such a fleet in 1634.[91] It was difficult enough just getting the merchants to load their merchandise for the 1634 fleets. Seville complained that Cádiz merchants were loading more than they were allowed, which was hurting Seville. Moreover, they complained that the Cádiz merchants wanted to send too many goods altogether. The more conservative merchant consulado in Seville preferred to send very little merchandise, keeping prices high and sales brisk. The fact was that business was down all over. The Tierra Firme fleets would require only 1,500 toneladas in 1634. The New Spain fleet, although it was allocated close to 5,000 toneladas, had great trouble finding enough merchandise to load. Even the House of Trade became exasperated with merchants who dragged their feet waiting for the arrival of more attractive goods.[92]

Despite the expressed need for twenty galleons for defense, the 1634 Armada de la Guardia would have only twelve galleons, heavily laden with men and supplies, including reinforcements for the island of San Martín, taken by Cadereyta the previous year. Nonetheless, the House of Trade proposed that the galleons carry merchandise equal to about one-fifth of their tonnage, so that the merchants could prepare fewer ships. Oquendo categorically refused to do this, and again protested having to carry even mercury. For the latter there was no remedy. The fleet ended up carrying 4,500 boxes of it, three times as much as Oquendo had planned.[93] The 1634 fleets were further proof that the interests of trade and imperial defense did not necessarily benefit one another. Preparations and the tug of war over merchandise continued through March and April for the Tierra Firme fleet, which finally left in fairly good time on May 9, with particular instructions to the purveyor to prevent fraud with special diligence.[94] The New Spain fleet would not leave until July 8, escorted by two large naos as its capitana and almiranta. The Tierra Firme fleet, accompanied by the Armada de la Guardia, left with most provisions for eight months, but only enough salt pork, dried codfish, and cheese for the three-month voyage. The remaining five months' worth of the more perishable items would be bought in the Indies, with money waiting there for the crown. In all, the Armada de la Guardia of twelve galleons, two tartans, and two dispatch boats had cost more than 350,000 ducados, including arms, ammunition, and food. The items still to be supplied in the Indies would raise the cost even higher.[95] The crown ordered the Armada de la Guardia to make the round trip in one sailing season, as in more normal times, but enemy movements and the weather would conspire to ruin these plans.

The previous year's New Spain fleet under don Lope de Hoces y Córdoba had wintered over in Veracruz. In July 1634 he prepared to bring it home, fighting resistance from the merchants who wished to stay even longer, spending their profits on trade in the Indies rather than risking confiscation by taking it home. Escorted by a dubious war fleet of eight urcas de guerra, they headed for Havana, arriving August 2. There Hoces heard that Oquendo had reached Cartagena on June 23 and hoped he and the Armada de la Guardia would make Havana by mid-August, so that they could return home together. His hopes vanished when a dispatch boat at the end of the month reported that Oquendo was still in Cartagena, kept there by reports of Dutch warships in various harbors, and not wanting to risk the treasure shipment until he knew that the approaches to Havana were clear. The Dutch had taken Curaçao near Tierra Firme in May and were still cruising throughout the area. Hoces knew the way to Havana was clear, but he could not relay the information to Oquendo in time—another example of the frustration inherent in long-distance communication in the seventeenth century. He could stay with his fleet in Havana until spring, but it would be a waste of time and money, considering that there were no materials there to careen his ships. Hoces called a council with his fleet officers and the governor of Havana, and they decided to take the New Spain fleet home without the Armada de la Guardia, though the season was dangerously late. They would leave the treasure and valuable merchandise in Havana, taking only some dyestuffs and silk on the capitana and almiranta.

Hoces and a tiny New Spain fleet left Havana on September 8—just the capitana, the almiranta, five large merchant ships, and one small one. As they neared the mouth of the Bahama Channel they hit a punishing series of storms from the northeast, which separated the almiranta and four of the ships from the capitana and the other two. Unsure where they were and in shallow water, three of the ships refused to follow the almiranta, which continued alone to Cádiz, arriving safely with its dispatch boat on November ninth, under the command of Francisco Díaz Pimienta. The three wandering ships miraculously found the capitana again and were sent back together to Havana; Lope de Hoces continued alone to Cádiz, where he arrived in mid-December. All things considered, luck had been on their side. None of the ships was lost, and the only valuable cargo reached Spain safely. Otherwise, the voyage was a classic example of why fleets avoided sailing in the Caribbean after August.[96]

Getting bottled up in Cartagena by reports of enemy ships was only one of the problems don Antonio de Oquendo and the Armada de la Guardia of 1634 faced. The voyage went uneventfully at first. After resupplying the island of San Martín, the fleet sailed on to Cartagena as usual. There the ships took on fresh provisions and supplies for their trip to Portobelo.[97] Then their troubles began. On returning from Portobelo, the galleon *Los Tres Reyes,* one of those built by Martín de Arana, was wrecked at the entrance to Cartagena harbor on August 4. It is not clear just where the accident happened, but both entrances to the protected harbor are shallow and blocked by sandbars. Recognizing the ship as lost, Oquendo ordered the dismal work of salvage to begin. Various local boats manned by black slaves did most of the work. The ship may not have carried any of the treasure when it was wrecked; at least none is mentioned in the extensive salvage records.[98] There is no doubt, however, that everything of value was salvaged, carefully inventoried, and temporarily warehoused in Cartagena. The heavy cables, extra anchors, and artillery came off first, including twenty-two guns and their carriages. Eleven of the artillery pieces would remain in Cartagena; the rest would be distributed among other ships of the fleet. The bulk of the unloading took place from August 10 on, and by Sunday, August 13, nearly everything was gone, including food, medicines, and most of the sails. The rowboats made their last trips on Monday morning. Although many of the workers were clearly identified as slaves, they were paid directly for their work, at something like 3 reales a day.

Every piece of equipment was identified in detail as it entered the warehouse; the list included assessed valuations as well. Masters on other ships in the fleet signed receipts for items released to them. Most of the artillery and extra equipment went to the other silver galleons, some for their own use, some to be carried back to Spain. Once the salvage finished, Oquendo announced a public sale of the hull and the remaining equipment by public crier. After several days of announcements, he awarded the final salvage to Captain Augustín de Baraona, a citizen of Cartagena and owner of many of the slaves who had done the salvage work. For 5,600 reales, Baraona got the hull with its mainmast, foremast, mizzen, and bowsprit, with their standing rigging. After some of the warehoused salvage was sold to various local buyers, Baraona made a deal for the rest of it, paying about 14,000 reales for 134 hundredweight of rigging and sail canvas. In all, the crown made 26,385 reales from the sales, about 2,400 ducados. There is no way that the minimal amount recovered from the salvage could compensate for the loss of *Los Tres Reyes,* which had cost nearly seven times that amount to build, but at least it meant that Oquendo's galleons would have plenty of supplies to repair their own ships, should they have to winter over in the Indies.

When the Armada de la Guardia came back from Portobelo in August, Oquendo found messages from various governors in the Indies, warning him of enemy ships in their areas. Sickness struck the Armada de la Guardia during August as well, even affecting some of Oquendo's own gentlemen attendants.[99] As he waited for more auspicious circumstances for moving the fleet and its treasure to Havana, Oquendo faced the reality that he could not return to Spain before the new year without running great risks. Repairing his ships and supplying his men with food for the unwelcome layover then became his main priority. Oquendo sent two hulks to New Spain to purchase food and made plans to sail to Havana as soon as possible, with the Tierra Firme fleet under don Nicolás de Judice y Fiesco. At least one of the galleons, *El Angel de la Guardia,* had been careened in Cartagena, but most of the work had to wait for Havana, which had more shipwrights and better facilities and protection. On the way from Cartagena in late October or early November, the fleet hit a series of storms. The voyage took thirty-six days to cover the 1,500-kilometer distance from Cartagena to Havana, about two weeks longer than usual. Miraculously, all the ships came through safely.[100] Once in Havana, Oquendo began careening four of his galleons, including *Begoña, San Juan Baptista,* and *San Felipe,* the last still serving as almiranta of the Tierra Firme fleet. Even with the extra equipment from *Los Tres Reyes,* the careening was expensive. A major reason was the wage scale in the Indies. A master caulker or carpenter earned 30 reales a day in Havana, Portobelo, or Cartagena. Journeymen earned 16 reales a day in Havana, 18 in Cartagena, and 20 in Portobelo, and ordinary workers earned half those rates.[101] That was about three times higher than wages for the same work in Spain.

To pay for the work and wages for his men, Oquendo stretched his authority as captain-general to the limit. For a start, he simply ordered the master of silver of the galleon *Nuestra Señora de la Concepción,* almiranta of the Armada de la Guardia, to release some 23,000 ducados of the treasure he carried. That unlucky man, named Lorenzo Enríquez, protested that he had only private treasure and refused to release it. Royal officials then went to Enríquez's home and searched it. Not finding any treasure, they proceeded to the jail, where they found the money stored in a locked cell. Enríquez protested that he did not have the keys, so the officials broke the lock, took the money, and testified to the entire incident before a notary. Enríquez was one master of silver who took his job quite seriously. Others obeyed Oquendo's order without protest, or at least without any protest that has been recorded.[102] In this way, Oquendo collected the funds for his men and ships.

The food crisis was solved when the hulks Oquendo had sent to New Spain arrived in Havana on January 17 with 1,200 hundredweight of biscuit. Without the new supplies, the galleons had only 620 hundredweight of good biscuit left, enough for only about 460 men on a three-month voyage.[103]

Careening and repairs continued through January, February and most of March, as Oquendo waited for the winter to pass. When the fleet was ready in late March, he told his captains that if any ship got off course on the way home, it should continue sailing, trying to pass windward of the Canary Islands at 41 degrees latitude. Considerably east of the Canaries, it should turn north to search for the Spanish coast and for some squadron of the Armada del Mar Océano as escort. If it saw an enemy squadron, it should head for port as soon as possible.[104] The *Begoña* was to have been capitana of the silver galleons on the way home, but it was replaced with a larger ship before they sailed. The only mishap on the voyage occurred when the galleon *Nuestra Señora de la Anunciada* began taking on water at such a rapid rate that it had to be abandoned. No more than the crew and two bars of silver could be removed before it sank, but evidently it had not carried much to begin with. All the other ships in the fleet reached Spain safely on June 10.[105] In all, the fleet returning with Oquendo brought back less than 2 million pesos of treasure and merchandise, disappointingly small but welcome all the same.[106]

Don Antonio de Oquendo found several distressing pieces of news awaiting his homecoming. First of all, France had made a pact with Holland in February, joining the Dutch in war against Spain. The Dutch would remain the major threat in the Indies, but open hostilities with France would create several new problems in Europe. Trade links between Spain and France were sure to be broken, at least for a while, and with the Thirty Years' War raging in central Europe, alternate trading partners would not be easy to find. The problems of resupplying Spanish armies in Flanders could only increase. Moreover, the vital naval stores that Spain imported from northern Europe would be harder to acquire, making it even more necessary to rely on foreign shipping.[107] To face the new situation in Europe, the Armada del Mar Océano needed to be at full strength. It could no longer afford to send its galleons to the Indies at the request of the House of Trade, even with the continued Dutch threat. A ship census taken just ten days after the 1635 Tierra Firme fleet returned to Cádiz showed *San Felipe, Santiago,* and *San Juan Baptista* reintegrated into the Armada del Mar Océano once more, among only nineteen ships that were clearly fit for service. The *Begoña* was to undergo careening in Cádiz shortly, but it too would be staying in European service for the foreseeable future.[108]

In discussing the most recent request from the House of Trade for galleons from the Armada del Mar Océano for the Indies fleets, several members of the Junta de Armadas vehemently opposed the idea. With the Armada de la Guardia and the expeditions to Brazil, the Indies had taken the best ships out of European service, much to the detriment of the Armada del Mar Océano. The House of Trade had sufficient time to supply its needs for 1636 from fortified merchant vessels, without relying on the Armada del Mar Océano. With the rupture in relations with France, the Armada del Mar Océano would need at least 30,000 toneladas of shipping; that would be difficult enough to find, without more drains from the Indies fleets. Because the crown was able to find money "for other things" (perhaps a pointed reference to the vast expenditure on the new Retiro Palace in Madrid), it was "only fair that money be found for this necessary and indispensable matter, and that the ships of the Armada del Mar Océano remain where they are needed."[109] Support from the royal bureaucracy for the Armada del Mar Océano came at a crucial time. The fleet not only faced greater challenges in Europe, but it faced a serious internal crisis as well, brought on by royal disfavor.

The other distressing news Oquendo received when he returned to Spain would have plunged a lesser man into despair. First of all, he was to be brought up on charges for disobeying orders by wintering over in the Indies. Even worse, while he was away, his superior officer in the Armada del Mar Océano, don Fadrique de Toledo y Osorio, had been imprisoned by the crown and had died in disgrace, stripped of his offices on land and sea.

NINE

The Struggle for Survival, 1635–1640

he difficulties that Fadrique de Toledo had with the crown and its ministers began to worsen shortly after his triumphant return from the Indies in 1630. While he was still aboard his ship in Cádiz Bay, the crown ordered him to report to Lisbon to join the Armada del Mar Océano, which he commanded, without rest or time to visit his home and attend to family business. Eventually he received a brief official leave, which he overstayed to attend to a lawsuit in Madrid; he had to be ordered back to Lisbon.[1] After a lifetime of service and military honors, he was arguably the most distinguished commander of his day. In addition to having been born into the exalted noble clan that included the Duke of Alba, don Fadrique had become the Marquis of Villanueva de Baldueza in 1624 and owned a collection of landholdings. Yet his relations with the central government had often been stormy, in part because of professional concerns over inadequate men, money, and supplies for the navy, and in part because he shared the aristocracy's animosity toward the king's chief minister, the Count-Duke of Olivares. Many times in the past he had ignored orders from Madrid that he disapproved, or had delayed carrying them out. His repeated requests for additional resources for the 1629 "galiflota" and his notable advocacy on behalf of the men in his command had done nothing to endear him to the chief minister, and he had come close to open disobedience several times.

Matters approached a crisis in the fall of 1633, when don Fadrique was ordered to mount another expedition to Brazil—the same expedition to which four of Arana's galleons had been tentatively assigned. Don Fadrique protested that his health had been ruined in royal service and that he needed to supervise urgent family matters, neglected in his many years at sea. He probably also assumed that the fleet would be inadequately supplied. The dispute evidently simmered long after the Junta de Armadas urged abandoning plans to send a war fleet to Brazil in 1634, arguing that the crown lacked the resources.[2] In July 1634 Olivares and don Fadrique had a heated argument overheard by several witnesses. Olivares refused to honor don Fadrique's request to be relieved from the expedition to Brazil because of his previous service, pointedly reminding him that he had received great financial rewards for that service—the same attitude other ministers had voiced about the Vallecilla brothers. Deeply offended, don Fadrique responded in kind. "Sir," he said, according to one version, "I beg to differ. And even if it were true, I did it by risking life and limb, unlike Your Excellency who by sitting in a chair makes more in a day than I do in a lifetime."[3] That, at least, is the story.

Whatever the provocation, he was tried by the Council in Castile for disobedience to royal orders, with the rising legal star don Diego de Riaño y Gamboa presenting the case against him. The council found him guilty according to the laws of the kingdom and obtained a royal decree for his imprisonment. After he had served a brief period under house arrest, the country was treated to the scandal of the great Spanish naval hero being imprisoned in the fort of Santa Olalla, an action that caused public consternation and aristocratic outrage. Just a few months earlier don Juan de Benavides had been executed in Seville. By early September don Fadrique had fallen ill in prison and received grudging permission from the council to come back to Madrid, but not to his own house or to that of any relative. Barred as well from staying with a prominent Madrid family, he was forced to lodge instead in the modest home of his faithful secretary while a special Junta de Obediencia of the council considered his sentence.

Olivares and the other ministers did all they could to keep don Fadrique's case from becoming a rallying point for the growing sentiment against the chief minister's policies. Guards had standing orders to let no one see don Fadrique but his wife and his doctors, as his condition continued to worsen. At the end of October the Duke of Alba and his son were ordered from the court; no reason was given, but it must have had to do with don Fadrique, to whom they were related. In early November the full council had several long meetings before deciding on his sentence—perpetual exile from the realm, the loss of all offices and official income, a 10,000-ducado fine, and all court costs. Although the sentence was official on November 12, don Fadrique's wife would not permit anyone to deliver it to her husband. His rapidly failing health finally evoked the mercy of the king, who allowed him to return to his home on November 15, where he died three weeks later, just over fifty years of age.

On December 11 mourners crowded the house to pay their respects as don Fadrique lay in state, richly attired and lying on cloth of gold, with his general's baton of office and his sword. Olivares supposedly denied him honor even in death, ordering the baton removed from his hands. In addition, the Jesuits were forced to cancel the public funeral planned for him at their Imperial College in Madrid, settling instead for a private ceremony in a chapel of their congregation. The family members who served as pallbearers included an impressive sampling of the high aristocracy of Spain, and the funeral procession to the church, like the burial honors accorded Juan de Benavides in May, served as a spectacular mute protest against the policies of

Figure 30. "The Recapture of Bahia" painted by Juan Bautista Maino. Don Fadrique de Toledo, the hero of Bahia, appears in the right center of the composition, pointing to a tapestry in which King Philip IV is being crowned with laurels by the Count-Duke of Olivares. Although the event occurred in 1625, the painting was not commissioned until 1635. By that time don Fadrique had died in disgrace, which explains his somewhat insignificant role in the composition. Note the galleons in the background, one of which carries a fourth mast (the bonaventure mizzen) and may have a spritsail topsail as well. (Courtesy of the Prado Museum, Madrid.)

Olivares.[4] This time the popular manifestation against Olivares was more vocal, with crowds in the street chanting that don Fadrique "had died from the envy of a court favorite."[5] That is how the Armada del Mar Océano came to be without its leader in 1635, just when it would need its full strength. (See figure 30.)

There is no question that don Fadrique was guilty of insubordination in 1634, just as he probably had been several times in the past. In that sense, the royal decree for his arrest had the force not only of law, but of justice. At this most critical time for Spanish power, the king and his chief minister simply could not allow royal orders to be flouted openly. Yet it is not difficult to sympathize with don Fadrique, especially given the shameful way he was treated in the final months of his life. His long and distinguished service, his endless correspondence on behalf of his men, his struggles against Madrid's ignorance of naval realities, his indignation that a lifetime of service meant so little—all these things must have weighed on his mind. When he crossed the line between respectful noncompliance and open insubordination, it is perhaps fairer to say that he was pushed. In the years that followed, Madrid would continue pushing its best naval commanders to the limits of loyalty, asking them to do the impossible and giving them inadequate tools to accomplish it. The surprising thing is that they often succeeded, overcoming insufficient equipment and manpower by sheer force of will. In other words, Spanish commanders often were forced to be heroes, because the crown gave them so little to work with. That would be demonstrated fully in the European battles of the 1630s.

Because of the continuing struggle in Europe, there were many tasks that could be performed only by a war fleet, such as the transfer of large numbers of troops and the protection of royal treasure and merchant fleets to the Indies. By the late 1620s, Spain had largely abandoned plans to extend its power to the Baltic, working instead for a balance of power that was friendly or at least not hostile to its interests. The main aim was still to recapture the northern provinces of the Netherlands, or at least to achieve a favorable position from which to negotiate a truce.

In the immediate aftermath of Matanzas, officials in the Spanish southern Netherlands worried that their cause would soon be lost. Yet the wherewithal arrived from Spain in time, spurred by heroic efforts on the part of the king's ministers to find money and send it north safely. By 1631 the crisis had passed, and regular payments for the European war again became the norm.[6] One of the results of this was military success in the Germanies, most notably the great victory at Nördlingen in 1634. With France at war with Spain after 1635, the Armada del Mar Océano became crucial to the fight in the Netherlands, ferrying troops and money by sea to reinforce the Spanish and Flemish forces there. Such voyages in wartime required careful planning and gave rise to the same agonized debates in the king's councils as did the Indies fleets, and for the same reason: the stakes were very high and the cost of failure enormous. As soon as the galleons of the Armada del Mar Océano returned from the Indies in 1635, several of them were earmarked for a fleet to Flanders in 1636. It would be the first major test of the channel since the French declaration of war. Ships would be gathered from Cádiz and elsewhere and sent to La Coruña for final preparations, with food for forty-five days.[7] In all, the fleet planned on forty-two ships with more than 19,000 toneladas capacity, ranging from small dispatch boats of 120 toneladas to war galleons as large as 1,000 toneladas.[8]

Everything depended on the timely arrival of ships completing other duties. After the Indies fleets arrived, seven ships were sent to Barcelona and on to Italy with troops raised in Andalusia and money for Spain's allies in the Thirty Years' War. Included in their number were the galleons *Santiago* and *San Juan Baptista,* two of the six built by Arana.[9] Evidently, ten ships originally had been planned for the trip. Before leaving for Barcelona on October 2, both ships underwent repairs and careening in Cádiz and their masters exchanged old and broken equipment for replacements from the royal warehouses.[10] They did not return from the Italian mission in time to go to Flanders. Of the other ships we have been following, the *Begoña* was being careened in Cádiz, a process that lasted off and on from August 26, 1635, to March 26, 1636. Thereafter, although it stayed in the Armada del Mar Océano, it did not go to Flanders either.[11] The *San Felipe* also underwent repairs and careening in Cádiz after returning from the Indies in 1635, receiving nine new masts and several new sails.[12] It would have a prominent position in the Flanders armada of 1636. Eight ships from the squadron of Flanders were also expected to join the expedition. They were particularly important, given the shortage in Spain of pilots familiar with the Flemish coast.[13]

Commanding the armada with the title of gobernador would be the Marquis of Fuentes, a member of the king's Council of War and captain-general of the armada in Flanders. The Duke of Veraguas had the courtesy title of captain-general of the expedition. As a member of the highest rank of Spain's nobility, he had a right to this distinction, but there was no question that Fuentes would be in actual command. When Fuentes's official instructions mentioned calling a council of his senior officers, the duke's name was crossed off the list.[14] The *San Felipe* and four smaller ships left Cádiz on March 20, 1636, with the Duke of Veraguas.[15] Don Antonio de Isasi was captain-general for the voyage to La Coruña and would serve as admiral of the combined fleet.[16] The Navarrese Captain Miguel de Horna, with a distinguished service record behind him, joined them in La Coruña with the squadron of Flanders. By mid-April there were twenty warships ready and by mid-June thirty, although not all were destined for Flanders.[17]

Most had been given a normal careening and refitting, but the *San Felipe* had received special treatment because it would be the flagship of the Duke of Veraguas. The Count of Montalvo, supervising the careening in Cádiz, wrote that he had not embellished any of the ships he had prepared in the last few years for expeditions to Barcelona, Italy, Flanders, or Curaçao—none, that is, except the *San Felipe*. He had added decoration to the galleon that would carry the duke, "mindful of his being a grandee of Castile, and going with the title of general of that armada, and having to arrive in an area where he will be closely scrutinized by foreigners, who decorate their ships with more costly embellishment than his will have." Despite standing orders against painting and gilding on Spanish warships of the time, the king approved Montalvo's extra expenses for the *San Felipe*—a final bill of 9,025 reales—besides the usual expense for colored bunting for display and battle dress. Pomp and circumstance were important tools of foreign policy, even when funds were scarce. To avoid such expenses in the future, however, one practical member of the Junta de Armadas suggested making a fancy set of hangings that could be moved around from one ship to another, for the poop chambers of important flagship commanders.[18]

The fleet finally left La Coruña August 19 with twenty-six ships totaling 8,550 toneladas, far short of the forty-two ships planned but typical of the compromises made in those years. Besides the eight ships from Dunkirk, there were four from the squadron of Galicia, six from the Armada del Mar Océano, and eight leased hulks and frigates. They carried 1,578 sailors, 733 experienced soldiers, and 3,774 newly levied recruits.[19] The Flemish ships were generally smaller than the Spanish ones and in questionable repair, but they would be invaluable companions through the difficult shallows of the Flemish coast, distributed among the rest of the fleet as guides. Fuentes's orders specifically mentioned that everyone should treat the men of the Flemish squadron well, so that they would be content and fight zealously in any enemy encounter.[20]

The main aim of the fleet was to ferry troops to Flanders, but it also carried the king's general victualler, Bartolomé Spínola, a member of the Councils of War and Finance, along with money and public and private letters of credit. The troops were to join the forces of the king's brother, the Cardinal-Infante Ferdinand, military commander in Flanders, but the money was nearly as important as they were.[21] From one end to the other, the channel teemed with Spain's enemies. Only the English were not openly hostile; they had maintained a cautious neutrality in the continental wars since 1630, benefiting from neutral status by carrying goods, passengers, and even silver between Spain and the Netherlands.[22] Nonetheless, the Spanish government had no illusions about English friendship and ordered Fuentes's fleet to stay clear of the English coast if at all possible.

By August 22, the ships were 40 leagues from La Coruña, and, on August 27, they came in sight of the English coast near Plymouth. Some forty-two ships reconnoitered them, finally identified as French. The Spanish fired one cannon and the French withdrew. The next day eight English ships observed them, and in the following days they passed many more vessels from England and Hamburg, but none made a hostile move. The most dangerous part of the voyage was undoubtedly the approach to the Flemish coast, but Fuentes successfully reached Mardick on September 1 and took all his vessels safely into port the next day, "without losing a single plank of his majesty's ships."[23]

The trip had taken just twelve days, and Fuentes was able to deliver 1.5 million ducados in silver and more than 4,500 soldiers under the Marquis of Velada.[24] Fuentes, the Duke of Veraguas, and the Dunkirk squadron all remained in Flanders; presumably, the leased foreign vessels went their own way, having fulfilled their contract. The Spanish ships returned home under don Antonio de Isasi as captain-general, with additional orders to reconnoiter the coasts of Normandy and offer aid to local rebels against the French crown. Though there were disturbances in Rouen and Rennes at the time, the Spanish evidently found no takers for their offer and returned to La Coruña by mid-October, ready for another assignment.[25]

It should thus be obvious that the Armada del Mar Océano was stretched very thin with the entry of France into the war. The king had appointed the Duke of Maqueda to head the Armada del Mar Océano after the disgrace and death of Fadrique de Toledo, but Maqueda was not a naval expert. The French meanwhile had brought together a fleet of some seventy or eighty ships and sixteen galleys, combining forces from Brittany and Marseilles. The king ordered Maqueda to create a force of thirty-six galleons to fight the French in the Mediterranean. Not surprisingly, this took longer than expected to accomplish, whereupon the royal government ordered don Antonio de Oquendo to take whatever ships were ready and join the squadron of Naples in the summer of 1636 to do battle with the French. Oquendo was not at all convinced of the wisdom of the plan. In terms strikingly similar to those used by other Spanish officers asked to do the impossible, he patiently explained the difficulties to the king and his ministers. The French had an enormous fleet of seventy ships, he wrote, forty of them large, and some above 2,000 toneladas, "something never before seen on the sea."[26] All had abundant artillery and men. His ships, on the other hand, were few, small, short-handed, ill-equipped, and not provisioned at all. He had only two galleons from Vizcaya that were over 700 toneladas, two at about 600, and the *Begoña* at 500—the galleon Arana had built that had recently undergone careening in Cádiz. The rest were much smaller. The chances of defeating the French in such a situation were virtually nonexistent.

Giving Madrid a small lesson in naval warfare, Oquendo also noted that, even had the fleet been ready, he could not simply sail into the Mediterranean looking for the French before intelligence reports told him where to look. Only galleys could easily reconnoiter from port to port. If the king still insisted on his leaving immediately, he should send very specific instructions for the voyage. That way, if the mission succeeded, Oquendo "would deserve no credit from it except the reward [he] had from serving the king, and if it failed, [he] would not be held at fault nor be the subject of an official inquiry such as the one that currently burdened [him]"—a clear reference to the inquiry over his 1634–35 Indies voyage.[27] The king and his chief minister seem so wrong-headed in this matter that Oquendo's biographer implies that Olivares concocted the plan simply to force Oquendo to appear a coward.[28] However it made him appear, Oquendo made his point and stayed in Cádiz through the winter of 1636–37. By mid-March, he and his squadron sailed to the Bay of Alcudia on Spain's east coast, traveling on to the port of Mahon in the Balearic Islands by the end of the month. That would be Oquendo's base until July 1638, in between various missions in the Mediterranean.[29] By the time he returned to Spain, the situation in northern Europe would demand even greater services to the crown.

Meanwhile the Indies fleets continued to sail as usual—that is to say, they were outfitted and sent off more or less regularly, but in an atmosphere of perpetual crisis. Don Lope de Hoces y Córdoba led a small relief expedition to Pernambuco in September 1635, just three months after he had arrived in Spain with a fleet from New Spain.[30] His combined Portuguese and Spanish fleet successfully captured Curaçao from the Dutch in 1636, which increased confidence in the viability of the Indies trade. The merchant fleets reestablished a somewhat regular rhythm. War with France made it hard to secure enough merchandise at first, but the merchants soon found alternate sources of supply. In 1636 the Spanish and French governments even concluded an arrangement allowing French goods back into the Indies trade despite the war, and diplomacy continued to assure the safety of trade with Flanders.[31] Though the Indies trade showed continuing signs of depression in 1635, there were also some signs of an upward trend, with substantial treasure returns from 1635 to 1638.[32]

Shortly after don Lope de Hoces returned from the Indies, the king required his services in northern Europe. The Cardinal-Infante Ferdinand, brother of Philip IV and his military commander in Flanders, desperately needed money and men by 1637, despite the successful relief mission in 1636. This time the Dutch were determined to prevent the Spaniards from reaching Flanders. Intelligence reports intercepted from the Dutch in mid-May said that a large Dutch squadron, fully equipped, was prepared to block their way. Nothing but a very large fleet could hope to combat the Dutch, and the Spanish were well advised not to make the attempt. Nonetheless, Olivares and others in Madrid favored a bold approach. A squadron of Dunkirk warships in La Coruña could form the nucleus of a Spanish fleet, under their courageous commander Jacques Colart. Olivares ordered Colart to leave for Flanders as soon as possible with the sixteen best ships he had, but Colart died before he could carry out the orders. Luckily for the crown, Lope de Hoces was available to take his place. Reports of an ever-larger Dutch fleet lying in wait caused more delays, exacerbated when businessmen declined to load their silver for the voyage. Relations with England offered no guarantees of a safe haven; lately Charles I had even threatened to join forces with the Dutch.

As Philip IV's councils debated the matter in Madrid, the situation in Flanders worsened. In September, the Spanish tried a diversionary tactic, sending Lope de Hoces and part of the squadron on a punitive mission to the French coast and the island of Ré. With only eleven galleons and two frigates, Hoces did considerable damage to the French and was back in La Coruña by September 28. The great hope was that the Dutch would believe that was their last action for the year, because the sailing season was so late. But, whatever the Dutch believed, the Spanish had no choice. The Cardinal-Infante sent a desperate letter on October 10 that his campaign would collapse utterly without more troops. After more frantic consultations in Madrid, the king sent the order in mid-November for Hoces to sail with the first favorable wind. All together, his fleet carried 1.8 million ducados and more than twelve thousand men on thirty-eight ships. It was less impressive than it sounded, however. Only twelve of the ships were large galleons; the rest were small galleons and merchant vessels.[33]

When at last they left La Coruña on December 8, the fleet was as well prepared as it could be, and even the English had promised the right of asylum should they need it. This time, at least, luck was on their side. A strong following wind blew them up the channel and blew the Dutch away from their patrol. The Spanish fleet arrived on December 13, in the incredible time of five days; Flanders was saved. The troops would soon distinguish themselves in battle, among other places, at St. Omer, where the French suffered a tremendous defeat. After two months in Flanders, Hoces and his fleet began the return voyage with sixteen galleons from Spain, three private corsairs, and twelve corsairs from the royal squadron of Dunkirk to escort them through the channel. Though they lost one ship in the shallows, on March 7 they chased a fleet of thirty ships and captured fifteen of them, including a pirate, before the wind blew them back into Mardick on March 9. Hoces left again on March 24, and the next day came upon forty merchant ships escorted by a strong Dutch squadron. In the subsequent battle, the Dutch lost two warships and ten of the merchants. When wind forced the Spanish to take refuge on the English coast at Portland, they captured another ship along the way. Despite damage from a severe storm, they pursued and captured three more Dutch vessels near Plymouth. At the southern mouth of the channel, the Dunkirk ships turned homeward. Two days later, just 60 leagues from Spain, the rest of the fleet met fifteen ships from France, which they pursued and fought, capturing seven. In all Lope de Hoces and his fleet had captured thirty-eight prizes on the way home.[34]

In addition, the period from 1635 to 1638 saw an estimated 200,000 toneladas of enemy shipping captured or sunk by corsairs sailing for Spain. In one expedition in 1635, some two hundred Dutch fishing busses were either captured or sunk, for a total of 16,000–18,000 toneladas. As Colart reported, "Such were the lamentations and complaints in Holland over this that members of the States General could scarcely dare to leave their houses."[35]

Under the Marquis of Fuentes, the new admiral in Flanders, the royal squadron grew larger and bolder. Admiral Miguel de Horna and Captain Salvador Rodríguez both distinguished themselves in sinking enemy vessels.[36] Holland heard dark rumors that Admiral Van Dorp, responsible for blockading Dunkirk, was in Spanish pay, and the Dutch became so angry at the French for their poor showing that they threatened to make a separate peace with the Habsburgs. These successes did not come cheaply, however. In addition to regular naval expenses, Philip IV subsidized each corsair to the tune of 6,000–10,000 ducados per year. To fight corsairing cost the Dutch about the same amount as the yearly average of Indies treasure from 1621 to 1640. That was admittedly during a slump in the Indies trade, but it was still three times the annual income of the English crown. At the height of Spanish corsairing in 1635–40, the Dutch were spending about 60,000 escudos each for some twenty-five to thirty anticorsairing vessels.[37] They would get no relief unless they could smash Spanish naval power in the channel.

On the Franco-Spanish side of the war, the five years from 1635 to 1640 had decidedly mixed results for the Spanish, with several victories and one major disaster. In October 1636, Spanish forces invaded France and took St. Jean de Luz on the coast, but the ill-prepared invasion bogged down in the winter and had to withdraw. Spanish actions by sea against southern France had more success.[38] In response to the Spanish invasion, France launched a major invasion of its own in 1637, sending the Prince of Condé with twenty thousand troops into the Basque province of Guipúzcoa. The Spanish had only two thousand local troops to stand against them, and in three days they had fallen back to San Sebastián. The French avoided trying to take that large town, instead settling for smaller villages in the area and the fort of Higuer at the mouth of the Bidasoa River on the Franco-Spanish border, which was defended by only ten soldiers. They also attacked the local shipyards, capturing four new galleons and burning four still in the framework; another four galleons escaped.

Then, in the summer of 1638 they prepared to take the fort of Fuenterrabía between the border and San Sebastián. Seven hundred able-bodied men defended the fort, aided by local men and women as auxiliaries. With supplies and plenty of ammunition, they prepared for a siege.[39] Madrid sent reinforcements by land and ordered don Antonio de Oquendo from Lisbon and don Lope de Hoces from La Coruña by sea. Oquendo had been preparing for an expedition to Brazil and could not put to sea immediately. Since Hoces was closer anyway, he was urged to leave immediately with the Irish infantry he had brought with him from Flanders. The orders were simple enough, but the reality of the situation was not. France had already blockaded Fuenterrabía by closing the mouth of the Bidasoa with a line of launches chained together. Several Spanish attempts to force the blockade had failed, but France was taking no chances. The Archbishop of Bordeaux was ordered back from the Mediterranean with the French fleet he commanded, the same force that Oquendo had already encountered there. The sixty-four ships in the French fleet included forty-four large warships, notable among them *La Couronne* at 2,000 toneladas and *Le Vaisseau du Roy* at 1,000. There were also a dozen each of transports and fireships, plus the usual contingents of supply and dispatch boats.[40]

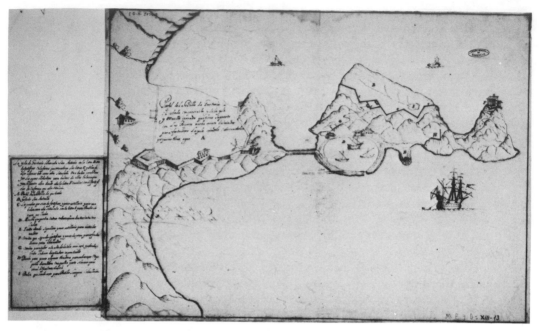

Figure 31. The town of Guetaria and its island of San Antonio, with proposed fortifications, 1667. (AGS, Mapas, Planos y Dibujos, XIII-13, from Guerra Antiqua, lég. 2136. Courtesy of the Archivo General de Simancas, Simancas, Valladolid.)

In La Coruña, Lope de Hoces had twelve ill-supplied ships and some of the Irish soldiers from Flanders. He had sent many of the men and a good part of his gunpowder to San Sebastián to outfit the four new galleons that had recently escaped from the French. Like the excellent naval commander he was, Hoces knew his situation was hopeless, but he prepared to carry out his orders. As a measure of the respect Lope de Hoces commanded from other mariners, some of the finest officers in the Spanish navy volunteered to go with him as simple captains. The group included ten men who had served as captains-general and admirals in fleets of their own. It was a touching show of loyalty to Hoces, and also to the crown, even though they can hardly have had much faith in the enterprise.

From the port of Santoña near Santander, Hoces wrote to Madrid asking that he be allowed to wait for Oquendo, because sending his meager force in alone meant certain defeat, given the strength of the French. The crown repeated the order to proceed to Fuenterrabía, noting that the French fleet could not possibly be as large as Hoces said. Even if it were, he could at least force the blockade, or anchor in a nearby port and send his men ashore in small boats.[41] The orders from Madrid allowed no further discussion. Hoces called a council of his officers at sea on August 19, 1638. Some argued for obedience to the spirit, rather than the letter, of the king's order—in effect urging delay until Oquendo arrived. Others, including Hoces himself, had to disagree. Kings want to be obeyed and not interpreted; disobedience is honored only if it succeeds, whereas obedience can at least be an excuse for failure.[42] Hoces headed for Guetaria (see figure 31), the best small port available; San Sebastián was too shallow for some of his ships. When he later learned the French had left the best port at Pasajes, he was already in Guetaria and becalmed.

In the port of Guetaria, Hoces lined his ships up broadside, with the strongest in the front line, closing the port. The French arrived with thirty-three ships, and on August 22, the battle of Guetaria took place.[43] After fighting from nine in the morning until four in the afternoon, the Spanish realized they could not win, though they had captured ten of the French captains. At that point a parlay of the Spanish officers voted to leave the ships and go ashore with the artillery. Sea and land forces together might have a chance to win, whereas sea forces alone were bound to lose. It was too late. Under the cover of artillery smoke, the French sent fire ships to grapple with the outer line of the Spanish vessels, setting them afire. As the flames spread to other ships, many men panicked and jumped into the water. To avoid having the French capture any prizes, Hoces ordered the capitana set afire and scuttled, and the other ships as well. He salvaged none of his personal belongings and reached shore half-drowned, with nothing more than the shirt on his back. The scene became horrific: powder magazines blew sky high, and masts, rigging, and dead bodies rained down on the living. Only one thousand of the four thousand men escaped death, later to wander dazed and wounded through the streets of Fuenterrabía, asking alms of the residents. One of Hoces's captains disobeyed orders and refused to scuttle his ship, instead raising sails and challenging the French alone. As luck would have it, he succeeded, escaping the French fleet and coming safely to port, his ship dismasted and full of cannon holes, but with flags bravely flying.

Unfortunately, this personal act of bravery cast doubts on the courage and ability of all the other captains, Hoces included. Neither his recent successes in Pernambuco and the channel, nor a lifetime of victorious and courageous command could save Lope de Hoces from the vilification heaped on him after Guetaria. The successful raising of the siege of Fuenterrabía by land shortly thereafter only made it worse. At Guetaria eleven large ships had been lost, and three thousand men, many of them with distinguished families and naval careers. Included in the roster were two former captains-general, four former admirals, five sea captains, four infantry captains, and the chief pilot, to mention only the first rank officers. Among them was Cristóbal de Garnica, long-time master of the *San Felipe*.[44] Ironically, he had been promoted to captain and transferred to another ship just in time for the ill-fated mission to Guetaria.[45]

In his anguished defense, Lope de Hoces argued that he had done all he could to win against impossible odds, before finally deciding to rob the French of the fruits of victory by destroying his ships. Given the odds against him, that was the best he could do. It would have been infinitely worse to have allowed everything to be captured, as the French Prince of Condé recently had done. "Ask those who censure me if I am the first general who has lost in such circumstances. How many emperors and kings and princes have been similarly defeated?"[46] In response, the king sent don Diego de Riaño y Gamboa to report on the battle and its losses.[47] Had Riaño, the successful prosecutor of don Fadrique de Toledo, found any discrepancies in Lope de Hoces's story, that unhappy man surely would have had to face charges, but he did not. In the public imagination, however, Hoces took the blame for Guetaria, because those to whom it really belonged—the king and his ministers—would not accept it.

With the relief of Fuenterrabía by land, the serious French threat to northern Spain lessened considerably. The Archbishop of Bordeaux did manage to bottle up a Spanish fleet at La Coruña, with Lope de Hoces in command—a continuation of his bad luck with the French. The French fleet, large though it was, attempted no major actions, however, and the Dutch had so little confidence in their French allies that they would not help. The crucial task for the Spanish remained in keeping the channel open to the transport of troops and money for Flanders. Without resupply, there could be no hope of regaining the northern Netherlands, and even the Spanish southern Netherlands would be jeopardized. Early in 1639 the government in Madrid decided that another major resupply fleet had to force the channel. Leasing ships from Flanders as troop transports could do only a small part of the job.[48] In the spring of 1639, recruiting went on in southern Spain for troops to send to Flanders, the Indies, and the North African forts.[49] From May 20 on, all the Cantabrian and Galician ports were closed to international traffic and set under military government, and from mid-June through July, the government's plans for the Flanders armada took shape.[50] Don Antonio de Oquendo was in Cádiz preparing the fleet, though at first the government was not sure where he could best serve—in the expedition to Flanders or in another Indies fleet. The Duke of Maqueda, titular head of the Armada del Mar Océano, contributed little to the plans.

Everything depended on the timely arrival of treasure from the Indies—as always. At the end of August 1638, just a week after the losses at Guetaria, don Carlos de Ibarra and seven galleons of the Armada de la Guardia encountered a Dutch fleet as they carried the New Spain treasure to Havana. The Dutch had seventeen heavily armed ships and were able to do considerable damage to the Spanish, but they suffered even more. After hard combat on and off for several days, the Dutch disengaged and did not return. Ibarra, wounded and apprised of more Dutch in the area, returned to Veracruz for the winter.[51] On his return home in the spring of 1639, Ibarra carried two and a half years of Indies treasure. To avoid the enemy, he used an old route back to Spain, which meant that his escort waiting in the eastern Atlantic missed the fleet and feared the worst.[52] When Ibarra and the fleet arrived safely in July 1639, confounding gloomy expectations, all Spain celebrated, from sailors in the harbor at Cádiz to the court in Madrid. The fleet's arrival enabled the crown to put about 3 million escudos aboard the fleet bound for Flanders.[53]

On July 17, the same day Ibarra arrived in Cádiz, the Junta de Armadas in Madrid gave the Count-Duke of Olivares a list of ships available for the Flanders voyage. Oquendo had twenty-four appropriate vessels in Cádiz, with 10,577 toneladas. Hoces had sixty-three ships in La Coruña, with 24,143 toneladas. Another twenty ships or so could be added to the fleet by various means, and the Indies fleets would add another twenty-seven.[54] By the end of July 1639 the government had made the resupply of Flanders its top priority, deciding to combine the squadrons of Oquendo and Hoces as the nucleus of the fleet.[55] As ships were shifted around to one duty and another, the potential list changed, and there has been considerable disagreement among scholars about the final composition of the fleet.[56] The most careful estimate to date, based on a thorough search of archival documents, puts the total at sixty-seven combat ships of all sizes in seven squadrons. The twenty-one ships of the squadron of Flanders had an average size of just 245 toneladas per ship. The eleven ships of the squadron of San José averaged 624 toneladas, and all the others averaged between 400 and about 480 toneladas per ship. The *San Felipe* was one of the eight ships of the squadron of La Coruña, where it had been based since 1636. The ships were of unequal soundness as well as varying sizes, and many were embargoed vessels of unknown utility in warfare. Counting combat ships and support vessels, the fleet would have about one hundred ships with 36,000 toneladas and would carry about twenty thousand men.[57] Don Antonio de Oquendo would command the combined fleet as captain-general (see figure 32). Don Lope de Hoces would serve as captain-general of the squadron of La Coruña and as admiral of the combined fleet, sailing on the 1,100-tonelada *Santa Teresa*. The *San Felipe,* listed at 560 toneladas, evidently served as almiranta of the La Coruña contingent.[58] Oquendo left Cádiz on August 2 for La Coruña, a voyage that took over a month because of bad weather. When he arrived, Hoces was standing out to sea to join him, to save time, and the combined fleet began its voyage on September 5.[59]

Figure 32. Don Antonio de Oquendo, ca. 1639. (Drawing by Michael Etoll.)

In Madrid nearly a month earlier, the Count-Duke of Olivares had met with the Junta de Armadas to lay out the objectives for the fleet. Its main mission was the transport of money and troops to Flanders, but Olivares proposed that such a large fleet had to do more than that—a good deal more. If possible, it was to defeat the French fleet on its way up the coast and deliver aid to French rebels in Normandy. Then it was to follow the Dutch to the English anchorage at the Downs north of Dover, where they often took refuge, and send reinforcements to Flanders from there. The varying drafts of the Spanish ships and the shortage of Flemish pilots made that the best plan. Although the English were still neutral, they had not broken relations with the Dutch after an earlier Dutch attack on Spanish ships near the Downs in neutral waters. Olivares reasoned that they probably would not break with Spain if it did likewise. In short, he proposed violating English neutrality to attack the Dutch at the Downs, believing that they would do the same if they had the chance. It was an audacious plan, because potentially Spain would be taking on all three of the other major naval powers of the time, and certainly two of them.[60] Olivares gambled not only on English neutrality, but on a considerable degree of luck as well. Unfortunately, Spain's luck was running out.

With the whole north coast of Spain closed to outsiders since late May, it was no secret to her enemies that Spain was preparing a major fleet, although they did not know just how large it was.[61] The Dutch and the French were waiting separately for it, but once at sea the Spanish got word that the French had decided not to take them on, instead retiring to their ports to preserve their fleet.[62] The Dutch under Maarten Tromp never even considered that alternative, although they originally set out to meet the Spanish with only seventeen large combat ships.[63] There are widely divergent accounts of the battle that followed.

As the encounter began on September 16, Oquendo, like other Spanish naval commanders before him, sought to engage in close combat with the Dutch, his flagship matched with Tromp's, and the others following their lead. The Spanish had an advantage within harquebus and musket range, and with grappling techniques. But Tromp had other plans. He escaped Oquendo's attempt to grapple and board and kept little closer than cannon range of the Spanish, inflicting much damage.[64] One Dutch ship was destroyed when its powder magazine exploded.[65] Although this heartened the Spaniards, they could do little more than chase the Dutch in a running artillery duel and get the worst of it. The next day the two fleets did not engage, but the day after, the battle recommenced. The Dutch fleet had increased to thirty ships with the arrival of reinforcements.[66] They captured two hopelessly disabled ships from the Spanish fleet, but Oquendo pursued the Dutch vessel towing one of the ships and won it back.[67]

During those sixty hours of often fierce and bloody combat, the fleets continued to move northward, coming 270 kilometers closer to Dunkirk, Oquendo's destination. The Dutch had lost at least two ships. The Spanish had lost many more men than the Dutch but only one ship, and that one a hired transport.[68] This would enable Spanish pamphleteers to claim a great victory over the Dutch in the channel.[69] The fact was that the larger Spanish fleet had been heavily battered by Dutch artillery and badly needed repairs. Moreover, both sides were out of ammunition by then. After watching Oquendo recapture one of the Dutch prizes, Tromp broke off the encounter and headed to Calais to resupply.[70] The Spanish were too far from Mardick to resupply there, so they headed for the Downs, planning to purchase ammunition in England with the aid of the Spanish ambassador in London. An English squadron of thirty ships under Admiral Pennington also arrived at the Downs, from Plymouth. Meanwhile the Dutch resupplied, unloaded their wounded men, and took on replacements in Calais—all in a few hours, thanks to their French allies.[71] Then they, too, sailed for the Downs, anchoring within harquebus shot of the Spanish and effectively blocking their exit.

Two of the hired English ships carrying troops for the Spanish were easily taken by the Dutch, which suggested collusion to Oquendo. It meant he would have one thousand fewer men.[72] Upon his arrival at the Downs, Oquendo sent emissaries to London and Flanders to coordinate his own resupply and the delivery of money and troops to the Cardinal-Infante.[73] In the month that the Spanish waited for powder, Oquendo managed to send about six thousand soldiers safely through to Flanders, and perhaps 3–3.5 million escudos.[74] To accomplish this, small Flemish and English ships slipped in and out of the Downs at night and under cover of fog. Experienced sailors in small boats could easily cover the 80 kilometers from the Downs to Mardick during the night. With the resupply of Flanders, Oquendo's fleet kept diminishing. Once the embargoed troop transports delivered their men, they left, their obligations over. Most of the squadron of Flanders returned to their home base carrying troops. Of the forty-seven warships in the Spanish squadrons that had come from La Coruña, only thirty-eight were still in condition to sail. The other nine had either been left without crew to bring other crews to full strength, gutted to repair other ships, or captured. Under the circumstances, repairs were very difficult to accomplish.[75]

In the meantime, the Dutch fleet kept growing, eventually rising to about 120 ships, including fireboats.[76] Pennington's English fleet of thirty ships had orders to enforce England's neutrality, but neither the Dutch nor the

Spanish took that very seriously. The Dutch had unequivocal orders to attack the Spanish fleet and knew that the English lacked the strength to prevent it.[77] The Spanish suspected that the English favored the Dutch and therefore lacked the will as well as the strength. Because of this, Oquendo's relations with Pennington were less than cordial—barely even correct— though Pennington seems to have done little to deserve such treatment. The English even helped assure that Spanish money and troops landed in Flanders got to their destination.[78] The fact was that the Spanish position was desperate, and Oquendo preferred to rely on no one but himself and his men. He called a war council and persuaded his officers that they could not trust the Dutch to respect England's neutrality, nor trust the English to prevent a Dutch attack. There was, of course, no question of carrying out Olivares's plan to attack the Dutch first. It was better to make a break for the open sea as soon as powder and supplies arrived, fighting and dying at sea rather than being trapped at anchorage. The memory of Guetaria was too strong to risk that particular sort of disaster again, as Lope de Hoces must certainly have agreed. On October 20 an English merchant arrived with the necessary gunpowder (at exhorbitant prices), and the Dutch decided to attack the next day, having resolved on October 11 to attack at the first favorable opportunity.[79] According to Spanish sources, several times before the Dutch had raised sail in an attitude of attack, and the English had responded as if to try to prevent it. This time, the Dutch Admiral Witte C. de With and thirty ships were charged with seeing that Pennington did not come to the aid of the Spanish.[80]

Before daybreak on October 21, Tromp gave the signal to set sail. His ships were under way at dawn, "and at about half-past eight we opened fire on the enemy who cut their cables and made sail; shortly after the action began it became very misty, so that we remained driving with our sails laid aback on the mast for a good half-hour, until it began to clear somewhat, so that we saw the enemy; we fought him again and drove the enemy, to the total of 23 ashore, close under the castles; . . ."[81] In dangerously shallow waters and blinded by the morning fog, more than half the Spanish ships had run aground. When the Dutch attacked, the English opened fire to dissuade them, but de With cut them off and they retired, rather than risk being destroyed along with the Spanish. When the fog cleared, only twenty-one Spanish warships had made it to the open sea.

Combat began with odds of greater than five to one. The Dutch again stood off and sent in fireboats in groups against individual Spanish ships. The septuagenarian Lope de Hoces on the *Santa Teresa* fought eight Dutch ships simultaneously. Although he lost an arm and a leg, he continued on deck directing the fighting. One Dutch fireboat got through and the *Santa Teresa* began to burn. Lope de Hoces and 550 of the 600 men on board died in the conflagration, firing their guns until the last minute.[82] In death, at least, he regained the reputation taken from him at Guetaria. Admiral Feijóo on the capitana of the squadron of Galicia fought an entire Dutch squadron for eighteen hours. He finally surrendered at two in the morning, when there were only thirteen men left alive on his ship. The ship itself was so damaged that it sank on the way to Holland. In all the Dutch took nine Spanish warships, six of which sank before reaching port, so damaged were they by the time they surrendered.[83]

On board *Nuestra Señora de la Concepción y Santiago,* Captain-General Oquendo refused all counsel to surrender. The sun set amid the smoke and wreckage of the battle, as Oquendo lowered sail and waited to be boarded. Instead, the Dutch stood off and increased their artillery barrage, anxious to take the capitana and seal their victory, but not anxious enough to risk boarding her. The capitana had already escaped four fireships, but the heat and intensity of the barrage panicked even Oquendo's seasoned crew, some of whom fled into the hold in terror. Oquendo pursued them and rallied his men once again. If their only choice left was how to die, they must choose to die with honor. Don Miguel de Horna, from the squadron of Flanders but sailing with Oquendo, completed their inspiration. With one eye knocked out and a bloody rag around half his head, he led the defense. Various Dutch ships moved in to try to board the capitana, but the men fought like demons to avoid encirclement. By nightfall, the galleons of Nicolás de Massibradi and the squadron of Flanders had freed the capitana. As Tromp ruefully admitted later, with Oquendo on board, the ship was invincible.[84]

The next day, October 22, a storm dispersed the Dutch ships and ended the battle. Kept afloat by five pumps, Oquendo's capitana limped toward Mardick, followed by Massibradi's galleons and seven from Dunkirk. Oquendo's ship was the largest that had ever tried to enter Mardick, but Miguel de Horna's expert pilotage brought it in safely on October 23, still flying the royal standard. An inventory of the damage showed that it had taken 1,700 hits. Contemplating the ship and his bitter loss to the Dutch, Oquendo remarked, "Nothing remains for me but to die, for I have brought the flagship and its standard in good repute to this port."[85]

Of the twenty-three ships grounded at the Downs before the final battle, only nine could be saved. Some had been burned by the Dutch, others were too damaged to repair and had been plundered by local residents of the English coast. Captain Andrés de Castro had kept up a furious fight from the grounded *almiranta real San Agustín,* in which half the crew died. Later stories would accuse Castro and other captains of deliberately grounding their ships to avoid battle, but there seems to have been no basis for the stories except anger and disappointment on the part of the Spanish and misinformation on the part of others.[86] Although Castro was no match for Oquendo or Hoces, he was an experienced commander and a member of the Council of War. After the battle, he refloated and repaired what ships he could and had them ready to sail in five days. Because the English had taken the artillery from the grounded ships, Castro at first accepted an English offer of an escort across the channel. Once he learned the Dutch had left the area, however, he preferred to go alone. In early November, the survivors met in Mardick, to carry out repairs over the winter. Oquendo put together a fleet of twenty-five ships for the return voyage, and by February he was heading home, with the squadron of Dunkirk under don Miguel de Horna in the lead. On the way to Spain they captured fifteen small corsairs from St. Malo and entered La Coruña on March 17.

Although Oquendo succeeded in his primary mission of resupplying Flanders with troops and money, there is no question that the Battle of the Downs was a major defeat for the Spanish. Figures differ wildly for the Spanish losses, the count being complicated by the comings and goings in the fleet once it anchored at the Downs. The best estimate is that, of the forty-seven Spanish combat ships that left La Coruña, thirty-two were lost. That was over 15,000 tons of shipping, some 68 percent of the Spanish contingent of the fleet. Only fifteen galleons survived the voyage and returned to La Coruña in March 1640. Among them was the *San Felipe* built by Martín de Arana, first commissioned twelve years before. About six thousand men died on the Spanish side in the final battle, a horrendous toll, but less than half of some of the estimates given. Very few officers survived, and some ships lost all but a handful of the men they carried. Counting those who died in the two days of battle in September, and from illness, the best estimate is that between nine and ten thousand men perished from mid-September to the end of October. Oquendo himself would last only another three months; he succumbed to illness in La Coruña and died on June 7, the Day of Corpus Christi. The Dutch lost only about one thousand men and ten ships.[87]

The deleterious effects on the Spanish war effort went far beyond mere numbers, however tragic they were. We know, from the perspective of several centuries, that the Dutch had proven themselves masters of the channel, though they would continue to suffer heavy losses from privateers. After 1640, the Spanish would be fighting for the survival of their provinces in the southern Netherlands, with no possibility of regaining the northern provinces. It would also be increasingly difficult for Spain to supply its forces in northern Europe. What we often forget, however, is that this was not immediately apparent. The documentary records show no break in their customary rhythm. While acknowledging the serious losses at the Downs, the Junta de Armadas and the rest of the royal bureaucracy continued with business as usual, refitting the Indies fleets, repairing the *San Felipe* and the other ships in La Coruña and Cádiz.[88] In 1641 Fulvio Testi, an Italian writer who was no friend of Spain, could still remark, "Thus it is that the power of the Catholic King is vast, immense, infinite."[89] Just a few years later, with the treaties that ended the Thirty Years' War in 1648, it was suddenly clear that Spain's hegemony in Europe was finished.

The same realization came slowly but inexorably to Spain, as it struggled during the 1640s with rebellions in Catalonia and Portugal, in addition to the increasing difficulties of keeping its war machine functioning. Fleets came from the Indies, but with disappointing returns; crews and ships were found, but with even greater difficulty than before. The multiple responsibilities of maintaining a global empire and at the same time fighting what some have called the first global war, simply could no longer be borne. In the critical period from about 1625 to 1640, Spain was fatally overextended abroad, just as its internal economy entered a steep decline. The two phenomena are related, though not in ways that are easy to sort out. It is clear, however, that external responsibilities and internal economic crisis exacerbated one another.

In trying to protect the empire and fight a global war at the same time, the Spanish government displayed remarkable resourcefulness and adaptability. Time and again, needed funds were secured in desperation from a multitude of sources, though often at a high cost in interest fees and good will. High taxation and the confiscation of private wealth combined with a cheeseparing mentality in many military expenditures. This two-sided approach aimed to extract the most revenue from loyal subjects and to spend it as frugally as possible. Yet the approach had many problems, not the least of which was that the crown often had to spend more in the long run, because it lacked ready cash in the short run or delayed spending money until prices had risen.

When all else failed, the loyalty and talents of bureaucrats, nobles, and military officers were pushed to the limit. Faced with inadequate money and supplies, they were in effect called upon to make up for these deficiencies with their zeal. The best of them rose to the challenge, but the cost was high. In just over a decade from 1631 to 1641, Spain lost practically its entire naval officer corps. Among the highest ranks we can count Francisco de Vallecilla in 1631, Tomás de Larráspuru in 1632, Fadrique de Toledo y Osorio and Juan de Benavides in 1634, Martín de Vallecilla in 1635, a dozen high-ranking career officers at Guetaria in 1638, Lope de Hoces in 1639, Antonio de Oquendo in 1640, and Carlos de Ibarra and Roque Centeno in 1641. One cannot escape the suspicion that they wore themselves out before their time by one superhuman effort after another, when they were not simply sent into a slaughter.

In the end, no amount of personal sacrifice or administrative talent could sustain Spain's power in the world. The odds against it were too great. Yet by using every possible resource, the government and its loyal servants were able to hang on to a great deal. By determined efforts in protecting the Indies fleets and the integrity of the Spanish colonies, Spain effectively kept other Europeans out of the heart of its empire. Although the Dutch created havoc in the New World in the 1630s and maintained a strong presence in Brazil until the early 1640s, they could not alter the reality of Iberian dominance in the New World. The colonial activities of England and France, as well, were driven to the fringes of Spain's American empire in the early seventeenth century, and that would change very little in the centuries that followed.

In Europe, Spain's hegemony crumbled in the same period; its predominant role was first assumed by France, in the late seventeenth century, and later by England. Yet Spain retained various European territories until the early eighteenth century and, by its continued possession of the American colonies, would retain some vestiges of its former power.

The great test of the early seventeenth century forced Spain to recognize the value of the navy in the defense and governance of its empire, despite the lack of naval expertise displayed by the king and his chief minister and the strong land-based traditions of Castile. The strains of defending and developing its empire in the sixteenth century had already engaged the crown in naval matters, though it continued to rely on embargoes of private vessels to meet some of its vast needs for shipping tonnage. In the seventeenth century, the crown began to regulate private ship construction, hoping to devise multi-purpose vessels that could serve the needs of both trade and defense. It also launched a major effort to increase the size of the fleet owned by the state. Luckily, long-standing traditions of seafaring and shipbuilding were there to be tapped.

The contract between the crown and Martín de Arana drew on the materials and traditions of the north coast, and on the linkage between service and personal advancement that defined Spanish society. The galleons that Arana built were generally sleeker and shallower than traditional merchant ships, but they did not represent the most advanced thinking about warship design. Instead, they were the product of a century of evolution from the earliest Spanish galleons in the 1520s, and of the changing, often conflicting, needs of Atlantic trade and defense. Because they could carry cargo and serve as warships at the same time, they were well suited to the needs of the empire at that particular juncture.

In contracting with Arana to build the ships, the crown relinquished part of its control over the finished product, but royal officials monitored the construction and its costs with great care. Moreover, in return for royal privileges for himself and his family, Arana gladly spent a great deal of his own money on the construction. The evidence encountered for this study suggests that using private contractors for public business benefited both the crown and its loyal servants.

The bureaucracy that oversaw Arana's ship construction also coordinated the selection, provisioning, and refitting of the Spanish fleets. In the desperate shortage of money that developed after the loss of the New Spain fleet in 1628, the bureaucracy showed remarkable agility, dedication, and inventiveness in keeping the fleets supplied. Private contractors and public officials worked together in that mutual task—not always harmoniously, but in general fruitfully. At the very least, they kept a wary eye on one another, which from the crown's point of view was even more useful than harmony.

The chain of command on the fleets, involving civilian officials as well as navy and infantry hierarchies, exemplified a similar creative tension. Each official had specific duties, but the functions of one often overlapped those of another. In a positive sense, this forced individuals to share responsibility for the ships and their contents. In a negative sense, it meant that derelictions of duty could be more easily noticed and reported. In the cramped and difficult conditions of an Atlantic crossing, hierarchy and regulations fostered an orderly routine that served the fleets well.

The provisioning records for the 1620s and 1630s offer no evidence that the crown cut rations or otherwise scrimped on food or supplies for the men who served in the royal fleets. Money might be late in coming, private contractors might not be paid promptly or in full, but the intent was to provide sailors and soldiers with nutritious food and good medical care. Analysis of the official diet shows plentiful calories and adequate nutritional content, by both ancient and modern standards.

Law and custom demanded a great deal in return. Even at the highest levels of society, royal policy dealt harshly with presumed malfeasance in office and even with human error. In the crisis that developed in the 1620s and 1630s, the stakes were too high to tolerate either. We can see this in the severe discipline meted out to fleet commanders and bureaucrats alike, whereas compassion and an understanding of naval affairs might have dictated a milder course. Yet in the traditional society of Habsburg Spain, loyal subjects continued to serve the crown willingly, even at great personal cost.

In the end, when the strains of maintaining a global empire became overwhelming, Spain relied heavily on such individuals. They served at home and they served in the royal fleets composed of ships such as Arana's six galleons. Faced by the serious challenges of the early seventeenth century, Spain managed to hold on to as much as it did largely because of the protection afforded by the imperial fleets. The ships built by Arana participated in most of the major naval actions of the time, both in the Indies and in Europe, beginning their service in time to meet the challenge posed by

Matanzas and continuing through the disastrous encounter at the Downs. The survival of the *San Felipe* after the Battle of the Downs can stand as a symbol of Spain itself in that period. To the nation and its leaders, the loss of power and prestige came as a hard lesson on the dangers of overextension. Still, by exhausting every available material and human resource, the empire at least survived. Spain had hoped for more from such sacrifices, but perhaps survival was enough.

Appendixes

Appendix A. Inventories of the Six Galleons Built by Martín de Arana[a]

San Felipe	Nuestra Señora de Begoña
Ship	
Rudder, tiller; whipstaff; compass box	Same as *San Felipe*
Mainmast and foremast, each with its masthead, topmast, yards; topgallant	
Bowsprit, mizzenmast with their yards and topmasts (gavias)	
Gangway from poop to prow and railings from port to starboard to hang the waistclothes during battle	
3 pumps, 2 of them with all their fittings, and one in reserve	
2 capstans, each with 6 beams	
2 timber-head tackles (guindastes) with their sheaves (roldanas) and bolts (pernos)	
All the curved knee timbers (corbatones) of bowline and braces required (one is broken)	Without the broken knee timber
Post with two knobs projecting from the deck to secure lines, cables, etc. (bita con dos tetas)	
Poop galleries painted in oil with appropriate decoration and the image of San Felipe	. . . image of Nuestra Señora de Begoña
Chambers on the poop planked in oak and partitioned with pine, the larger with its storage box (cajon) on the galleries, and the smaller on the inside	
The storerooms for bread and gunpowder planked and closed; ship lacks a larder (despensa) and the storeroom for the sails	Lacks a larder
Artillery storeroom (Rancho de Santa Barbara) lacks sides to protect the cartridges and other items from hot embers	
Holes for mainmast and foremast through both decks, the larger with four iron rings (argollas)	
Four rope ladders, to climb up and down	
Beakhead (espolón) with its figure of a rampant lion with a golden crown	
Compartments for the pumps	
16 ports between decks, with 7 iron rings each	
14 ports on the quarterdeck (plaza de armas), with 5 iron rings each	13 ports on quarterdeck, 7 on the larboard side and 6 on the starboard
Bitt from port to starboard on the forecastle, with a boom to secure the foremast	
7 iron posts (macarrones) on each side of the ship, with their iron chains (2 at 180 lb.)	
2 "ynquetes" [?] of iron with their belaying pins (cabillas) attached, for the capstans	
Hatchways with their covers and iron bars	
5 iron rings, the one below with its "candados"[?]	
4 cat-heads to secure the raised anchors	
1 rope ladder for the gangway	
Davit (gaviete) to raise the anchors	
All the standing rigging and tackle necessary, in working order	
2 cookstoves (fogones)	
Missing: 24 small blocks to rig the topgallant; 2 *bocas* for the mainmast and 2 for the foremast, for the yards during battle, each one 12 brazas [about 66 feet] long and 80 threads thick	Missing bocas for yards of foremast and mainmast for use during battle, each 12 brazas long and 80 threads thick. These are being sent, along with planks and nails to make shot-lockers in the Rancho de Santa Barbara.

Los Tres Reyes	San Juan Baptista	San Sebastián	Santiago
Same as *San Felipe*	Same as *San Felipe*	Same as *San Felipe*	Same as *San Felipe*
			2 capstans, each with 3 beams
Without the broken knee timber	Without the broken knee timber	Without the broken knee timber	Without the broken knee timber
. . . image of the Tres Reyes	. . . image of San Juan Baptista	. . . image of San Sebastián	. . . image of Santiago
Lacks a larder	Lacks a larder	Lacks a larder and room for sails Rancho de Santa Barbara complete	Lacks a larder Rancho de Santa Barbara complete
14 ports between decks, with 7 rings each 15 ports on quarterdeck, with 5 rings each	14 ports between decks, with 7 rings each 12 ports on quarterdeck, with 5 rings each	12 ports between decks, with 7 rings each 10 ports on quarterdeck, with 5 rings each	12 ports between decks, with 7 rings each 10 ports on quarterdeck, with 5 rings each
		5 iron posts on each side, with chains	5 iron posts on each side, with chains
No davit	No davit	No davit	No davit
Missing bocas for the yards and mainmast, 12 brazas long and 80 threads thick. They are being sent to the ship's master.	Same as *Los Tres Reyes*	Missing bocas for the yards and four for the anchors, 12 brazas long and 80 threads thick. They are being sent to the ship's master.	Missing bocas for the yards of the mainmast, each of the two 12 brazas long and 80 threads thick. They are being sent to the ship's master.

San Felipe		Nuestra Señora de Begoña	

Sails

San Felipe	Nuestra Señora de Begoña
2 lower sails for the mainmast, with their bonnets; bolt-ropes attached (relingadas)	Same as *San Felipe*
2 lower sails for the foremast, with their bonnets; bolt-ropes attached	
2 topsails for the mainmast (gavia mayor)	
2 topsails for the foremast (borriquete)	
2 spritsails	
1 mizzen sail	
2 topgallant sails for the mainmast and a spritsail topsail (sobrecebadera)	
All with their rope-band and furling line (envergue and princeo). One skiff has no rope-band on the sail.	

Cables (from Calatayud unless otherwise noted)

San Felipe		Nuestra Señora de Begoña	
1 ayuste	504 threads	1 ayuste	540 threads
1 ayuste	540 threads	1 ayuste	459 threads
1 cable	450 threads	1 cable	450 threads
1 mooring cable	360 threads	1 mooring cable	450 threads
1 mooring cable	432 threads	1 mooring cable	450 threads
1 cable	360 threads	1 cable	504 threads
1 cable	306 threads	1 hawser	48 threads
1 laid rope (calabrote) from Cherba	108 threads	12 bocas for anchors	
1 laid rope from San Macari (France)	153 threads	1 laid rope from Cherba	180 threads
6 bocas of tackle (jarcia) from San Macari, except one which is from Calatayud, plus two buoy ropes in the water, making the required total of 8			

Anchors

San Felipe	Nuestra Señora de Begoña
4 iron anchors (ancoras) mooring the ship; two with buoys; all four with their buoy ropes	5 iron anchors, with stocks and buoy ropes
1 anchor with its anchor stock	
1 stream anchor or kedge (anclote), with stock	1 stream anchor, with buoy ropes
1 grappling iron or mud anchor (arpeo)	1 grappling iron, missing its chain

Other Equipment

San Felipe	Nuestra Señora de Begoña
1 poop lantern covered with gilded copper	1 lantern
1 skiff, with its covered stowage areas (tillas), rudder with tiller, 1 mast and its sail, and 12 oars and grappling iron	1 small skiff, with grappling iron and 5 oars
5 buckets (baldes)	13 buckets
2 white linen flags painted with the royal arms	2 linen flags, one on the mast-head
1 running lantern of tin-plate	
2 large chests, one for muskets and one for balls	1 chest for muskets, harquebuses, and powder-flasks, and an *arcada* for balls
	604 *varas* (yards) of colored bunting in 11 pieces, for all six galleons

Los Tres Reyes	San Juan Baptista	San Sebastián	Santiago
Same as *San Felipe*, but with	Same as *San Felipe*, but with	Same as *San Felipe*	Same as *San Felipe*

no topsails for the foremast

2 mizzen sails

Los Tres Reyes	San Juan Baptista	San Sebastián	Santiago
1 skiff sail has rope-bands and furling line; the other doesn't	1 skiff sail with bolt-ropes and furling lines		

Los Tres Reyes		San Juan Baptista		San Sebastián		Santiago	
1 ayuste	450 threads	1 ayuste	450 threads	1 ayuste	450 threads	1 ayuste	450 threads
1 mooring cable	324 threads	1 mooring cable	350 threads	1 mooring cable	324 threads	1 mooring cable	306 threads
1 cable	360 threads	1 mooring cable	450 threads	1 mooring cable	306 threads	1 cable	306 threads
1 cable	360 threads	1 mooring cable	360 threads	1 mooring cable	324 threads	1 mooring cable	288 threads
1 mooring cable	360 threads	1 hawser	54 threads	1 cable	306 threads	1 cable	324 threads
1 cable	360 threads	1 top rope "de cubierta"		1 hawser	45 threads	1 cable	306 threads
1 top rope (virador)		1 laid rope from Cherba	252 threads	1 laid rope from San Macari	96 threads	1 hawser	48 threads
1 laid rope from San Macari	126 threads	1 laid rope from San Macari	99 threads			1 top rope	
						1 laid rope from San Macari	90 threads

Los Tres Reyes	San Juan Baptista	San Sebastián	Santiago
5 iron anchors, with stocks, 4 with buoy ropes	5 iron anchors, with stocks and buoy ropes	5 anchors . . .	5 anchors . . .
1 stream anchor with stock	1 stream anchor with stock	1 stream anchor . . .	1 stream anchor . . .
1 grappling iron, missing its chain	1 grappling iron, with iron chain	1 grappling iron, missing its chain	1 grappling iron, missing its chain
4 bocas for anchors	6 bocas for anchors		6 bocas for anchors

Los Tres Reyes	San Juan Baptista	San Sebastián	Santiago
1 skiff with grappling iron and 9 oars	1 skiff with grappling iron and 9 oars	1 skiff with grappling iron and 9 oars	1 skiff with grappling iron and 9 oars
6 buckets			6 buckets
1 linen flag	1 linen flag	1 linen flag	1 linen flag
1 running lantern of tin-plate	1 running lantern of tin-plate	1 running lantern of tin-plate	1 running lantern of tin-plate
1 chest for muskets, harquebuses, and powder flasks	1 chest for muskets, harquebuses, and powder flasks	1 chest for muskets, harquebuses, powder flasks	1 chest for muskets, harquebuses, powder flasks
1 arcada for balls	1 arcada for balls	1 arcada for balls	1 arcada for balls

[a]Bell Library, University of Minnesota "Spanish Shipping," f1628, dated July 31, 1628. Each of the six delivery invoices follows the same form, the only differences being the varying equipment on each ship. Here the list of equipment is transcribed fully only for the *San Felipe*. The equipment on the other ships was the same, except for the differences noted.

Appendix B.
Some Weights, Measures, and Coinage in Use in Seventeenth-Century Spain

Weight and Volume

Arroba   25 Castilian pounds of 16 ounces; 8 azumbres; 11.5 kilograms.

Azumbre   Liquid measure divisible into 4 cuartillos; 4 pints.

Bota   Liquid measure often used for wine; size and weight varied widely, in a range of 15–30 arrobas.

Cántara   Liquid measure most commonly divisible into 8 azumbres.

Celemín   Dry measure divisible into 4 cuartillos; about 4.625 liters; weight varied.

Fanega   Dry measure divisible into 12 celemines; 55.5 liters; weight varied, depending upon the item measured.

Libra   Castilian pound; 16 ounces; 460.1 grams.

Libra carnicera   Butchers' pound of 32 ounces, sometimes used for meat.

Pipa   Pipe, a measure used for water and wine; about 27.5 arrobas in the documents used for this study, but sometimes calculated as 30 arrobas.

Quintal   100 Castilian pounds; 1 hundredweight.

Tonel   Often called the tonel macho or the tonel de Vizcaya; measure of a ship's carrying capacity used in the province of Vizcaya. Equal to 2 botas of 30 cántaras each, or 15 quintales mayores of 150 libras each, according to a document around 1530 (AGS, Estado, leg. 441). There is general agreement that the tonel macho was 1.2 times larger than the tonelada then in use in Andalusia. From 1590 on, the tonel macho became the official tonelada. It was equal to 8 cubic codos, or about 1.42 cubic meters. This is equivalent to the French sea ton (tonneau de mer) used in Bordeaux.

Tonelada   Measure of a ship's carrying capacity in Andalusia and the Indies trade. Equal to 2 pipas of 27.5 arrobas each, according to Juan Escalante de Mendoza in 1575. A royal decree dealing with ship measurement, dated August 20, 1590, effectively adopted the tonel macho (sometimes called the tonelada larga) as the standard tonelada, though both large and small toneladas continued in use.

Linear Measure

Braza   5.5 feet or 1.67 meters.

Codo   The codo *real* used in ship construction was 22 inches or 565 millimeters long. It was generally subdivided into either 33 dedos or 27.5 pulgadas, although the meaning of these terms varied. See the discrepancies under *pie* and *vara*.

Dedo   One-sixteenth of a foot (*pie*); about 0.67 inches or 17 millimeters.

Palmo   One-fourth of a vara, subdivided into 9 pulgadas; equal to about 8.2 inches or 209 millimeters.

Paño   Length of cloth equal to about 24 varas.

Pie   Foot; divided into 16 dedos or 12 pulgadas; about 11 inches or 278 millimeters.

Pulgada   One-twelfth of a foot; about 0.8 inches or 20.4 millimeters.

Vara   Castilian yard; commonly divisible into 3 feet (*pies*), 4 palmos, 48 dedos, or 40 pulgadas; about 33 inches or 835 millimeters.

Coinage and Monetary Equivalents

Ducado   Money of account worth 11 reales or 375 maravedís.

Escudo   Gold coin worth 10 reales or 340 maravedís in the accounts used for this study, although it was usually worth about 12–15 reales in the early seventeenth century.

Maravedí   The smallest unit of money of account.

Peso   Silver coined in the New World. The famous "piece of eight" (peso de ocho) was worth 8 reales or 272 maravedís.

Real   Silver coin worth 34 maravedís.

Appendix C. Tables

Table 1. Principal Measures of Arana's Galleons Compared to 1618 and 1626 Rules
(in codos of 22 inches each)

	Beam	Keel	Length on Deck	Depth in Hold	Floor	Toneladas Method 1[a]	Method 2[b]	Given in Document[c]	Keel to Beam	Depth to Beam	Length to Beam	Floor to Beam
Begoña	18.0	44	56.75	8.50	8.5	542.67	618.65	541.50	2.44	0.47	3.15	0.47
Felipe	18.0	44	56.00	8.50	8.5	535.50	610.47	537.38	2.44	0.47	3.11	0.47
Baptista	17.0	42	53.50	8.00	8.0	454.75	518.42	455.75	2.47	0.47	3.15	0.47
Reyes	17.0	42	53.33	8.00	8.0	453.31	516.77	455.00	2.47	0.47	3.14	0.47
Santiago	15.2	38	49.50	7.12	7.0	334.82	381.69	338.50	2.50	0.47	3.26	0.46
Sebastián	15.0	38	48.67	7.17	7.0	327.15	372.96	330.25	2.53	0.48	3.24	0.47
1618 Rules	18.0	46	59.00	8.50	9.0	564.19	643.17	624.50	2.56	0.47	3.28	0.50
	17.0	44	56.00	8.00	8.5	476.00	542.64	530.00	2.59	0.47	3.29	0.50
	15.0	40	50.50	7.00	7.5	331.41	377.80	371.50	2.67	0.47	3.37	0.50
1626 Rule changes	18.0	46	59.00	9.00	8.1	597.38	681.01	———	2.56	0.50	3.28	0.45
	17.0	44	56.00	8.50	7.7	505.75	576.56	———	2.59	0.50	3.29	0.45
	15.0	40	50.50	7.50	6.8	355.08	404.79	———	2.67	0.50	3.37	0.45

[a] (Depth × beam) divided by 2; the result times length on deck; product divided by 8. My calculations.

[b] (Depth × beam) divided by 2; the result times length on deck; minus 5 percent; divide result by 8, then add 20 percent. My calculations.

[c] AGS, Guerra Antigua, leg. 3149, no. 2 provided these figures.

Table 2. Measures, Ratios, and Estimated Tonnages Prescribed by Nautical Experts and Government Ordinances

	Beam	Keel	Length on Deck	Depth in Hold	Floor	Toneladas		Given in Document[a]	Keel to Beam	Depth to Beam	Length to Beam	Floor to Beam
						Method 1	Method 2					
Escalante de Mendoza (1575)	19.4	44	61.60						2.27		3.18	
	18.5	42	58.80						2.27		3.18	
	16.7	38	53.20						2.27		3.18	
García de Palacio (1587)	16.0	34	51.75	7.75		401.06	457.21	400.00	2.13	0.48	3.23	
Ordenanzas (1507)	19.0	47	65.00	10.00		771.88	879.94	897.38	2.47	0.53	3.42	
	18.0	44	62.00	9.50		662.63	755.39	755.00	2.44	0.53	3.44	
	17.0	43	60.00	9.25		589.69	672.24	669.38	2.53	0.54	3.53	
	16.0	42	57.00	8.75		498.75	568.58	567.88	2.63	0.55	3.56	
	15.0	40	52.00	8.00		390.00	444.60	487.13	2.67	0.53	3.47	
	14.0	39	50.00	7.50		328.13	374.06	373.38	2.79	0.54	3.57	
Ordenanzas (1613)	20.0	51	66.00	10.00		825.00	940.50	833.63	2.55	0.50	3.30	
	18.0	48	61.50	9.00		622.69	709.86		2.67	0.50	3.42	
	17.0	46	58.75	8.50		530.59	604.87	539.25	2.71	0.50	3.46	
Ordenanzas (1618)	20.0	49	63.00	9.50	10.00	748.13	852.86	821.88	2.45	0.48	3.15	0.50
	19.0	48	61.50	9.00	9.50	657.28	749.30	721.75	2.53	0.47	3.24	0.50
	18.0	46	59.00	8.50	9.00	564.19	643.17	624.50	2.56	0.47	3.28	0.50
	17.0	44	56.00	8.00	8.50	476.00	542.64	530.00	2.59	0.47	3.29	0.50
	16.0	42	53.00	7.50	8.00	397.50	453.15	444.50	2.63	0.47	3.31	0.50
	15.0	40	50.50	7.00	7.50	331.41	377.80	371.50	2.67	0.47	3.37	0.50
	14.0	38	48.00	6.50	7.00	273.00	311.22	309.50	2.71	0.46	3.43	0.50
Ordenanzas (¿666)	18.5	53	65.00	8.75		657.62	749.68	700.00	2.86	0.47	3.51	
	17.5	50	62.00	8.25		559.45	637.78	500.00	2.86	0.47	3.54	
Ordenanzas (¿679)	19.0	56	67.50	9.25		741.45	845.25	800.00	2.92	0.49	3.55	
Garrote (1691)	22.0	66	75.62	8.69		903.56	1030.06	894.25	3.00	0.40	3.44	
	18.0	54	61.80	7.14		496.41	565.91	487.88	3.00	0.40	3.43	

[a]These figures were provided in the source listed. They are useful as comparisons with my calculations according to methods 1 and 2.

Table 3. Masts, Yards, and Sails According to 1618 Rules[a]

	Length in Codos[b]	Maximum Girth in Palmos,[c] Tapering to:	
Mainmast	Keel plus 2 codos	.5 beam	60%
main yard	2.25 beam	tip of mainmast	40%
main-topmast	1.67 beam	tip of mainmast minus 1 pulgada	60%
main-topmast yard	1 beam	tip of main-topmast	40%
Foremast	mainmast minus 4 codos	5/6 mainmast	60%
fore yard	2 beam	tip of foremast minus 1 pulgada	40%
fore-topmast	main-topmast minus 20%	tip of foremast minus 1 pulgada	60%
fore-topmast yard	beam minus 20%	tip of fore-topmast	40%
Bowsprit	mainmast minus 6 codos	foremast minus 1 palmo	60%
bowsprit yard	2 beam minus 20%	tip of bowsprit	40%
Mizzenmast	main-topmast plus 3 codos	main-topmast	60%
mizzen yard	2 beam		
Main-topgallant[d]	1 beam for lower arch		
	1 beam minus 1.5 codos for upper arch		
Fore-topgallant[d]	1 beam minus 1.5 codos for lower arch		
	1 beam minus 2.5 codos for upper arch		

[a] AGM, C.F. 134.

[b] 1 codo = 22 inches or 560 millimeters.

[c] 1 palmo = 8.2 inches or 9 pulgadas.

[d] The word used is gavias, which usually meant topsails. The size of the sails could only pertain to topgallants, however.

Table 4. Masts, Yards, and Sails on Arana's Ships According to 1618 Rules

	Begoña and San Felipe			Los Tres Reyes and Baptista			Santiago			San Sebastián		
	Length (codos)[a]	Girth (palmos)[b]	Tip	Length (codos)	Girth (palmos)	Tip	Length (codos)	Girth (palmos)	Tip	Length (codos)	Girth (palmos)	Tip
Mainmast	46.00	9.00	5.40	44.00	8.50	5.10	40.00	7.60	4.56	40.00	7.50	4.50
main yard	40.05	5.40	2.16	38.25	5.10	2.04	34.20	4.56	1.82	33.75	4.50	1.80
main-topmast	30.06	5.29	3.17	28.39	4.99	2.99	25.38	4.45	2.67	25.05	4.39	2.63
main-topmast yard	18.00	3.17	1.27	17.00	2.99	1.20	15.20	2.67	1.07	15.00	2.63	1.05
Foremast	42.00	7.50	4.50	40.00	7.08	4.25	36.00	6.33	3.80	36.00	6.25	3.75
fore yard	36.00	4.39	1.76	34.00	4.14	1.66	30.40	3.69	1.48	30.00	3.64	1.46
fore-topmast	24.05	4.39	2.63	22.71	4.14	2.48	20.30	3.69	2.21	20.04	3.64	2.18
fore-topmast yard	14.40	2.63	1.05	13.60	2.48	0.99	12.16	2.21	0.88	12.00	2.18	0.87
Bowsprit	40.00	6.50	3.90	38.00	6.08	3.65	34.00	5.33	3.80	34.00	5.25	3.75
bowsprit yard	28.80	3.90	1.56	27.20	3.65	1.46	24.32	3.80	1.52	24.00	3.75	1.50
Mizzenmast	33.06	5.29	3.17	31.39	4.99	2.99	28.38	4.45	2.67	28.05	4.39	2.63
mizzen yard	36.00			34.00			30.40			30.00		
Main-topgallant, lower arch	18.00			17.00			15.20			15.00		
upper arch	16.50			15.50			13.70			13.50		
Fore-topgallant, lower arch	16.50			15.50			13.70			13.50		
upper arch	15.50			14.50			12.70			12.50		

[a] 1 codo = 22 inches.
[b] 1 palmo = 8.2 inches.

Table 5. Masts and Yards on Royal Galleons

	Arana's *San Felipe,* 1636				Galleons Planned for Barlovento Patrol, 1609			
	Length (codos)	Girth (palmos)	Length (feet)	Girth (feet)	Length (codos)	Girth (palmos)	Length (feet)	Girth (feet)
Mainmast	43	10.00	78.82	6.85	39	9.50	71.50	6.51
main yard	39	6.50	71.49	4.45	39	7.00	71.50	4.79
main-topmast	38	7.00	69.65	4.79	26	7.50	47.67	5.14
main-topmast yard					19	4.00	34.83	2.74
main-topgallant mast	19	3.50	34.83	2.40				
Foremast	44	10.30	80.65	7.05	35	7.50	64.17	5.14
fore yard	37	7.50	67.82	5.14	31	6.50	56.83	4.45
fore-topmast	35	7.25	64.16	4.97	21	6.00	38.50	4.11
fore-topmast yard					19	4.00	34.83	2.74
fore-topgallant yard	35	7.25	64.16	4.97				
Bowsprit	41	9.50	75.15	6.51	38	7.50	69.67	5.14
bowsprit yard					25	5.00	45.83	3.42
yard of spritsail top-sail	19	3.50	34.83	2.40				
Mizzenmast	38	7.25	69.67	4.97	31	7.00	56.83	4.79
mizzen yard	19	3.50	34.83	2.40	35	4.00	64.17	2.74
mizzen topgallant	19	3.50	34.83	2.40				

Table 6. Sails on Arana's *Santiago,* 1634

	Maximum Width in Paños[a]	Length in Codos[b]	Square Measure in Codos	Percentage of Maximum Area Aloft
Mainsail				
with bonnet	34.0	20	816.0	23.99
without bonnet	30.0	15	540.0	15.88
Foresail				
with bonnet (1)	25.0	18	540.0	15.88
with bonnet (2)	29.0	15	522.0	15.35
Spritsail	20.0	13	312.0	9.17
Mizzen	12.0	19	273.6	8.05
Main-topsail				
(1)	25.0	24	720.0	21.17
(2)	23.0	23	634.8	
Fore-topsail				
(1)	23.0	22	607.2	17.85
(2)	20.0	19	456.0	13.41
Topgallant				
(1)	10.0	11	132.0	3.88
(2)	8.0	10	96.0	2.82
(3)	7.5	9	81.0	2.38
(4)	6.5	8	62.4	1.83
Maximum sail area aloft at one time (in square codos)			3400.8	

Source: AGS, CMC 3a, leg. 1323.

[a] 1 paño = 1.2 codos.

[b] 1 codo = 22 inches.

Table 7. Estimated Cost of Building Arana's Six Galleons, 1625–28

		Percentage	Ducados
Contract price for 2,658.4 toneladas at 30 ducados			
per tonelada		100.00	79,752
Including:			
Wood: 155,402 codos plus braces, knees, etc.	22,067	27.67	
Iron	11,962.8	15.0	
Sails: All materials and labor	5,248.7	6.58	
Cables and rigging	21,373.2	26.8	
Oil, tar, pitch, tow	3,987.3	5.0	
Pulleys, tackle	797.5	1.0	
Labor	14,315.5	17.95	
Additional Costs			
Decoration, etc.			3,403.6
Reserve supplies, careening, miscellaneous			6,618.5
Six new cables			1,800
Final preparations for the first voyage			2,600
Subtotal Paid by the Crown			94,174.1
35.4 ducados per tonelada			
15,695.7 ducados per ship			
Contributed by Arana from his personal funds (not reimbursed)			6,000
Total Cost			**100,174.1**
37.7 ducados per tonelada			
16,695.7 ducados per ship			

Table 8. Calibers and Weights of Artillery Produced at Liérganes, 1628–46[a]

Number of Cannons with Weight Listed[b]	Caliber (ball fired in pounds)	Average Gun Weight (pounds)	Weight Range (pounds)		Ratio of Barrel Length to diameter		Pounds Gun to Each Pound of Ball
			Low	High	Low	High	
98	24	5,187	4,775	5,950	19.5	19.5	216.1
283	16	4,020	3,918	4,562	20.0	21.5	251.2
23	12	3,300					275
180	10	3,300	2,850	4,450	23.5	24.5	330
43	8	2,579					322.4
101	7	2,377					339.6
106	6	2,124	2,050	2,150			354
7	5	1,868					373.6
40	3	1,395	1,300	1,575			465

Other Weapons

Name and Number		Caliber	Average Weight (pounds)	Weight Range (pounds)	
				Low	High
Trabuco					
(catapult)	2	280	1,567	1,533	1,600
	5	100	828	720	925
	2	75	825	806	844
	2	45	584	530	638
Mortero					
(mortar)	2	360	3,000		
	2	200	2,000		
	2	100	814		
Petardo					
(petard)	3	68			

(cont'd)

Table 8. Calibers and Weights of Artillery Produced at Liérganes, 1628–46[a] (*cont.*)

Ammunition

Number	Caliber	Average Weight (pounds)	Low	High
6,564	40	40.89	40.54	41.38
1,000	38	37.06		
1,427	35	34.43	34.25	34.50
1,200	33	32.50	32.00	33.00
500	32	32.00		
3,316	25	24.75	24.69	25.00
7,374	24–25	24.38		
21,754	24	23.45	22.00	24.38
2,000	20	18.25		
100	18	17.00		
800	17	17.00		
42,580	16	15.55	15.30	18.19
1,400	14	13.51	13.44	13.69
9,092	12	11.80	11.50	15.00
39,606	10	9.81	9.50	13.00
1,400	8	8.00		
800	7.5	7.13		
10,860	7	7.20	6.78	9.81
18,017	6	5.98	5.94	7.43
17,029	5	5.00		
700	4.5	4.13		
935	4	3.91		
10,389	3	2.95	2.88	3.00
1,750	2.5	2.50		
2,750	2	1.88		
1,500	1.5	1.43		

Bombas de Fierro (iron bombs for the mortars)

Number	Caliber	Weight (pounds)
812	280	280
290	264	264
400	200	200
270	150	150
500	120	120
650	100	100
200	75	75
200	45	45
99	16	16

Granadas (grenades)

Number	Caliber	Weight
3,000	5	[c]

[a] AGS, CMC 3a, leg. 30.

[b] The document provided weights only for these cannons. Others were mentioned without specifications.

[c] A document from 1674 mentioned that each 5-pound caliber grenade should weigh 2.5 lbs. AGS, CMC 3a, leg. 2101, no. 10.

Table 9. Mariners (*gente de mar*) in the Armada de la Guardia, 1601, 1613

| | 1601[a] | | 1613[b] | |
	Number	Percentage	Number	Percentage
Oficiales (officers)	87	15.4	93	17.1
Marineros (seamen)	136	24.2	178	32.8
Grumetes (apprentices)	119	21.1	110	20.3
Pajes (pages)	85	15.1	42	7.7
Artilleros (gunners)	136	24.2	120	22.1
Total men	563	100.0	543	100.0
Total ships	6		6	

[a] Chaunu, *Séville et l'Atlantique,* 4:122.
[b] Navarrete, *Colección de documentos,* 24(2):79.

Table 10. Wages of Mariners on Spanish Treasure Fleets
(in silver reales per month)

	1514	1550–64	1567–1623
Captain (master?)[a]	38.2	73.5	88.2
Mate (contramaestre?)	33.8	55.1	66.2
Watchman (guardian?)	—	55.1	66.2
Water bailiff (alguacil)	—	55.1	55.1
Carpenter	—	55.1	66.2
Caulker	—	—	66.2
Cooper	—	—	66.2
Notary	33.1	44.1	66.2
Dispenser	—	44.1	66.2
Artilleryman (gunner)		44.1	55.1
First-class sailor (seaman)	26.5	30.9	44.1
Second-class sailor (apprentice)	17.6	20.6	29.4
Cabin boy (page)	13.2	15.4	22.0

Source: Hamilton, "Wages and Subsistence."
[a] Probable Spanish equivalents of Hamilton's labels are in parentheses, unless such equivalents are obvious.

Table 11. Mariners' Wages on Ships of the Armada del Mar Océano, 1633 (in reales per month[a])

	Capitana[b]	Almiranta	Other Galleons	Galeoncetes	Embargoed Vessels
Mariners per 100 toneladas	18	16	16	16	—
Number of officials	23	21	14	13	—
Owner	—	—	—	—	250
Captain	400	300	250	200	—
Master	300	250	200	150	250
Contramaestre	250	180	150	120	60
Guardian	180	120	120	82	50
Chief pilot	250	250	200	200	—
Pilot	200	—	—	—	—
Chaplain	132	132	132	132	—
Surgeon	120	100	—	—	—
Water bailiff	66	66	66	66	—
Dispenser	66	66	66	66	—
Cooper	66	66	66	66	—
Caulker	66	66	66	66	60
Carpenter	66	66	66	66	60
Notary	66	66	66	66	60
Trumpeter	66	66	66	66	—
Diver	66	66	—	—	—
Barber/surgeon	66	66	66	66	60
Flageolet players: 4 at	66	—	—	—	—
2 at	88				
Sail Master	—	—	—	—	50
Master Gunner	68	68	68	60	—
Gunners	66	66	66	50	—
Seamen	44	44	44	25	—
Apprentices	29.4	29.4	29.4	15	—
Pages	22	22	22	10	—

Source: Ordenanzas . . . Armada del Mar Océano 1633, pp. 29v–30, 39.

[a] Wages were listed in escudos of 10 reales, except those of the master gunner, listed as 2 ducats, and the apprentices, listed as 1,000 maravedís.

[b] The capitana and the almiranta each carried 2 coopers, 2 caulkers, and 2 carpenters. The capitana carried 4 trumpeters and 6 flageolet players; the almiranta carried 2 trumpeters and no other musicians.

Table 12. Mariners' Wages, ca. 1628–35 (in reales per month)

Captain-general of galleons	5,000	*a*
Admiral of galleons	2,750	*a*
Captain-general of merchant fleet	1,833	*b*
Admiral of merchant fleet	1,375	*b*
Joint captain, sea and land	440	*c*
Sea captain	250	*d*
Master	250	*d*
Master of rations	200	*e*
Pilot	220	*d*
Contramaestre	110	*d*
	150	*e*
Diver	110	*d*
Guardian	88	*d*
	130	*e*
Master gunner	88	*d, e*
Water bailiff	66	*d, e*
Dispenser of provisions	66	*d, e*
Notary	66	*d, e*
Chaplain	66	*d*
Carpenter	66	*d, e*
Caulker	66	*d, e*
Cooper	66	*d*
Gunner	66	*d, e*
Drummer	66	*e*
Barber/surgeon	55	*d*
	66	*e*
Common seaman	44	*d, e*
Apprentice seaman	29	*d*
	30	*e*
Page	22	*d, e*

[a] AGS, Guerra Antigua, leg. 3150, memorandum January 14, 1632.

[b] Estimated from Veitia Linaje, *Rule of Trade*, pp. 165–66.

[c] "Diálogo," in Fernandez Duro, *Disquisiciones náuticas*, 6:156–57.

[d] AGI, Consulados, legs. 1040, 1046, 1048.

[e] AGS, CMC 3a, leg. 627, Arana's six galleons, 1628.

Table 13. Wages of Spanish Infantrymen (in reales per month)

	1578[a]	1633[b]	1634–35[c]
Maestre de campo (commander of a new regiment)	880	1,160	—
Gobernador de tercio (regimental commander)	—	—	500
Capitán de mar y guerra (sea and infantry captain)	—	—	440
Capitán de guerra (infantry captain)	440	400	250
Alférez (lieutenant)	132	150	150
Cabo principal (head squadron leader)	—	—	90
Cabo ordinario (squadron leader)	66	70	80
Sargento (sergeant)	55	80	80
Pífano (fife player)	33	60	60
Tambor (drummer)	33	60	60
Mosquetero (musketeer)	66	60	60
Arcabucero (harquebusier)	44	40	40
Coselete (pikeman)	44	—	—
Abanderado (standard bearer)	—	30	40
Alabardero (halberdier)	44	—	—
Soldado (soldier)	33	30–80	35–60
Artillero (gunner)	88	—	—
Odrero (wine-skin maker)	88	—	—
Tonelero (cooper)	88	—	—
Herrero (smith)	88	—	—
Cordelero (rope-maker)	88	—	—
Minador (sapper)	88	—	—
Carpintero (carpenter)	88–110	—	—
Albañil (mason)	88–110	—	—
Barbero (barber/surgeon)	—	30	—
Capellán (chaplain)	—	120	—

[a] Planned Hispano-Portuguese expedition to Africa. In Sánchez-Albornoz, "Gastos," p. 159.
[b] *Ordenanzas* . . . 1633, fols. 21v–22, for the *Armada del Mar Océano.*
[c] AGI, *Consulados*, legs. 1040, 1046, 1048; AGM, Mss. 471, fols. 157–74; "Diálogo," in Fernández Duro, *Disquisiciones Náuticas*, 6:156–57.

Table 14. Nutritional Content of Spanish Shipboard Dietaries in the Early Seventeenth Century

	Energy (calories)	Protein (grams)	Fat (grams)	Carbohydrate (grams)	Calcium (mg.)
Meat Days (19 per month)					
Biscuit (1.5 lbs.)	1,639.50	62.00	17.70	335.40	571.50
Wine (2 pts.)	1,007.00	1.00	0	54.00	77.00
Rice (1 oz.)	102.94	1.90	0.11	22.79	6.81
Chickpeas (1 oz.)	102.06	5.81	1.36	17.29	42.50
Salt pork (6 oz.)	1,278.80	6.38	138.80	0	trace
Total	4,130.30	77.09	157.97	429.48	697.81
Fish Days (9 per month)					
Biscuit (1.5 lbs.)	1,639.50	62.00	17.70	335.40	571.50
Wine (2 pts.)	1,007.00	1.00	0	54.00	77.00
Rice (1 oz.)	102.94	1.90	0.11	22.79	6.81
Chickpeas (1 oz).	102.06	5.81	1.36	17.29	42.50
Dried cod (6 oz.)	637.90	139.10	4.80	0	382.90
Olive oil (1 oz.)	253.60	0	28.40	0	0
Vinegar (2.67 oz.)					
Total	3,743.00	209.81	52.37	429.48	1,080.71
Cheese Days (3 per month)					
Biscuit (1.5 lbs.)	1,639.50	62.00	17.70	335.40	571.50
Wine (2 pts.)	1,007.00	1.00	0	54.00	77.00
Rice (1 oz.)	102.94	1.90	0.11	22.79	6.81
Chickpeas (1 oz.)	102.06	5.81	1.36	17.29	42.50
Cheese (6 oz.)	630.68	37.84	51.99	3.24	1,244.32
Olive oil (.5 oz.)	126.80	0	14.20	0	0
Total	3,608.98	108.55	85.36	432.72	1,942.13
Daily Average	3,967.41	118.67	120.29	429.79	929.39
Recommended Daily Allowance (moderately active male, 143 lbs.)	3,000.00	37.00			400–500

(cont'd)

Table 14. Nutritional Content of Spanish Shipboard Dietaries in the Early Seventeenth Century (*cont.*)

Phosphorus (mg.)	Iron (mg.)	Sodium (mg.)	Potassium (mg.)	Retinol (I.U.)	Thiamine (mg.)	Riboflavin (mg.)	Niacin (mg.)	Ascorbic Acid (mg.)
1,728.00	15.60	3,606.00	1,742.00	trace	2.06	0.70	19.00	trace
45.00	1.80	41.00	757.00		0.05	0.13	0.11	
26.62	0.22	1.44	26.06	0	0.21	0.01	0.45	0
93.81	1.96	7.38	225.94	14.38	0.09	0.04	0.58	
trace	0.98	1,979.20	68.60	0	0.29	0.06	1.46	
1,893.43	20.56	5,635.02	2,819.60	14.38	2.70	0.94	21.60	0
1,728.00	15.60	3,606.00	1,742.00	trace	2.06	0.70	19.00	trace
45.00	1.80	41.00	757.00		0.05	0.13	0.11	
26.62	0.22	1.44	26.06	0	0.21	0.01	0.45	0
93.81	1.96	7.38	225.94	14.38	0.09	0.04	0.58	
1,515.80	6.10	13,778.00	272.20	0	0.14	0.76	18.50	0
0	0	0	0		0	0	0	0
3,409.23	25.68	17,433.82	3,023.20	14.38	2.55	1.64	38.64	0
1,728.00	15.60	3,606.00	1,742.00	trace	2.06	0.70	19.00	trace
45.00	1.80	41.00	757.00		0.05	0.13	0.11	
26.62	0.22	1.44	26.06	0	0.21	0.01	0.45	0
93.81	1.96	7.38	225.94	14.38	0.09	0.04	0.58	
775.57	1.53			2,113.64		0.77	0.17	0
0	0	0	0	0	0	0	0	0
2,669.00	21.11	3,655.82	2,751.00	2,128.02	2.41	1.65	20.31	0
2,408.56	22.10	8,868.94	2,872.07	218.93	2.63	1.21	26.42	0
	5–9			2,500	1.2	1.8	19.8	30

Table 15. Costs of Spanish Military Rations in Seville, 1626 (in maravedís)

		Price	
		Low	High
Meat days			
Biscuit	1.50 pounds	16.30	17.70
Wine	2.00 pints	23.80	25.50
Rice	1.00 ounce	1.50	1.70
Chickpeas	1.00 ounce	0.71	0.78
Salt pork	6.00 ounces	17.70	20.40
Total		60.01	66.08
Fish days			
Biscuit	1.50 pounds	16.30	17.70
Wine	2.00 pints	23.80	25.50
Rice	1.00 ounce	1.50	1.70
Chickpeas	1.00 ounce	0.71	0.78
Dried cod	6.00 ounces	8.42	8.42
Oil	1.00 ounce	1.43	1.53
Vinegar	2.67 ounces	1.36	1.53
Total		53.52	57.16
Cheese days			
Biscuit	1.50 pounds	16.30	17.70
Wine	2.00 pints	23.80	25.50
Rice	1.00 ounce	1.50	1.70
Chickpeas	1.00 ounce	0.71	0.78
Cheese	6.00 ounces	15.00	17.80
Oil	0.50 ounce	0.72	0.77
Total		58.03	64.25
Total monthly cost			
Meat	19 days	1,140.19	1,255.52
Fish	9 days	481.68	514.44
Cheese	3 days	174.08	192.74
Total	31 days	1,795.95	1,962.70
Daily average		57.93	63.31

Price Source: AGI, Contaduria, leg. 555, ramos 1, 2.

Table 16. Prices of Food Bought for Royal Armadas

Item	Year	Place	Price
Ordinary ship's biscuit	1554	Seville	13–14 reales per 100 lbs.
	1626	Seville	32.4 reales per 100 lbs.
	1635	Seville	64–80 reales per 100 lbs.
White biscuit	1554	Seville	20 reales per 100 lbs.
	1626	Seville	64–70 reales per 100 lbs.
Wine	1554	Seville	118.7–218.2 maravedís per arroba (25 lbs.)
	1626	Seville	357–409.1 maravedís per arroba (25 lbs.)
	1628	Andalusia	188 maravedís per arroba (25 lbs.)
	1628	Bilbao	531.6 maravedís per arroba (25 lbs.)
Salt pork	1562	Seville	40 maravedís per libra carnicera (32 oz.)
	1626	Seville	102 maravedís per libra carnicera (32 oz.)
Salt cod	1540	North coast	26.2 maravedís per libra carnicera (32 oz.)
	1567	North coast	30 maravedís per libra carnicera (32 oz.)
	1626	Seville	45.5 maravedís per libra carnicera (32 oz.)
	1635	Seville and Cádiz	47.6 maravedís per libra carnicera (32 oz.)
Cheese	1562	North and south	377 maravedís per arroba
	1626	Seville	1,096.5 maravedís per arroba
Rice	1562	Seville	10.5 maravedís per lb.
	1626	Seville	25.5 maravedís per lb.
Chickpeas and broad beans	1554	Andalusia	272 maravedís per fanega (1.5 bushels each)
	1626	Andalusia	1,360 maravedís per fanega (1.5 bushels each)
Olive oil	1554	Seville	248.4 maravedís per arroba (25 lbs.)
	1626	Seville	587.1 maravedís per arroba (25 lbs.)
Vinegar	1554	Seville	98.5 maravedís per arroba (25 lbs.)
	1626	Seville	218.2 maravedís per arroba (25 lbs.)

Sources: 1540 AGS, Estado, leg. 497, fol. 221.
1554 AGI, Contaduría, leg. 279.
1562 AGI, Contaduría, leg. 548.
1567 AGS, Contaduría del Sueldo, leg. 197.
1626 AGI, Contaduría, leg. 555, ramos 1 and 2.
1628 AGS, Guerra Antigua, leg. 3149, no. 2.
1635 AGI, Consulados, legs. 1051, 1052.

Notes

Archival Sections and Abbreviations Cited in the Notes[a]
AGI   Archivo General de Indias, Seville
   Contaduría
   Contratación
   Consulados
   Escribanía de Cámara
   Indiferente General
   Mapas y Planos
   Patronato Real
   Santo Domingo

AGM   Archivo General de la Marina, Madrid (Museo Naval)
   Caja Fuerte: C.F.
   Colección Navarrete
   Colección Guillén
   Colección Vargas Ponce
   Colección Sanz—Simancas
   Colección Sanz—Barcelona

AGS   Archivo General de Simancas
   Consejo y Juntas de Hacienda: CJH
   Contaduría del Sueldo
   Contaduría Mayor de Cuentas, 1a Época: CMC 1a
   Contaduría Mayor de Cuentas, 2a Época: CMC 2a
   Contaduría Mayor de Cuentas, 3a Época: CMC 3a
   Contadurías Generales: CG
   Diversos de Castilla
   Patronato Real

Secretaría de Estado: Estado
Guerra Antigua
Mapas, Planos y Dibujos

AHN   Archivo Histórico Nacional
  Órdenes Militares
    Alcántara
    Santiago

ARCV   Archivo de la Real Chancillería de Valladolid

BN   Biblioteca Nacional, Madrid

RAH   Real Academia de la Historia, Madrid
  Colección Salazar

Additional Identifying Information
  expedientillo: exp.
  legajo: leg.
  libro: lib.
  ramo
  título: tit.
[a] See the Bibliography for a discussion of the archives and their holdings.

Chapter ONE. Challenge and Response

1. AGI, Escribanía de Cámara, legajo (hereafter leg.) 968, contains Benavides's official sentence, which prescribed his execution in great detail, from the route of the procession to the height of the scaffold. The event itself is described by an eyewitness in Cesáreo Fernández Duro, *Disquisiciones náuticas,* 6 vols. (Madrid: Sucesores de Rivadeneyra, 1876–81), 2:285–89. Unless otherwise noted, the description of Benavides's execution comes from this eyewitness account.

2. C. R. Boxer, *Salvador de Sá and the Struggle for Brazil and Angola, 1602–1686* (London: Athlone Press, 1952), pp. 56–67, has a good summary of Dutch actions before and after Matanzas, though he errs in writing (page 66) that Benavides was executed in Cádiz.

3. Fernández Duro, *Disquisiciones náuticas,* 2:279–83; Samuel Pierre L'Honoré Naber and Irene A. Wright, *Piet Heyn en de Zilvervloot, Bescheiden uit Nederlandsche en Spaansche archieven* (Utrecht: Kemink and Zoon, 1928), pp. 93–100, contains Heyn's report of the incident, which is consistent with this account. Various reports from Spaniards present at Matanzas, including Benavides and Leoz, appear on pages 19–34 of the Spanish appendixes in Naber and Wright.

4. Naber and Wright, *Piet Heyn,* pp. 157–58, list the booty sold at auction. The official Spanish manifests, dated July 19, 1628, appear on pages 9–14 of the Spanish appendixes.

5. The full case is contained in AGI, Escribanía de Cámara, leg. 968. See also the correspondence of the merchant consulado in AGI, Contratación, leg. 5118.

6. The site of the old fortress of Carmona now contains a luxurious government-owned hotel.

7. Fernández Duro, *Disquisiciones náuticas,* 2:285–86.

8. "Os aseguro, que siempre que hablo [del desastre] se me revuelve la sangre en las venas." Quoted in Antonio Domínguez Ortiz, "Los caudales de Indias y la política exterior de Felipe IV," *Anuario de Estudios Americanos* 13 (1956):341.

9. Abbott Payson Usher, "Spanish Ships and Shipping in the Sixteenth and Seventeenth Centuries," *Facts and Factors in Economic History: For Edwin Francis Gay*

(Cambridge, Mass.: Harvard University Press, 1932; reprint, New York: Russell and Russell, 1967), p. 212, citing Walther Vogel, "Zur Grösse der europäischen Handelsflotten im 15, 16, and 17 Jahrhundert," *Forschungen und Versuche zur Geschichte des Mittelalters und der Neuzeit: Festschrift Dietrich Schäfer* (Jena, 1915), p. 331.

10. Fernand Braudel, *The Structures of Everyday Life,* vol. 1 of *Civilization and Capitalism 15th–18th Century,* trans. Siân Reynolds (New York: Harper and Row, 1981), p. 363.

11. Tomé Cano, *Arte para fabricar y aparejar naos (1611),* ed. Enrique Marco Dorta (La Laguna, Canary Islands: Instituto de Estudios Canarios, 1964), p. 96.

12. Huguette and Pierre Chaunu, *Séville et l'Atlantique,* 8 vols. in 12 (Paris: A. Colin, 1955–59).

13. Ernst Schäfer, *El Consejo Real y Supremo de las Indias: Su historia, organización y labor administrativo hasta la terminación de la Casa de Austria,* 2 vols. (Seville: Publicaciones de la Escuela de Estudios Hispano-Americanos, 1935–47), p. 366, citing AGI, Contratación, leg. 5009.

14. See Guillermo Céspedes del Castillo, *La avería en el comercio de Indias* (Seville: Publicaciones de la Escuela de Estudios Hispano-Americanos, 1945), for the complex history of this tax.

15. Fernández Duro, *Disquisiciones náuticas,* 2:167–68.

16. AGS, Guerra Antigua, leg. 3154, letter of June 5, 1630.

17. Schäfer, *Consejo de las Indias,* pp. 371–73.

18. Pierre Chaunu with Huguette Chaunu, *Séville et l'Amérique aux XVIe et XVIIe siècles* (Paris: Flammarion, 1977), pp. 232–33.

19. Auguste Antoine Thomazi, *Les flottes de l'or: Histoire des galions d'Espagne,* rev. ed. (Paris: Payot, 1956), pp. 133–37; Chaunu, *Séville et l'Atlantique,* vols. 4 and 5.

20. Eufemio Lorenzo Sanz, *Comercio de España con América en la época de Felipe II,* 2 vols. (Valladolid: Servicio de Publicaciones de la Diputación Provincial de Valladolid, 1980), 2:275–82. See also Francisco-Felipe Olesa Muñido, "La marina oceánica de los Austrias," in *El buque en la armada española* (Madrid: Silex, 1981), p. 130.

21. Clarence Henry Haring, *Trade and Navigation between Spain and the Indies in the Time of the Hapsburgs* (Cambridge, Mass.: Harvard University Press, 1918), p. 208, blames deviations from the timetable on the "incurable dilatoriness of the Spaniard," a position that betrays a lack of comprehension of the complexity of the process, as well as an obvious prejudice.

22. Chaunu, *Séville et l'Amérique,* p. 229, estimates that 85 percent of the goods traveled in convoys.

23. Haring, *Trade and Navigation,* p. 210, and those who use his work as their principal source.

24. AGI, Patronato Real, leg. 260, no. 2, ramo 48; Fernández Duro, *Disquisiciones náuticas,* 2:327–30; Lorenzo Sanz, *Comercio,* p. 355.

25. Haring, *Trade and Navigation,* p. 210.

26. Thomazi, *Flottes de l'or,* p. 120. See also AGI, Patronato Real, leg. 260, no. 2, ramo 17.

27. Federico Castro y Bravo, *Las naos españolas en la carrera de las Indias: Armadas y flotas en la segunda mitad del siglo XVI* (Madrid: Editorial Voluntad, 1927), pp. 41–42; Francisco-Felipe Olesa Muñido, *La organización naval de los estados mediterráneos y en especial de España durante los siglos XVI y XVII,* 2 vols. (Madrid: Editorial Naval, 1968, p. 597.

28. I. A. A. Thompson, *War and Government in Habsburg Spain* (London: Athlone Press, 1976), tables A and B, pp. 288–89, has a good summary of income and expenditures from 1559 to 1623.

29. Ibid., p. 33, and tables, pp. 295–303. See the discussion of the tonelada in Chapters 2 and 3.

30. Olesa Muñido, "Marina oceánica," p. 134; Lorenzo Sanz, *Comercio,* p. 360.

31. Olesa Muñido, "Marina oceánica," pp. 134–40.

32. Cesáreo Fernández Duro, *Armada española desde la unión de los reinos de Castilla y de León*, 9 vols. (Madrid, 1895–1903), 4:8–9.

33. José Alcalá-Zamora y Queipo de Llano, *España, Flandes y el Mar del Norte (1618–1639): La última ofensiva europea de los Austrias madrileños* (Barcelona: Editorial Planeta, 1975, p. 313. See also Jonathan Israel, *The Dutch Republic and the Hispanic World, 1606–1661* (Oxford: Clarendon Press, 1982), pp. 192–96, 263–71.

34. Lorenzo Sanz, *Comercio*, pp. 357–60; Thompson, *War and Government*, p. 33; Schäfer, *Consejo de las Indias*, pp. 389–94.

35. *Colección de documentos inéditos relativos al descubrimiento, conquista y organización de las antiguas posesiones españolas de Ultramar*, 25 vols. (Madrid: Real Academia de la Historia, 1864–1932), 14:94, mentions a plan in 1630 that raised the avería 6 percent to increase the Armada de la Guardia to twenty ships.

36. Domínguez Ortiz, "Caudales de Indias," pp. 339–40.

37. Chaunu, *Séville et l'Atlantique*, 5:176. There is general agreement that contraband trade was an important part of the Indies market, though by nature it is difficult to study in detail. We know that Spanish colonists and foreign interlopers were involved at all levels in thwarting the monopoly of trade and colonization claimed by Castile. What we do not know is the extent of their activity and how it changed over time, although Chaunu frequently includes commentary about it in his text and in the extensive notes to the tables.

38. Bibiano Torres Ramírez, *La Armada de Barlovento* (Seville: Publicaciones de la Escuela de Estudios Hispano-Americanos, 1981), pp. 1–47; Chaunu, *Séville et l'Atlantique*, 5:270–71.

39. Gabriel Porras Troconis, "Cartagena de Indias, antemural de la hispanidad," *Revista de Indias* 28 (1968):337. Archival references to increased pirate activity are common in official dispatches of the period. See, for example, AGI, *Santo Domingo*, leg. 132 for 1620.

40. Kenneth Andrews, *The Spanish Caribbean: Trade and Plunder, 1530–1630* (New Haven: Yale University Press, 1978), pp. 198–208. See Israel, *Dutch Republic*, pp. 92–3, 123–4, 203–4, for Dutch attempts to secure salt in the New World.

41. Andrews, *Spanish Caribbean*, pp. 209–15.

42. Domínguez Ortiz, "Caudales de Indias," p. 377; see also Chaunu, *Séville et l'Atlantique*, 8:1573–75, 1689, 1713–14. John C. TePaske and Herbert Klein, "The Seventeenth-Century Crisis in New Spain: Myth or Reality?" *Past and Present* 90 (February 1981): 116–35, present new evidence and a good summary of the continuing debate on the New World economy.

43. Rafael Estrada y Arnáiz, "La influencia del mar en la historia de España," conference paper (Zaragoza: Consejo Superior de Investigaciones Científicas, 1950), p. 22; Ricardo Cappa, *Estudios críticos acerca de la dominación española en América*, 3rd ed., 26 vols. (Madrid: Librería Católica, 1889–   ), 12:302–4.

44. See Jonathan Brown and J. H. Elliott, *A Palace for a King. The Buen Retiro and the Court of Philip IV* (New Haven: Yale University Press, 1980), p. 164, for the military victories centered around the year 1625.

Chapter TWO. Spanish Shipbuilding and the Contract of Martín de Arana

1. The Junta de Armadas dated from about 1550, according to Francisco-Felipe Olesa Muñido, and was charged with regulating and overseeing the Atlantic fleets. *La organización naval de los estados mediterráneos y en especial de España durante los siglos XVI y XVII*, 2 vols. (Madrid: Editorial Naval, 1968), p. 401. I. A. A. Thompson, on the other hand, dated it from 1594. *War and Government in Habsburg Spain* (London: Athlone Press, 1976), p. 40. Whenever it was founded, the Junta was well established by 1625, and played a central role in negotiations with Martín de Arana and other shipbuilders.

2. AGS, Guerra Antigua, leg. 3149, no. 2. Unless otherwise mentioned, all documents dealing with Arana's contract come from this source. Most of the packet is composed of minutes of the Junta de Armadas and supplementary material for the items discussed. There is often a scribbled addendum in the king's hand indicating his decision on matters forwarded to him from the Junta. Private requests sent to the Junta are labeled "de parte" to distinguish them from the official business, labeled "de oficio."

3. See appendix B, for Spanish equivalents in the seventeenth century.

4. See also the 1616 contract with don Juan de Amassa to build four galleons in Pasajes (Guipúzcoa) on the north coast. Martín Fernández de Navarrete, *Colección de documentos y manuscriptos compilados,* 32 vols. (Nendeln, Lichtenstein: Kraus-Thompson Organization, 1971), 24(1), no. 18, pp. 159–74. Philip III's government also contracted in 1617 with Captain Alonso Herrera, a citizen of Havana, to build four galleons there at the expense of the avería. The cost was a very high 47.3 ducados per tonelada, as most of the materials had to be brought from Europe. AGI, Santo Domingo, leg. 132; Indiferente General, leg. 2525. See Lawrence A. Clayton, *Caulkers and Carpenters in a New World: The Shipyards of Colonial Guayaquil* (Athens: Ohio University Center for International Studies, 1980), pp. 22–23, 154–56, for shipbuilding contracts in Guayaquil in the same period. Contracts after 1625 often explicitly used Arana's contract as a model. Navarrete, *Colección de documentos,* 24(2), doc. 49.

5. Teófilo Guiard y Larrauri, *Historia del Consulado y Casa de Contratación de la villa de Bilbao,* 2 vols. (Bilbao: J. de Astuy, 1913–14; facsimile edition in 3 vols., Bilbao: Editorial La Gran Enciclopedia Vasca, 1972), 1:viii–ix, provides evidence for the Basques. Cantabrian contributions are discussed in Antonio Ballesteros y Beretta, *La marina cántabra y Juan de la Cosa* (Santander: Diputación de Santander, 1954), pp. 20–33, and Florentino Pérez Embid, "La marina real castellana en el siglo XIII," in *Estudios de historia marítima,* ed. Francisco Morales Padrón (Seville: Real Academia Sevillana de Buenas Letras, 1979), pp. 71–127.

6. Pierre Chaunu, "Les routes espagnoles de l'Atlantique," *Colloque international d'histoire maritime, 9th, Seville 1967* (Paris: S.E.V.P.E.N., 1969), pp. 99–108; J. A. García de Cortázar, *Vizcaya en el siglo XV: Aspectos económicos y sociales* (Bilbao: Ediciones de la Caja de Ahorros Vizcaína, 1966).

7. Cesáreo Fernández Duro, *La marina de Castilla, desde su orígen y pugna con Inglaterra hasta la refundición en la armada española* (Madrid, 1893), pp. 22–49, 226–27; María del Carmen Carlé, "Mercaderes en Castilla (1252–1512)," *Cuadernos de historia de España* 21–22 (1954):230–40.

8. Wendy R. Childs, *Anglo-Castilian Trade in the Later Middle Ages* (Manchester, Eng.: Manchester University Press, 1978), pp. 152–55; Jacques Heers, *L'Occident aux XIV et XVe siècles: Aspects économiques et sociaux,* 2d ed. (Paris: Presses Universitaires de France, 1966), pp. 172–73, and "Commerce des Basques en Méditerranée au XVe siècle (d'après les archives de Gênes)," *Bulletin hispanique* 57 (1955):292–324.

9. Heers, "Commerce des Basques," pp. 295–305.

10. Carlé, "Mercaderes en Castilla," pp. 261–317; Richard Konetzke, *El imperio español,* trans. from German (Madrid, 1946) pp. 21–68; Carla Rahn Phillips, "Spanish Merchants and the Wool Trade in the Sixteenth Century," *Sixteenth Century Journal* 14 (Fall 1983):259–82.

11. Ballesteros, *Marina cántabra,* p. 120, reports a shortage of shipping as early as 1436 on the north coast, clearly the result of increased demands for tonnage for the Flanders trade. Royal support for shipbuilding is exemplified by a 1458 law granting an annual subsidy to those who built and maintained ships of 1,000 toneles, enormous compared to many later ships. Josephe de Veitia Linaje, *Norte de la contratación de las Indias occidentales* (Seville, 1672), translated in abridged form as *The Spanish*

Rule of Trade to the West-Indies (London, 1702; reprint, New York: AMS Press, 1977), book 2, chap. 14.

12. Ramón Carande Thobar, *Carlos V y sus banqueros, 1516–1556*, 3 vols. (Madrid: Sociedad de Estudios y Publicaciones, 1943–67), 1:278–79.

13. The commercial privileges of Bilbao are listed in AGS, CJH, leg. 76, fols. 202–3.

14. AGS, Diversos de Castilla, leg. 9, fol. 4.

15. Fernández Duro, *Marina de Castilla,* p. 293.

16. See AGS, Diversos de Castilla, leg. 42, fol. 26; *Colección de documentos inéditos para la historia de España,* 112 vols. (Madrid, 1842–1895), 1:337.

17. Gervasio de Artiñano y de Galdácano, *La arquitectura naval española (en madera)* (Madrid, 1920), pp. 67–68; Emiliano Fernández de Pinedo, *Crecimiento económico y transformaciones sociales del País Vasco, 1100–1850* (Madrid, 1974), pp. 30–33.

18. Pedro de Medina, *Libro de las grandezas y cosas memorables de España* (Alcalá de Henares, 1566; first published 1543), fols. 128v–129.

19. AGS, Guerra Antigua, leg. 13, fol. 128; and Estado, leg. 65, fol. 152.

20. Artiñano, *Arquitectura naval,* p. 67.

21. Estánislao Jaime de Labayru y Goicoechea, *Historia general del Señorío de Vizcaya* (Bilbao: La Gran Enciclopedia Vasca, 1968–72), 4:349.

22. Navarrete, *Colección de documentos,* vol. 22(1), doc. 26, fols. 78–79v; doc. 31, fols. 112–113v.

23. See, for example, Auguste Antoine Thomazi, *Les flottes de l'or: Histoire des galions d'Espagne,* rev. ed. (Paris: Payot, 1956), pp. 118–19.

24. AGS, Guerra Antigua, leg. 71, fols. 115, 227; CJH, leg. 49, fol. 211, dated May 6, 1563. Labayru, *Historia general,* 4:368. William D. Phillips, Jr., "Spain's Northern Shipping Industry in the Sixteenth Century," *Journal of European Economic History* (forthcoming).

25. See construction accounts in AGI, Contaduría, leg. 462, no. 8 for 1577–78 in Bilbao; and leg. 561, no. 4 for 1578 in Guipúzcoa, the Basque province whose capital was San Sebastián. Navarrete, *Colección de documentos,* 22(1), no. 10. Barros himself built ships for the crown. AGS, CMC 3a, leg. 3532, no. 3.

26. Juan Escalante de Mendoza, *Itinerario de navegación de los mares y tierras occidentales* (Madrid, 1575; reprinted in Cesáreo Fernández Duro, *Disquisiciones náuticas,* 6 vols. [Madrid: Sucesores de Rivadeneyra, 1876–81], 5:413–515). A government memorandum on the causes of the decline appears in AGI, *Patronato Real,* leg. 260, no. 2, ramo 29.

27. AGM, Colección Vargas Ponce, vol. II, doc. 11, fols. 13–14v.

28. Modesto Ulloa, "Unas notas sobre el comercio y la navegación españoles en el siglo XVI," *Anuario de historia económica y social de España* (1969): 203.

29. Richard W. Unger, *Dutch Shipbuilding before 1800: Ships and Guilds* (Atlantic Highlands, N.J.: Humanities Press, 1978), p. 44, sets the inventive phase of Dutch shipbuilding at 1570–1630.

30. Tomé Cano, *Arte para fabricar y aparejar naos (1611),* ed. Enrique Marco Dorta (La Laguna, Canary Islands: Instituto de Estudios Canarios, 1964), pp. 96–97.

31. AGM, Colección Vargas Ponce, vol. II, docs. 11, 15, 16 on fols. 13–14v, 20–26, for the 1580s. See also a memorandum of Cristóbal de Barros in 1583. AGS, CJH, leg. 210, no. 22.

32. Cano, *Arte para fabricar naos,* p. 96.

33. Wilfred Brulez, "Shipping Profits in the Early Modern Period," *Acta Historiae Neerlandicae* 14 (1981):67–68. See also Frederic Chapin Lane, *Venetian Ships and Shipbuilders of the Renaissance* (Baltimore: Johns Hopkins University Press, 1934), p. 263.

34. See accounts for ship construction in 1568 in AGI, Contaduría, leg. 459, ramo 1.

35. Huguette and Pierre Chaunu, *Séville et l'Atlantique*, 8 vols. in 12 (Paris: A. Colin, 1955–59), 5:32, 8(2)(2):1597, 1682.

36. Earl J. Hamilton, *American Treasure and the Price Revolution in Spain, 1501–1650* (Cambridge, Mass.: Harvard University Press, 1934; reprint, New York: Octagon Books, 1965). Harry A. Miskimin, "Agenda for Early Modern Economic History," *The Journal of Economic History* 31 (March 1971):172–83, gives an introduction to the vast literature on this topic.

37. Cano, *Arte para fabricar naos*, pp. 94–95.

38. E. W. Petrejus, "The Dutch Flute," in Joseph Jobé, ed. *The Great Age of Sail*, trans. Michael Kelly (Lausanne: Edita, 1967), p. 81.

39. Fernández Duro, *Disquisiciones náuticas*, 2:474–77.

40. Richard Unger, *The Ship in the Medieval Economy, 600–1600* (Montreal: McGill-Queen's University Press, 1980), pp. 267–71.

41. Cano, *Arte para fabricar naos*, p. 95.

42. Brulez, "Shipping Profits," p. 78–80.

43. AGM, ms. 2106.

44. See documents in AGS, Estado, leg. 97, fol. 51; leg. 97, fol. 53; leg. 95, fol. 258, all from 1552, and numerous other documents from the 1550s in the sections CJH, CMC, Estado and Guerra Antigua.

45. Clarence Henry Haring, *Trade and Navigation between Spain and the Indies in the Time of the Hapsburgs* (Cambridge, Mass.: Harvard University Press, 1918), p. 283, for figures in the early sixteenth century; AGM, Colección Vargas Ponce, vol. I, doc. 21, fols. 23–26 for later figures.

46. AGM, ms. 580, doc. 13, fols. 40–48v.

47. AGM, Colección Vargas Ponce, vol. II, doc. 66, fols. 100–104; AGI, Patronato Real, leg. 259, ramo 19; AGS, CJH, leg. 210, no. 12, contains various arguments against large ships, including a memorial of Andrés Poza to the king in 1596, also printed in Cesáreo Fernández Duro, *Armada española desde la unión de los reinos de Castilla y de León*, 9 vols. (Madrid, 1895–1903), 2:443–48. AGS, Patronato Real, leg. 85, nos. 501–2, provides arguments against small ships by the merchants in Seville.

48. Labayru, *Historia general*, 5:51–52.

49. AGS, Diversos de Castilla, leg. 40, no. 36; CJH, leg. 210, no. 22, and leg. 82, no. 122.

50. Eufemio Lorenzo Sanz, *Comercio de España con América en la época de Felipe II*, 2 vols. (Valladolid: Servicio de Publicaciones de la Diputación Provincial de Valladolid, 1980), 2:293–95.

51. Cano, *Arte para fabricar naos*, pp. 93–94.

52. Lane, *Venetian Ships and Shipbuilders*, pp. 124–28; Ruggiero Romano, "Economic Aspects of the Construction of Warships in Venice in the Sixteenth Century," in *Crisis and Change in the Venetian Economy in the Sixteenth and Seventeenth Centuries*, ed. Brian Pullan (London: Methuen, 1968), pp. 61–80.

53. Valentín Vázquez de Prada, *Historia económica y social de España*, vol. 3, *Los siglos XVI y XVII* (Madrid, 1978), p. 628.

54. Thompson, *War and Government*, pp. 256–73; table K, pp. 304–6, is a useful list of shipping built between 1588 and 1623, unfortunately designated only as built by *administración* or by *asiento*. More complete information on the construction contracts appears in Fernández Duro, *Armada española*, especially 4:10–11 and 432–41 for the period 1622–36.

55. Thompson, *War and Government*, pp. 195–97.

56. Lawrence A. Clayton, "Ships and Empire: The Case of Spain," *Mariner's Mirror* 62 (August 1976):235–48, subscribes to a negative judgment of its effects.

57. See one contract for 1582 in AGI, Patronato Real, leg. 260, no. 1, ramo 8.

58. AGM, Colección Sanz—Simancas, ms. 388, doc. 670, fol. 399; Pierre

Chaunu, with Huguette Chaunu, *Séville et l'Amérique aux XVIe et XVIIe siècles* (Paris: Flammarion, 1977), pp. 244–45.

59. Escalante de Mendoza, *Itinerario*. Escalante favored a beam-keel-length ratio of 2.2–5–7, roughly equivalent to the 1–2–3 ratio favored for Mediterranean sailing ships. See below for a discussion of the changing ideal proportions for the hull.

60. Diego García de Palacio, *Instrucción náutica para navegar (1587)* (Madrid: Cultura hispánica, 1944). Fernández Duro, *Disquisiciones náuticas*, 1:133, identifies García as a member of the king's Council of War. The Portuguese Fernando de Oliveira's detailed nautical treatise *Livro da fabrica das naus* was evidently written in about 1565, but the manuscript languished in the Biblioteca Nacional in Lisbon until the late nineteenth century. Henrique Lopes de Mendonça published it as part of his *O padre Fernando Oliveira e a sua obra nautica* (Lisbon, 1898).

61. Haring, *Trade and Navigation,* p. 270. Francisco-Felipe Olesa Muñido, *Organización naval,* pp. 376–78, has a slightly more positive view. An excellent summary of the naval reform movement under Philip III appears in Jesús Varela Marcos, "El Seminario de Marinos: Un intento de formación de los marineros para las Armadas y Flotas de Indias," *Revista de Historia de América 87* (January–June 1979): 9–36.

62. AGS, CMC 3a, leg. 2214–17. Unless otherwise noted, all references to Bertendona's ships are from this source.

63. For example, AGS, Estado, leg. 2025, a memorandum from Padre Joseph Cresuelo of October 2, 1608, recommended the "gallones de Stado" built in Florence.

64. Navarrete, *Colección de documentos,* 23(1), doc. 47, pp. 575–93. AGM, Marqués de la Victoria, *Diccionario,* plate 5. The proportional rule was called "as, dos, tres" in Spanish, in which "as" (one) was the beam, "dos" (two) the keel, and "tres" (three) the length.

65. Lane, *Venetian Ships and Shipbuilders*, pp. 235–37, has a table comparing the measures of various ships in the sixteenth century.

66. Haring, *Trade and Navigation,* pp. 264–65. A memorandum giving the measurements of the ships, dated December 17, 1575, appears in AGI, Patronato Real, leg. 260, no. 2, ramo 34.

67. Artiñano, *Arquitectura naval,* pp. 91–98. Escalante mentioned that Bazán's experiments with very large merchant ships in the Indies trade had not been successful. Escalante de Mendoza, *Itinerario,* in Fernández Duro, *Disquisiciones náuticas,* 5:446.

68. Fernández Duro, *Disquisiciones náuticas*, 5:50–52.

69. Ibid., 5:376.

70. Ibid., 5:50–55.

71. Ibid., 5:378, citing AGM, Colección Vargas Ponce.

72. Veas offered to build several of the ships in Havana, presumably as part of the Armada de Barlovento planned to guard the Caribbean. Even though that plan was abandoned, the seventeenth century saw increasing use of shipyards in the Indies. Navarrete, *Colección de documentos,* 23(1), doc. 45, pp. 559–63; 24(2), doc. 49. The beam-keel-length ratio Veas proposed was 1–2.9–3.7. See AGI, Contratación, leg. 554, for estimated costs and sources of supply for the ships.

73. Cano, *Arte para fabricar naos.* Cano published in 1611, but the book was finished and approved in 1608.

74. Royal cédula of May 19, 1609, giving privileges to those who built ships larger than 200 toneladas.

75. Artiñano, *Arquitectura naval,* pp. 128–29; Navarrete, *Colección de documentos,* 24(1), doc. 15, pp. 133–42.

76. Francisco-Felipe Olesa Muñido, "La marina oceánica de los Austrias," in *El buque en la armada española* (Madrid: Silex, 1981), p. 140.

77. Olesa Muñido, *Organización naval,* pp. 853–58. AGI, Consulados, leg. 1052, has a list of payments for the crown's use of private ships in 1635.

78. Fernández Duro, *Disquisiciones náuticas,* 5:65–69; AGM, Colección Vargas Ponce, vol. II, docs. 69–71.

79. Navarrete, *Colección de documentos,* 24(1), docs. 11–14, pp. 93–131. The inspection took place February 4, 1614.

80. AGM, C.F. 134.

81. Escalante de Mendoza, *Itinerario,* in Fernández Duro, *Disquisiciones náuticas,* 5:438–46. Unger, *The Ship in the Medieval Economy,* p. 265.

82. Fernández Duro, *Disquisiciones náuticas,* 5:378, citing a document dated December 19, 1610, at Sanlúcar de Barrameda.

83. AGS, Guerra Antigua, leg. 3152; Fernández Duro, *Disquisiciones náuticas,* 5:378–85. Chaunu, *Séville et l'Atlantique,* 6(1):168, has a table showing the slowly rising average ship size in the Indies trade from 1504 to 1650.

84. The figures are derived from the table in Abbott Payson Usher, "Spanish Ships and Shipping in the Sixteenth and Seventeenth Centuries," *Facts and Factors in Economic History: For Edwin Francis Gay* (Cambridge, Mass.: Harvard University Press, 1932; reprint, New York: Russell and Russell, 1967), p. 201, citing AGI, Contratación, 41-1-2/13.

85. Quoted from Rafael Estrada y Arnáiz, *El Almirante don Antonio de Oquendo* (Madrid: Espasa Calpe, 1943), pp. 128–30.

86. Jorge Juan y Santacilia, *Examen marítimo theórico práctico, o tratado de mechánica aplicado a la construcción, conocimiento y manejo de los navíos y demás embarcaciones,* 2 vols. (Madrid, 1771; facsimile edition, Madrid: Instituto de España, 1968).

87. Juan Sorapán de Rieros, *Medicina española contenida en proverbios vulgares de nuestra lengua,* ed. Antonio Castillo de Lucas (Madrid: Cosano, 1949), p. 123.

88. John F. Guilmartin, *Gunpowder and Galleys: Changing Technology and Mediterranean Warfare at Sea in the Sixteenth Century* (Cambridge: Cambridge University Press, 1974), is the best work on the characteristics and uses of the galley in the early modern period.

89. See the excellent series of etchings, woodcuts, and plates in Artiñano, *Arquitectura naval,* and in *El buque en la armada española* (Madrid: Silex, 1981).

90. Lane, *Venetian Ships and Shipbuilders,* p. 37, citing Giovanni Villani, *Cronica* (ed. Francesco Gherardi Dragomanni, Florence, 1845), 2:101.

91. *The Lore of Ships,* rev. ed. (New York: Crescent, 1975), p. 18.

92. Unger, *The Ship in the Medieval Economy,* pp. 216–19; José María Martínez-Hidalgo y Terán, *Columbus's Ships,* trans. and ed. Howard I. Chapelle (Barre, Mass.: Barre Publishing Co., 1966), pp. 28–34; Pedro Castiñeiras Múñoz, "La época de los descubrimientos geográficos," in *El buque en la armada española,* pp. 74–75.

93. Martínez-Hidalgo, *Columbus's Ships,* p. 30; Lane, *Venetian Ships and Shipbuilders,* pp. 39–41; G. B. Rubin de Cervin, *Bateaux et batellerie de Venise* (Lausanne: Edita, 1978), p. 24.

94. Enrique Manera Regueyra, "La marina de Castilla," in *El buque en la armada española,* p. 25. There is a particularly fine illustration of one in an early thirteenth-century Spanish vulgate bible in the library of the Biblioteca del Monasterio del Escorial. The bible originally belonged to the Duke of Escalona.

95. Lionel Casson, *Ships and Seamanship in the Ancient World* (Princeton, N.J.: Princeton University Press, 1971), pp. 208–10; J. H. Parry, *The Age of Reconnaissance. Discovery, Exploration and Settlement 1450 to 1650* (New York: Praeger Publishers, 1969), pp. 56–64.

96. Lane, *Venetian Ships and Shipbuilders,* pp. 39–41.

97. Manera Regueyra, "Marina de Castilla," pp. 32–33.

98. Unger, *The Ship in the Medieval Economy,* pp. 222–23.

99. José María Martínez-Hidalgo, "La marina catalanoaragonesa," in *El buque en*

la armada española, p. 42; G. B. Rubin de Cervin, "The Catalan Ship," in Jobé, *Great Age of Sail*, pp. 16–19.

100. Rubin de Cervin, *Bateaux*, pp. 20–28, suggests that it would have been either a cog or a galleon, but it seems to me that the ship has more in common with a carrack or what the Spanish would call a nao.

101. Rubin de Cervin in Jobé, *Great Age of Sail*, p. 16; Lane, *Venetian Ships and Shipbuilders*, pp. 40–41.

102. Unger, *Dutch Shipbuilding*, pp. 32–33.

103. Unger, *The Ship in the Medieval Economy*, p. 229.

104. Unger, *Dutch Shipbuilding*, pp. 36–50; E. W. Petrejus in Jobé, *Great Age of Sail*, p. 81; R. Morton Nance, "A Sixteenth-Century Sea-Monster," *Mariner's Mirror* 2 (1912):97–104; Parry, *Age of Reconnaissance*, p. 67.

105. Castiñeiras, "Época de los descubrimientos," in pp. 76–77. Louis-André Vigneras, *The Discovery of South America and the Andalusian Voyages* (Chicago: University of Chicago Press, 1976), p. 38, credits the lateen-rigged caravels to the Spanish and the full-rigged version to the Portuguese, but this is surely mistaken. Various authors trace the origins of the lateen caravel back as far as the thirteenth century, though little firm evidence has emerged yet on this fascinating topic. See, for example, Fernández Duro, *Disquisiciones náuticas*, 1:99–130, and Carlos Etayo Elizondo, *Naos y carabelas de los descubrimientos y las naves de Colón* (Pamplona, 1971), pp. 93–98.

106. See Martínez-Hidalgo, *Columbus's Ships*, pp. 87–88.

107. See Ibid., pp. 96–100, for estimated configurations of the two caravels. Etayo, *Naos*, pp. 121–23, 155–66, 217–41 and *La expedición de la "Niña II"* (Barcelona: Plaza y Janes, 1963), pp. 129–30, present a different set of configurations and argues that the *Niña* on Columbus's second voyage was a different ship from the *Niña* on the first voyage in 1492. Most other scholars disagree. Eugene Lyon has found documentary evidence that the *Niña* that sailed with Columbus on his third voyage in 1498 had been fitted with a fourth mast (bonaventure), but that still leaves open the question of whether this was the same *Niña* as on the first voyage. Paper presented to the American Historical Association Annual Meeting, December 28–30, 1985, New York City.

108. Castiñeiras, "Época de los descubrimientos," pp. 76–84; Parry, *Age of Reconnaissance*, pp. 65–66.

109. BN, ms. 2811, fols. 164–170.

110. Olesa Muñido, "Marina oceánica," p. 111; Harry Albert Morton, *The Wind Commands: Sailors and Sailing Ships in the Pacific* (Middletown, Conn.: Wesleyan University Press, 1975, pp. 98–101. See Carlo Cipolla, *Guns, Sails, and Empires: Technological Innovation and the Early Phases of European Expansion, 1400–1700* (New York: Pantheon, 1965), pp. 88–89, for the unwieldy nature of the large carracks.

111. Oliveira, *Livro da fabrica das naus* in Mendonça, *O padre Fernando Oliveira*, p. 168. Much of the confusion among modern writers can be traced to John Charnock, *A History of Marine Architecture*, 3 vols. (London, 1801), whose dating and identification of illustrations often obscure more than they clarify. For example, in vol. 2 he identifies as a Genoese carrack of 1542 a ship that appears much more likely to have been a war vessel from the late seventeenth century. Those who follow his interpretations repeat the confusion. See Alfred Sternbeck, *Filibusters and Buccaneers*, trans. Doris Mudie (New York: Robert M. McBride and Company, 1930), p. 112, for a reproduction of Charnock's supposed carrack. Sternbeck uses as his frontispiece a ship he calls a sixteenth-century "man-of-war," which has the characteristic high castles and cut waist of the carrack. Mendel Peterson, *The Funnel of Gold: The Trials of the Spanish Treasure Fleets . . .* (Boston: Little, Brown, 1975), identifies a similar illustration as a carrack, which would seem to be accurate. Then he, too, adds to the confusion on page 109, by including the illustration Sternbeck had as a frontispiece

and calling it a "galleon and galley" (there is also a smaller oared ship in the picture). The illustration in question is almost certainly an etching by Pieter Brueghel from the mid-sixteenth century of a carrack and a small oared barge. In addition, Peterson, pp. 58–59, describes the illustration of a two-masted cog with a lateen mizzen as a late fifteenth-century carrack, "the prototype of the carracks that sailed in the early treasure fleets to and from America." In contrast, Chaunu, *Séville et l'Amérique,* pp. 240–43, does not even mention the carrack among the ship types sailing to the Indies from 1504 to 1650.

112. Martínez-Hidalgo, *Columbus's Ships,* pp. 28–34. The nao followed the traditional ship proportions of "as, dos, tres," described above (n. 64). Castiñeiras, "Época de los descubrimientos," pp. 65–70. By the time Veitia Linaje wrote in 1672, nao was clearly a generic term. Veitia Linaje, *Norte de la contratación,* book 2, chap. 14.

113. Escalante de Mendoza, *Itinerario* in Fernández Duro, *Disquisiciones náuticas,* 5:449.

114. Discussion following Gille, "Navires lourds," pp. 180–182.

115. Lane, *Venetian Ships and Shipbuilders,* pp. 50–51, 63, 133; Frederic Chapin Lane, "Venetian Naval Architecture about 1550," *Mariner's Mirror* 20 (1934):39–42; Cipolla, *Guns, Sails, and Empires,* p. 79.

116. AGS, CMC 1a, leg. 436.

117. Diego Ribero, "Carta Universal en que se contiene todo lo que del mundo se ha descubierto fasta agora," Seville, 1529.

118. Jacques Bernard, "Les types de navires ibériques et leur influence sur la construction navale, dans les ports du Sud-Ouest de la France (XVe–XVIe siècles)," *Colloque international d'histoire maritime, 5th, Lisbon, 1960* (Paris: S.E.V.P.E.N., 1966), p. 205.

119. I am indebted to Professor García for several stimulating conversations and correspondence on this subject. See Thomazi, *Flottes de l'or,* p. 13, for a similar point of view.

120. See, for example, Thomazi, *Flottes de l'or,* pp. 13–14.

121. Martínez-Hidalgo, *Columbus's Ships,* pp. 96–100.

122. Castiñeiras, "Época de los descubrimientos," pp. 66–69. Olesa Muñido, "Marina oceánica," pp. 111–12.

123. Illustrations from 1520 show these altered naos, in the prayerbook of Charles I, Monasterio del Escorial, Spain.

124. Olesa Muñido, "Marina oceánica," pp. 117–18.

125. For example Haring, *Trade and Navigation,* p. 263, writes of the galleon: "Constructed with keel and beam in the proportion of three to one or less, and with towering 'castles' at either extremity, its sailing qualities were of the very worst." Clearly, he is describing a carrack and not a galleon here, so one must discard his statement entirely. Similarly, Robert Marx, *The Treasure Fleets of the Spanish Main* (Cleveland: World Publishing Co., 1968), p. 30, identifies an enormous carrack as a Spanish galleon, repeating an error from Paul Farnham, a twentieth-century artist of maritime scenes. According to Farnham, it was built by the Portuguese Pero Menéndez Marquez and first sailed in 1578. Nicknamed the *Cacafuego,* it was captured by Francis Drake in the South Seas. The Portuguese origin of the ship also suggests that it was a carrack, rather than the "Spanish Galleon" designation painted on the frame of Farnham's portrait. The error is hardly surprising, however. Farnham noted that Charles V, whose portrait also appears on the frame, ordered the ship built and had it commissioned in 1578—quite a feat, considering that Charles died twenty years earlier. Library of Congress, Prints and Drawings, Farnham's copyright file from 1923.

126. Unger, *The Ship in the Medieval Economy,* p. 276; Rubin de Cervin, in Jobé, *Great Age of Sail,* p. 46; Moya Blanco, "Arquitectura naval," p. 149.

127. Unger, *The Ship in the Medieval Economy,* p. 253.

128. João da Gama Pimentel Barata, *O traçado das naus e galeões portugueses de 1550–80 a 1640* (Lisbon: Junta de Investigaçao do Ultramar, 1970), pp. 5–20. The distinction may have become less clear in the seventeenth century, as the Portuguese gradually abandoned the large carrack. C. R. Boxer, "Admiral João Pereira Corte-Real and the Construction of Portuguese East-Indiamen in the Early Seventeenth Century," *The Mariner's Mirror* 26 (1940):400–404. Joaquim Serrão, *História de Portugal*, 6 vols. (Lisbon: Editorial Verbo, 1978), 4:160, contains a color illustration of a seventeenth-century Portuguese galleon, taken from the contemporary *Livro de traça de carpinteria* of Manuel Fernandes. My colleague Stuart Schwartz kindly provided this reference.

129. Fernández Duro, *Disquisiciones náuticas,* 2:362. Outside Spain, this interchangeability was recognized as well. For example, a Spanish galleon turned up in Bordeaux in southern France in 1548, bought by a local merchant for his business. Bernard, "Constructions navales," p. 42.

130. Pierre and Huguette Chaunu, *Séville et l'Atlantique,* 6(1):159–68; and Pierre Chaunu, "La *tonelada* espagnole au XVI et XVII siècles," *Colloque international d'histoire maritime, 1st and 2nd, 1956, 1957* (Paris: S.E.V.P.E.N., 1957), p. 84.

131. AGS, CMC 1a, leg. 1875.

132. Olesa Muñido, "Marina oceánica," pp. 111–12. Manning ratios on merchant ships in the sixteenth-century Mediterranean fell from 20.8 to 13.3 men per 100 toneladas. Lane, *Venetian Ships and Shipbuilders,* p. 39.

133. AGS, Estado, leg. 441.

134. AGS, Guerra Antigua, leg. 11, fol. 178.

135. Olesa Muñido, "Marina oceánica," pp. 118–20.

136. AGS, Guerra Antigua, leg. 53, no. 206.

137. AGS, CMC 1a, leg. 780.

138. AGS, CG, leg. 3019; AGM, Sanz-Simancas, ms. 1949, doc. 4, fols. 15–17.

139. AGS, Estado, leg. 496, fols. 61–62.

140. Olesa Muñido, "Marina oceánica," pp. 120–22. See Artiñano, *Arquitectura naval,* pp. 91–94, for other experimental ships he built after 1550, which were evidently failures.

141. AGS, *Contaduría del Sueldo,* leg. 197, no. 1.

142. AGS, *Estado,* leg. 559, no. 67.

143. Unger, *Dutch Shipbuilding,* p. 44.

144. AGM, ms. 471, fols. 157–74.

145. Cipolla, *Guns, Sails, and Empires,* pp. 83–84.

146. *Oxford Companion to Ships and the Sea,* ed. Peter Kemp (London: Oxford University Press, 1976), p. 334.

147. *Letters and Papers, Foreign and Domestic, of the Reign of Henry VIII, Preserved in the Public Records Office, the British Museum, and Elsewhere in England,* 21 vols. (Great Britain, Public Records Office), vol. 20(1), no. 543. My thanks to Stephen R. Alvin for this reference.

148. AGS, Guerra Antigua, leg. 75, no. 95.

149. Ibid., leg. 76, no. 1.

150. AGM, Colección Vargas Ponce, II, doc. 66, fols. 100–104, from 1614.

151. Navarrete, *Colección de documentos,* vol. 22(1), no. 31.

152. AGS, Contaduría del Sueldo, leg. 280, fols. 2106–7.

153. See the illustrations in Theodore de Bry, *Grand voyages* (Frankfort, 1606); Gerard Mercator, *Atlas sive cosmographicae* (Amsterdam, 1628), 1:210–35; and the paintings and etchings of Pieter Brueghel the Elder.

154. Unger, *The Ship in the Medieval Economy,* pp. 258–59.

155. Federico Castro y Bravo, *Las naos españolas en la carrera de las Indias: Armadas y flotas en la segunda mitad del siglo XVI* (Madrid: Editorial Voluntad, 1927), pp. 43–45.

156. Chaunu, *Séville et l'Atlantique,* 1:276–79.

157. Artiñano, *Arquitectura naval,* p. 98.

158. Clayton, *Caulkers and Carpenters,* pp. 45–52, 108.

159. Olesa Muñido, *Organización naval,* p. 846.

160. AGS, Guerra Antigua, leg. 3152, memoranda of July 6 and 12, 1628. The changing terminology as well as the multiple uses of ships can easily mislead. In an otherwise very informative article commenting on Spanish shipping, John D. Harbron mistakenly writes that galleons in the Habsburg period were "commercial vessels" whereas navíos were "warships." "The Spanish Ship of the Line," *Scientific American* 251 (December 1984):116. A similar misapprehension appears in Clayton, *Caulkers and Carpenters,* pp. 70–71, which uses lists of ships from 1615, 1695, and 1736 as if the names and characteristics of ship types had not changed in 120 years.

161. AGM, ms. 471, fols. 157–74.

Chapter THREE. The Construction of Arana's Six Galleons

1. Carlos Clavería Arza, *Los vascos en el mar* (Pamplona, 1967), p. 58. Surnames are a fairly good—but not always certain—indication of lineage from the fifteenth century on. Julio Caro Baroja, *Vasconiana* 2d. ed. (San Sebastian: Editorial Txertoa, 1974), pp. 27–28.

2. María del Carmen Carlé, "Mercaderes en Castilla (1252–1512)," *Cuadernos de historia de España* 21–22 (1954):253.

3. Jacques Heers, "Commerce des Basques en Méditerranée au XVe siècle (d'après les archives de Gênes)," *Bulletin hispanique* 57 (1955):321. There was a Diego de Arana on Columbus's first voyage, whose crew was gathered entirely in southern Spain, but there is no proof that he had relatives in the Basque country. José María Martínez-Hidalgo y Terán, *Columbus's Ships,* trans. and ed. Howard I. Chapelle (Barre, Mass.: Barre Publishing Co., 1966), p. 72.

4. AGS, CMC la, leg. 780.

5. Estánislao Jaime de Labayru y Goicoechea, *Historia general del Señorío de Vizcaya* (Bilbao: La Gran Enciclopedia Vasca, 1968–72), 4:349.

6. AHN, Órdenes Militares, Alcántara, expedientillo 13.346.

7. Francisco-Felipe Olesa Muñido, *La organización naval de los estados mediterráneos y en especial de España durante los siglos XVI y XVII,* 2 vols. (Madrid: Editorial Naval, 1968), pp. 378–80; Clarence Henry Haring, *Trade and Navigation between Spain and the Indies in the Time of the Hapsburgs* (Cambridge, Mass.: Harvard University Press, 1918), p. 270; José Cervera Pery, "Dos facetas navales del reinado de Felipe IV," *Revista de Historia Naval* 1(1982): 150–52.

8. Jacques Bernard, *Navires et gens de mer à Bordeaux (vers 1400–vers 1500),* 3 vols. (Paris: S.E.V.P.E.N., 1968), 1:317–47.

9. Frederic Mauro, "Navires et constructions navales en Europe occidentale aux XVIe et XVIIe siècles: Points de départ pour une étude comparée," *Études economique sur l'expansion portugaise (1500–1900)* (Paris, 1970). For Spanish shipyards, see also Florentino Pérez Embid, "La marina real castellana en el siglo XIII," *Estudios de historia marítima,* ed. Francisco Morales Padrón (Seville: Real Academia Sevillana de Buenas Letras, 1979), pp. 94–97; Lawrence A. Clayton, "Ships and Empire: The Case of Spain," *Mariner's Mirror* 62 (August 1976):238; and José Alcalá-Zamora y Queipo de Llano, *España, Flandes y el Mar del Norte (1618–1639): La última ofensiva europea de los Austrias madrileños* (Barcelona: Editorial Planeta, 1975), pp. 91–93.

10. Nicolaes Witsen, *Architectura navalis et Regimen Nauticum,* 2 ed. (Amsterdam, 1690), p. 179.

11. Pedro Texeira, "Descripción de las costas y puertos de España (1630)," ed. A. Blázquez, *Boletín de la Real Sociedad Georgráfica* (1910):36–138, 180–233.

12. Pedro de Medina, *Libro de las grandezas y cosas memorables de España (Alcalá de Henares,* 1566; first published Seville, 1548), pp. 128v–129.

13. Document in the Archive of the Spanish Embassy in Rome, dated San Lorenzo del Escorial, September 23, 1617, and printed in the *Boletín de la Real Sociedad Vascongada de Amigos del País* (1950):359–61.

14. Martín Fernández de Navarrete, *Colección de documentos y manuscriptos compilados,* 32 vols. (Nendeln, Lichtenstein: Kraus-Thompson Organization, 1971), 23(1), doc. 47.

15. AGI, Patronato Real, leg. 260, no. 2, ramo 41, describes the wood requirements for each part of a ship in some detail. See also Juan Escalante de Mendoza, *Itinerario de navegación de los mares y tierras occidentales* (Madrid, 1575), in Fernández Duro, *Disquisiciones náuticas,* 5:413–515, 5:451–53; Navarrete, *Colección de documentos* 23(1), doc. 47, pp. 575–93; AGM, Marqués de la Victoria, *Diccionario,* plates 21–26.

16. Jorge Juan y Santacilia, *Examen marítimo theórico práctico, o tratado de mechánica aplicado a la construcción, conocimiento y manejo de los navíos y demás embarcaciones,* 2 vols. (Madrid, 1771; facsimile reprint, Madrid: Instituto de España, 1968, plate 2, fig. 7. Lionel Casson, *Ships and Seamanship in the Ancient World* (Princeton, N.J.: Princeton University Press, 1971), pp. 208–13, describes shipbuilding techniques in the ancient Mediterranean that would still have been familiar to seventeenth-century shipwrights.

17. AGM, Marqués de la Victoria, *Diccionario,* plate 8.

18. Escalante de Mendoza, *Itinerario,* in Fernández Duro, *Disquisiciones náuticas,* 5:454–55.

19. AGM, C.F. 134, paragraph 23, and Marqués de la Victoria, *Diccionario,* plates 35–37.

20. AGM, C.F. 134.

21. Juan y Santacilia, *Examen marítimo,* 2:12–23.

22. AGM, C.F. 134.

23. Navarrete, *Colección de documentos,* 23(1), doc. 45, pp. 559–63. This lends some credence to the widely held idea that Spanish ships at the time of the Great Armada in 1588 were not as heavily braced as they should have been for their size. On the other hand, the maritime archeology that has been done to date on Great Armada wrecks is not conclusive, and there has been a tendency to speculate and assume far beyond the limits of proof that historians generally accept. See, for example, Keith Muckelroy, *Maritime Archeology* (Cambridge and New York: Cambridge University Press, 1978), pp. 100–104.

24. AGM, Colección Vargas Ponce, leg. 3, doc. 90, fols. 347–347v.

25. AGS, Guerra Antigua, leg. 3149, no. 2.

26. Ibid.

27. Auguste Antoine Thomazi, *Les flottes de l'or: Histoire des galions d'Espagne,* rev. ed. (Paris: Payot, 1956), p. 119.

28. Navarrete, *Colección de documentos,* 23(1), doc. 47; AGM, C.F. 134, paragraphs 92–101.

29. AGM, Marqués de la Victoria, *Diccionario,* plates 27 and 98, illustrate many of the tools in use.

30. Josephe de Veitia Linaje, *Norte de la contratación de las Indias occidentales* (Seville, 1672), translated as *The Spanish Rule of Trade to the West-Indies* (London, 1702; reprint, New York: AMS Press, 1977), book 1, chap. 16, no. 4.

31. AGM, Marqués de la Victoria, *Diccionario,* plates 38–41.

32. Ibid., plates 51–53.

33. Frederic Chapin Lane, *Venetian Ships and Shipbuilders of the Renaissance* (Baltimore: Johns Hopkins University Press, 1934), pp. 98–99.

34. "Galafatería," in Fernández Duro, *Disquisiciones náuticas,* 6:243–71.

35. AGM, Marqués de la Victoria, *Diccionario,* plate 55, illustrates various types of pumps.

36. Navarrete, *Colección de documentos,* 23(1), doc. 59.

37. AGS, Guerra Antigua, leg. 3149, No. 2, letter of January 15, 1627.

38. AGM, Colección Vargas Ponce, XXVI, doc. 10, fol. 15.

39. AGS, Guerra Antigua, leg. 3149, no. 2. All the documents dealing with the official measurement (arqueamiento) are dated March 23, 1627, and located at various places in the bundle.

40. Ibid., letters dated April 5, 1627, in Bilbao.

41. AGM, Colección Guillén, ms. 1294. Rivaherrera had served the crown on the north coast at least since 1593, and the AGM contains a notable number of documents from his official career.

42. AGS, Guerra Antigua, leg. 3149, no. 2, letter from Fernando de la Rivaherrera to the king, dated April 6, 1627, in Santander.

43. AGM, Colección Guillén, ms. 1294, doc. 1. Rivaherrera had owned his office. When he died and a young nephew inherited the estate, the king appointed an official to serve in the naval posts at half salary until the nephew came of age. AGS, Guerra Antigua, leg. 3157, Junta de Armadas memorandum of January 24, 1631.

44. AGM, ms. 471, fols. 157–74.

45. Juan y Santacilia, *Examen marítimo,* 2:12–13 and plate 3, fig. 8.

46. Barros's 1590 rules are printed in Fernández Duro, *Disquisiciones náuticas,* 5:150–54. Clarification of the method was issued in 1607. Navarrete, *Colección de documentos,* 23(1), doc. 47. The official duties and methods of the measurer of ships (arqueador de navíos) in Seville ca. 1574 appear in AGI, Patronato Real, leg. 260, no. 2, ramo 35.

47. Tomé Cano, *Arte para fabricar y aparejar naos (1611),* ed. Enrique Marco Dorta (La Laguna, Canary Islands: Instituto de Estudios Canarios, 1964), pp. 91–92.

48. The formula can be expressed as $.5Pu(.75M + .5Pl) \times .5(E + Q)$, in which Pu is puntal (depth in the hold); M is manga (beam); Pl is plan (floor); E is eslora (length on deck); and Q is quilla (keel). The resulting figure in cubic codos was divided by 8 to give toneladas.

49. Fernández Duro, *Disquisiciones náuticas,* 5:383. In 1633 the 1613 rules would be reinstituted. Ibid., 5:154–60; AGM, Colección Vargas Ponce, XXVI, doc. 42, fol. 67.

50. AGS, Guerra Antigua, leg. 3149, no. 2; AGM, Colección Vargas Ponce, leg. 3a, doc. 90, fols. 347–47v. Appendix B briefly describes the evolution of the tonelada in Spanish usage. The definition is complicated by the coexistence of two methods of calculation long after the crown had officially adopted, in 1590, the formula I have called Method 2. Chaunu has argued that the tonelada after 1590 was equivalent to 2.6 cubic meters of displacement, slightly smaller than the modern international ton. Pierre Chaunu, "La *tonelada* espagnole au XVI et XVII siècles," *Colloque international d'histoire maritime, 1st and 2nd, 1956, 1957* (Paris: S.E.V.P.E.N., 1957), pp. 77–78. This would seem much too large. More logical is the calculation of Michel Morineau that the official tonelada was 1.42 cubic meters of displacement, equal to the sea ton (tonneau de mer) in use in Bordeaux. Michel Morineau, *Jauges et méthodes de jauge anciennes et modernes* (Paris: Armand Colin, 1966), pp. 31–34, 64, 115–16. Both the arqueamiento formulas I have called Method 1 and Method 2 assume that the tonelada was equal to 8 cubic codos of displacement, which is very close to 1.42 cubic meters.

51. See the illustration in AGM, Marqués de la Victoria, *Diccionario,* plates 47–48.

52. Diego García de Palacio, *Instrucción náutica para navegar (1587)* (Madrid: Cultura hispánica, 1944), p. 93. H. S. Vaughan, "The Whipstaff," *Mariner's Mirror* 3 (1913):236.

53. AGM, C.F. 134.

54. "Diálogo entre un vizcaíno y un montañés," in Fernández Duro, *Disquisiciones náuticas,* 6:106–222. The year 1623 is often given erroneously as the approximate date of the treatise. See Ramón Carande Thobar, *Carlos V y sus banqueros,*

1516–1556 (Madrid: Sociedad de Estudios y Publicaciones, 1943–67), 1:366; and Abbott Payson Usher, "Spanish Ships and Shipping in the Sixteenth and Seventeenth Centuries," *Facts and Factors in Economic History: For Edwin Francis Gay* (Cambridge, Mass.: Harvard University Press, 1932; reprint, New York: Russell and Russell, 1967), p. 197. It is not clear how these authors arrived at 1623, since the "Diálogo" mentions a notorious salt tax imposed in Vizcaya in 1631 and rescinded in 1632. "Diálogo," in Fernández Duro, *Disquisiciones náuticas,* 6:211–12. Huguette and Pierre Chaunu, *Seville et l'Atlantique,* 8 vols. in 12 (Paris: A. Colin, 1955–59), 5:212 assume it dates from around 1630. Fernández Duro, *Disquisiciones náuticas,* 5:387–88 lists it tentatively among other documents of the period as 1640. There is little question that it is from the decade of the 1630s, earlier rather than later.

55. AGM, Colección Vargas Ponce, XVII, doc. 262.

56. Surprisingly, the brief discussion by Anders Franzen in Joseph Jobé, ed. *The Great Age of Sail,* trans. Michael Kelly (Lausanne: Edita, 1967), pp. 65–69, still calls the sinking "inexplicable."

57. AGS, Guerra Antigua, leg. 3149, no. 2, letter of June 13, 1627, from Bilbao.

58. Ibid., letter of June 15, 1627.

59. Ibid., leg. 3151, memorandum of July 14, 1627.

60. Ibid., letters of June 25 and July 7, 1627.

61. Ibid., letter of August 7 from Portugalete.

62. Ibid.

63. Ibid., testimony before the notary of Portugalete, Pedro de Gordón, October 11, 1627.

64. Ibid., letters of October 16 and 20, 1627.

65. Ibid., leg. 3152, memoranda of February 13 and 23, 1628, discuss the food and supplies sent to Santander; Cesáreo Fernández Duro, *Armada española desde la unión de los reinos de Castilla y de León,* 9 vols. (Madrid, 1895–1903), 4:144.

66. AGS, Guerra Antigua, leg. 3149, no. 2, reports of March 16 and 20, and Junta comments of April 2, 1628.

67. Ibid., letters of December 17, 1627, and March 27, 1628.

68. Ibid. See his letter of May 5, 1628, mentioning they were increased in size from 18 to 21 codos.

69. Ibid., letters of April 7, 17, and 24, 1628; Earl J. Hamilton, *American Treasure and the Price Revolution in Spain, 1501–1650* (Cambridge, Mass.: Harvard University Press, 1934; reprint ed., New York: Octagon Books, 1965), pp. 82–85, 217–18.

70. AGS, Guerra Antigua, leg. 3149, no. 2, letters of April 10, 1628.

71. Ibid., letter of April 14, 1628.

72. Ibid., letter of April 17, 1628. Coloma was a secretary of state, acting as secretary of the Junta de Armadas. AGS, Estado, leg. 2051.

73. AGS, Guerra Antigua, leg. 3149, no. 2, letters of April 10, 21, and 24, 1628, from Domingo Ochoa de Yrazagorria and Aparicio de Recalde y Hormaeche.

74. Ibid., letters of May 5, 8, and 13, from Arana to the king and to his secretary Coloma.

75. AGM, Marqués de la Victoria, *Diccionario,* plates 69–70.

76. AGS, Guerra Antigua, leg. 3149, no. 2, letters of May 8, 12, and 13, 1628.

77. Ibid., letter of May 12 from Ochoa to Pedro de Coloma, and May 13, 1628, letter from Arana to the king.

78. Ibid., letters of June 2 and 16, and July 3, 1628.

79. Ibid., letter of July 9.

80. Ibid., letter of July 10, 1628. See Olesa Muñido, *Organización naval,* pp. 280–330, for artillery on Spanish warships.

81. Ibid., letter of July 3, 1628, with comments in the margin.

82. Ibid., letter from Ochoa, July 25, 1628.

83. Bell Library, University of Minnesota, "Spanish Shipping," f 1628. Julio Ortega Galindo consulted these documents, or copies of them, somewhere in Spain before 1947. He cites no precise location, but one assumes it was in Bilbao. A brief précis of one of the inventories and two other brief royal documents dealing with Arana and the six galleons form the substance of his article "Los seis galeones de la plata," *Boletín de la Real Sociedad Vascongada de Amigos del País* 3(1947):221–24.

84. Fernández Duro, *Disquisiciones náuticas*, 1:231–34.

85. Ibid., "Diálogo entre un vizcaíno y un montañés," 6:151–53.

86. AGM, ms. 1311, fol. 86.

87. AGS, Guerra Antigua, leg. 3152, letters of July 6 and 12, 1628.

88. Santa Barbara's appeal for artillerymen has persisted into the twentieth century. Artillery officers of the United States Marine Corps honor her every year in late November. *Los Angeles Times,* November 30, 1982, "San Diego at Large."

89. *Recopilación de Leyes de los reynos de las Indias, mandadas imprimir y publicar por el Magestad católica del rey don Carlos II,* 3 vols. (Madrid, 1681; reprint, Madrid: Consejo de la Hispanidad, 1943), 3:337. AGM, Marqués de la Victoria, *Diccionario,* plate 8.

90. Francisco-Felipe Olesa Muñido, "La marina oceánica de los Austrias," in *El Buque en la armada española* (Madrid: Silex, 1981), pp. 142–44; Carlos Moya Blanco, "La arquitectura naval de los Austrias," in *Buque,* p. 163.

91. AGI, Mapas y Planos, Panamá 45.

92. R. C. Anderson, *The Rigging of Ships in the Days of the Spritsail Topmast, 1600–1720* (Salem, Mass.: Marine Research Society, 1927), pp. 210–30. For a contemporary account of English sails, cables, and rigging, see Edward Hayward, *The Sizes and Lengths of Riggings for all the States Ships and Frigats* (London, 1655; facsimile edition, London: Francis Edwards, 1967).

93. Selma Huxley Barkham, "The Basques: Filling a Gap in Our History Between Jacques Cartier and Champlain," *Canadian Geographical Journal* 96 (February–March 1978):15.

94. *Recopilación de Leyes de Indias,* 3:337–38.

95. AGM, Marqués de la Victoria, *Diccionario,* plates 58, 60, 63–66, illustrates cable making in Spain and the numerous sizes and varieties of the finished products.

96. AGI, Contaduría, leg. 554.

97. "Diálogo," in Fernández Duro, *Disquisiciones náuticas,* 6:149.

98. Olesa Muñido, "Marina oceánica," pp. 145–47; AGM, C.F. 134.

99. Cano, *Arte para fabricar naos,* pp. 72–76.

100. AGI, Contaduría, leg. 554.

101. AGS, CMC 3a, leg. 2910, no. 8.

102. Cano, *Arte para fabricar naos,* pp. 72–76.

103. García de Palacio, *Instrucción náutica para navegar,* fols. 102v–107v. See the illustrations in AGM, Marqués de la Victoria, *Diccionario,* plates 42, 43, 63, 65, 69, 118–20 for sails and sail plans.

104. AGS, CMC 3a, leg. 1323, new sails for the *Santiago* in 1634.

105. Olesa Muñido, "Marina oceánica," in *Buque,* pp. 139–47; AGM, Marqués de la Victoria, *Diccionario,* plate 104. Some ships of the Armada del Mar Océano were undoubtedly more lavishly adorned, though the ordinances of 1633 restricted decoration on all but the capitanas of squadrons. *Ordenanzas del buen govierno de la armada del mar océano de 24 de henero de 1633* (facsimile edition, Madrid: Instituto Histórico de Marina, 1974), paragraphs 17, 329–30. An excellent depiction of galleons of the period is the series of six battle scenes by Juan de la Corte, commemorating the 1635 Indies fleet of Captain-General don Lope de Hoces. They now hang in the Archivo Museo del Viso del Marqués.

106. AGS, Guerra Antigua, leg. 3149, no. 2, letter of August 2, 1628, from Portugalete.

107. Ibid., letters from Arana to the king and to the royal secretary Coloma, August 3, 1628, from Bilbao.

108. At normal high tide the channel below Portugalete was only about 14 feet deep in the middle. At low tide it dropped to only 6 feet. A storm tide might rise to 17 or 18 feet, but that created other problems. AGS, *Mapas, Planos, y Dibujos,* IX-18, IX-24.

109. AGS, Guerra Antigua, leg. 3149, no. 2, letter from Ochoa and Hormaeche, August 4, 1628.

110. Ibid., letter of August 9, 1628; leg. 3152, a memorandum of March 25, 1628, mentioned the *Santiago* and other ships on the north coast not fit for service.

111. Ibid., leg. 3149, no. 2, letter of August 14, 1628, from Arana in Bilbao.

Chapter FOUR. Reckoning the Cost

1. AGS, CMC 3a, leg. 627.

2. AGS, Guerra Antigua, leg. 3149, no. 2, March 14, 1625.

3. Martín Fernández de Navarrete, *Colección de documentos y manuscriptos compilados,* 32 vols. (Nendeln, Lichtenstein: Kraus-Thompson Organization, 1971), 23(1):589–92.

4. AGM, C.F. 134.

5. AGI, Consulados, leg. 1050, accounts for careening and repairs in Portobelo and Havana in the mid-1630s.

6. Jonathan Brown and J. H. Elliott, *A Palace for a King: The Buen Retiro and the Court of Philip IV* (New Haven, Conn.: Yale University Press, 1980), p. 93.

7. Cesáreo Fernández Duro, *Disquisiciones náuticas,* 6 vols. (Madrid: Sucesores de Rivadeneyra, 1876–81), 5:68–69.

8. I. A. A. Thompson, *War and Government in Habsburg Spain* (London: Athlone Press, 1976), p. 332, citing AGS, Guerra Antigua, leg. 347.

9. Frederic Chapin Lane, *Venetian Ships and Shipbuilders of the Renaissance* (Baltimore: Johns Hopkins University Press, 1934), pp. 264–65. The cost of a galleon built in Venice in 1560 came to the following: "Wood, masts, yards, and carpenters' labor—40.6 percent; tow, pitch, iron, and caulkers—19.9 percent; rigging and sails—39.5 percent."

10. AGS, Estado, leg. 2039.

11. Cited in José Alcalá-Zamora y Queipo de Llano, *España, Flandes y el Mar del Norte (1618–1639): La última ofensiva europea de los Austrias madrileños* (Barcelona: Editorial Planeta, 1975), pp. 269–70. The cost ranged from 37 ducados per tonelada for a 600-tonelada ship to 43 ducados per tonelada for a 300-tonelada ship.

12. AGI, Indiferente General, leg. 2525. The figures cited by Lawrence A. Clayton, *Caulkers and Carpenters in a New World: The Shipyards of Colonial Guayaquil* (Athens: Ohio University Center for International Studies, 1980), pp. 87–92, for ship construction are so high as to be incredible—140 to 218 ducados per tonelada in the early seventeenth century.

13. AGM, C.F. 134, the 1618 ordinances.

14. AGS, Guerra Antigua, leg. 3149, no. 2, contract of March 14, 1625.

15. "Diálogo," Fernández Duro, *Disquisiciones náuticas,* 6:150.

16. Etienne Taillemite, "Royal Glories," in *The Great Age of Sail,* ed. Joseph Jobé (Lausanne: Edita, 1967), p. 77, said that it took approximately 100,000 cubic feet of oak, or 4,000 trees, to build a ship of 110 guns, which was several times the size of the ships Arana built. John D. Harbron estimated that it took 3,000 trees, each yielding 600 board feet (double Jobé's estimate), to build a warship about the average size of Arana's six galleons. Forty pine trees would be required for the spars alone. "The Spanish Ship of the Line," *Scientific American* 251 (December 1984): 119. Jobé had much smaller trees in mind than Harbron.

17. AGS, Estado, leg. 81, fols. 81, 84, 89.

18. Ibid., Estado, leg. 97, fol. 96. Evidently, there was even wood suitable for masts in Vizcaya, but too far from the coast—10 leagues or so—to transport cheaply or efficiently. AGS, Guerra Antigua, leg. 3150, document of May 16, 1626.

19. Estánislao Jaime de Labayru y Goicoechea, *Historia general del Señorío de Vizcaya* (Bilbao: La Gran Enciclopedia Vasca, 1968–72), 4:365–66.

20. AGS, Guerra Antigua, leg. 71, fols. 111, 121, 124, and leg. 72, fols. 297–300; CJH, leg. 81, fols. 219–27.

21. AGM, mss. 580, doc. 13, fols. 40–48v and mss. 2099, doc. 15, fol. 123; RAH, Colección Vargas Ponce, vol. 29.

22. Federico Castro y Bravo, *Las naos españolas en la carrera de las Indias: Armadas y flotas en la segunda mitad del siglo XVI* (Madrid: Editorial Voluntad, 1927), p. 201.

23. AGM, Colección Vargas Ponce, XX, doc. 70, fol. 168; AGM, ms. 2099, doc. 15, fols. 119–20, 123; AGS, Guerra Antigua, leg. 3157, memorandum of September 27, 1631, regarding Arana and forest conservation.

24. See Paul W. Bamford, *Forests and French Sea Power* (Toronto: University of Toronto Press, 1956), pp. 70–94, for the depletion of French forests and the regulations to conserve what was left.

25. AGS, Guerra Antigua, leg. 3149, no. 2, January 15, 1627.

26. AGM, Colección Vargas Ponce, XXVI, doc. 26, pp. 37–41v.

27. AGI, Contaduría, leg. 459, ramo 1.

28. Ricardo Cappa, *Estudios críticos acerca de la dominación española en América,* 3rd ed., 26 vols. (Madrid: Librería católica, 1889–), 10:128–31; Fernández Duro, *Disquisiciones náuticas,* 5:376, 381.

29. See, for example, a refitting in Lisbon in 1606 in AGS, CMC 3a, leg. 2214, no. 7.

30. See AGM, Marqués de la Victoria, *Diccionario,* plates 51–53.

31. AGS, Guerra Antigua, leg. 3149, no. 2, reports of June 2, 1628, January 15, 1629, April 20, 1629. See the illustrations of anchors in AGM, Marqués de la Victoria, *Diccionario,* plates 72 and 76.

32. AGI, Contaduría leg. 459, ramo 1. AGS, CMC 3a, leg. 1383. Iron was 19.1 percent of the cost of a Venetian merchant ship built in 1586. Lane, *Venetian Ships and Shipbuilders,* pp. 264–65.

33. AGS, Guerra Antigua, leg. 3149, no. 2, memorandum of June 2, 1628.

34. AGI, Contaduría, leg. 462, no. 2.

35. "Diálogo," in Fernández Duro, *Disquisiciones náuticas,* 6:149–50.

36. AGI, Contratación, leg. 4048, document of August 10, 1634.

37. Cappa, *Estudios críticos,* 10:128–31.

38. AGS, CMC 3a, leg. 2204, no. 11.

39. AGM, Colección Vargas Ponce, XVII, doc. 263.

40. AGS, Guerra Antigua, leg. 3149, no. 2 account of January 15, 1629.

41. Ibid., reports of June 2 and November 12, 1628, and the inventory of July 31.

42. "Diálogo," in Fernández Duro, *Disquisiciones náuticas,* 6:149.

43. AGI, Contaduría, leg. 554.

44. AGM, Colección Vargas Ponce, II, doc. 4, fols. 4–5 and doc. 34, fols. 47–48v; AGI, Contaduría leg. 459, ramo 1.

45. AGS, Guerra Antigua, leg. 3149, no. 2, account of June 2, 1628. The replacement cables ordered by Admiral Vallecilla were priced at 18 ducados the quintal, but all other references to cable and rigging price them at about 12 ducados.

46. AGS, CMC 3a, leg. 2204, no. 11.

47. AGI, Contaduría, leg. 459, *ramo* 1; AGS, CMC 3a, leg. 1383.

48. Ibid. and Lane, *Venetian Ships and Shipbuilders,* passim.

49. AGS, Guerra Antigua, leg. 3149, no. 2, reports of October 17 and November 12, 1628, and January 15, 1629.

50. Ibid., report of September 20, 1628.

51. Carlos Moya Blanco, "La arquitectura naval de los Austrias," in *El buque en la armada española* (Madrid: Silex, 1981), p. 164.

52. AGS, Guerra Antigua, leg. 3149, no. 2, report of September 20, 1628.

53. Ibid., letter of October 17, 1628, from Arana.

54. Ibid., report of November 12, 1628.

55. Ibid.

56. Ibid.

57. Ibid., letter of December 15, 1628.

58. Ibid., letter of December 23, 1628.

59. Ibid., report of January 15, 1629.

60. Ibid., report of Martín de Aróztegui, March 5, 1629.

61. Ibid., meeting of March 17, 1629, with don Fernando Girón, don Luis Brabo, Martín de Aróztegui, and Pedro de Arce attending.

62. Ibid., memoranda of March 23 and April 1, 1628.

63. Ibid., memoranda of March 27 and April 5, 20, and 27, 1629.

64. Ibid., memorandum of May 22, 1629.

65. Ibid., undated memorandum mentioning the June 5, 1629, decree.

66. Ibid., letter of Arana of June 7, 1629, and Junta meeting of June 27, referring the matter to the king.

67. Ibid., letter from Arana on August 20, and Junta meetings of August 25 and September 11.

68. Quoted in Julio Ortega Galindo, "Los seis galeones de la plata," *Boletín de la Real Sociedad Vascongada de Amigos del País* 3 (1947): 224.

Chapter FIVE. Preparations for the Indies Fleet of 1629

1. AGI, Contaduría, leg. 555.

2. Gervasio Artiñano y de Galdácano, *La arquitectura naval española (en madera)* (Madrid, 1920), pp. 43–44, claims that Catalan merchantmen carried artillery by 1381.

3. See, for example, the hundreds of accounts of mayordomos de artillería in AGS, CMC 3a. Fairly complete accounts for several mayordomos of the Armada del Mar Océano in the 1630s can be found in legs. 637, 1345, and 1447.

4. Nicolás Sánchez-Albornoz, "Gastos y alimentación de un ejército en el siglo XVI según un presupuesto de la época," *Cuadernos de Historia de España* 14 (1950): 156.

5. AGM, mss. 2413, doc. 3. Unfortunately, one folio is missing from the document.

6. Martín Fernández de Navarrete, *Colección de documentos y manuscriptos compilados,* 32 vols. (Nendeln, Lichtenstein: Kraus-Thompson Organization, 1971), 24(2), doc. 49, pp. 736–48.

7. I. A. A. Thompson, *War and Government in Habsburg Spain* (London: Athlone Press, 1976), pp. 234–55. The author chooses to regard this as a negative development—another abrogation of sovereignty—a position with which I disagree.

8. AGS, CMC 3a, leg. 1447. These accounts of Juan de la Sierra Rubalcava, mayordomo de la artillería de la Armada Real for 1632–36, begin with an alphabetical table of contents listing the categories.

9. Ibid., leg. 30.

10. AGI, Contaduría, leg. 279. See Josephe de Veitia Linaje, *Norte de la contratación de las Indias occidentales* (Seville, 1672), abridged and translated as *The Spanish Rule of Trade to the West-Indies* (London, 1702; reprint, New York: AMS Press, 1977), book 1, chap. 10 for *factores.* Also in 1554 a fleet supplied in Laredo on the north coast relied upon royal officials rather than private factors. AGM, Colección Navarrete, vol. 21, doc. 43, fols. 143–46.

11. AGS, Estado, leg. 513, fols. 165–68.

12. AGM, Colección Vargas Ponce, has copies of some of the purveyors' accounts and other documents, but the main collections are in the financial papers of the AGS, Contaduría Mayor de Cuentas, and the AGI, Contaduría.

13. Thompson, *War and Government,* pp. 207–33, describes the system well but finds more harm than good in the trend toward private contracts for government functions. A comprehensive contract for provisioning and maintaining thirteen galleons in royal service appears in Navarrete, *Colección de documentos,* 9, doc. 23, fols. 251–66, minutely specifying the responsibilities of the contractor.

14. AGS, Guerra Antigua, leg. 3149, Junta meeting of May 18, 1625.

15. Ibid., memo of June 30, 1625.

16. AGM, Colección Vargas Ponce, XXVI, doc. 6, fol. 10, letter of May 4, 1626, to Fernando de la Rivaherrera, acting for his brother Francisco as purveyor of armadas. Manuel Gomez y Acosta died before the end of November 1626, leaving his heirs to sort out the accounts. AGS, Guerra Antigua, leg. 3150.

17. AGS, CMC 3a, legs. 1870, no. 3; 2125, no. 11; 2279, no. 8; 2287, no. 4; and 2715, no. 2. Levanto had previously served as treasurer of the Royal Mint in Granada. AGS, Guerra Antigua, leg. 3150, document dated October 3, 1626.

18. AGS, CMC 3a, legs. 1323; 2873, no. 11; 2951, no. 22; and 3012, no. 20. Veitia Linaje, *Rule of Trade,* book 1, chap. 16.

19. AGI, Contratación, leg. 4222; Consulados, leg. 1051. See also the accounts in AGS, CMC 3a, inventoried by the name of the official filing the accounts. Francisco-Felipe Olesa Muñido, *La organización naval de los estados mediterráneos y en especial de España durante los siglos XVI y XVII,* 2 vols. (Madrid: Editorial Naval, 1968), pp. 488–98, discusses the bureaucratic apparatus for fleet provisioning, including a useful flow chart of the chain of command on pages 494–95.

20. AGS, Estado, leg. 513, fols. 165–68. Earl J. Hamilton, "Wages and Subsistence of Spanish Treasure Ships, 1503–1660," *Journal of Political Economy* (1929), p. 440, shows that the standard ration in 1556–57 cost 30 maravedís for ordinary seamen and 40 maravedís for the captain-general of a fleet.

21. AGS, Guerra Antigua, leg. 3149.

22. AGS, CMC 3a, legs. 1870, no. 3; 2229, no. 9. Navarrete, *Colección de documentos* 9, doc. 23, fols. 251–66, mentions ración costs of 51 maravedís in silver in 1638. Olesa Muñido, *Organización naval,* p. 893, notes the value of a ration as 12–24 maravedís, but that is clearly too low for the seventeenth century.

23. AGS, Guerra Antigua, leg. 3152, memorandum of June 5, 1628, estimates a cost of 68 maravedís in silver and mentions that provisions on Spain's north coast could run as high as 85 maravedís in the same period. Another document from October of the same year estimated 60 maravedís (ibid.), as did an estimate from January 1632 (ibid., leg. 3159). The figure of 2 reales, or 68 maravedís, is mentioned in ibid., leg. 3154 for an October 1630 provisioning in Lisbon.

24. "Diálogo entre un vizcaíno y un montañés," in Cesáreo Fernández Duro, *Disquisiciones náuticas,* 6 vols. (Madrid: Sucesores de Rivadeneyra, 1876–81), 6:158–60. A document from 1631 mentions rations costing just 57 maravedís each in copper vellón. AGS, Guerra Antigua, leg. 3158. Another estimates a cost of 51 maravedís in silver for late 1635, demonstrating the considerable range of provisioning costs in this period. Ibid., leg. 3164.

25. L. Denoix, "Charactéristiques des navires de l'époque des grandes découvertes," *Colloque International d'Histoire Maritime, 5th, Lisbon, 1960* (Paris: S.E.V.P.E.N., 1966), pp. 137–48.

26. John F. Guilmartin suggested this comparison.

27. *Recopilación de Leyes de los reynos de las Indias, mandadas imprimir y publicar por el Magestad católica del rey don Carlos II,* 3 vols. (Madrid, 1681; reprint, Madrid: Consejo de la Hispanidad, 1943), 3:394–97.

28. AGM, Colección Vargas Ponce, XII, doc. 89, has a representative list of provisions, and there are hundreds of other such lists in the AGM, the AGS, and the AGI.

29. Hamilton, "Wages and Subsistence," pp. 431–32.

30. RAH, Colección Salazar, A-14, fols. 122–23.

31. See AGS, Guerra Antigua, leg. 12, fols. 179–80, leg. 13, fol. 121; and Estado, leg. 442 for provisioning accounts in the reign of Charles I.

32. AGS, Estado, leg. 497, fol. 221; AGS, Guerra Antigua, leg. 15, no. 45.

33. AGS, CMC 1a, leg. 1052.

34. Ibid., leg. 1193.

35. See AGI, Contaduría, leg. 462, no. 2, for French wheat supplied to an armada of Pedro Menéndez de Avilés in 1568.

36. RAH, Colección Salazar, A-50, fol. 58.

37. AGS, CMC 3a, leg. 1828, no. 1.

38. AGS, Estado, leg. 2045. The city of Burgos tried to take advantage of the scarcity, charging 35 reales for each fanega (about 1.5 bushels) of wheat delivered to Santander over the mountains. AGS, Guerra Antigua, leg. 3156, memorandum of May 29, 1631.

39. AGS, Guerra Antigua, leg. 3149, no. 2, letters from the inspector Ochoa and the purveyor Hormaeche to the king and his secretary, dated February 21 and April 3, 1628; leg. 3152, memorandum dated February 23, 1628.

40. Ibid., leg. 3149, no. 2, letter from Ochoa and Hormaeche to the king, dated Bilbao March 10, 1628.

41. Ibid., May 12, 1628.

42. Ibid., June 16 and July 3, 1628.

43. Ibid., letter from Ochoa to the king, dated Bilbao July 25, 1628.

44. AGI, Contaduría, leg. 279.

45. AGS, CMC 1a, leg. 1193.

46. AGI, Contaduría, leg. 462, no. 2.

47. Earl J. Hamilton, *American Treasure and the Price Revolution in Spain, 1501–1650* (Cambridge, Mass.: Harvard University Press, 1934; reprint, New York: Octagon Books, 1969).

48. AGI, Contaduría, legs. 279; 555, ramos 1–2. In 1628 wheat sold for 33 reales the fanega in Andalusia, 28.7 reales in New Castile, and 15 reales in Old Castile. Hamilton, *American Treasure,* pp. 364–81. In the same year in Bilbao, even moisture-damaged wheat cost 24.5 reales, further proof of the scarcity of grains on the north coast. AGS, Guerra Antigua, leg. 3149, no. 2; CMC 3a, leg. 627; AGI, Consulados, leg. 1051.

49. Hamilton, *American Treasure,* pp. 237–42.

50. John F. Guilmartin, *Gunpowder and Galleys: Changing Technology and Mediterranean Warfare at Sea in the Sixteenth Century* (Cambridge: Cambridge University Press, 1974), pp. 222–24, notes that military rations cost more in Spain than in Italy.

51. AGI, Contaduría, legs. 279 (for 1554), 548 (for 1562). Hamilton, *American Treasure,* p. 335, has the comparable market prices in Seville.

52. AGI, Contaduría, leg. 555, ramos 1 and 2; AGS, Guerra Antigua, leg. 3149, no. 2, letter to the king on March 10, 1628; Hamilton, *American Treasure,* pp. 365, 381.

53. AGI, Contaduría legs. 548; 555, ramos 1 and 2; Hamilton, *American Treasure,* p. 365.

54. AGI, Contaduría, legs. 279; 548; 555, ramos 1 and 2; Consulados, legs. 1051, 1052; AGS, Estado, leg. 497, fol. 221; Contaduría del Sueldo, leg. 197. Fish drying in Conil near Cádiz is illustrated in Georgius Braun and Franz Hogenberg, *Civitates Orbis Terrarum* (Cologne, 1572.) Cervantes briefly describes the large tuna fishery at Zahara on the same coast. Miguel de Cervantes Saavedra, "Ilustre fregona," *Novelas*

ejemplares, ed. Francisco Rodríguez Marín (Madrid: Espasa Calpe, 1962), 1:219–324, especially the notes on pp. 224–25.

55. AGI, Contaduría, legs. 548; 555, ramos 1 and 2; AGS, Estado, leg. 497, fol. 221; Hamilton, *American Treasure,* pp. 336, 364.

56. AGI, Contaduría, legs. 279; 548; 555, ramos 1 and 2.

57. Ibid.

58. AGI, Consulados, legs. 1046, 1052.

59. Ibid., legs. 1046, 1049, 1051, 1052; Contaduría, legs. 279; 555, ramos 1 and 2; AGS, Estado, leg. 497, fol. 221; CMC 3a, leg. 1103, no. 1. Sugar, bought in small quantities for dietas, was one of the few items that cost less in the Indies than in Spain, because important sugar plantations flourished in the Caribbean Islands and in Mexico.

60. Navarrete, *Colección de documentos,* 24(1), no. 16, pp. 148–49.

61. See, for example, AGI, Contaduría, leg. 548 for 1562; and AGM, Colección Sanz—Simancas, ms. 1949, fols. 9–17 for 1575, accounts that list neither wine, nor cider, nor containers for water.

62. AGI, Contaduría, legs. 279 for 1554 and 548 for 1562; AGM, Colección Sanz—Simancas, ms. 1949, fols. 9–17 for 1575; AGS, CMC 1a, leg. 1193 for 1557; RAH, Colección Salazar, B-4, fols. 238–38v for 1624; AGS, Guerra Antigua, leg. 3152 for 1628, CMC 3a, leg. 1870, no. 3 for 1629; AGI, Contratación, leg. 4053 for 1638–39; AGS, CMC 3a, leg. 1828, no. 1 for 1638–42; AGM, Colección Guillén, ms. 1311, doc. 7, fol. 86 for 1646; Colección Vargas Ponce, XIII, doc. 194 for ca. 1650; XVIII, doc. 210, fols. 356–57v for 1666; XII, docs. 176, fol. 287 and doc. 178, fols. 289–289v for ca. 1671.

63. See chapter 7 for the contents of the daily ration of food and drink, and its nutritional value.

64. Valentín Vázquez de Prada, "Las escalas en la navegación española a América," *Colloque international d'histoire maritime, 10th, Brussels, 1968* (Brussels: Société Jean Bodin pour l'histoire comparative des Institutions; Recueils, vol. 33), pp. 109–13.

65. "Diálogo," in Fernández Duro, *Disquisiciones náuticas,* 6:158–60, has the menu on which these calculations were based.

66. AGS, CMC 3a, leg. 1870, no. 3, contains the provisioning accounts.

67. AGI, Contaduría, legs. 548, 555, ramos 1 and 2; AGS, Guerra Antigua, leg. 3153.

68. AGI, Contaduría, legs. 548, 555, ramos 1 and 2; Contratación, leg. 4048; AGS, Guerra Antigua, leg. 3149, no. 2; CMC 3a, legs. 1103, no. 1 and 2204, no. 11; Ricardo Cappa, *Estudios críticos acerca de la dominación española en América,* 3rd ed., 26 vols. (Madrid: Librería católica, 1889–), 10:128–31.

69. AGI, Contaduría, leg. 555, ramos 1 and 2; AGS, CMC 3a, leg. 2204, no. 11.

70. AGI, Contaduría, leg. 555, ramos 1 and 2.

71. AGS, Guerra Antigua, leg. 3149, no. 2, reports of October 17 and November 12, 1628, and January 15, 1629.

72. *Recopilación de Leyes de Indias,* libro 9, título 31, 3:394–96 of the 1943 edition.

73. AGS, Estado, leg. 497, fol. 221; Guerra Antigua, leg. 3149, no. 2; CMC 3a, leg. 2204, no. 11.

74. AGI, Contaduría, leg. 555, ramos 1 and 2.

75. Huguette and Pierre Chaunu, *Séville et l'Atlantique,* 8 vols. in 12 (Paris: A. Colin, 1955–59), 5:175.

76. AGI, Contaduría, leg. 555.

77. Chaunu, *Séville et l'Atlantique,* 5:116.

78. Pierre Chaunu, with Huguette Chaunu, *Séville et l'Amérique aux XVIe et XVIIe siècles* (Paris: Flammarion, 1977), pp. 229–39; *Séville et l'Atlantique,* 6(1), tables 18–128.

79. Chaunu, *Séville et l'Atlantique,* 4:248–409.

80. Ibid., 4:478–591.

81. Ibid., 5:6–25. Ordinarily, the Armada de la Guardia would have a captain-general in command and an admiral as second in command.

82. Ibid., 5:26–37, 58–65. The bulk of the treasure carried on *Nuestra Señora de Atocha,* one of the silver galleons lost to the storm, was located in the summer of 1985 by private salvors. Its value in modern terms will be tens of millions of dollars, at least.

83. Ibid., 5:52. The best-known chronicle of the voyage is Antonio Vázquez de Espinosa, "Tratado verdadero del viaje y navegación de este año de seiscientos y veinte y dos que hizo la flota de Nueva España y Honduras," *Revista de Indias* 36 (January–June 1976): 287–352. Twenty-seven ships left Havana, but four went to Florida. See also Oliver Dunn, "Trouble at Sea: The Return Voyage of the Fleet of New Spain and Honduras in 1622," *Terrae Incognitae* 11 (1979): 29–42, and the sources cited therein. The author mentions "annual return voyages" (p. 29), perhaps unaware that the merchant fleets habitually wintered over. Less well known is the harrowing voyage of another fleet in 1642, chronicled by Pedro de Fontiveros, in Fernández Duro, *Disquisiciones náuticas,* 2:219–21.

84. Chaunu, *Séville et l'Atlantique,* 5:44–55, 84–95.

85. AGI, Contratación, leg. 5173, letter to the Junta de Armadas of December 11, 1628.

86. Chaunu, *Séville et l'Atlantique,* 5:152–83.

87. *Ibid.,* 5:208–12.

88. Ignacio de Arzamendi Orbegozo, *Almirante D. Antonio De Oquendo* (San Sebastián: Sociedad Guipuzcoana de Ediciones y Publicaciones, 1981), pp. 224–29, contains a full account of the case.

89. AGS, Guerra Antigua, leg. 3152, Junta de Armadas minutes of October 17, 1628.

90. AGI, Contratación, leg. 5189, letter to Don Gaspar de Montezer, December 6, 1628.

91. Ibid., letter of December 15, 1628.

92. Samuel Pierre L'Honoré Naber and Irene A. Wright, *Piet Heyn en de Zilvervloot, Bescheiden uit Nederlandsche en Spaansche archieven* (Utrecht: Kemink and Zoon, 1928), pp. 113–17. Mendel Peterson, *The Funnel of Gold: The Trials of the Spanish Treasure Fleets . . .* (Boston: Little, Brown, 1975), pp. 259–63, says that Piet Heyn's official report did not reach Holland until mid-May 1629, but the Dutch surely knew unofficially by late November of the previous year.

93. AGI, Contratación leg. 5173, letter of January 4, 1629.

94. AGI, Indiferente General, leg. 2567, letters of December 17 and 29, 1628.

95. AGI, Contratación leg. 5173, memorandum of December 11, 1628.

96. AGS, Guerra Antigua, leg. 3152, memorandum of December 16, 1628.

97. Ibid., letter from him on October 18, 1628; AGI, Indiferente General, leg. 2567, memoranda of January 15 and March 5, 1629, discuss the final selection of don Fadrique to accompany the fleet to the Indies. Because the 1629 armada was essentially a war fleet, the Junta de Guerra de Indias helped to plan its mission, along with the Junta de Armadas. Formed in 1609 to deal with the particular problems of war and defense in the Indies, the Junta de Guerra de Indias was composed of four councilors each from the Council of War and the Council of the Indies, though formally annexed to the latter. Olesa Muñido, *Organización naval,* pp. 423, 1300. Much of the correspondence regarding the 1629 fleet is in AGI. Indiferente General, leg. 2567.

98. AGS, Guerra Antigua, leg. 3153, letter from Oquendo in Lisbon, December 29, 1628; memorandum of the Junta de Armadas, January 5, 1629, Madrid; letter from Tomás de Ibio Calderón, the inspector general in Lisbon, dated December 28, 1628.

99. AGS, Guerra Antigua, leg. 3153, letter from Oleaga in Cádiz to the king, January 27, 1629.

100. AGS, Guerra Antigua, leg. 3153, Junta de Armadas minutes and letters in January 1629. Oleaga would die in office about ten years later, ca. 1639. AGS, CMC 3, leg. 3511-6.

101. AGI, Contratación, leg. 5173, lib. 17, fols. 396v–400; lib. 18, fols. 7–14, 397–400. Commercial debts had been postponed until the arrival of the fleet, but that was little help. *Colección de documentos inéditos relativos al descubrimiento, conquista y organización de las antiguas posesiones espanõles de Ultramar,* 25 vols. (Madrid: Real Academia de la Historia, 1864–1932), 15:42. Correspondence about the impossibility of sending merchant fleets in 1629 can be found in AGI, Indiferente General, leg. 2567, letters during February 1629.

102. AGS, Guerra Antigua, leg. 3153, letter from Oquendo in Cádiz, January 27, 1629; AGI, Contratación, leg. 5173, lib. 17.

103. AGS, Guerra Antigua, leg. 3153; AGI, Indiferente General, leg. 2567, dated February 12, 1629.

104. AGI, Indiferente General, leg. 2567, memorandum of December 17, 1628; AGS, Guerra Antigua, leg. 3152, memoranda dated August 25 and September 1, 1628.

105. AGS, Guerra Antigua, leg. 3153, letters of October 21, 1629, January 8 and 20, 1630; Junta de Armadas minutes of December 21, 1629. See also the memorandum of March 9, 1628, sending him to Cádiz. Ibid., leg. 3152. Unlike most other naval commanders of his rank, Roque Centeno almost certainly did not enjoy noble status. He is never referred to with the honorific *don* in any document I have seen. Bibiano Torres Ramírez, *La Armada de Barlovento* (Seville: Publicaciones de la Escuela de Estudios Hispano-Americanos, 1981), p. 42, accords Centeno the honorific, but it is unclear if this came from a documentary source or was merely based on the author's assumption that he held noble rank.

106. AGS, Guerra Antigua, leg. 3153, Junta de Armadas minutes of January 27 and February 1, 1629; letter from Oleaga in Cádiz on January 7, 1629.

107. Ibid., leg. 3154, Junta de Armadas minutes of August 30 and enclosed letters.

108. Ibid., leg. 3153, Junta de Armadas minutes of February 1, 1629.

109. AGS, CMC 3a, leg. 1870, no. 3.

110. AGS, Guerra Antigua, leg. 3153, Junta de Armadas minutes of February 1, 1629, and enclosed letters.

111. Ibid., Junta de Armadas list of February 19 and minutes of March 7, 1629.

112. Ibid., Junta de Armadas minutes of March 3, 1629, with don Antonio de Oquendo's estimates of February 23 sent from Cádiz.

113. Auguste Antoine Thomazi, *Les flottes de l'or: Histoire des galions d'Espagne,* rev. ed. (Paris: Payot, 1956), pp. 131–32. Regulations for the royal officials engaged in the work appear in *Recopilación de Leyes de Indias,* libro 8, titulo 32, 3:398–99 in the 1943 edition.

114. AGS, Guerra Antigua, leg. 3153, Junta de Armadas minutes of March 7, 1629.

115. Ibid., Junta de Armadas minutes of March 7, 1629; AGI, Indiferente General, leg. 2567, letters of March 10 and 24, 1629.

116. AGS, Guerra Antigua, leg. 3153, Junta de Armadas minutes of April 27, 1629, with the king's annotation, "si no, se perderá todo."

117. AGI, Indiferente General, leg. 2567, memorandum of March 15, 1629. See Antonio Domínguez Ortiz, "Los caudales de Indias y la política exterior de Felipe IV," *Anuario de Estudios Americanos* 13 (1956): 343–44, for a discussion of the treasure Larráspuru brought with him.

118. AGS, Guerra Antigua, leg. 3153, Junta de Armadas minutes of April 27, 1629; letter of don Juan de Castro y Castilla from Seville, April 24, 1629.

119. AGI, Contratación leg. 5189, memoranda of April 2, May 4, 1629. José Goñi Gaztambide, *Historia de la bula de cruzada en España* (Vitoria, 1958).

120. AGS, Guerra Antigua, leg. 3153, Junta de Armadas minutes of May 17; AGI, Indiferente General, leg. 2567, memoranda of April 11 and May 14, 1629.

121. AGS, Guerra Antigua, leg. 3152. In June 1628, he had asked to be relieved of duty for a while, to attend to family business.

122. Ibid., leg. 3153, letter of Horacio Levanto from Jerez de la Frontera, May 20, 1629; AGI, Indiferente General, leg. 2567, letters of May 14–16, 1629.

123. AGS, Guerra Antigua, leg. 3153, letter from Cádiz, May 22, 1629; Junta de Armadas minutes of May 28, 1629, responding to a letter from don Fadrique de Toledo in Cádiz, May 22, 1629.

124. Ibid., letters of May 30 and June 29 from don Fadrique de Toledo in Cádiz. See also AGI, Indiferente General, leg. 2567, letters and memoranda during the month of June 1629. Many of the papers are marked "extremely urgent" ("luego, luego, luego"); the modern phrase is "con tres luegos."

125. AGS, Guerra Antigua, leg. 3153, letters from don Fadrique de Toledo in Cádiz, June 29, 1629.

126. Ibid., Junta de Armadas minutes of July 5, 1629.

127. Ibid., Junta de Armadas minutes of July 7 and August 12, 1629; AGI, Indiferente General, leg. 2567, memoranda of May 7 and July 11, 1629.

128. AGS, Guerra Antigua, leg. 3153, report of don Juan de Castro y Castilla from Cádiz, August 12, 1629. See also Thompson, *War and Government,* pp. 154–59, for the role Medina-Sidonia and other aristocrats played in military levies.

129. AGI, Indiferente General, leg. 2567, memorandum of June 30, 1629.

130. AGS, Guerra Antigua, leg. 3153, report of October 4, 1629.

131. Ibid., estimate sent from Cádiz by don Juan de Castro and Sebastián de Oleaga, September 8, 1629.

132. Ibid., Junta de Armadas minutes of September 21, 1629.

133. Ibid., Junta de Armadas minutes of October 16, 1629.

134. Ibid., Junta de Armadas minutes of October 25, 1629.

135. Ibid., Junta de Armadas minutes of November 6, 1629.

136. Chaunu, *Séville et l'Atlantique,* 5:154, 178, 184, names a Francisco Díaz Pimienta as the owner of record of two ships sailing in 1628–30.

137. AGS, Guerra Antigua, leg. 3153, Junta de Armadas minutes of October 25 and 28, 1629.

138. Ibid., Junta de Armadas minutes of December 12, 1629.

139. Chaunu, *Séville et l'Atlantique,* 5:170–95.

140. AGS, Guerra Antigua, leg. 3153, Junta de Armadas minutes of October 11, 1629.

141. Ibid., Junta de Armadas minutes of October 11, 1629.

142. Chaunu, *Séville et l'Atlantique,* 5:184–95, 214–24, 242–57, 276–83.

Chapter six. Officers and Men

1. *Recopilación de Leyes de los reynos de las Indias, mandadas imprimir y publicar por el Magestad católica del rey don Carlos II,* 3 vols. (Madrid, 1681; reprint, Madrid: Consejo de la Hispanidad, 1943), 3:207–43. Josephe de Veitia Linaje, *Norte de la contratación de las Indias occidentales* (Seville, 1672), abridged and translated as *The Spanish Rule of Trade to the West-Indies* (London, 1702; reprint, New York: AMS Press, 1977), bk. 1, chaps. 9, 16, defines the jobs of some of these officials.

2. AGI, Consulados, leg. 554. Bureaucratic appointments in a fleet were often made before those of the fleet officers. See AGS, CMC 1a, leg. 1193, for a fleet in northern Spain in 1557.

3. AGI, Consulados, leg. 554; *Recopilación de Leyes de Indias,* 3:221–32.

4. *Recopilación de Leyes de Indias,* 3:207–21.

5. AGS, CMC 3a, leg. 2910, no. 8.

6. An inventory of his goods appears in CMC 3a, leg. 1103, no. 22 in 1638, which may indicate he was in trouble with the crown again. Typically, when a royal official had to answer charges of fraud or mismanagement, his goods were inventoried, in case they were later confiscated to compensate for his malfeasance in office.

7. See Francisco-Felipe Olesa Muñido, *La organización naval de los estados mediterráneos y en especial de España durante los siglos XVI y XVII,* 2 vols. (Madrid: Editorial Naval, 1968), p. 874, for a flow chart of the chain of command. Huguette and Pierre Chaunu, *Séville et l'Atlantique,* 8 vols. in 12 (Paris: A. Colin, 1955–59), 5:170–77.

8. Veitia Linaje, *Rule of Trade,* bk. 2, chap. 1, no. 2.

9. Olesa Muñido, *Organizacion naval,* pp. 423, 597–98; *Colección de documentos inéditos relativos al descubrimiento, conquista y organización de las antiguas posesiones españoles de Ultramar,* 25 vols. (Madrid: Real Academia de la Historia, 1864–1932), 25:242–43; Federico Castro y Bravo, *Las naos españolas en la carrera de las Indias: Armadas y flotas en la segunda mitad del siglo XVI* (Madrid: Editorial Voluntad, 1927), p. 42.

10. Robert Marx, *The Treasure Fleets of the Spanish Main* (Cleveland: World Publishing Co., 1968), pp. 35–38. Mendel Peterson, *The Funnel of Gold: The Trials of the Spanish Treasure Fleets . . .* (Boston: Little, Brown, 1975), p. 65.

11. Juan Escalante de Mendoza, *Itinerario de navegación de los mares y tierras occidentales* (Madrid, 1575), in Cesáreo Fernández Duro, *Disquisiciones náuticas,* 6 vols. (Madrid Sucesores de Rivadeneyra, 1876–81), 5:482–83.

12. Escalante de Mendoza, *Itinerario,* in Fernández Duro, *Disquisiciones náuticas,* 5:484–91; Fernández Duro, *Disquisiciones náuticas,* 3:208–10, 2:126, discusses instructions for the 1629 and 1631 Indies voyages. For laws pertaining to captains-general, see *Recopilación de Leyes de Indias,* 3:141–207, and Veitia Linaje, *Rule of Trade,* bk. 2, chap. 1.

13. Escalante de Mendoza, *Itinerario,* in Fernández Duro, *Disquisiciones náuticas,* 5:484–88; Castro, *Naos españolas,* pp. 91–96.

14. Chaunu, *Séville et l'Atlantique,* 1:115–16; Olesa Muñido, *Organización naval,* pp. 596–97.

15. *Recopilación de Leyes de Indias,* 3:169–74.

16. Olesa Muñido, *Organización naval,* p. 99.

17. Ibid., pp. 598–99; Cesáreo Fernández Duro, *Armada española desde la unión de los reinos de Castilla y de León,* 9 vols. (Madrid, 1895–1903), 4:145.

18. A royal decree in 1647 set a scale of bonds to be posted, with 5,000 ducados for the captain-general of the Armada de la Guardia, 4,000 for his admiral and for captains-general of merchant fleets, and 300 for minor officials. Veitia Linaje, *Rule of Trade,* bk. 2, chap. 1. Some lower officials paid considerably more than the fleet officers, because they handled valuable goods. See the discussion of ships' masters and masters of silver, later in this chapter.

19. Escalante de Mendoza, *Itinerario,* in Fernández Duro, *Disquisiciones náuticas,* 5:492–93.

20. If that was not possible, each fleet had a set list of code words to follow for each day of the week. Fernández Duro, *Disquisiciones náuticas,* 3:209–10.

21. AGI, Patronato Real, leg. 260, no. 2, ramo 44.

22. AGS, Guerra Antigua, leg. 3152, memoranda of April and May 1628. Unless otherwise noted, all debate over the capitanes de mar y guerra appears here.

23. Fernández Duro, *Disquisiciones náuticas,* 2:341–47. The 1633 ordinances of the Armada del Mar Océano continued this practice. *Ordenanzas del buen govierno de la armada del mar océano de 24 de Henero de 1633* (Barcelona, 1678; facsimile edition, Madrid: Instituto Histórico de Marina, 1974), fol. 7.

24. "Diálogo entre un vizcaíno y un montañés," ca. 1635, in Fernández Duro, *Disquisiciones náuticas,* 6:218–20.

25. AGI, Indiferente General, leg. 2567, Junta de Guerra de Indias memorandum of January 15, 1629.

26. The autobiography of Alonso de Contreras presents one of the more colorful recorded careers for a Spanish infantry soldier, an example of the picaresque as well as the edifying. See below, note 29.

27. AGI, Indiferente General, leg. 2589.

28. "Diálogo," in Fernández Duro, *Disquisiciones náuticas,* 6:169–72.

29. Diego García de Palacio, *Instrucción náutica para navegar (1587)* (Madrid: Cultura hispánica, 1944), fol. 111v. Alonso de Contreras, *The Life of Captain Alonso de Contreras, Knight of the Military Order of St. John, Native of Madrid, Written by Himself (1582 to 1633),* trans. Catherine Alison Phillips (New York: Alfred A. Knopf, 1926), pp. 193–95, describes how he kept order as a capitán de mar y guerra among men he calls "death's chosen instruments throughout Andalusia."

30. Louis-André Vigneras, *The Discovery of South America and the Andalusian Voyages* (Chicago: University of Chicago Press, 1976), p. 39.

31. See the ships in a wool fleet under the Duke of Medinaceli in 1571. ARCV, Masas, legs. 260–61.

32. Escalante de Mendoza, *Itinerario,* in Fernández Duro, *Disquisiciones náuticas,* 5:493–515; Chaunu, *Séville et l'Atlantique,* 1:275.

33. García de Palacio, *Instrucción,* fols. 111–12.

34. Olesa Muñido, *Organización naval,* pp. 847–50, has a full discussion of the nautical duties of the master.

35. Escalante de Mendoza, *Itinerario,* in Fernández Duro, *Disquisiciones náuticas,* 5:495.

36. *Actas de la Universidad de Mareantes de Sevilla,* transcribed by María del Carmén Borrego Plá (Seville: Diputación Provincial de Sevilla, 1972).

37. Clarence Henry Haring, *Trade and Navigation between Spain and the Indies in the Time of the Hapsburgs* (Cambridge, Mass.: Harvard University Press, 1918), pp. 314–15.

38. Escalante de Mendoza, *Itinerario,* in Fernández Duro, *Disquisiciones náuticas,* 5:494–99.

39. AGI, Patronato Real, leg. 260, no. 2, ramo 2.

40. *Recopilación de Leyes de Indias,* 3:287–99. Among the many manuscript "fianzas de maestres" (masters' bonds) in the Archive of the Indies, there are often printed documents, with blanks to fill in for the specific master and voyage. See AGI, Contratación, leg. 24, dated June 16, 1635. One ship's master in the 1631 Indies fleet paid just 4,000 ducados, which may have been an individual concession, based on his past record. AGI, Consulados, leg. 1069.

41. Juan de Hevia Bolaños, *Laberinto de comercio terrestre y naval* (Madrid, 1619), pp. 526–36.

42. Veitia Linaje, *Rule of Trade,* bk. 2, chap. 8.

43. Olesa Muñido, *Organización naval,* p. 860; Fernández Duro, *Disquisiciones náuticas,* 2:322, contains a document from 1666 mentioning the ill treatment of masters.

44. Chaunu, *Séville et l'Atlantique,* 1:275. AGI, Consulados, leg. 554, contains instructions for the masters of rations of the 1618 Indies fleets.

45. "Diálogo," in Fernández Duro, *Disquisiciones náuticas,* 6:174–75.

46. Chaunu, *Séville et l'Atlantique,* vol. 5. Eufemio Lorenzo Sanz, *Comercio de España con América en la época de Felipe II,* 2 vols. (Valladolid: Servicio de Publicaciones de la Diputación Provincial de Valladolid, 1980), 2:77–79, attempts to sort out the confusion, but instead adds to it.

47. *Recopilación de Leyes de Indias,* 3:287–99.

48. Veitia Linaje, *Rule of Trade,* bk. 2, chap. 9, no. 1. *Recopilación de Leyes de Indias,* 3:288.

49. Escalante de Mendoza, *Itinerario*, in Fernández Duro, *Disquisiciones náuticas*, 5:509.

50. Ibid., 5:512–13.

51. "Diálogo," in Fernández Duro, *Disquisiciones náuticas*, 6:176–77.

52. García de Palacio, *Instrucción*, fols. 112v–113v.

53. "Diálogo," in Fernández Duro, *Disquisiciones náuticas*, 6:177–78. The 1633 ordinances for the Armada del Mar Océano even required pilots to question sailors on their nautical skills as they signed on for the voyage. *Ordenanzas*, fol. 30v.

54. Pedro Porter y Casanate, *Reparo a errores de la navegación española* (Zarazoza, 1634; facsimile edition, Madrid: Ediciones J. Porrua Tarranzas, 1970), pp. 29–30.

55. Charles Howard Carter, *Secret Diplomacy of the Habsburgs, 1598–1625* (New York: Columbia University press, 1964), p. 35; *Recopilación de Leyes de Indias*, 3:280–81.

56. One list appears in AGI, Patronato Real, leg. 260, no. 2, ramo 30.

57. Veitia Linaje, *Rule of Trade*, bk. 2, chap. 12; Fernández Duro, *Disquisiciones náuticas*, 2:330–41.

58. Porter, *Reparo*, p. 35.

59. AGI, Contratación, leg. 5189, illustrates the selection process.

60. Olesa Muñido, *Organización naval*, pp. 868–71.

61. Hevia Bolaños, *Laberinto*, p. 537.

62. AGI, Patronato Real, leg. 260, no. 1, ramo 33.

63. Pedro de Medina, *Arte de navegar* (Valladolid, 1545), fol. ii.

64. Martín Cortés, *Breve compendio de la sphera y de la arte de navegar* (Seville, 1551; facsimile edition, Zaragoza: Institución Fernando el Católico, 1945).

65. García de Palacio, *Instrucción*, fols. 112v–113v.

66. "Diálogo," in Fernández Duro, *Disquisiciones náuticas*, 6:176–77.

67. Porter, *Reparo*, dedication. See also Salvador García Franco, *Historia del arte y ciencia de navegar*, 2 vols. (Madrid: Instituto Histórico de Marina, 1947).

68. Rodrigo Zamorano, *Arte de navegar* (1581, facsimile edition, Madrid: Instituto Bibliográfico Hispánico, 1973).

69. Porter, *Reparo*, pp. 29–78.

70. See, for example, Haring, *Trade and Navigation*, pp. 298–314. Authors writing in English have been particularly prone to this error, since they often relied on hostile sources such as Thomas Gage, *Travels in the New World* (London, 1648; Norman: University of Oklahoma Press, 1958, and many other editions.) Peterson, *Funnel of Gold*, pp. 75–77, and Timothy Severin, *The Golden Antilles* (New York: Alfred A. Knopf, 1970), pp. 116–17, use Gage heavily.

71. David Watkin Waters, *The Art of Navigation in England in Elizabethan and Early Stuart Times* (London: Hollis and Carter, 1958), pp. 102–7, 313–15.

72. Harry Albert Morton, *The Wind Commands: Sailors and Sailing Ships in the Pacific* (Middletown, Conn.: Wesleyan University Press, 1975), p. 180.

73. AGI, Contratación, leg. 5189, letters of June 15 and 27, 1629.

74. See *Recopilación de Leyes de Indias*, 3:276–86; Veitia Linaje, *Rule of Trade*, bk. 2, chap. 11. Castro, *Naos españolas*, pp. 104–05; AGI, Patronato Real, leg. 260, no. 2, ramo 2. The following discussion is based on many individual pilot examinations for the period in AGI, Contratación, legs. 55A, 55B, 5781.

75. Castro, *Naos españolas*, p. 105.

76. Porter, *Reparo*, p. 120.

77. See, for example, AGI, Contratación, leg. 55B for the 1638 armada, when pilots were particularly scarce.

78. Castro, *Naos españolas*, pp. 108–9.

79. Escalante de Mendoza, *Itinerario*, in Fernández Duro, *Disquisiciones náuticas*, 5:500–502; García de Palacio, *Instrucción*, fols. 113v–115; "Diálogo," in Fernández Duro, *Disquisiciones náuticas*, 6:179–81. The duties of the contramaestre are strikingly

close to those of the loadmaster on a modern cargo aircraft. According to John Guilmartin, who kindly provided this information, the loadmaster is "charged with making out the cargo and passenger manifest, recording the weights and locations of everything loaded, security of stowage and the care and maintenance of the cargo and passenger handling gear."

80. Escalante de Mendoza, *Itinerario,* in Fernández Duro, *Disquisiciones náuticas,* 5:502.

81. García de Palacio, *Instrucción,* fol. 115. The ordinances of the Armada del Mar Océano in 1633 noted that some contramaestres and guardians abused their disciplinary powers, and specified dismissal for those who did not treat their men well. *Ordenanzas,* fols. 8–8v.

82. García de Palacio, *Instrucción,* fols. 115–115v; "Diálogo," in Fernández Duro, *Disquisiciones náuticas,* 6:181–82. Olesa Muñido, *Organización naval,* pp. 871–75.

83. Escalante de Mendoza, *Itinerario,* in Fernández Duro, *Disquisiciones náuticas,* 5:500–502.

84. "Diálogo," Fernández Duro, in *Disquisiciones náuticas,* 6:184.

85. Olesa Muñido, *Organización naval,* p. 882.

86. *Recopilación de Leyes de Indias,* 3:287–99. Haring, *Trade and Navigation,* pp. 200–201. Papers dealing with appointments of masters of silver in the early 1630s appear in AGI, Indiferente General, leg. 2593.

87. AGI, Contratación contains most of the extant registers, although there are also some in Consulados. They have been used by modern treasure hunters to identify the names and cargoes of shipwrecks off the coasts of North and South America and in the Caribbean.

88. AGI, Contratación, leg. 588A.

89. AGI, Indiferente General, leg. 2593, memorandum of the Council of the Indies, dated April 13, 1633.

90. *Recopilación de Leyes de Indias,* 3:289.

91. AGI, Consulados, leg. 554, documents from 1618–1620 fleets.

92. Castro, *Naos españolas,* pp. 110–11; Hevia Bolaños, *Laberinto,* pp. 542–44.

93. "Diálogo," in Fernández Duro, *Disquisiciones náuticas,* 6:186.

94. Ibid., pp. 185–86; *Recopilación de Leyes de Indias,* 3:237–43. See *Ordenanzas,* fol. 38, for the well-known delays of masters in presenting their accounts in the Armada del Mar Océano.

95. Olesa Muñido, *Organización naval,* pp. 883–84, says the chaplain earned several times the wages of an ordinary seaman, but that was not always the case. See appendix C, table 10. According to John F. Guilmartin, *Gunpowder and Galleys: Changing Technology and Mediterranean Warfare at Sea in the Sixteenth Century* (Cambridge: Cambridge University Press, 1974), appendix 5, pp. 293–94, the position of chaplain rose dramatically in pay and status on Spanish galleys during the course of the sixteenth century.

96. Fernández Duro, *Disquisiciones náuticas,* 2:366; *Ordenanzas,* fols. 28v–29.

97. "Diálogo," in Fernández Duro, *Disquisiciones náuticas,* 6:166–67; *Ordencnzas,* fol. 29.

98. Castro, *Naos españolas,* pp. 107–8. Olesa Muñido, *Organización naval,* pp. 883–84.

99. "Diálogo," in Fernández Duro, *Disquisiciones náuticas,* 6:188–89; García de Palacio, *Instrucción,* fols. 117–117v.

100. García de Palacio, *Instrucción,* fols. 116v–117; "Diálogo," in Fernández Duro, *Disquisiciones náuticas,* 6:189–90.

101. Escalante de Mendoza, *Itinerario,* in Fernández Duro, *Disquisiciones náuticas,* 5:505; García de Palacio, *Instrucción,* fol. 117; Veitia Linaje, *Rule of Trade,* bk. 1, chap. 16; "Diálogo," in Fernández Duro, *Disquisiciones náuticas,* 6:189–91.

102. "Diálogo," in Fernández Duro, *Disquisiciones náuticas,* 6:191–92.

103. García de Palacio, *Instrucción,* fol. 128; "Diálogo," in Fernández Duro, *Disquisiciones náuticas,* 6:192; Olesa Muñido, *Organización naval,* p. 889.

104. AGS, Estado, leg. 559, no. 67, a document from 1570.

105. Nicolás Sánchez-Albornoz, "Gastos y alimentación de un ejército en el siglo XVI según un presupuesto de la época," *Cuadernos de Historia de España* 14 (1950): 153.

106. Olesa Muñido, *Organización naval,* pp. 850–53. AGI, Patronato Real, leg. 260, no. 2, ramo 42, describes manning ratios on Indies merchant vessels.

107. AGS, CMC 1a, leg. 1563. Estánislao Jaime de Labayru y Goicoechea, *Historia general del Señorío de Vizcaya* (Bilbao: La Gran Enciclopedia Vasca, 1968–72), 4: 499–501.

108. AGS, Guerra Antigua, leg. 3152, memorandum of October 17, 1628, expressed as 16 mariners and 26 infantrymen for each 100 toneladas.

109. *Ordenanzas,* fol. 2v. The 1631 decree is in AGM, mss. 2095, doc. 10, fol. 50, expressed as 18 mariners and 25 infantrymen for each 100 toneladas.

110. "Diálogo," in Fernández Duro, *Disquisiciones náuticas,* 6:154–55.

111. Olesa Muñido, *Organización naval,* pp. 850–53, expressed as 20.4 mariners and 24 infantrymen for each 100 toneladas.

112. AGM, mss. 471, fols. 167–74.

113. For mentions of crew shortages in various periods, see Labayru, *Historia General,* 4:504–5 for 1583; I. A. A. Thompson, *War and Government in Habsburg Spain* (London: Athlone Press, 1976), pp. 204–05; AGM, Colección Vargas Ponce, I, for the 1580s; AGS, Guerra Antigua, legs. 3149–53 for the 1620s; and "Diálogo," in Fernández Duro, *Disquisiciones náuticas,* 6:210–12 for about 1635.

114. AGS, Guerra Antigua, leg. 3149 contains the preliminary discussions of this matter in the Junta de Armadas, and numerous other documents dealing with its provisions. Gervasio de Artiñano y de Galdácano, *Gente de mar* (Barcelona, 1934), pp. 127–28, mentions a similar decree dated October 5, 1605, although this may not have been put into effect. Some sixteenth-century lists are in Martín Fernández de Navarrete, comp., *Colección de documentos y manuscriptos compilados,* ed. by Julio Guillén Tato, 32 vols. (Nendeln, Lichtenstein: Kraus-Thompson Organization, 1971), 22(1), docs. 34, 36, fols. 118–122v.

115. AGS, Guerra Antigua, leg. 3149, memorandum of October 31, 1625. AGS, CMC 3a, leg. 627, which includes expenses for building Arana's ships, also mentions the costs for parchment and other supplies for libros de matrícula in Bilbao.

116. Escalante de Mendoza, *Itinerario,* in Fernández Duro, *Disquisiciones náuticas,* 5:473–74.

117. Quoted by M. J. Ferreira David, "Aperçu historique des types de navires à travers les siècles et influence des navires ibériques sur la construction naval européenne," *Colloque international d'histoire maritime, 5th, Lisbon, 1960* (Paris: S.E.V.P.E.N., 1966), p. 149.

118. AGS, Guerra Antigua, leg. 3153, Junta de Armadas memorandum of October 25, 1629.

119. García de Palacio, *Instrucción,* fols. 119–119v.

120. Contreras, *Life,* p. 25.

121. "Diálogo," in Fernández Duro, *Disquisiciones náuticas,* 6:199–200.

122. Hevia Bolaños, *Laberinto,* pp. 537–41.

123. See AGI, Consulados, leg. 554, documents dated July 24, 1618, for the fleet that left Cádiz July 6. See *Recopilación de Leyes de Indias,* 3:299–306, for laws pertaining to sailors.

124. Escalante de Mendoza, *Itinerario,* in Fernández Duro, *Disquisiciones náuticas,* 5:477–78. See also García de Palacio, *Instrucción,* fols. 119v–120, and "Diálogo," in Fernández Duro, *Disquisiciones náuticas,* 6:201.

125. García de Palacio, *Instrucción,* fol. 120.

126. Escalante, *Itinerario*, in Fernández Duro, *Disquisiciones náuticas*, 5:479–82; García de Palacio, *Instrucción*, fol. 120; "Diálogo," in Fernández Duro, *Disquisiciones náuticas*, 6:201–2. The will of a page who died on the homebound voyage in 1631 is in AGI, Contratación, leg. 5581, no. 8.

127. Castro, *Naos españolas*, pp. 120–21; Olesa Muñido, *Organización naval*, pp. 884–85; Francisco-Felipe Olesa Muñido, "La marina oceánica de los Austrias," in *El buque en la armada española* (Madrid: Silex, 1981), pp. 128–29, 136.

128. "Diálogo," in Fernández Duro, *Disquisiciones náuticas*, 6:196.

129. Olesa Muñido, *Organización naval*, p. 886.

130. Castro, *Naos españolas*, p. 120.

131. "Diálogo," in Fernández Duro, *Disquisiciones náuticas*, 6:196–97.

132. Ibid., 6:192–95.

133. Olesa Muñido, *Organización naval*, p. 888.

134. AGI, Consulados, leg. 1040, book of the *San Juan Baptista*.

135. Ibid., book of the *San Felipe*.

136. *Recopilación de Leyes de Indias*, 3:243–61, has laws about the infantry companies. Sánchez-Albornoz, "Gastos," discusses a 1577–78 infantry regiment (tercio) containing ten companies of 200 pikemen and two companies of 250 harquebusiers.

137. Veitia Linaje, *Rule of Trade*, bk. 2, chap. 2.

138. Castro, *Naos españolas*, pp. 119–20.

139. Haring, *Trade and Navigation*, pp. 219–20; Olesa Muñido, Organización naval, pp. 890–92.

140. AGI, Indiferente General, leg. 2567, memorandum of the Junta de Guerra de Indias, January 15, 1629.

141. "Diálogo," in Fernández Duro, *Disquisiciones náuticas*, 6:160–62.

142. René Quatrefages, *Los tercios españoles (1567–77)* (Madrid: Fundación Universitaria Española, 1979), pp. 147–51. See pp. 133–77 for the duties on land of all infantry officers.

143. "Diálogo," in Fernández Duro, *Disquisiciones náuticas*, 6:164.

144. AGM, Colección Sanz—Simancas, mss. 1949, fols. 40–42.

145. "Diálogo," in Fernández Duro, *Disquisiciones náuticas*, 6:163. Unless otherwise noted, discussion of the infantry comes from pages 160–68 of this source and from Veitia Linaje, *Rule of Trade*, bk. 2, chap. 2. According to John Guilmartin, muskets of the time were around .82–.92 caliber, harquebuses around .69.

146. "Diálogo," in Fernández Duro, *Disquisiciones náuticas*, 6:168.

147. See AGI, Consulados, legs. 1038–41, and libs. 497–541 for dozens of these books from the 1630s.

148. AGI, Consulados, leg. 1040, the company of Captain Vicente de la Torre, 1634–35.

149. Chaunu, *Séville et l'Atlantique*, 4:510. See also Fernández Duro, *Disquisiciones náuticas*, 2:168.

150. Castro, *Naos españolas*, p. 120.

151. AGI, Consulados, legs. 1040, 1048.

152. Olesa Muñido, *Organización naval*, pp. 867–71.

153. Olesa Muñido, "Marina oceánica," p. 112, for estimates in about 1500; AGS, Estado, leg. 559, fol. 67, for wages on a voyage to Flanders in 1570. Olesa Muñido, *Organización naval*, pp. 875–76.

154. Earl J. Hamilton, "Wages and Subsistence on Spanish Treasure Ships, 1503–1660," *Journal of Political Economy* (1929): 447–50, said that ordinary seamen's wages rose faster than those of officers in the middle third of the sixteenth century, cushioning the effects of inflation.

155. See Frederic C. Lane, *Venice: A Maritime Republic* (Baltimore, Md.: Johns Hopkins University Press, 1973), pp. 166–70, 364–74, for the parallel degradation of galley crews in Venice.

156. AGS, Guerra Antigua, leg. 3152, Junta de Armadas memorandum of October 17, 1628.

157. Ibid. Quatrefages, *Los tercios españoles,* p. 170.

158. AGM, mss. 471, fols. 157–74.

159. "Diálogo," in Fernández Duro, *Disquisiciones náuticas,* 6:155–56, Auguste Antoine Thomazi, *Les flottes de l'or: Histoire des galions d'Espagne,* rev. ed. (Paris: Payot, 1956), p. 75.

160. "Diálogo," in Fernández Duro, *Disquisiciones náuticas,* 6:155–56. The ordinances for the Armada del Mar Océano charged soldiers only 18.75 reales and infantry captains 45 reales for their rations, with other ranks in between. *Ordenanzas,* fol. 37v. See also Sánchez-Albornoz, "Gastos," pp. 151–55.

Chapter SEVEN. Shipboard Life

1. AGM, C.F. 134.

2. "Diálogo entre un vizcaíno y un montañés" (ca. 1635), in Cesáreo Fernández Duro, *Disquisiciones náuticas,* 6 vols, (Madrid: Sucesores de Rivadeneyra, 1876–81), 6:172–78.

3. Ibid. pp. 181–82.

4. Ibid. pp. 188–89.

5. Ibid. pp. 200–01.

6. Ibid. pp. 162–63.

7. Alonso de Contreras, *The Life of Captain Alonso de Contreras, Knight of the Military Order of St. John, Native of Madrid, Written by Himself (1582 to 1633),* trans. Catherine Alison Phillips (New York: Alfred A. Knopf, 1926), pp. 192–94.

8. Nicolas Louis Scrattish, "New Perspectives on Castilian Migration to the *Audiencias* of Mexico and Lima, 1540–1580" (Ph.D. diss., University of California, San Diego, 1975), p. 58.

9. In Lope de Vega's original, the passage is:

Lo que es más razón que alabés,
es ver salir destas naves
Tanta diversa nación,
Las cosas que desembarcan,
El salir y entrar en ellas,
y el volver después a vellas
Con otras muchas que embarcan.
Por cuchillos el francés,
Mercerías y Ruán,
Lleva aceite; el alemán
Trae lienzo, fustán, llantes;
Carga vino de Alanís.
Hierro trae el vizcaíno,
El cuartón, el tiro, el pino;
El indiano el ambar-gris,
La perla, el oro, la plata,
Palo de Campeche, cueros.
Toda esta arena es dineros.
        "El arenal de Sevilla," Act I, scene 1.

10. Scrattish, "New Perspectives," p. 91; Antonio Domínguez Ortiz, *Orto y Ocaso de Sevilla: Estudio sobre la prosperidad y decadencia de la ciudad durante los siglos XVI y XVII* (Seville: Diputación Provincial, 1946), p. 89.

11. Eugenio de Salazar, "Carta escrita al Licenciado Miranda de Ron, 1573," in Fernández Duro, *Disquisiciones náuticas,* 2:178–200.

12. Ibid., p. 181.

13. Ibid., pp. 181–84.

14. Fernández Duro, *Disquisiciones náuticas,* 2:161.

15. *Ibid.,* pp. 160–61.

16. Salazar, in Fernández Duro, *Disquisiciones náuticas,* 2:179.

17. Juan Escalante de Mendoza, *Itinerario de navegación de los mares y tierras occidentales* (Madrid, 1575), printed in Fernández Duro, *Disquisiciones náuticas,* 5:514–15.

18. Fernández Duro, *Disquisiciones náuticas,* 2:163–64.

19. Cited in Federico Castro y Bravo, *Las naos españolas en la carrera de las Indias: Armadas y flotas en la segunda mitad del siglo XVI* (Madrid: Editorial Voluntad, 1927), pp. 140–41.

20. Antonio de Guevara, *Arte de marear* (Valladolid, 1539), in Cesáreo Fernández Duro, *Disquisiciones náuticas,* 2:33.

21. Fernández Duro, *Disquisiciones náuticas,* 2:408–54. See also the lament of an Italian apothecary aboard the Manila galleon in 1697, quoted at length in Warren L. Cook, *Floodtide of Empire: Spain and the Pacific Northwest, 1543–1819* (New Haven, Conn.: Yale University Press, 1973), pp. 6–7.

22. Fernández Duro, *Disquisiciones náuticas,* 2:148–49; Cristóbal de Villalón, *Viaje a Turquía, 1552–55,* 3rd ed. (Buenos Aires and Mexico City: Espasa Calpe, 1942), p. 46; Pedro María González, *Tratado de las enfermedades de la gente de mar* (Madrid: Imprenta Real, 1805), pp. 367–85. See the detailed description of French galley life in Paul W. Bamford, *Fighting Ships and Prisons: The Mediterranean Galleys of France in the Age of Louis XIV* (Minneapolis: University of Minnesota Press, 1973), pp. 200–24.

23. Samuel Eliot Morison, *Admiral of the Ocean Sea: A Life of Christopher Columbus* (Boston: Little, Brown and Company, 1942), pp. 125, 177.

24. González, *Tratado,* pp. 385–98; Fernández Duro, *Disquisiciones náuticas,* 2:262–64.

25. Fernández Duro, *Disquisiciones náuticas,* 2:382–88, 472–90. The date of the stories is not clear in Fernández Duro. According to John Guilmartin, primers such as fulminate of mercury were not in use before 1750 or so.

26. Salazar in Fernández Duro, *Disquisiciones náuticas,* 2:393.

27. Antonio Vázquez de Espinosa, "Tratado verdadero del viaje y navegación de este año de seiscientos y veinte y dos que hizo la flota de Nueva España y Honduras" (Malaga, 1623), in *Revista de Indias* 36(January–June 1976):287–352, discourse X, pp. 318–21; discourse XI, pp. 321–23.

28. Castro, *Naos españolas,* p. 136, citing don García de Toledo.

29. José M. Gella Iturriaga, *Refranero del mar,* 2 vols. (Madrid: Instituto Histórico de la Marina, 1944), 1:42. "Contra fortuna no hay arte ninguna."

30. Ibid. "Contra las adversidades y del tiempo la inclemencia, el escudo es la paciencia."

31. Ibid., 1:16–17. One version is "Anda por mar y aprenderás a orar."

32. Quoted from the picaresque novel *Guzmán de Alfarache* in Castro, *Naos españolas,* pp. 152, 156–59.

33. Gella, *Refranero,* 1:66. "Dinero guardado, barco amarrado."

34. Ibid., p. 30. "Buque sobrecargado, capitán abandonado."

35. Ibid., p. 82, "En buen tiempo no faltan pilotos"; p. 51, "Cuando la nave está perdida, todos son pilotos."

36. Ibid., p. 82. "Viento en popa y mar bonanza, navegaría Sancho Panza."

37. Quoted in Castro, *Naos españolas,* p. 148.

38. Salazar, in Fernández Duro, *Disquisiciones náuticas,* 2:183–4. Guevara, *Arte de marear,* pp. 43–44, described nautical jargon purely for comic effect, and the English renegade Thomas Gage remembered only "the hideous noise of the mariners hoisting up sails." Thomas Gage, *Travels in the New World,* ed. J. Eric S. Thompson (Norman: University of Oklahoma press, 1958), p. 35.

39. Salazar, in Fernández Duro, *Disquisiciones náuticas,* 2:184–86.

40. Fernández Duro, *Disquisiciones náuticas,* 2:265–66.

41. Gella, *Refranero,* 1:71.

42. "Diálogo," in Fernández Duro, *Disquisiciones náuticas,* 6:178.

43. Samuel Eliot Morison, *The Great Explorers: The European Discovery of America* (New York: Oxford University Press, 1978), p. 498, without mentioning a source. It is difficult to reconcile the accepted interpretation with several mentions in the "Diálogo" written about 1635 that the watch shifts were three hours long, rather than four. "Diálogo," in Fernández Duro, *Disquisiciones náuticas,* 6:168, 199. Because there are numerous other errors in the "Diálogo," however, it is possible that the original was transcribed incorrectly.

44. Fernández Duro, *Disquisiciones náuticas,* 2:179–80. Unless otherwise noted, the translations are mine.

> Bendita sea la luz,
> y la Santa Veracruz,
> y el Señor de la verdad,
> y la Santa Trinidad;
> Bendita sea el alma,
> y el Señor que nos la manda;
> Bendito sea el día
> y el Señor que nos le envía.

45. "Dios nos dé buenos dias; buen viaje; buen pasaje haga la nao, señor Capitán y maestre y buena compaña, amén; así faza buen viaje, faza; muy buenos días de Dios a vuestras mercedes, señores de popa y proa." Salazar, in Fernández Duro, *Disquisiciones náuticas,* 2:179–80.

46. "Buena es la que va, mejor es la que viene; una es pasada y en dos muele, mas molerá si Dios quisiere; cuenta y pasa, que buen viaje faza." Salazar, in Fernández Duro, *Disquisiciones náuticas,* 2:191.

47. "Una va pasada, y en dos muele; mas molerá si mi Dios querrá; a mi Dios pidamos, que buen viaje hagamos; y a la que es Madre de Dios y abogada nuestra, que nos libre de agua de bomba y tormentas." Fernández Duro, *Disquisiciones náuticas,* 2:261. It is possible that the bell Fernández Duro mentioned actually came into use later, because Morison did not find it in the sixteenth-century documents he used. Morison, *Great Explorers,* p. 498.

48. Castro, *Naos españolas,* p. 146.

49. "Al cuarto, al cuarto, señores marineros de buena parte; al cuarto, al cuarto, en buen hora de la guardia del señor piloto, que es la hora; leva, leva, leva." Salazar, in Fernández Duro, *Disquisiciones náuticas,* 2:192.

50. "Amén, y Dios nos dé buenas noches; buen viaje, buen pasaje haga la nao, señor capitán y maestre y buena compañía." Ibid., 2:191.

51. Ibid.

> Bendita la hora en que Dios nació,
> Santa María que le parió,
> San Juan que le bautizó.
> La guarda es tomada;
> La ampolleta muele,
> Buen viaje haremos,
> Si Dios quisiere.

52. Salazar, in Fernández Duro, *Disquisiciones náuticas,* 2:195. The compass rose on traditional nautical maps was divided into thirty-two positions, each designating a possible wind direction.

53. Vázquez, "Tratado," discourse IX, pp. 315–18.

54. Castro, *Naos españolas,* pp. 142–43. Fernández Duro, *Disquisiciones náuticas,* 3:212–19, includes a list of rules for religious observations on board Mediterranean galleys. Gage, *Travels,* pp. 18–19, describes a series of elaborate religious observations on the 1625 fleet going to New Spain.

55. AGM, Colección Vargas Ponce, XVII, doc. 217, fols. 370–71, contains accounts for a shipboard holiday in 1667.

56. Miguel de Cervantes Saavedra, "La española inglesa," *Novelas ejemplares,* 2 vols. (Madrid: Fenicia, 1970), 2:251–5.

57. Gella, *Refranero,* 1:74. "El muerto es del mar, cuando la tierra lejos está," and "Al que muere en el barco, lo reclama el charco." The funeral of a friar poisoned by an Indian arrow in 1625 featured a requiem mass sung by his companion friars. Gage, *Travels,* p. 28.

58. Salazar, in Fernández Duro, *Disquisiciones náuticas,* 2:192–94.

59. Gage, *Travels,* p. 29.

60. Auguste Antoine Thomazi, *Les flottes de l'or: Histoire des galions d'Espagne,* rev. ed. (Paris: Payot, 1956), pp. 192–93. Castro, *Naos españolas,* pp. 150–52; Gage, *Travels,* pp. 15–38.

61. Gella, *Refranero,* 1:62. "De popa a proa, cuanto se embarca se empeora," but "Mareado el buen vino de Jerez; si valía a cinco, vale a diez." This was true even on voyages in the Mediterranean. See Guevara, *Arte de marear,* pp. 27–31, 41, 50–52.

62. Fernández Duro, *Disquisiciones náuticas,* 2:162–63.

63. Earl J. Hamilton, "Wages and Subsistence on Spanish Treasure Ships, 1503–1660," *Journal of Political Economy* (1929): 435.

64. Vázquez, *Tratado,* discourse XI, pp. 321–23.

65. Harry Albert Morton, *The Wind Commands: Sailors and Sailing Ships in the Pacific* (Middletown, Conn.: Wesleyan University Press, 1975), p. 305.

66. AGM, C.F. 134, fol. 10.

67. Fernández Duro, *Disquisiciones náuticas,* 2:366–67.

68. Morison, *Admiral of the Ocean Sea,* p. 620.

69. Fernández Duro, *Disquisiciones náuticas,* 2:142–43.

70. Villalón, *Viaje a Turquía,* p. 45.

71. Contreras, *Life,* 161.

72. Vázquez, *Tratado,* discourse XI, pp. 321–23.

73. AGI, Patronato Real, leg. 260, no. 2, *ramo* 14. González, *Tratado,* pp. 435–44, discusses ways to preserve foods for long voyages.

74. Vázquez, "Tratado," discourse IX, p. 305, discourse X, p. 320.

75. "A quien no trabaja, una gallina; a quien trabaja, una sardina." Gella, *Refranero,* 1.8. "Quien trabaja come pan; y quien no trabaja, salmón y faisán." Ibid., p. 184.

76. In 1621, the crown banned all livestock from the galleons, because they not only fouled the decks but hindered the ship's military exercises. *Recopilación de Leyes de los reynos de las Indias, mandadas imprimir y publicar por el Magestad católica del rey don Carlos II,* 3 vols. (Madrid: 1681; reprint, Madrid: Consejo de la Hispanidad, 1943), 3:338. The ban cannot have been very effective, however, since chickens, at least, appear in nearly every account I have seen for Indies fleets.

77. Vázquez, "Tratado," discourse X, p. 320.

78. Diego García de Palacio, *Instrucción náutica para navegar (1587)* (Madrid: Cultura hispánica, 1944), fols. 115v–116v.

79. Gella, *Refranero,* 1:166. "Pescado salado, bien cocido y mal asado."

80. Scrattish, "New Perspectives," p. 54, citing a document from 1576.

81. *Ordenanzas del buen govierno de la armada del mar océano de 24 de Henero de 1633* (facsimile edition, Madrid: Instituto Histórico de Marina, 1974), fols. 36v–37, 43v. Cooking arrangements and the danger from fire are not as well known as they should be. Ship model makers, purporting to represent Spanish ships of the period,

sometimes show large brick stoves deep in the hold, which would have been highly improbable in the days of wooden ships.

82. *Recopilación de Leyes de Indias,* 3:338.

83. AGS, Guerra Antigua, leg. 3153, letter of May 30, 1629.

84. Quoted in Fernández Duro, *Disquisiciones náuticas,* 2:99–101.

85. García de Palacio, *Instruccion náutica,* 115v–116v.

86. Salazar, in Fernández Duro, *Disquisiciones náuticas,* 2:187–88. On some ships in the Mediterranean, the crew may have gone below decks to eat. Alonso Enríquez de Guzmán, *The Life and Acts of Don Alonso Enríquez de Guzmán, a Knight of Seville, of the Order of Santiago, A.D. 1518 to 1543,* trans. Clements R. Markham (London: Hakluyt Society, 1st ser., 1862), 29:25–26, clearly describes such a mealtime from the early sixteenth century.

87. Salazar, in Fernández Duro, *Disquisiciones náuticas,* 2:188–89.

88. Enríquez de Guzmán, *Life,* pp. 80–81.

89. AGS, Estado, leg. 513, fol. 165.

90. AGS, Guerra Antigua, leg. 49, fol. 305.

91. AGS, Estado, leg. 513, fols. 165–68, provisions bought in 1555 for the homecoming voyage of Charles I from Flanders.

92. See Nicolás Sánchez-Albornoz, "Gastos y alimentación de un ejército en el siglo XVI según un presupuesto de la época," *Cuadernos de Historia de España* 14 (1950): 165–69, for a comparison of land and sea diets in 1578.

93. AGS, CG, leg. 3019. There are hundreds of provisioning accounts and dietaries for European fleets in AGI, Contaduría; AGS, CMC 1a, 2a, 3a, and CG.

94. Gregorio Marañón, "La vida en las galeras en tiempo de Felipe II," *Vida e historia,* pp. 67–97 (Buenos Aires, 1937); Fernández Duro, *Disquisiciones náuticas,* 2:134–35; Castro, *Naos españolas,* pp. 166–67, 186–88.

95. Villalón, *Viaje a Turquía,* p. 45.

96. Luis Ortiz, *Memorial del contador Luis Ortiz a Felipe II (1558)* (Madrid: Instituto de España, 1970), p. 94.

97. See the complete list in Martín Fernández de Navarrete, *Colección de viajes y descubrimientos que hicieron por mar los españoles,* 5 vols. (Madrid: Imprenta Nacional, 1829–59), 4:10–11.

98. Hamilton, "Wages and Subsistence," p. 434.

99. See, for example, Robert Marx, *The Treasure Fleets of the Spanish Main* (Cleveland: World Publishing Co., 1968), p. 38; Mendel Peterson, *The Funnel of Gold: The Trials of the Spanish Treasure Fleets . . .* (Boston: Little, Brown, 1975), p. 85, both of which mention rations that bear little resemblance to information in the documentary sources.

100. Hamilton, "Wages and Subsistence," p. 438. Daily rations in the early nineteenth century allowed only eighteen ounces of biscuit daily, about four ounces of salted meat and five ounces of menestra, which suggests that there had been a decline from the sixteenth century standards. González, *Tratado,* pp. 12–13.

101. "Diálogo" in Fernández Duro, *Disquisiciones náuticas,* 6:158–60. There are numerous mathematical errors and other confusing elements in the "Diálogo" dietary, but it is still helpful if used with care. Rations for the 1630 Indies fleet allowed four meat days, two fish days, and one cheese day each week. AGS, Guerra Antigua, leg. 3153, memorandum dated October 11, 1629.

102. AGS, CMC 3a, leg. 2229, no. 9.

103. AGM, Colección Vargas Ponce, IX, doc. 157, fol. 213; XII, doc. 176, fol. 287; XII, doc. 178, fols. 289–289v. Fernández Duro, *Disquisiciones náuticas,* 2:134–35, mentions a similar cut in the biscuit ration on galleys in 1678 and 1679.

104. Hamilton, "Wages and Subsistence," p. 435.

105. Scrattish, "New Perspectives," pp. 115–16.

106. AGS, CMC 3a, leg. 1103, no. 1; AGI, Contaduria, leg. 555, ramos 1 and 2.

107. Hamilton, "Wages and Subsistence"; Sánchez-Albornoz, "Gastos"; Frank Spooner, "Régimes alimentaires d'autrefois: Proportions et calculs en calories," *Annales: E. S. C.* 16 (1961):568–74; "Régimes alimentaires d'autrefois: Deux nouveaux cas espagnols," *Annales: E. S. C.* 17 (1962):93–94.

108 Unless otherwise noted, modern calculations of food content come from Bernice K. Watt and Annabel L. Merrill, et al., for the United States Department of Agriculture, *Handbook of the Nutritional Contents of Foods* (New York: Dover Publications, Inc., 1975). Modern nutritional information comes from R. Passmore et al., *Handbook on Human Nutritional Requirements* (Rome: Food and Agriculture Organization, United Nations, 1974).

109. Fernández Duro. *Disquisiciones náuticas,* 2:142–43. Ship's biscuit in the British navy was evidently almost unleavened, or at least was not allowed to rise. James Lind, *A Treatise of the Scurvy,* excerpted in Christopher Lloyd, ed., *The Health of Seamen: Selections from the works of Dr. James Lind, Sir Gilbert Blane and Dr. Thomas Trotter* (London: Navy Records Society, 1965), p. 15. Detailed directions for making ship's biscuit in France appear in Jacques Savary des Bruslons, *The Universal Dictionary of Trade and Commerce,* trans. Malachy Postlethwayt, 2 vols. (London: J. and P. Knapton, 1751–55), 1:285–86.

110. Villalón, *Viaje a Turquía,* p. 45.

111. Lind, *Treatise of the Scurvy,* in Lloyd, p. 15.

112. R.-J. Bernard, "Peasant Diet in Eighteenth-Century Gévaudan," in *European Diets from Pre-Industrial to Modern Times,* ed. Elborg and Robert Forster (New York: Harper Torchbooks, 1975), p. 28, thought the pigs in southcentral France in the mid-eighteenth century were "very poorly nourished" but at the same time he judged their salt pork to be extremely fat.

113. AGM, Colección Sanz—Simancas, ms. 1949, fols. 9–17; AGS, CMC 3a, leg. 1103, no. 1.

114. Passmore, et al., *Human Nutritional Requirements,* p. 9.

115. Sánchez-Albornoz, "Gastos,", pp. 171–72.

116. Bernard, "Peasant Diet," p. 35.

117. Hamilton, "Wages and Subsistence," pp. 434–38.

118. Spooner, "Régimes alimentaires: Deux nouveaux cas," pp. 93–94; Passmore, et al., *Human Nutritional Requirements,* p. 21.

119. Passmore, et al., *Human Nutritional Requirements,* pp. 16–21.

120. Ibid.

121. See the discussion in John K. Evans, "*Plebs rustica.* The Peasantry of Classical Italy. II: The Peasant Economy," *American Journal of Ancient History* 5 (1980):148. An example of an overly high standard was the one set by the Food and Nutrition Board of the National Academy of Sciences in 1974 for "the maintenance of good nutrition of practically all healthy people in the U.S.A." in the *Sourcebook on Food and Nutrition,* eds. Ioannis S. Scarpa and Helen Chilton Kiefer (Chicago: Marquis Academic Media, 1978), p. 100.

122. Bernard, "Peasant Diet," pp. 37–39; Spooner, "Régimes alimentaires: Deux nouveaux cas," p. 94.

123. Passmore, et al, *Human Nutritional Requirements,* p. 19.

124. Ibid., pp. 25–28. *Nutritional Requirements of Man: A Conspectus of Research* (New York: Nutrition Foundation, 1980), pp. 79, 81.

125. Passmore, et al., *Human Nutritional Requirements,* pp. 43–45.

126. Ibid., p. 35; *Nutritional Requirements of Man,* pp. 249–52.

127. Lind, *Treatise of the Scurvy,* in Lloyd, *Health of Seamen,* p. 9; Passmore, et al., *Human Nutritional Requirements,* p. 33; *Nutritional Requirements of Man,* pp. 249–60.

128. Morton, *The Wind Commands,* p. 275; Navarrete, *Colección de viajes y descubrimientos,* 4:10–11, 182–183.

129. *The First Voyage Round the World, by Magellan, Translated from the Accounts of*

Pigafetta, and other Contemporary Writers, comp. and trans. Lord Stanley of Alderley (London: Hakluyt Society, 1st ser., 1874), 52:64–66.

130. See descriptions of Vizcaíno's expedition in *Colección de diarios y relaciones* (Madrid: Archivo General de la Marina, 1944–47), 4:39–68; Donald C. Cutter, ed. *The California Coast: A Bilingual Edition of Documents from the Sutro Collection,* trans. George Butler Griffin in 1891 (Norman: University of Oklahoma Press, 1969), pp. 64–117.

131. Lind, *A Treatise of the Scurvy* (Edinburgh, 1753).

132. An excellent summary of Anson's harrowing voyage and Lind's subsequent search for a preventive for scurvy is in James Watt, "Some Consequences of Nutritional Disorders in Eighteenth-century British Circumnavigations," in *Starving Sailors,* ed. James Watt et al. (London: National Maritime Museum, 1981), pp. 51–59. Several other articles in the volume touch on the story as well.

133. Julián de Zulueta and Lola Higueras, "Health and Navigation in the South Seas: The Spanish Experience," in Watt, ed., *Starving Sailors,* pp. 95–97; Cook, *Floodtide of Empire,* pp. 57, 119; Cutter, ed., *California Coast,* pp. 188–273.

134. González, *Tratado,* pp. xxxiii–xxxiv, 213–80.

135. Andrés Cristóbal Cruz, "The Manila Galleons," *Orientations* (February 1970):67.

136. González, *Tratado,* pp. 213–15.

137. Passmore, et al., *Human Nutritional Requirements,* p. 33.

138. González, *Tratado,* p. 427.

139. [Magellan], *First Voyage,* 52:65.

140. Henry Kamen, *Spain in the Later Seventeenth Century, 1665–1700* (London and New York: Longman, 1980), pp. 165–67.

141. M. Desamparados Sánchez Vilar, *Viaje desde Estella a Sevilla: Cuentos de un viaje (1352)* (Valencia, 1962).

142. Juan Sorapán de Rieros, *Medicina española contenida en proverbios vulgares de nuestra lengua (Granada, 1615),* ed. Antonio Castillo de Lucas (Madrid: Cosano, 1949), pp. 117–25, 131.

143. María del Carmen Simón Palmer, *Alimentación y sus circunstancias en el Real Alcázar de Madrid* (Madrid: Instituto de Estudios Madrileños, 1982).

144. Charles Lawrence Carlson, "The Vulgar Sort: Common People in *Siglo de Oro* Madrid" (Ph.D. diss., University of California, Berkeley, 1977), pp. 83–102; Vicente Palacio Atard, "Alimentación y abastecimiento de Madrid en la segunda mitad del siglo XVIII" (Madrid: Ayuntamiento de Madrid, 1966).

145. Gella, *Refranero,* 1:34. "Carne y pescado en una comida, acortan la vida."

146. Sorapán, *Medicina,* pp. 215–20.

147. See Luisa Cogliato Arano, *The Medieval Health Handbook "Tacuinum Sanitatis"* (New York: George Braziller, 1976) for the general properties of foods according to the doctrine of humors.

148. Sorapán, *Medicina,* pp. 238–55. When the third Duke of Alba held his posting in the Netherlands, he had his wife send him fresh limes, presumably for their value in the kitchen rather than for their antiscorbutic properties. William S. Maltby, *Alba: A Biography of Fernando Álvarez de Toledo, Third Duke of Alba, 1507–1582* (Berkeley, Los Angeles, and London: University of California Press, 1983), p. 254. Nonetheless, they could have helped him avoid scurvy in the winter.

149. Sorapán, *Medicina,* pp. 291–94, has a full discussion of the refrain, "El queso es sano, que da el avaro."

150. Ibid., pp. 281–91. See Evans, *"Plebs rustica,"* for the growing seasons of many of the same plants in Italy.

151. Contreras, *Life,* p. 137.

152. Sorapán, *Medicina,* pp. 261–69; Juan Dantín Cereceda, *La alimentación española, sus diferentes tipos* (Madrid: Colección geográfica, 1, 1934), pp. 56–61.

153. Estánislao Jaime de Labayru y Goicoechea, *Historia general del Señorío de Vizcaya* (Bilbao: La Gran Enciclopedia Vasca, 1968–72), 4:288.

154. Dantín, *Alimentación,* pp. 20–21.

155. Fernández Duro, *Disquisiciones náuticas,* 2:134–35; Marañón, "Vida," pp. 72–75; Passmore, *Human Nutritional Requirements,* pp. 36–39.

156. González, *Tratado,* pp. 104–327.

157. Marañón, "Vida," p. 85.

158. Gella, *Refranero,* 1:74.

159. An eighteenth-century collection of instruments is illustrated in AGM, Marqués de la Victoria, *Diccionario,* pl. 100.

160. AGI, Contaduría, leg. 279, no. 1, medicines from 1554.

161. Lists of ships' medicines from the 1630s to the 1660s can be found in AGS, CMC 3a, legs. 627, 1323, 1934, 3337; AGI, Consulados, leg. 1051 bis; AGM, Colección Vargas Ponce, XII, doc. 78, fols. 115–116v; AGM, mss. 580, fols. 107–115.

162. AGM, Colección Vargas Ponce, XII, doc. 78, fols. 115–116v.

163. *Ordenanzas del buen govierno de la armada del mar océano de 24 de Henero de 1633* (Barcelona, 1678; facsimile edition, Madrid: Instituto Histórico de Marina, 1974), fol. 29.

164. Sorapán, *Medicina,* pp. 404–28, discusses the medicinal properties of many ordinary foods and gives recipes of cures for various ailments.

165. AGS, CMC 3a, leg. 1870, no. 3.

166. Sorapán, *Medicina,* p. 220.

167. Hamilton, "Wages and Subsistence," p. 441, citing AGI, Contratación, 36-3-19/7. The remedies had not changed much by the nineteenth century, although items such as chocolate had been added. González, *Tratado,* pp. 362–66.

168. *Ordenanzas, fols.* 28v–29; and chapter 6.

169. Sorapán, *Medicina,* pp. 219–20.

170. Ibid., pp. 271–73.

171. "Diálogo," in Fernández Duro, *Disquisiciones náuticas,* 6:212–18.

172. Sánchez-Albornoz, "Gastos," p. 155.

173. Labayru, *Historia General,* 5:65–67.

174. AGM, Colección Vargas Ponce, XX, docs. 146–50, fols. 312–316v.

175. AGS, Guerra Antigua, leg. 3164. The corregidor was still trying to get funds from the crown in 1635, although a yearly income for the hospital had been donated in 1622.

176. AGS, Guerra Antigua, leg. 3152.

177. Scrattish, "New Perspectives," pp. 105–13.

178. AGI, Consulados, leg. 1040. See other records in legs. 1047, 1050, 1052.

179. Ibid., leg. 1052, fleet of Captain-General Carlos Ibarra in 1635.

180. Ibid.

181. Ibid., leg. 1050. Gage, *Travels,* p. 325, mentions Spanish colonists growing oranges and lemons on one of the Caribbean islands.

182. Hamilton, "Wages and Subsistence," p. 439.

183. AGI, Consulados, leg. 1040.

184. Continuing work in European demographic history indicates that a death rate of 30–40 per 1,000 members of the total population can be considered a normal range. Age-specific rates require very detailed records to calculate precisely, and one is often forced to rely on statistical projections rather than documentary evidence. In the commonly used work of Ansley J. Coale and Paul Demeny, *Regional Model Life Tables and Stable Populations* (Princeton, N.J.: Princeton University Press, 1966), appropriate tables for Europe project adult male death rates of about 20–30 per 1,000. For example, the table often used for sixteenth-century Spain is Model South, Mortality Level 4, Growth rate 5.00. This projects a death rate for males between

the ages of fifteen and forty-nine of 2.74 percent, or 27.4 per 1,000. Thus, in any given year, one might expect 27.4 deaths among 1,000 males between the ages of fifteen and forty-nine.

Chapter EIGHT. The Struggle for the Indies, 1629–1635

1. Huguette and Pierre Chaunu, *Séville et l'Atlantique,* 8 vols. in 12 (Paris: A. Colin, 1955–59), 8(2)(2):1657–64.

2. Anguste Antoine Thomazi, *Les flottes de l'or: Histoire des galions d'Espagne,* rev. ed. (Paris: Payot, 1956), pp. 143–44; Clarence Henry Haring, *Trade and Navigation between Spain and the Indies in the Time of the Hapsburgs* (Cambridge, Mass.: Harvard University Press, 1918), p. 223; Valentín Vázquez de Prada, "Las escalas en la navegación española a América," *Colloque international d'histoire maritime, 10th, Brussels, 1968* (Brussels: Société Jean Bodin pour l'histoire comparative des institutions. Recueils, vol. 33), pp. 109–12; Ernst Schäfer, "Comunicaciones marítimas y terrestres de las Indias españolas," *Anuario de Estudios Americanos* 3 (1946):969–70.

3. Cesáreo Fernández Duro, *Disquisiciones náuticas,* 6 vols. (Madrid: Sucesores de Rivadeneyra, 1876–81), 3:208. See also AGM, Colección Vargas Ponce, XIII, doc. 106, fols. 133–136v and doc. 108, fols. 139–139v, for the 1628 instructions given to Captain-General Tomás de Larráspuru.

4. AGS, Guerra Antigua, leg. 3153, Junta de Armadas minutes of July 5, 1629; AGI, Indiferente General, leg. 2567, memoranda of May 14, June 30, and August 13, 1629, reveal the process of formulating don Fadrique's orders in the Junta de Guerra de Indias.

5. Fernández Duro, *Disquisiciones náuticas,* 2:166.

6. Ernst Schäfer, *El Consejo Real y Supremo de las Indias: Su historia, organización y labor administrativo hasta la terminación de la Casa de Austria,* 2 vols. (Seville: Publicaciones de la Escuela de Estudios Hispano-Americanos, 1935–47), pp. 346–49, mentions an unsuccessful petition from the Spanish Netherlands in 1613 to allow the direct importation of tobacco from Venezuela to Flanders.

7. Kenneth Andrews, *The Spanish Caribbean: Trade and Plunder, 1530–1630* (New Haven, Conn.: Yale University Press, 1978), pp. 224–39.

8. AGM, Colección Sanz—Barcelona, mss. 367, fols. 319–321v.

9. Ibid., citing official reports to the crown, claims one sinking and seven captures.

10. AGS, Guerra Antigua, leg. 3153, report of November 21, 1629. Cesáreo Fernández Duro, *Armada española desde la unión de los reinos de Castilla y de León,* 9 vols. (Madrid, 1895–1903), 4:109–10, citing no source, reports only a skirmish and one small navío captured.

11. AGS, Guerra Antigua, leg. 3153, Oleaga's report of November 21, 1629, mentioning the letter dated August 27, 1629, from don Luis Jorge de Rivera Baena, the governor's son.

12. AGM, Colección, Sanz—Barcelona, mss. 367, fols. 319–321v. Fernández Duro, *Armada española,* 4:477, cites a similar account in a printed pamphlet from 1629.

13. Unless otherwise noted, the sources for the fleet's actions in the Caribbean come from Fernández Duro, *Armada española,* 4:109–11, and Rafael Estrada y Arnáiz, *El Almirante don Antonio de Oquendo* (Madrid: Espasa Calpe, 1943), pp. 105–10.

14. AGI, Contratación, leg. 5101.

15. Philip Ainsworth Means, *The Spanish Main* (New York: Charles Scribner's Sons, 1935), pp. 161–62.

16. AGI, Contratación, leg. 5101, letter of April 9, 1630, from Hernán Gómez de

Sandoval, captain-general of the New Spain fleet in Veracruz, reporting on dispatches from Fadrique de Toledo in Cartagena dated in February.

17. Juan Manuel Zapatero, *Fortalezas españoles en América: Cartagena de Indias* (Madrid: Editorial Revista Geográfica Española, 1967), pp. 21–22, citing papers in the RAH.

18. AGI, Mapas y Planos, Panamá 45; Panamá 48 is a sketch of the city's fortifications.

19. AGI, Contratación, leg. 5101, don Fadrique de Toledo's letter of February 14, 1630.

20. AGS, Guerra Antigua, leg. 3154, reports dated June 5 from Havana, July 26 from the capitana at sea, and July 30 from a temporary anchorage in the Bahama Channel. AGI, Contratación legs. 2251–54 contains records of silver carried by don Martín de Vallecilla's silver galleons.

21. AGS, Guerra Antigua, leg. 3154, don Fadrique de Toledo's report of August 2, 1630, with Junta de Armadas minutes of August 14.

22. Antonio Domínguez Ortiz, "Los caudales de Indias y la política exterior de Felipe IV," *Anuario de Estudios Americanos* 13 (1956):344, citing Blas Fernández de Santiesteban, "Relación de la venida de la Flota de Nueva España y galeones" (Granada, 1630); AGI, Contratación, leg. 5189, letter from the House of Trade, August 2, 1630.

23. AGS, Guerra Antigua, leg. 3154, report of July 26, 1630, with a total of 5,057,997 pesos. AGI, Contratación, leg. 2251 contains silver accounts from several of the galleons in the fleet.

24. AGS, Guerra Antigua, leg. 3153, various memoranda from October and November 1629, and leg. 3154, memoranda from January 1630. See chapter 5 for a discussion of the preparations for Larráspuru's fleet.

25. AGI, Consulados, leg. 1047; AGI, Contratación, legs. 2243–50 contains the records of Larráspuru's fleet; Fernández Duro, *Armada española*, 4:112; Chaunu, *Séville et l'Atlantique*, 5:184, 200, 204 ff, 224 ff.

26. AGM, Colección Vargas Ponce, XXVI, doc. 35, fol. 56; AGI, Contratación, leg. 4922. Martín Fernández de Navarrete, comp., *Colección de documentos y manuscriptos compilados*, ed. Julio Guillén Tato, 32 vols. (Nendeln, Lichtenstein: Kraus-Thompson Organization, 1971), 24(2), doc. 49.

27. AGI, Contaduría, leg. 548, accounts of August 26 and 31, 1630.

28. AGI, Contratación, leg. 4534, ramo 4.

29. Domínguez Ortiz, "Caudales," pp. 345–47.

30. Chaunu, *Séville et l'Atlantique*, 5:191–92, 208–12. Navarrete, *Colección de documentos*, 24(2), doc. 49, has the 1631 fleet negotiations.

31. Chaunu, *Séville et l'Atlantique*, 8(2)(2):1670–71.

32. AGS, Guerra Antigua, leg. 3154, letter of August 2, 1630, from Cádiz Bay, and memorandum of the Junta de Armadas dated August 14, 1630.

33. Ibid., Junta de Armadas minutes of October 22, 1630.

34. Ibid., memoranda of September 8 and 14.

35. Ibid., undated list accompanying memoranda from September.

36. Chaunu, *Séville et l'Atlantique*, 5:172.

37. AGS, Guerra Antigua, leg. 3159, list of ships dated January 14, 1632.

38. Ibid., leg. 3158, memoranda and lists of December 1631 and July 1632.

39. Ibid., leg. 3154, memoranda of September 14, October 23 and 26, and November 8, 1630, with Levanto's contract dated January 18, 1630.

40. AGI, Contratación, leg. 5101, letter of December 1, 1630; Chaunu, *Séville et l'Atlantique*, 5:190.

41. Unless otherwise noted, the account of Oquendo's fleet in Brazil comes from Estrada, *Almirante Oquendo*, pp. 111–20; Fernández Duro, *Armada española*, 4:122–23.

42. AGS, Guerra Antigua, leg. 3156, memoranda in September 1631 dealing with resupply.

43. Domínguez Ortiz, "Caudales," pp. 347–48; Chaunu, *Séville et l'Atlantique,* 5:221.

44. Fernández Duro, *Armada española,* 4:136; Domínguez Ortiz, "Caudales," pp. 347–49; Chaunu, *Séville et l'Atlantique,* 8(2)(2):1705–13.

45. Chaunu, *Séville et l'Atlantique,* 5:218–20.

46. AGS, Guerra Antigua, leg. 3159, letter of March 11, 1632, from Cádiz, confirming earlier reports.

47. Chaunu, *Séville et l'Atlantique,* 5:220–21.

48. AGS, Guerra Antigua, leg. 3158, memorandum of February 5, 1632.

49. Chaunu, *Séville et l'Atlantique,* 8(2)(2):1729–30.

50. AGS, Guerra Antigua, leg. 3158, memorandum of February 5, 1632. Other ship censuses for the period are in legs. 3157, 3158, from December 1631 through February 1632.

51. AGI, Indiferente General, leg. 2593, memorandum of February 12, 1632.

52. AGS, Guerra Antigua, leg. 3158, memoranda of December 1631, January 1632; leg. 3159, memoranda of February 1632.

53. Ibid., leg. 3158, numerous letters, accounts, and memoranda from January through October 1632.

54. AGI, Indiferente General, leg. 2593, Council of War minutes of February 27, March 3, and 9, 1632.

55. AGS, Guerra Antigua, leg. 3159, memoranda of March 10 and 18, 1632.

56. Ibid., Junta de Armadas minutes of March 18, 1632.

57. Ibid., dozens of letters and memoranda.

58. AGI, Contratación, leg. 5174, fols. 9v–10; AGS, CMC 3a, leg. 1103, no. 1.

59. Chaunu, *Séville et l'Atlantique,* 5:221, citing AGI, Contratación, leg. 5173, lib. 17, fols. 332–335v.

60. AGI, Contratación, leg. 5189, memoranda from late May 1632; Chaunu, *Séville et l'Atlantique,* 5:221–23, lists the mercury carried on each ship.

61. AGI, Contratación, leg. 5189, letter of June 2, 1632.

62. AGS, Guerra Antigua, leg. 3159, memoranda and letters from April through July 1632, and complaints about the shortage of officers available in late January. *Ordenanzas del buen govierno de la armada del mar océano de 24 de Henero de 1633* (Barcelona, 1678; facsimile edition, Madrid: Instituto Histórico de Marina, 1974), fol. 43, paragraph 348.

63. AGS, Guerra Antigua, leg. 3158, memorandum of September 9, 1632, giving the figure as 272.75 reales.

64. Ibid., memoranda of September 9 and October 26, 1632, with the cost given as 7,877,514 reales.

65. AGI, Contratación, leg. 4534, fols. 57–58.

66. AGS, Guerra Antigua, leg. 3159, memorandum of July 28, 1632.

67. Ibid., leg. 3158, memorandum of October 23, 1632.

68. Ibid., leg. 3161, memoranda of December 8, 1632 and June 20, 1633. Velasco served simultaneously as inspector, purveyor, comptroller, and comptroller of artillery for the fleet—in short, the king's fiscal watchdog.

69. Ibid., memoranda and letters of December 8, 1632, June 20, July 31, and August 26, 1633. Navarrete, *Colección de documentos,* 12, doc. 37, fols. 172–73, contains Oquendo's report from Cartagena, dated December 10, 1632.

70. *Colección de documentos inéditos relativos al descubrimiento, conquista y organización de las antiguas posesiones españolas de Ultramar,* 25 vols. (Madrid: Real Academia de la Historia, 1864–1932), 14:53.

71. AGI, Contratación, leg. 4534, fols. 57–58.

72. Ibid., legs. 2262; 5174, fols. 42–42v.

73. Ibid., legs. 2262–66. Chaunu, *Séville et l'Atlantique,* often lists maestres de plata and maestres indiscriminantly in his fleet tables.

74. AGI, Indiferente General, leg. 2593, various memoranda from September through December 1632; AGS, Guerra Antigua, leg. 3158, memoranda from the same period.

75. AGS, Guerra Antigua, legs. 3160, 3161, memoranda and letters from December 1632 through the spring of 1633.

76. Ibid., leg. 3161, memoranda through the spring of 1633; AGI Contratación, leg. 5189, for the same period; Chaunu, *Séville et l'Atlantique,* 5:236–39.

77. AGI, Contratación, leg. 5101.

78. Ibid., leg. 5174, lib. 1633–36, fol. 26; Chaunu, *Séville et l'Atlantique,* 5:230.

79. Fernández Duro, *Armada española,* 4:113–15; Jonathan Israel, *The Dutch Republic and the Hispanic World, 1606–1661* (Oxford: Clarendon Press, 1982), pp. 203–4.

80. Chaunu, *Séville et l'Atlantique,* 5:258–60. The military successes of 1633, both in Europe and in the New World, figured prominently in the decoration scheme for the Retiro Palace being built in Madrid. Jonathan Brown and J. H. Elliott, *A Palace for a King: The Buen Retiro and the Court of Philip IV* (New Haven, Conn.: Yale University Press, 1980), p. 166.

81. AGI, Contratación, leg. 4534, fols. 58–62.

82. Chaunu, *Séville et l'Atlantique,* 5:237–38; Navarrete, *Colección de documentos,* 24(2), doc. 49.

83. AGS, Guerra Antigua, leg. 3161, memoranda of October and November 1633.

84. AGI, Contratación, leg. 5101, letter from Oquendo in Cádiz, February 12, 1634; AGS, Guerra Antigua, leg. 3162, letters from January and February 1634.

85. AGS, Guerra Antigua, leg. 3162, memoranda of mid-January and early February 1634.

86. Chaunu, *Séville et l'Atlantique,* 5:237–38.

87. *Ordenanzas,* fol. 43, paragraph 348.

88. The accounts for the redistribution of old sails and rigging from the ships are in AGS, CMC 3a, leg. 1323.

89. Ibid., legs. 1870, no. 3, 2287, no. 4; AGI, Contratación, leg. 4048.

90. AGS, Guerra Antigua, leg. 3161, memoranda and letters from February 1633.

91. AGI, Contratación, leg. 5189, memoranda and letters of January through March 1634; AGS, CMC 3a, leg. 3521, no. 9.

92. Chaunu, *Séville et l'Atlantique,* 5:254–55; 8(2)(2):1723–32; AGI, Contratación, leg. 5189, letters of January and February 1634.

93. Chaunu, *Séville et l'Atlantique,* 5:255, citing AGI, Contratación, leg. 5101.

94. AGS, Guerra Antigua, leg. 3162, memoranda from March and April, 1634; AGI, Consulados, leg. 1051.

95. AGS, Guerra Antigua, leg. 3162, accounts of May 29 and August 9, 1634.

96. AGI, Contratación, leg. 5101, letters of Francisco Díaz Pimienta, dated November 6, and of Lope de Hoces y Córdoba, dated December 22, 1634.

97. AGI, Consulados, leg. 1051, document of July 23: supplies for the galleon *Los Tres Reyes.*

98. AGI, Contratación, leg. 4048. All information on the salvage operation comes from this source.

99. Ibid., documents from August 1634; Consulados, legs. 1048, 1051.

100. See Vázquez de Prada, "Escalas," pp. 116–17 for distances and voyaging times across the Caribbean.

101. AGI, Consulados, legs. 1049, 1051 bis, accounts from 1635–36.

102. AGI, Contratación leg. 4048, documents of December 12 and 20, 1634, and January 22, 1635.

103. Ibid., leg. 4048, memorandum of February 9, 1635, Havana.

104. Estrada, *Almirante Oquendo,* p. 121.

105. AGI, Contratación, legs. 2275–82 contain the silver registers for the fleet. Ibid., leg. 4048, document dated June 17, 1635, is a list of all the boxes of documents sent with the fleet, including physical descriptions of each box. A confirming list, sent separately, also appears in the same bundle. The masters of silver for every galleon in the armada are named in a document dated June 17, 1635.

106. Domínguez Ortiz, "Caudales," p. 350.

107. Chaunu, *Séville et l'Atlantique,* 5:268–72.

108. AGS, Guerra Antigua, leg. 3164, documents of June 20, 1635; CMC 3a, leg. 1323.

109. AGS, Guerra Antigua, leg. 3164, memorandum of July 21, 1635.

Chapter NINE. *The Struggle for Survival, 1635–1640*

1. Cesáreo Fernández Duro, *Armada española desde la unión de los reinos de Castilla y de León,* 9 vols. (Madrid, 1895–1903), 4:143; Cesáreo Fernández Duro, *Disquisiciones náuticas,* 6 vols. (Madrid: Sucesores de Rivadeneyra, 1876–81), 2:299.

2. AGS, Guerra Antigua, leg. 3162, memoranda of mid-January and early February 1634.

3. Jonathan Brown and J. H. Elliott, *A Palace for a King: The Buen Retiro and the Court of Philip IV* (New Haven, Conn.: Yale University Press, 1980), p. 173. Fernández Duro, *Disquisiciones náuticas,* 2:299–300, has a more prosaic version of the same incident.

4. AGM, ms. 507, fols. 226–30.

5. Fernández Duro, *Armada española,* 4:143.

6. José Alcalá-Zamora y Queipo de Llano, *España, Flandes y el Mar del Norte (1618–1639): La última ofensiva europea de los Austrias madrileños* (Barcelona: Editorial Planeta, 1975), pp. 251–65. Jonathan Israel, *The Dutch Republic and the Hispanic World, 1606–1661* (Oxford, Eng.: Clarendon Press, 1982), p. xiv, argues, "There can no longer be any doubt that the Spanish crown had come to accept the principle of Dutch political and religious independence by 1606, and that there was never subsequently any Spanish ambition or plan for reconquering the break-away northern Netherlands." The position seems rather extreme. The government responded to the political and military situation as it developed, and it is difficult to imagine that it would not have pursued a plan for a full reconquest, should the situation ever have been favorable enough. The vast expenditure of men and money during the eighty-year struggle with the northern Netherlands is testimony enough to the Spanish strength of purpose. See Geoffrey Parker, *The Army of Flanders and the Spanish Road, 1567–1659: The Logistics of Spanish Victory and Defeat in the Low Countries' Wars* (Cambridge, Eng.: Cambridge University Press, 1972), esp. pp. 139–57, 263–68.

7. AGS, Guerra Antigua, leg. 3164, memoranda of December 15, 1635.

8. Ibid., leg. 3167, memorandum of January 2, 1636.

9. Ibid.

10. AGS, CMC 3a, leg. 1323.

11. Ibid., careening accounts.

12. Ibid., leg. 2910, no. 8.

13. AGS, Estado, leg. 2051, discusses this and other matters related to the fleet.

14. AGS, Guerra Antigua, leg. 3166, instructions from Madrid dated May 4, 1636.

15. AGS, CMC 3a, legs. 1323, 2910, no. 8.

16. AGS, Guerra Antigua, leg. 3166, instructions to Fuentes, dated May 4, 1636, in Madrid.

17. Alcalá-Zamora, *España, Flandes,* p. 390.

18. AGS, Guerra Antigua, leg. 3167, memorandum of May 4, 1636; AGS, CMC 3a, leg. 1323.

19. AGS, Guerra Antigua, leg. 3167, official report of Fuentes at sea August 28, 1636. Alcalá-Zamora, *España, Flandes,* p. 390, mentions thirty-eight ships, but the figure was taken from printed sources.

20. AGS, Guerra Antigua, leg. 3166; CMC 3a, leg. 3303, no. 1 has some of the provisioning accounts for the voyage.

21. AGS, Guerra Antigua, leg. 3166, instructions dated May 4, 1636, in Madrid.

22. Alcalá-Zamora, *España, Flandes,* pp. 348–58; Israel, *Dutch Republic,* p. 267.

23. AGS, Guerra Antigua, leg. 3167, Fuentes's report dated October 6, 1636.

24. Ibid.; Alcalá-Zamora, *España, Flandes,* p. 390.

25. Alcalá-Zamora, *España, Flandes,* pp. 390–91.

26. Oquendo's letter to the king from Cádiz, July 26, 1636, transcribed in full in Rafael Estrada y Arnáiz, *El Almirante don Antonio de Oquendo* (Madrid: Espasa Calpe, 1943), pp. 128–30. I mention the size of the French ships in Chapter 2.

27. Ibid. Various authors have quoted Oquendo's letter but dated it incorrectly, the most misleading being Artiñano, who writes as if Oquendo were discussing the Dutch and Spanish fleets near Brazil in 1631. Gervasio de Artiñaño y de Galdácano, *La arquitectura naval española (en madera)* (Madrid, 1920), p. 104.

28. Estrada, *Almirante Oquendo,* pp. 124–28.

29. Ibid., pp. 124–30; Jaime Salvá, "La armada de Oquendo en Mallorca (1637–1638)," *Bolletí de la Sociétat Arqueológica Juliana* 28(1942–43):421–40; AGS, Guerra Antigua, leg. 3154, various memoranda and accounts.

30. AGS, Guerra Antigua, leg. 3164, documents from late summer and fall 1635; Huguette and Pierre Chaunu, *Séville et l'Atlantique,* 8 vols. in 12 (Paris: A. Colin, 1955–59), 5:291.

31. AGS, Estado, leg. 2052.

32. AGI, Contratación, leg. 5174, fols. 325–363v; Chaunu, *Séville et l'Atlantique,* 8(2)(2):1733–92.

33. Alcalá-Zamora, *España, Flandes,* pp. 391–94.

34. Ibid., pp. 395–96; Fernández Duro, *Armada española,* 4:169–71.

35. Alcalá-Zamora, *España, Flandes,* pp. 384–85, citing AGS, Estado, leg. 3860.

36. See AGS, Guerra Antigua, leg. 3170, memorandum of April 21, 1638, for one of Horna's victories.

37. Alcalá-Zamora, *España, Flandes,* pp. 386–88; The monetary value of the Dutch losses is analyzed in R. Baetens, "The Organisation and Effects of Flemish Privateering in the Seventeenth Century," *Acta Historiae Neerlandicae* 9 (1976):48–75.

38. Fernández Duro, *Armada española,* 4:169–71.

39. Ibid., pp. 171–72.

40. Ibid., p. 173; Auguste Jal, *Abraham du Quesne et la marine de son temps,* 2 vols. (Paris: H. Plon, 1873), 1:87–88, lists thirty-seven of the large ships, which averaged 399 toneladas. A somewhat fanciful estimate of the precise measurements of *La Couronne* appears in Edmond Pâris, *Souvenirs de marine* (Paris: Gauthier-Villars, 1882).

41. Fernández Duro, *Armada española,* 4:174–75.

42. A report on that meeting is printed in full in Ibid., pp. 175–76.

43. Unless otherwise noted, the following account of the battle comes from Fernández Duro, *Armada española,* 4:175–88, including the report later filed by Captain-General don Lope de Hoces.

44. A partial list of officers killed appears in Fernández Duro, *Armada española,* 4:186.

45. Alcalá-Zamora, *España, Flandes,* p. 400.

46. Fernández Duro, *Armada española,* 4:182–83.

47. AGS, Guerra Antigua, leg. 3171, memorandum of November 7, 1638.

48. AGS, Estado, leg. 2054.

49. AGS, Guerra Antigua, leg. 3172, letter of May 19, 1639, from the Duke of Ciudad Real, in Cádiz.

50. Alcalá-Zamora, *España, Flandes,* p. 416.

51. Ibid., pp. 400–401.

52. Juan de Laínez, "Carta . . . en que le da cuenta del viaje de los galeones (1639)," in Fernández Duro, *Disquisiciones náuticas,* 2:223–58.

53. Alcalá-Zamora, *España, Flandes,* pp. 420–21.

54. AGS, Guerra Antigua, leg. 3174, including careening documents for the *San Felipe* in La Coruña.

55. Alcalá-Zamora, *España, Flandes,* pp. 420–21.

56. See lists in Fernández Duro, *Armada española,* 4:224–27, taken from documents in the AGM; and a list in Estrada, *Almirante Oquendo,* pp. 146–47, which is very similar but not identical.

57. Alcalá-Zamora, *España, Flandes,* pp. 429–33. Dutch and English sources confirm this total, with minor discrepancies. See C. R. Boxer, trans. and ed., *The Journal of Maarten Harpertszoon Tromp, anno 1639* (Cambridge: Cambridge University Press, 1930), pp. 38, 163. Peter White, *A Memorable Sea-fight . . . or A Narrative of all the Principall Passages which were trans-acted in the Downes, in the Year, 1639* (London, 1649), mentioned only sixty-six large ships.

58. Alcalá-Zamora, *España, Flandes,* pp. 430–32, has the entire list of ship names and sizes. The Coruña squadron is designated the Portugal squadron in some sources, presumably because it was part of the Armada del Mar Océano, officially based in Lisbon. However, it was outfitted in La Coruña, which made it, in Spanish usage, the squadron of La Coruña for that particular voyage.

59. Ibid., p. 423; Estrada, *Almirante Oquendo,* p. 154.

60. Alcalá-Zamora, *España, Flandes,* pp. 423–27. See also Boxer/Tromp, *Journal,* p. 14.

61. Boxer/Tromp, *Journal,* pp. 160–61.

62. Ibid., p. 11.

63. Ibid., p. 38.

64. Estrada, *Almirante Oquendo,* pp. 155–56; Alcalá-Zamora, *España, Flandes,* pp. 440–41.

65. Boxer/Tromp, *Journal,* p. 165.

66. Ibid., p. 44.

67. Ibid., pp. 164–65.

68. Alcalá-Zamora, *España, Flandes,* pp. 437–42.

69. Fernández Duro, *Armada española,* 4:496, lists such a pamphlet printed in Seville shortly after the event.

70. Boxer/Tromp, *Journal,* pp. 45–46, 164–65.

71. Ibid., p. 48.

72. Estrada, *Almirante Oquendo,* pp. 158–59.

73. White, *Sea-fight,* gives a running account of Spanish negotiations with the English. The desire of Charles I and his ministers to extract every benefit they could from enforcing their neutrality provides a rather sordid footnote to the Battle of the Downs. Boxer/Tromp, *Journal,* pp. 55–56.

74. Alcalá-Zamora, *España, Flandes,* pp. 443–44; Estrada, *Almirante Oquendo,* pp. 159–60. Boxer/Tromp, *Journal,* p. 49, mentions the early dispatch of men and money.

75. Alcalá-Zamora, *España, Flandes,* pp. 443–46.

76. Admiral Tromp told Peter White on October 18 that he had 103 warships and 16 fireships. Boxer/Tromp, *Journal,* p. 51. More ships may have arrived before the final battle.

77. Boxer/Tromp, *Journal,* p. 53; White, *Sea-fight,* pp. 14, 39.

78. See Jon S. Kepler, *The Exchange of Christendom: The International Entrepot at Dover, 1622–1641* (Bristol, Eng., 1976), pp. 61–64.

79. Boxer/Tromp, *Journal,* p. 188.

80. Ibid., pp. 57–59, 187–88. Estrada, *Almirante Oquendo,* pp. 162–64; Alcalá-Zamora, *España, Flandes,* pp. 448–49.

81. Boxer/Tromp, *Journal,* pp. 195–96.

82. Alcalá-Zamora, *España, Flandes,* pp. 450–51. White, *Sea-fight,* p. 45.

83. Alcalá-Zamora, *España, Flandes,* pp. 450–51.

84. Ibid., pp. 451–52.

85. Ibid., p. 454.

86. C. R. Boxer heaped abuse on Castro, saying, "This poltroon was subsequently appointed Vice-Admiral of a fleet in 1640—an appointment which throws a lurid light on Spanish naval maladministration in the seventeenth century." Boxer/Tromp, *Journal,* p. 62. Clearly, a government that had executed don Juan de Benavides, imprisoned don Fadrique de Toledo, and disciplined don Antonio de Oquendo and dozens of other fleet officers, would not have hesitated to move against Castro had he been found culpable in the grounding.

87. Alcalá-Zamora, *España, Flandes,* pp. 455–57; Estrada, *Almirante Oquendo,* pp. 174–77.

88. AGS, Guerra Antigua, legs. 3174, 3175.

89. Quoted in Antonio Domínguez Ortiz, "Los caudales de Indias y la política exterior de Felipe IV," *Anuario de estudios americanos* 13 (1956):313.

Bibliography

Archives

The bulk of the sources for this study were concentrated in the large state archives devoted to early modern Spain, enormous storehouses of documents that provide persuasive evidence for the thoroughness of bureaucratic record-keeping during the Habsburg centuries.

The Archivo General de Simancas, somewhat unexpectedly, provided the most bountiful information. Because the six galleons I was studying served in the guard squadron for the Indies fleets in the early 1630s, I had assumed that most of the information about them would be in the Archivo General de Indias in Seville, the main depository for Indies documents, and the Archivo General de la Marina in the Museo Naval in Madrid, the most concentrated source of naval documents. Although those collections provided material of undoubted value, the richest and most varied sources are at Simancas. Scholars interested in naval affairs in the Habsburg centuries, anywhere in the empire, would be well advised to plan considerable time there.

Most valuable for this study was the Simancas archive's general section on War and Marine (Guerra y Marina), more commonly known as Guerra Antigua. Among other things, it contains papers from the Council of War and its Junta de Armadas (fleet committee), whose concern was Spain's Atlantic fleets; the equivalent for the Mediterranean was the Junta de Galeras (galley committee). The Junta de Armadas included experienced naval officers and senior ministers of the crown such as the presidents of the Council of the Indies and the Council of Finance. The Junta generally met three times a week at fixed hours. As a major part of its business, it regularly evaluated the seaworthiness of vessels in the Atlantic fleets and designated those that would accompany the merchant vessels to Spain's American empire. The galleons I was studying sailed in such escort fleets—the Armada de la Guardia de la Carrera de las Indias—in their first six years of service to the crown, although they were technically part of the European Atlantic fleet, the Armada del Mar Océano.

The minutes of the Junta de Armadas contain debates about the timing, size, and strength of Indies and European expeditions, lengthy nominations for the senior officers on each fleet, and endless concern over crew levies. As the advisory body for the administration of Spain's Atlantic fleets, in many ways the Junta de Armadas was the voice of the navy, often opposing unrealistic demands made by the crown on overextended naval resources. Another committee of the Council of War dealt with matters of military strategy regarding the Indies—the committee of war for the Indies (Junta de Guerra de Indias), with four members each from the Council of War and the Council of the Indies. Its papers, too, are in the general section called Guerra Antigua at Simancas. Although it lacks a modern detailed catalog, the section does have older manuscript inventories, and the generally chronological organization of the documents makes them fairly easy to use.

Financial papers at Simancas provided documentation on the construction, provisioning, salaries, repairs and careening, and shipboard diet for my six galleons. Most of the information came from the papers filed with royal accountants, in the sections called Contadurías Generales and Contaduría Mayor de Cuentas, 3a Época. The latter is the subject of a recent two-volume analytical catalog—ten years in the making—that indexes every document in more than three thousand large bundles. Because the papers were filed under the name of the royal official who drew up the accounts, it saves considerable time to know the officials involved. The cost of outfitting the guard squadron for the Indies fleets technically came from taxes called averías on merchandise shipped to and from the New World, administered by the House of Trade (Casa de Contratación) in Seville. In the late 1620s and 1630s, Dutch naval actions in the New World so disrupted trade that the merchant fleets could not hope to cover the costs of their military escorts. Consequently, the money came from a variety of sources, patched together by extraordinary efforts on the part of royal bureaucrats. The accounts filed for the fleets provide detailed evidence about all aspects of their cost and maintenance.

Several of my six galleons returned to the European Atlantic fleet in 1635, when France's entry into the Thirty Years' War placed even greater strains on Spanish naval resources. For the period after 1635, the papers of the Council of State in the section Secretaría de Estado (Estado), along with those of the Council of War and its committees, trace several of the galleons on duty in the Mediterranean and the English Channel. Printed catalogs and manuscript inventories provide a key for many of the subsections in Estado, though there is no catalog for the section as a whole.

The Archivo General de Indias in Seville contained considerable information on my six galleons, though its richest maritime holdings concern the merchant fleets of the Indies trade. A general rule of thumb is that the documents include detailed information about galleons in the guard squadrons only when they carried merchandise. The guard squadrons habitually carried mercury for silver refining and official documents to the New World, and treasure of all kinds on the way back, whether it belonged to private individuals or to the king. Otherwise they were forbidden by law from carrying anything but their men, munitions, and supplies. It is anyone's guess how much that law was observed in normal times. In the 1630s, when my six galleons sailed to the Indies, the existing state of war made them both more battleworthy and at the same time more likely to carry merchandise and extra supplies legally. In 1629, when no merchant vessels sailed, the large "galiflota" that included my six galleons carried the few trade goods that were sent. For that reason, the Archive of the Indies has considerable information on the galleons in that year. In other years, they appeared only briefly in the registers for the outward voyage, but more fully for the homeward voyage, because of the treasure they carried.

Most of the pertinent documents are contained in the section on trade (Contratación), including memoranda on the taxes used to pay for each fleet, the provisioning and warehousing of supplies, silver shipments, and officers of the fleets. Contratación also contains the actual registers of silver and other treasure. The officials in charge of registering treasure had to post bond with the House of Trade in order to take up their posts. In addition, Indies pilots were chosen, trained, and licensed by the House of Trade. Because of these requirements, copious records were generated and filed in Contratación. The House of Trade also played a crucial role in selecting the ships for the Indies fleets, inspecting and licensing the merchant vessels, and requesting certain ships for the guard squadrons.

The accounting section (Contaduría) also provided useful information, particularly on the costs of some of the fleets that interested me and the taxes used to pay for their escort squadrons. For my purposes, however, and for the 1630s in general, this was a rather disappointing section, much less rich than the financial records at Simancas. The section called Consulados consists of papers from the merchant organizations of Seville and Cádiz. Recently cataloged, it yielded a few very interesting documents, notably on the fleet returning in 1633 with my six galleons, some provisioning accounts, and instructions for royal inspectors of fleets in the seventeenth century.

A miscellaneous section (Indiferente General) held letters and memoranda on the first Indies fleet in which my six galleons sailed (1629), as well as lengthy documentation on officers and officials in other fleets. The section on royal patrimony (Patronato Real) contained documents on royal policies regarding ship construction and the administration of the Indies fleets, as well as several well-known sets of sailing instructions. Another section (Escribanía de Cámara) dealt with the formal inquiries faced by commanders of the Indies fleets, several of whom had dealings with my six galleons. Finally, the section of Maps and Plans (Mapas y Planos) included several helpful sailing charts illustrating ships and port cities of the epoch.

The Archivo General de la Marina in the Museo Naval in Madrid proved useful for royal ordinances, memoranda, and decrees dealing with ship construction. In addition, the archive's Colección Vargas Ponce contained dozens of references to officers in fleets that interested me, and many documents dealing with my six galleons. Some of these were copies of documents at Simancas, but others came from originals in various private archives. Without these copies made for the Archivo General de la Marina in the eighteenth century, I almost certainly would not have found them One of the private archives was the likely source of the ship inventories purchased by the James Ford Bell Library at Minnesota, which inspired this study. The Archivo General de la Marina also contains hundreds of documents dealing with shipboard diet and provisioning. Its lists of instructions for fleet commanders and armament on royal ships also helped my research. Although the same types of documents—and often the originals of the documents themselves—exist in far greater quantity at Simancas and Seville, those in the Archivo General de la Marina are more easily accessible: every document in the collection is inventoried and cross-indexed in one way or another.

The Archivo Histórico Nacional provided information about the builder of the six galleons, Martín de Arana, and his sons. From a distinguished Basque family of mariners and shipbuilders, Arana belonged to the middle ranks of the Spanish nobility, as a gentleman of the Military Order of Alcántara. Through building the six galleons he gained various favors from the king. These included appointment as a royal official on the north coast and preferment for his sons. Documents concerning the nobility and rising status of Arana's family are contained in various sections of the archive, easy to locate because they are usually cataloged by name. The Real Academia de la Historia provided material about distinguished naval commanders in the Habsburg period, as well as information about naval campaigns and fortified ports in the New World. The Biblioteca Nacional in Madrid and the Archivo de la

Real Chancillería in Valladolid each contributed several interesting documents for this study.

Notarial archives in Bilbao, where the six galleons were built, and in Seville, La Coruña, Lisbon, and Cádiz, where they were refitted and provisioned at various times, could undoubtedly provide more information about them, although it is possible that the results of the search would not compensate for the time required to carry it out. In any case, the documents in the larger archives were voluminous enough to dissuade me from that further effort. Closer to home, the James Ford Bell Library held not only the delivery invoices that initiated this study, but also an impressive collection of contemporary books and printed maps for the broader context of the history of navigation and exploration.

Published Primary Sources

Actas de la Universidad de Mareantes de Sevilla. Transcribed by María del Carmen Borrego Plá. Seville: Diputación Provincial de Sevilla, 1972.

Alemán, Mateo. *The Rogue, or The Life of Guzmán de Alfarache.* Translated by James Mabbe, 1623. 4 vols. London and New York: Alfred A. Knopf, 1924.

Arano, Luisa Cogliato, ed. *The Medieval Health Handbook "Tacuinum Sanitatis."* New York: George Braziller, 1976.

Blázquez, Antonio, ed. *"Descripción de las costas y puertos de España* de Pedro Texeira Albernas*"* (1630). *Boletín de la Real Sociedad Geográfica* (1910):36–138, 180–233.

Boxer, C. R., trans. and ed. *The Journal of Maarten Harpertszoon Tromp, anno 1639.* Cambridge: Cambridge University Press, 1930.

Calafatería. See "Tratado de la Galafatería."

Cano, Tomé. *Arte para fabricar y aparejar naos (1611).* Edited by Enrique Marco Dorta. La Laguna, Canary Islands: Instituto de Estudios Canarios, 1964.

Cervantes Saavedra, Miguel de. "La española inglesa." *Novelas ejemplares.* 2 vols. Madrid: Fenicia, 1970.

———. "Ilustre fregona," *Novelas ejemplares.* Edited by Francisco Rodríguez Marín, 1:219–324. Madrid: Espasa Calpe, 1962.

Colección de diarios y relaciones para la historia de los viajes y descubrimientos. Madrid: Archivo General de la Marina, 1944–47.

Colección de documentos inéditos para la historia de España. 112 vols. Madrid, 1842–95.

Colección de documentos inéditos relativos al descubrimiento, conquista y organización de las antiguas posesiones españoles de Ultramar. 25 vols. Madrid: Real Academia de la Historia, 1864–1932.

Contreras, Alonso de. *The Life of Captain Alonso de Contreras, Knight of the Military Order of St. John, Native of Madrid, Written by Himself (1582 to 1633).* Translated by Catherine Alison Phillips. New York: Alfred A. Knopf, 1926.

Cortés, Martín. *Breve compendio de la sphera y de la arte de navegar.* Seville, 1551. Reprinted, Zaragoza: Institución Fernando el Católico, 1945.

Cutter, Donald C., ed. *The California Coast: A Bilingual Edition of Documents from the Sutro Collection.* Translated by George Butler Griffin in 1891. Norman: University of Oklahoma Press, 1969.

Dassié, C. R. *L'architecture navale avec le routier des Indes orientales et occidentales.* 2 vols. in 1. Paris, 1677.

"Diálogo entre un vizcaíno y un montañés." (Written ca. 1635) In *Disquisiciones náuticas,* edited by Cesáreo Fernández Duro (see below), 6:106–222.

Documentary Sources for the Wreck of the New Spain Fleet of 1554. Edited and translated by David McDonald and J. Barto Arnold III. Austin: Texas Antiquities Committee, 1979.

Duhamel du Monceau, Henri-Louis. *The Elements of Naval Architecture, or A Practical Treatise on Ship-building.* Translated from the 1752 French edition and published in an abridged version by Mungo Murray. London, 1764.

————. *Traité de la fabrique des manoeuvres pour les vaisseaux, ou l'art de la corderie....* Paris, 1747.

Enríquez de Guzmán, Alonso. *The Life and Acts of Don Alonso Enríquez de Guzmán, a Knight of Seville, of the Order of Santiago, A.D. 1518 to 1543.* Translated by Clements R. Markham. 1st ser., vol. 29. London: Hakluyt Society, 1862.

Escalante de Mendoza, Juan. *Itinerario de navegación de los mares y tierras occidentales* (Madrid, 1575). In *Disquisiciones náuticas,* edited by Cesáreo Fernández Duro (see below), 5:413–515.

Fernández Duro, Cesáreo, ed. *Disquisiciones náuticas,* 6 vols. Madrid: Sucesores de Rivadeneyra, 1876–81.

Fontiveros, Pedro de. "Carta a don Antonio Martínez de Espinosa, 1642." In *Disquisiciones náuticas,* edited by Cesáreo Fernández Duro (see above), 2:219–222.

Furtenbach, Josef. *Architectura navalis: Das ist: Von dem Schiff-Gebäw, auff dem Meer und Seekusten zu gebrauchen....* Frankfort, 1629. Reprinted in *The Printed Sources of Western Art.* Edited by Theodore Besterman. Portland, Ore.: United Academic Press, 1972.

Gage, Thomas. *The English-American, his Travail by Sea and Land ... Or a New Survey of the West Indies.* London, 1648. Quotations are from the edition called *Travels in the New World,* edited by J. Eric S. Thompson. Norman: University of Oklahoma Press, 1958.

García de Céspedes, Andrés. *Regimento de navegación....* Madrid, 1606.

García de Palacio, Diego. *Instrucción náutica para navegar (1587).* Madrid: Cultura Hispánica, 1944.

Gella Iturriaga, José M., ed. *Refranero del mar.* 2 vols. Madrid: Instituto Histórico de la Marina, 1944.

Guevara, Antonio de. *Arte de marear* (Valladolid, 1539). In *Disquisiciones náuticas,* edited by Cesáreo Fernández Duro (see above), 2:11–164.

Hayward, Edward. *The Sizes and Lengths of Riggings for All the State's Ships and Frigats.* London, 1655. Facsimile edition, London: Francis Edwards, 1967.

[Hein, Pieter Pieterzoon]. *Nederlandsche reizen, tot bevordering van den koophandel, na de Westindien.* Amsterdam, 1787.

Hevia Bolaños, Juan de. *Laberinto de comercio terrestre y naval.* Madrid, 1619.

Hinojosa Montalvo, José, ed. *Cuentas de la industria naval, 1406, 1415.* Valencia: Universidad de Valencia, 1973.

Juan y Santacilia, Jorge. *Examen marítimo theórico práctico, o tratado de mechánica aplicado a la construcción, conocimiento y manejo de los navíos y demás embarcaciones.* 2 vols. Madrid, 1771. Facsimile edition, Madrid: Instituto de España, 1968.

Laínez, Juan de. "Carta ... en que le da cuenta del viaje de los galeones (1639)." In *Disquisiciones náuticas,* edited by Cesáreo Fernández Duro (see above), 2:223–58.

Linschoten, J. H. van. *Itinerarium ofte Schipvaert naer Oost ofte Portugals Indien.* Amsterdam, 1623.

[Magellan]. *The First Voyage Round the World, by Magellan. Translated from the Accounts of Pigafetta, and other Contemporary Writers.* Compiled and translated by Lord Stanley of Alderley. 1st ser., vol. 52. London: Hakluyt Society, 1874.

Medina, Pedro de. *Arte de navegar.* Valladolid, 1545.

————. *Libro de las grandezas y cosas memorables de España* (1543). Alcalá de Henares, 1566.

————. *Regimiento de navegación.* Seville, 1563. Reprinted 2 vols. Madrid: Instituto de España, 1964.

Naber, Samuel Pierre L'Honoré, and Irene A. Wright, eds. *Piet Heyn en de Zilvervloot, Bescheiden uit Nederlandsche en Spaansche archieven.* Utrecht: Kemink and Zoon, 1928.

Navarrete, Martín Fernández de, comp. *Colección de documentos y manuscriptos compilados.* Edited by Julio Guillén Tato. 32 vols. Nendeln, Lichtenstein: Kraus-Thompson Organization, 1971.

————. *Colección de viajes y descubrimientos que hicieron por mar los españoles.* 5 vols. Madrid: Imprenta Nacional, 1829–59.

Oliveira, Fernando de. *Livro da fabrica das naos.* Edited with a preliminary study by Henrique Lopes de Mendonça. *O padre Fernando Oliveira e a sua obra nautica.* Lisbon: Academia Real das Sciencias, 1898.

Ordenanzas del buen govierno de la armada del mar océano de 24 de Henero de 1633. Barcelona, 1678. Facsimile edition, Madrid: Instituto Histórico de Marina, 1974.

Ortiz, Luis. *Memorial del contador Luis Ortiz a Felipe II (1558).* Madrid: Instituto de España, 1970.

Parra, Antonio. *Descripción de diferentes piezas de historia natural las más del ramo marítimo.* Havana, 1771.

Paso y Troncoso, Francisco del, ed. *Epistolario de Nueva España, 1505–1817.* 16 vols. Mexico, 1939–42.

Porter y Casanate, Pedro. *Reparo a errores de la navegación española.* Zarazoza, 1634. Facsimile edition, Madrid: Ediciones J. Porrua Tarranzas, 1970.

Recopilación de Leyes de los reynos de las Indias, mandadas imprimir y publicar por el Magestad católica del rey don Carlos II. 3 vols. Madrid, 1681. Reprinted, Madrid: Consejo de la Hispanidad, 1943.

Salazar, Eugenio de. "Carta escrita al Licenciado Miranda de Ron, 1573." In *Disquisiciones náuticas,* edited by Cesáreo Fernández Duro (see above), 2:178–200.

Sánchez Vilar, M. Desamparados. *Desde Estella a Sevilla: Cuentos de un viaje (1352).* Valencia, 1962.

Sorapán de Rieros, Juan. *Medicina española contenida en proverbios vulgares de nuestra lengua* (Granada, 1615). Edited by Antonio Castillo de Lucas. Madrid: Cosano, 1949.

Texeira, Pedro. See Bláquez, Antonio.

Thorne, Robert. *The booke made by the Right Worshipful Master Robert Thorne, in the yeere 1527, in Sivill, to Doctor Ley, Lorde Ambassadour for King Henrie the eight, to Charles the Emperour, being an information of the parts of the world discovered by him and the King of Portingale* . . . 1st ser., vol. 7. London: Hakluyt Society, 1850.

"Tratado de la Galafatería y carena de las naos, y en la forma que se debe hacer" (ca. 1640). In *Disquisiciones náuticas,* edited by Cesáreo Fernández Duro (see above), 6:243–268.

Vázquez de Espinosa, Antonio. "Tratado verdadero del viaje y navegación de este año de seiscientos y veinte y dos que hizo la flota de Nueva España y Honduras." Malaga, 1623. Edited by B. Velasco Bayón. In *Revista de Indias* 36 (January–June 1976): 287–352.

Vega Carpio, Lope Félix de. "El arenal de Sevilla." In *Biblioteca de Autores Españoles,* 3:527–546. Madrid: Ediciones Atlas, 1950.

————. "El Brasil restituído." Edited by Gino Solenni. New York: Instituto de las Españas, 1929.

————. "La dragontea." 2 vols. Burgos: Museo Naval, 1935.

Veitia Linaje, Josephe de. *Norte de la contratación de las Indias occidentales.* Seville, 1672. Translated in an abriged version as *The Spanish Rule of Trade to the West-Indies.* London, 1702. Reprinted, New York: AMS Press, 1977.

Villalón, Cristóbal de. *Viaje a Turquía, 1552–55.* 3rd ed. Buenos Aires and Mexico City: Espasa Calpe, 1942.

Vizcaíno, Sebastián. See Cutter, Donald.

White, Peter. *A Memorable Sea-Fight* . . . *or a Narrative of all the Principall Passages which were trans-acted in the Downes, in the Year, 1639.* London, 1649.

Witsen, Nicolaes. *Architectura navalis et Regimen Nauticum, ofte Aeloude en Heden-daagsche Scheeps-bouw en Bestier* (1671). 2d ed. Amsterdam, 1690.

Wright, Irene A., ed. *Bescheiden over de verovering van de zilvervloot door Piet Heyn Uit Spaansche archieven bijeenverzameld en uitgegeven.* See also Naber, Samuel Pierre L'Honoré. Utrecht: Kemink and Zoon, 1928.

Zamorano, Rodrigo. *Arte de navegar* (1581). Facsimile edition, Madrid: Instituto Bibliográfico Hispánico, 1973.

Published Maps and Reference Works

Álvar López, Manuel. *Atlas lingüístico de los marineros peninsulares: Cuestionario.* Madrid: Instituto Histórico de Marina, 1973.

Braun, Georgius and Franz Hogenberg. *Civitates Orbis Terrarum.* Cologne, 1572.

Bry, Theodore de. *Grand voyages.* 13 vols. Frankfurt, 1606.

Coale, Ansley J., and Paul Demeny. *Regional Model Life Tables and Stable Populations.* Princeton, N. J.: Princeton University Press, 1966.

Cortesão, Armando, and Avelino Teixeira da Mota, comps. *Portugaliae monumenta cartographica.* 6 vols. Lisbon, 1960–62.

Crespo Rodríguez, Rafael. *Vocabulario de construcción naval Español-Inglés, Inglés-Español.* Madrid: Gráficas Lormo, 1975.

Diccionario de autoridades. 3 vols. Facsimile edition, Madrid: Gredos, 1963.

Doursther, Horace. *Dictionnaire universel des poids et mesures . . .* (1840). Reprinted, Amsterdam: Meridian Publishing Co., 1965.

Ewe, Herbert, ed. *Schöne Schiffe auf alten Karten.* Bielefeld: Verlag Delius, Klasing & Co., 1978.

Garmendia Berástegui, Ignacio. *Diccionario marítimo ilustrado castellanovasco, vascocastellano. . . .* Bilbao: Gran Enciclopedia Vasca, 1970.

Guéroult du Pas, Jacques. *Recueil de veües de tous les differens bastimens de la mer Mediterranée y de l'ocean.* Paris, 1710.

Guillén y Tato, Julio. *Monumenta chartographica indiana.* Vol. 1. Madrid: Ministerio de Asuntos Exteriores, 1942.

Jal, Auguste. *Glossaire nautique.* 3 vols. Paris, 1848.

Kemp, Peter, ed. *Oxford Companion to Ships and the Sea.* London: Oxford University Press, 1976.

Lorenzo, José, et al. *Diccionario marítimo español.* Madrid, 1965.

Manwayring, Henry. *The Seaman's Dictionary* (1644). Reprinted, Menston, Eng.: Scolar Press, 1972.

Mercator, Gerard. *Atlas sive cosmographicae meditationes de fabrica mundi et fabricati figura.* Amsterdam, 1628.

O'Scanlan, Timoteo. *Diccionario marítimo español* (1831). Reprinted in facsimile, Madrid: Museo Naval, 1974.

Pâris, Edmond. *Souvenirs de marine. Collection de plans ou dessins de navires et de bateaux anciens ou modernes existants ou disparus, avec les éléments numériques nécessaires à leur construction.* Paris: Bureau des Longitudes et de l'École Polytechnique, 1882.

Savary des Bruslons, Jacques. *Dictionnaire universel du commerce.* Paris, 1723–30. Published in English as *The Universal Dictionary of Trade and Commerce,* translated by Malachy Postlethwayt. 2 vols. London: J. and P. Knapton, 1751–55.

Watt, Bernice Kunerth, and Annabel Laura Merrill. *Handbook of the Nutritional Contents of Foods.* United States Department of Agriculture Handbook No. 8. New York: Dover Publications, 1975.

Ysita, Eugene. *Glosario de terminología marítima interamericana.* Washington, D.C.: Unión Panamericana, 1964.

Selected Secondary Works

Aláez Zazurca, José Antonio. *Resistencia viscosa de buques.* Madrid: Canal de Experiencias Hidrodinámicas de el Pardo, 1972.

Alcalá-Zamora y Queipo de Llano, José. *España, Flandes y el Mar del Norte (1618–1639): La última ofensiva europea de los Austrias madrileños.* Barcelona: Editorial Planeta, 1975.

Anasagasti, Pedro. "La célula de Bilbao: Los astilleros de Zorroza." *Boletín de la Real Sociedad Vascongada de Amigos del País* 6 (San Sebastián, 1950): 359–61.

Anderson, R. C. *The Rigging of Ships in the Days of the Spritsail Topmast, 1600–1720.* Salem, Mass.: Marine Research Society, 1927.

Andrews, Kenneth. *Elizabethan Privateering: English Privateering during the Spanish War, 1585–1603.* Cambridge and New York: Cambridge University Press, 1964.

———. *The Spanish Caribbean: Trade and Plunder, 1530–1630.* New Haven, Conn.: Yale University Press, 1978.

Artiñano y de Galdácano, Gervasio. *La arquitectura naval española (en madera).* Madrid, 1920.

———. *Gente de mar.* Barcelona, 1934.

Arzamendi Orbegozo, Ignacio de. *Almirante D. Antonio de Oquendo.* San Sebastián: Sociedad Guipuzcoana de Ediciones y Publicaciones, 1981.

Baetens, R. "The Organisation and Effects of Flemish Privateering in the Seventeenth Century." *Acta Historiae Neerlandicae* 9 (1976): 48–75.

Ballesteros y Beretta, Antonio. *La marina cántabra y Juan de la Cosa.* Santander: Diputación de Santander, 1954.

Ballesteros y Beretta, Antonio, et al. *La marina cántabra.* Vol. 1. *De sus orígenes al siglo XVI.* Santander: Diputación Provincial, 1968.

Bamford, Paul W. *Fighting Ships and Prisons: The Mediterranean Galleys of France in the Age of Louis XIV.* Minneapolis: University of Minnesota Press, 1973.

———. *Forests and French Sea Power, 1660–1789.* Toronto: University of Toronto Press, 1956.

Barkham, Selma Huxley. "The Basques: Filling a Gap in Our History Between Jacques Cartier and Champlain." *Canadian Geographical Journal* 96 (February–March 1978): 8–19.

———. "First Will and Testament on the Labrador Coast," *The Geographical Magazine* 49 (June 1977): 574–81.

———. "Guipuzcoan Shipping in 1571 with Particular Reference to the Decline of the Transatlantic Fishing Industry." In *Anglo-American Contributions to Basque Studies: Essays in Honor of Jon Bilbao,* edited by William A. Douglass, et al. Reno, Nev.: Desert Research Publications on the Social Sciences, no. 13, 1977.

Barreda y Ferrer de la Vega, Fernando. *La marina cántabra.* Vol. 2. *Desde el siglo XVII al ocaso de la navegación a vela.* Santander: Diputación Provincial, 1968.

Bautier, Robert-Henri. "Sources pour l'histoire du commerce maritime en Méditerranée du XIIe au XVe siècle." *Colloque international d'histoire maritime, 4th, Paris, 1959,* pp. 137–80. Paris: S.E.V.P.E.N., 1962.

Beaujouan, Guy, and Emmanuel Poulle. "Les origines de la navigation astronomique aux XIVe et XVe siècles." *Colloque international d'histoire maritime, 1st, Paris, 1956,* pp. 103–18. Paris: S.E.V.P.E.N., 1957.

Bernard, Jacques. *Navires et gens de mer à Bordeaux (vers 1400–vers 1550).* 3 vols. Paris: S.E.V.P.E.N., 1968.

———. "Les types de navires ibériques et leur influence sur la construction navale, dans les ports du Sud-Ouest de la France (XVe–XVIe siècles)." *Colloque international d'histoire maritime, 5th, Lisbon, 1960.* pp. 195–222. Paris: S.E.V.P.E.N., 1966.

Bernard, R.-J. "Peasant Diet in Eighteenth-Century Gévaudan." *European Diet from Pre-Industrial to Modern Times.* Edited by Elborg and Robert Forster. New York: Harper Torchbooks, 1975.

Boxer, C. R. "Admiral João Pereira Corte-Real and the Construction of Portuguese East-Indiamen in the Early Seventeenth Century." *The Mariner's Mirror* 26 (1940): 388–406.

———. *Salvador de Sá and the Struggle for Brazil and Angola, 1602–1686.* London: Athlone Press, 1952.

Braudel, Fernand. *The Structures of Everyday Life.* Vol. 1 of *Civilization and Capitalism*

15th–18th Century. Translated by Siân Reynolds. New York: Harper and Row, 1981.

Brown, Jonathan, and J. H. Elliott, *A Palace for a King: The Buen Retiro and the Court of Philip IV*. New Haven, Conn.: Yale University Press, 1980.

Brulez, Wilfred. "Shipping Profits in the Early Modern Period," *Acta Historiae Neerlandicae* 14 (1981).

El buque en la armada española. Madrid: Silex, 1981.

Cappa, Ricardo. *Estudios críticos acerca de la dominación española en América*. 3rd ed. 26 vols. Madrid: Librería Católica, 1889– .

Carande Thobar, Ramón. *Carlos V y sus banqueros, 1516–1556*. 3 vols. Madrid: Sociedad de Estudios y Publicaciones, 1943–67.

Carlé, María del Carmen. "Mercaderes en Castilla (1252–1512)," *Cuadernos de historia de España* 21–22 (1954): 146–328.

Carlson, Charles Lawrence. "The Vulgar Sort: Common People in *Siglo de Oro* Madrid." Ph.D. diss., University of California, Berkeley, 1977.

Caro Baroja, Julio. "La creencia en hombres marinos." In *Algunos mitos españoles*. 2d ed. Madrid, 1944.

———. *Vasconiana*. 2d ed. San Sebastián: Editorial Txertoa, 1974.

———. *Los vascos y el mar*. San Sebastián: Editorial Txertoa, 1981.

Carr-Laughton, L. G. "English and Spanish Tonnage in 1588." *Mariner's Mirror* 44 (1958): 151–54.

Carter, Charles Howard. *Secret Diplomacy of the Habsburgs, 1598–1625*. New York: Columbia University Press, 1964.

Casado Soto, José Luis. "Arquitectura naval en el Cantábrico durante el siglo XIII." *Altamira: Revista del Centro de Estudios Montañeses* (1975): 345–73.

Casson, Lionel. "More Evidence for the Lead Sheathing on Roman Craft." *Mariner's Mirror* 64 (1978): 139–42.

———. *Ships and Seamanship in the Ancient World*. Princeton, N. J.: Princeton University Press, 1971.

Castiñeiras Múñoz, Pedro. "La época de los descubrimientos geográficos." In *El buque en la armada española*, 63–86. Madrid: Silex, 1981.

Castro y Bravo, Federico. *Las naos españolas en la carrera de las Indias. Armadas y flotas en la segunda mitad del siglo XVI*. Madrid: Editorial Voluntad, 1927.

Cervera Pery, José. "Dos facetas navales del reinado de Felipe IV." *Revista de Historia Naval* 1 (1982): 148–57.

Céspedes del Castillo, Guillermo. *La avería en el comercio de Indias*. Seville: Escuela de Estudios Hispano-Americanos de la Universidad de Sevilla, 1945.

Charnock, John. *A History of Marine Architecture*. 3 vols. London, 1800–1802.

Chaunu, Pierre. "Les routes espagnoles de l'Atlantique." *Colloque international d'histoire maritime, 9th, Seville, 1967*, pp. 97–138. Seville: S.E.V.P.E.N., 1969.

Chaunu, Pierre, with Huguette Chaunu. *Séville et l'Amérique aux XVIe et XVIIe siècles*. Paris: Flammarion, 1977.

———. *Séville et l'Atlantique,* 8 vols. in 12. Paris: A. Colin, 1955–59.

Chaunu, Pierre. "La *tonelada* espagnole au XVI et XVII siècles." *Colloque international d'histoire maritime, 1st and 2nd, 1956, 1957*, pp. 71–84. Paris: S.E.V.P.E.N., 1957.

Chevalier, François. "Les cargaissons de flottes de la Nouvelle Espagne vers 1600." *Revista de Indias* 4 (Madrid, 1943): 323–30.

Childs, Wendy R. *Anglo-Castilian Trade in the Later Middle Ages*. Manchester, Eng.: Manchester University Press, 1978.

Cipolla, Carlo M. *Guns, Sails and Empire: Technological Innovation and the Early Phases of European Expansion, 1400–1700*. New York: Pantheon, 1965.

Clayton, Lawrence A. *Caulkers and Carpenters in a New World: The Shipyards of Colonial Guayaquil*. Athens: Ohio University Center for International Studies, 1980.

————. "Ships and Empire: The Case of Spain." *Mariner's Mirror* 62 (August 1976): 235–48.

Cook, Warren L. *Floodtide of Empire: Spain and the Pacific Northwest, 1543–1819.* New Haven, Conn.: Yale University Press, 1973.

Dantín Cereceda, Juan. *La alimentación española, sus diferentes tipos.* Madrid: Colección geográfica 1 (1934).

Denoix, L. "Charactéristiques des navires de l'époque des grandes découvertes." *Colloque international d'histoire maritime, 5th, Lisbon, 1960.* pp. 137–48. Paris: S.E.V.P.E.N., 1966.

Domínguez Ortiz, Antonio. "Los caudales de Indias y la política exterior de Felipe IV." *Anuario de Estudios Americanos* 13 (1956): 311–83.

————. *Orto y ocaso de Sevilla: Estudio sobre la prosperidad y decadencia de la ciudad durante los siglos XVI y XVII.* Seville: Diputación Provincial, 1946.

Dunn, Oliver. "Trouble at Sea: The Return Voyage of the Fleet of New Spain and Honduras in 1622." *Terrae Incognitae* 11 (1979): 29–41.

Earle, Peter. *The Treasure of the Concepción. The Wreck of the Almiranta.* New York: Viking Press, 1980

Estrada y Arnáiz, Rafael. *El Almirante don Antonio de Oquendo.* Madrid: Espasa Calpe, 1943.

————. "La influencia del mar en la historia de España," Conference paper. Zaragoza: Consejo Superior de Investigaciones Científicas, 1950.

Etayo Elizondo, Carlos. *La expedición de la "Niña II."* Barcelona: Plaza y Janes, 1963.

————. *Naos y carabelas de los descubrimientos y las naves de Colón.* Pamplona, 1971.

Evans, John K. "*Plebs rustica.* The Peasantry of Classical Italy. II. The Peasant Economy." *American Journal of Ancient History* 5 (1980): 134–73.

Fernández Duro, Cesáreo. *Armada española desde la unión de los reinos de Castilla y de León.* 9 vols. Madrid, 1895–1903.

————. *La marina de Castilla, desde su origen y pugna con Inglaterra hasta la refundición en la armada española.* Madrid, 1893.

Fernández Gaytán, José. *Las banderas de la marina de España.* Madrid: Museo Naval, 1985.

Fernández de Pinedo, Emiliano. *Crecimiento económico y transformaciones sociales del País Vasco, 1100–1850.* Madrid, 1974.

Ferreira David, M. J. "Aperçu historique des types de navires à travers les siècles et influence des navires ibériques sur la construction naval européenne." *Colloque international d'histoire maritime, 5th, Lisbon 1960,* pp. 149–70. Paris: S.E.V.P.E.N., 1966.

Fonseca, Quirino da. *A caravela portuguesa e a prioridade técnica das navegaçoes henriquinas.* Coimbra: Impresa da Universidade, 1934.

Gama Pimentel Barata, João da. *O traçado das naus e galeões portugueses de 1550–80 a 1640.* Coimbra: Junta de Investigaçoes do Ultramar. Printed Lisbon, 1970.

García de Cortázar y Ruiz de Aguirre, José Angel. *Vizcaya en el siglo XV: Aspectos ecónomicos y sociales.* Bilbao: Ediciones de la Caja de Ahorros Vizcaínos, 1966.

García Franco, Salvador. *Historia del arte y ciencia de navegar.* 2 vols. Madrid: Instituto Histórico de Marina, 1947.

Gille, Paul. "Jauge et tonnage des navires." *Colloque international d'histoire maritime, 1st, Paris, 1956,* pp. 85–102. Paris: S.E.V.P.E.N., 1957.

————. "Navires lourds et navires rapides, avant et après les caravelles." *Colloque international d'histoire maritime, 5th, Lisbon, 1960,* pp. 171–82. Paris: S.E.V.P.E.N., 1966.

Goldenberg, Joseph A. "Exploration and Status: The Changing Position of Iberian Seamen and Captains in the Voyage of Discovery." *Mariner's Mirror* 70 (February 1984): 65–73.

González, Pedro María. *Tratado de las enfermedades de la gente de mar.* Madrid: Imprenta Real, 1805.

Graham, Winston. *The Spanish Armadas.* London: George Rainbird, 1972.

Guiard y Larrauri, Teófilo. *Historia del Consulado y Casa de Contratación de la villa de Bilbao.* 2 vols. Bilbao: J. de Astuy, 1913–14. Facsimile edition in 3 vols., Bilbao: Editorial La Gran Enciclopedia Vasca, 1972.

————. *La industria naval vizcaína* (1913). 2d ed. rev. Bilbao: Librería Villar, 1968.

Guilleux de la Roërie [Commandant]. "Introduction à une histoire du navire." *Annales: Économies, Sociétés, Civilisations* 11 (Apr.–June 1956): 145–153.

Guilmartin, John F. *Gunpowder and Galleys: Changing Technology and Mediterranean Warfare at Sea in the Sixteenth Century.* Cambridge: Cambridge University Press, 1974.

————. "The Guns of the *Santíssima Sacramento.*" *Technology and Culture* 24, No. 4 (October 1983): 559–601.

Hamilton, Earl J. *American Treasure and the Price Revolution in Spain, 1501–1650.* Cambridge, Mass.: Harvard University Press, 1934. Reprinted, New York: Octagon Books, 1965.

————. "Wages and Subsistence on Spanish Treasure Ships, 1503–1660." *Journal of Political Economy* (1929): 430–50.

Harbron, John D. "The Spanish Ship of the Line." Scientific American 251 (December 1984): 116–29.

Haring, Clarence Henry. *Trade and Navigation between Spain and the Indies in the Time of the Hapsburgs.* Cambridge, Mass.: Harvard University Press, 1918.

Heers, Jacques. "Commerce des Basques en Méditerranée au XVe siècle (d'après les archives de Gênes)." *Bulletin hispanique* 57 (1955): 292–324.

————. *L'Occident aux XIV et XVe siècles: Aspects économiques et sociaux.* 2d ed. Paris: Presses Universitaires de France, 1966.

Hoffman, Paul E. *The Spanish Crown and the Defense of the Caribbean, 1535–1585.* Baton Rouge and London: Louisiana State University Press, 1980.

Horner, Dave. *The Treasure Galleons: Clues to Millions in Sunken Gold and Silver.* New York: Dodd, Mead & Company, 1971.

Ireland, J. de Courcey. "Ragusa and the Spanish Armada of 1588." *Mariner's Mirror* 64 (1978): 251–62.

Israel, Jonathan. *The Dutch Republic and the Hispanic World, 1606–1661.* Oxford: Clarendon Press, 1982.

Jal, Auguste. *Abraham du Quesne et la marine de son temps.* 2 vols. Paris: H. Plon, 1873.

Jeannin, Pierre. "Le tonnage des navires utilisés dans le Baltique de 1550 à 1640 d'après les sources prussiennes." *Colloque international d'histoire maritime, 3rd, Paris, 1958.* Paris: S.E.V.P.E.N., 1960.

Jobé, Joseph, ed. *The Great Age of Sail.* Translated by Michael Kelly. Lausanne: Edita, 1967.

Kamen, Henry. *Spain in the Later Seventeenth Century, 1665–1700.* London and New York: Longman, 1980.

Kepler, Jon S. *The Exchange of Christendom: The International Entrepot at Dover, 1622–1641.* Bristol, Eng., 1976.

Konetzke, Richard. *El imperio español.* Translated from German. Madrid, 1946.

Labayru y Goicoechea, Estánislao Jaime de. *Historia general del Señorío de Vizcaya.* Bilbao: La Gran Enciclopedia Vasca, 1968–72.

Lane, Frederic Chapin. "Venetian Naval Architecture about 1550." *Mariner's Mirror* 20 (1934): 24–49.

————. *Venetian Ships and Shipbuilders of the Renaissance.* Baltimore: Johns Hopkins University Press, 1934.

————. *Venice: A Maritime Republic.* Baltimore: Johns Hopkins University Press, 1973.

————. "Tonnages, Medieval and Modern." *Economic History Review* 17, 2d ser. (1964): 213–33.

Lethbridge, T. C. "Shipbuilding." In *A History of Technology,* edited by Charles Singer, et al., 2: 563–88. 7 vols. Oxford: Oxford University Press, 1954–1978.

Lewis, Archibald, and Timothy J. Runyan. *European Naval and Maritime History, 300–1500.* Bloomington: Indiana University Press, 1985.

Libros de náutica, cosmografía y viajes de la sección de raros del Museo Naval, sede del Instituto Histórico de Marina. Madrid: Año Internacional del Libro, 1972.

Lind, James. *A Treatise of the Scurvy.* Excerpted in Christopher Lloyd, ed., *The Health of Seamen: Selections from the works of Dr. James Lind, Sir Gilbert Blane and Dr. Thomas Trotter.* London: Navy Records Society, 1965.

López Piñero, José María. *El arte de navegar en la España del Renacimiento.* Barcelona: Editorial Labor, 1979.

————. *Ciencia y técnica en la sociedad española de los siglos XVI y XVII.* Barcelona: Labor Universitaria, 1979.

The Lore of Ships. Rev. ed. New York: Crescent, 1975.

Lorenzo Sanz, Eufemio. *Comercio de España con América en la época de Felipe II.* 2 vols. Valladolid: Servicio de Publicaciones de la Diputación Provincial de Valladolid, 1980.

Lynch, John C. *Spain Under the Habsburgs.* 2 vols. Oxford: Oxford University Press, 1964–69.

Maltby, William S. *Alba: A Biography of Fernando Álvarez de Toledo, Third Duke of Alba, 1507–1582.* Berkeley, Los Angeles, and London: University of California Press, 1983.

Manera Regueyra, Enrique. "La marina de Castilla." In *El buque en la armada española,* 21–39. Madrid: Silex, 1981.

Marañón, Gregorio, "La vida en las galeras en tiempo de Felipe II." In *Vida e historia,* 67–97. Buenos Aires, 1937.

Martínez Guitián, Luis. Naves y flotas de las Cuatro Villas de la Costa. Santander: Publicaciones del Centro de Estudios Montañeses, 1942.

————. *Viajes de las armadas de galeones y flotas a Tierra Firme y Nueva España, al mando de D. Juan de Echeverri, conde de Villa Alcázar de Sirga.* Madrid: Gráficas Uquina, 1949.

Martínez-Hidalgo y Terán, José María. *Columbus's Ships.* Edited and translated by Howard I. Chapelle. Barre, Mass.: Barre Publishing Co., 1966.

————. "La marina catalanoaragonesa." In *El buque en la armada española,* 41–61. Madrid: Silex, 1981.

Marx, Robert. *The Treasure Fleets of the Spanish Main.* Cleveland: World Publishing Co., 1968.

Mauro, Frederic. "Navires et constructions navales en Europe occidentale aux XVIe et XVIIe siècles: Points de départ pour une étude comparée." *Études économique sur l'expansion portugaise 1500–1900.* Paris, 1970.

Maza Solana, Tomás. "Cartas de Felipe II a don Pedro Enríquez de Cisneros, referentes a Santander y a los astilleros de Guarnizo." *Altamira: Revista del Centro de Estudios Montañeses* 1 (1951): 45–63.

Means, Philip Ainsworth. *The Spanish Main: Focus of Envy, 1492–1700.* New York: Charles Scribner's Sons, 1935.

Mendonça, Henrique Lopes de. *Estudos sobre navios portuguezes nos seculos XV e XVI.* Lisbon: Academia Real das Sciencias, 1892.

————. *O padre Fernando Oliveira e a sua obra nautica.* Lisbon: Academia Real das Sciencias, 1898.

Mercapide Compains, Nemesio. *Crónica de Guarnizo y su real astillero, desde sus orígenes hasta el año 1800.* Santander, 1974.

Moore, Alan. "Rigging in the Seventeenth Century." *Mariner's Mirror* 2 (1912): 301–8.

Morineau, Michel. *Jauges et méthodes de jauge anciennes et modernes.* Paris: Armand Colin, 1966.

Morison, Samuel Eliot. *Admiral of the Ocean Sea: A Life of Christopher Columbus.* Boston: Little, Brown and Company, 1942.

———. *The Great Explorers: The European Discovery of America.* New York: Oxford University Press, 1978.

Morton, Harry Albert. *The Wind Commands: Sailors and Sailing Ships in the Pacific.* Middletown, Conn.: Wesleyan University Press, 1975.

Moya Blanco, Carlos. "La arquitectura naval de los Austrias." In *El buque en la armada española,* 147–67. Madrid: Silex, 1981.

Muckelroy, Keith. *Maritime Archeology.* Cambridge and New York: Cambridge University Press, 1978.

Naish, G. P. B. "Ships and Shipbuilding." In *A History of Technology,* edited by Charles Singer, et al, 3:471–500. 7 vols. Oxford: Oxford University Press, 1954–1978.

Nance, R. Morton. "A Batch of Carracks." *Mariner's Mirror* 4 (1914): 275–82.

———. "Caravels." *Mariner's Mirror* 3 (1913): 265–71.

———. "The *Kraeck* of W. A." *Mariner's Mirror* 2 (1912): 225–32.

———. "A Mediterranean Carrack." *Mariner's Mirror* 2 (1912): 309–15.

———. "Northern Ships of *circa* 1340." *Mariner's Mirror* 3 (1913): 33–39.

———. "A Sixteenth-Century Sea-Monster." *Mariner's Mirror* 2 (1912): 97–104.

———. "Some French Carracks." *Mariner's Mirror* 9 (1923): 130–36.

North, Douglass C. "Sources of Productivity Change in Ocean Shipping, 1600–1850." *Journal of Political Economy* 76 (July–August 1968): 953–70.

Nutritional Requirements of Man: A Conspectus of Research. New York: Nutrition Foundation, 1980.

Olaechea Labayen, Juan B. "Evolución del código marítimo y sus afinidades con los códigos documentarios." *Revista de Archivos, bibliotecas y museos* 82 (1979): 437–48.

Olesa Muñido, Francisco-Felipe. "La marina oceánica de los Austrias." In *El buque en la armada española,* 109–45. Madrid: Silex, 1981.

———. *La organización naval de los estados mediterráneos y en especial de España durante los siglos XVI y XVII.* 2 vols. Madrid: Editorial Naval, 1968.

Ortega Galindo, Julio. "Los seis galeones de la plata." *Boletín de la Real Sociedad Vascongada de Amigos del País* 3 (1947): 221–24.

Palacio Atard, Vicente. "Alimentación y abastecimiento de Madrid en la segunda mitad del siglo XVIII." Madrid: Ayuntamiento de Madrid, 1966.

Parker, Geoffrey. *The Army of Flanders and the Spanish Road, 1567–1659: The Logistics of Spanish Victory and Defeat in the Low Countries' Wars.* Cambridge: Cambridge University Press, 1972.

Parry, John Horace. *The Age of Reconnaissance: Discovery, Exploration and Settlement 1450–1650.* New York: Praeger Publishers, 1969.

Passmore, R., et al. *Handbook on Human Nutritional Requirements.* Rome: United Nations Food and Agriculture Organization, 1974.

Pérez Embid, Florentino. *Estudios de historia marítima.* Edited by Francisco Morales Padrón. Seville: Homenaje de la Real Academia Sevillana de Buenas Letras, 1979.

Peterson, Mendel. *The Funnel of Gold: The Trials of the Spanish Treasure Fleets. . . .* Boston: Little, Brown, 1975.

Petrejus, E. W. "The Dutch Flute." In *The Great Age of Sail,* edited by Joseph Jobé. Lausanne: Edita, 1967.

Phillips, Carla Rahn. "Spanish Merchants and the Wool Trade in the Sixteenth Century." *Sixteenth Century Journal* 14 (Fall 1983): 259–82.

Phillips, William D., Jr. "Spain's Northern Shipping Industry in the Sixteenth Century." *Journal of European Economic History* (forthcoming).

Porras Troconis, Gabriel. "Cartagena de Indias, antemural de la hispanidad." *Revista de Indias* 28 (1968): 337.

Poujade, Jean. *La route des Indes et ses navires.* Paris: Payot, 1946.

Pulido Rubio, José. *El piloto mayor. Pilotos mayores, catedráticos de cosmografía y cosmógrafos de la Casa de la Contratación de Sevilla.* Seville: Consejo Superior de Investigaciones Científicas, 1950.

Quatrefages, René. *Los tercios españoles (1567–77).* Madrid: Fundación Universitaria Española, 1979.

Robinson, Gregory. "The Development of the Capital Ship." *Mariner's Mirror* 4 (1914): 14–19; 6 (1920): 44–50; 7 (1921): 108–17.

Romano, Ruggiero. "Economic Aspects of the Construction of Warships in Venice in the Sixteenth Century." In *Crisis and Change in the Venetian Economy,* edited by Brian Pullan. London: Methuen, 1968.

Rubin de Cervin, G. B. "The Catalan Ship." In *The Great Age of Sail,* edited by Joseph Jobé. Lausanne: Edita, 1967.

———. *Bateaux et batellerie de Venise.* Lausanne: Edita, 1978.

Salvá, Jaime. "La armada de Oquendo en Mallorca (1637–1638)," *Bolletí de la Societat Arqueológica Juliana* 28 (1942–43): 421–40.

Sánchez-Albornoz, Nicolás. "Gastos y alimentación de un ejército en el siglo XVI según un presupuesto de la época." *Cuadernos de historia de España* 14 (1950): 150–73.

Scammell, G. V. "European Seamanship in the Great Age of Discovery." *The Mariner's Mirror* 68 (1982): 357–76.

———. *The World Encompassed: The First European Maritime Empires.* Berkeley and Los Angeles: University of California Press, 1981.

Scarpa, Ioannis S., and Helen Chilton Kiefer, eds. *Sourcebook on Food and Nutrition.* Chicago: Marquis Academic Media, 1978.

Schäfer, Ernst. "Comunicaciones marítimas y terrestres de las Indias españolas." *Anuario de Estudios Americanos* 3 (1946): 969–83.

———. *El Consejo Real y Supremo de las Indias: Su historia, organización y labor administrativo hasta la terminación de la Casa de Austria.* 2 vols. Seville: Publicaciones de la Escuela de Estudios Hispano-Americanos, 1935–47.

Scrattish, Nicolas Louis. "New Perspectives on Castilian Migration to the *Audiencias* of Mexico and Lima, 1540–1580." Ph.D. diss., University of California, San Diego, 1975.

Severin, Timothy. *The Golden Antilles.* New York: Alfred A. Knopf, 1970.

Simón Palmer, María del Carmen. *Alimentación y sus circunstancias en el Real Alcázar de Madrid.* Madrid: Instituto de Estudios Madrileños, 1982.

Singer, Charles, et al., eds. *A History of Technology.* 7 vols. Oxford: Oxford University Press, 1954–78.

Sleeswyk, A. W., and Lehmann, L. Th. "Pintle and Gudgeon and the Development of the Rudder: The Two Traditions." *Mariner's Mirror* 68 (1982): 279–304.

Sluiter, Engel. "Dutch Maritime Power and the Colonial *Status Quo,* 1585–1641." *Pacific Historical Review* 11 (1942): 29–41.

———. "Dutch Spanish Rivalry in the Carribbean Area (1594–1609)." *Hispanic American Historical Review* 28 (1948): 165–96.

Sottas, Jules. "An Atlas of Drake's Last Voyage." *Mariner's Mirror* 2 (1912): 135–42.

———. "Guillaume le Testu and his Work." *Mariner's Mirror* 2 (1912): 65–75.

Spooner, Frank C. "Régimes alimentaires d'autrefois: Proportions et calculs en calories." *Annales: Économies, Sociétés, Civilisations* 16 (1961): 568–74.

————. "Régimes alimentaires d'autrefois: Deux nouveaux cas espagnols." *Annales: Économies, Sociétés, Civilisations* 17 (1962): 93–94.

Sternbeck, Alfred. *Filibusters and Buccaneers.* Translated by Doris Mudie. New York: Robert M. McBride and Company, 1930.

Suárez Fernández, Luis. *Navegación y comercio en el Golfo de Vizcaya: Un estudio sobre la política marinera de la Casa de Trastámara.* Madrid: Consejo Superior de Investigaciones Científicas, 1959.

Taillemite, Etienne. "Royal Glories." In *The Great Age of Sail,* edited by Joseph Jobé. Lausanne: Edita, 1967.

TePaske, John C., and Herbert Klein. "The Seventeenth-Century Crisis in New Spain: Myth or Reality?" *Past and Present* 90 (February 1981): 116–35.

Thomazi, Auguste Antoine. *Les flottes de l'or: Histoire des galions d'Espagne.* Rev. ed. Paris: Payot, 1956.

Thompson, I. A. A. *War and Government in Habsburg Spain.* London: Athlone Press, 1976.

————. "Spanish Armada Guns." *Mariner's Mirror* 61 (November 1975): 355–71.

Torres Ramírez, Bibiano. *La Armada de Barlovento.* Seville: Publicaciones de la Escuela de Estudios Hispano-Americanos, 1981.

Ulloa, Modesto. "Unas notas sobre el comercio y la navegación españoles en el siglo XVI." *Anuario de historia económica y social de España* (1969), pp. 191–237.

Unger, Richard W. *Dutch Shipbuilding before 1800: Ships and Guilds.* Atlantic Highlands, N. J.: Humanities Press, 1978.

————. *The Ship in the Medieval Economy, 600–1600.* Montreal: McGill–Queen's University Press, 1980.

Usher, Abbott Payson. "Spanish Ships and Shipping in the Sixteenth and Seventeenth Centuries." In *Facts and Factors in Economic History: For Edwin Francis Gay.* Cambridge, Mass.: Harvard University Press, 1932. Reprinted, New York: Russell and Russell, 1967.

Varela Marcos, Jesús. "El seminario de marinos: Un intento de formación de los marineros para las armadas y flotas de Indias." *Revista de Historia de América* 87 (January – June 1979): 9–36.

Vaughan, H. S. "The Whipstaff." *Mariner's Mirror* 3 (1913): 230–37.

Vázquez de Prada, Valentín. "Las escalas en la navegación española a América." *Colloque international d'histoire maritime, 10th, Brussels, 1968,* vol. 33, pp. 101–22. Brussels: Société Jean Bodin pour l'histoire comparative des institutions, Recueils, 1974.

————. *Historia económica y social de España.* Vol. 3. *Los siglos XVI y XVII.* Madrid: Confederación Española de Cajas de Ahorros, 1978.

Vigneras, Louis-André, *The Discovery of South America and the Andalusian Voyages.* Chicago, Ill.: University of Chicago Press, 1976.

Vogel, Walther. "Zur Grösse der europäischen Handelsflotten im 15, 16, und 17 Jahrhundert. Ein historisch-statistischer Versuch." *Forschungen und Versuche zur Geschichte des Mittelalters und der Neuzeit: Festschrift Dietrich Schäfer.* Jena: Verlag von Gustav Fischer, 1915.

Waters, David Watkin. *The Art of Navigation in England in Elizabethan and Early Stuart Times.* London: Hollis and Carter, 1958.

————. "The Elizabethan Navy and the Armada Campaign." *Mariner's Mirror* 35 (1949): 90–138.

Watt, James. "Some Consequences of Nutritional Disorders in Eighteenth-Century British Circumnavigations." In *Starving Sailors,* edited by James Watt, et al, pp. 51–72. London: National Maritime Museum, 1981.

————, ed. *Starving Sailors: The Influence of Nutrition upon Naval and Maritime History.* London: National Maritime Museum, 1981.

Zapatero, Juan Manuel. *Fortalezas españoles en América: Cartagena de Indias.* Madrid: Editorial Revista Geográfica Española, 1967.

Zulueta, Julián de, and Lola Higueras. "Health and Navigation in the South Seas: The Spanish Experience." In *Starving Sailors,* edited by James Watt, et al. pp. 85–100. London: National Maritime Museum, 1981.

Zumalacárregui, Leopoldo. "Contribución al estudio de la avería en el siglo XVI y principios del XVII." *Anales de economía* 4 (Madrid, 1944): 383–424.

Index

Carla Rahn Phillips is professor of European history at the University of Minnesota. She is also the author of *Ciudad Real, 1500-1750: Growth, Crisis, and Readjustment in the Spanish Economy.*